# CHI—THE SIXTH SENSE

Dr. Daniel Santos

**Contact**
Email: chithesixthsense@gmail.com
Website: chithesixthsense.com.

*"You need a body that is in good working order to realize the Self. Realizing the Self is the only useful and worthy activity in this life."* [1]
—Annamalai Swami

# CONTENTS

# INTRODUCTION

When we come into this world, we are suggestible and vulnerable. We are taught how to breathe and move in specific ways by those around us to become a thread in the social tapestry that we are born into. It is these breathing and moving patterns that create and anchor our story and way of perceiving, or our self-identity.

As we grow older, through repetition of these patterns, we move ever more deeply into our trained idea of "ourselves" and its manipulations. These tendencies seep ever more deeply into our breathing and moving. Our natural Self gradually becomes overshadowed and limited by this repetition of learned behavior. This begins to severely limit the range of our feelings and perceptions and can have a negative impact on our health and well-being.

But somehow, all the while, something in us knows we are more than our belief in who we are taught to be and the way that it has trained us to perceive and interact with the world around us. We begin to sense there is something missing. We begin to sense a beckoning to return to wholeness, to unite with the stream of the natural movement around us.

The feeling that there is more "beyond" us increases. This force begins to knock against our conditioning or learned behavior. It jolts us sometimes quite strongly. We somehow sense that this force is pulling us towards Union. As we proceed along this path, we become more keenly aware of the pull of this force of Life within us and how it manifests and presents itself—something ungraspable but there.

We also experience the difficulties that are caused by this force seeking to break through our learned behavior and the psychological and physiological imbalances that are produced as a result. It becomes more and more obvious that the biggest obstacle to our evolution is the rigidity of the story we have been taught, or who we are supposed to be in the world, as we are being called to sink deeper into ourselves.

What I focus on in *Chi—The Sixth Sense* is how to deal with disruption in the "normal functioning" of our learned body concept by the surfacing of the substrata of our being or our True nature. Or, to put it into other words, what our learned idea of the body and our learned perception goes through as it tries to stabilize itself when it is being barraged by the energy of our True nature trying to actualize. I look at what this process of integration looks like as we are being pulled towards our true or natural beingness and how to deal with the dismantling of this learned body concept and resultant physical and psychological dysfunctions that are created.

It is important to realize how deeply our social self is implanted in us through the moving and breathing patterns we adopt. Having had an acupuncture practice, a Chinese herb store, and teaching movement arts for many years, I have had the opportunity to see the negative effects that the limited patterns of relating given to us by our learned behavior have on our health and well-being.

I not only saw firsthand how we are limited, hampered and made ill by those learned patterns, but also how simultaneously there is a greater force working to loosen those bonds and free us to pursue our natural evolution.

This perspective gave me the opportunity to sense and explore how, when we begin to align properly—gravitationally with the Earth and the pressures it creates around us—we can enhance our ability to become whole with less reliance on others to "hold us up." And how this aligning allows us to move away from the suffocating social fabric engulfing us and to sense and merge with the life stream flowing around and through us. We begin to realize that true healing is to call on the knowledge of the Self to align with wholeness.

Working with our body concept is pivotal. In this book, I use Chi Gung that is focused on saturating and moving beyond our movement and breathing patterns as the vehicle for allowing the Earth's energy to flow more freely through us. Chi Gung used with this focus can be used to override the limited body concept given to us by our conditioning. By doing this we can enhance our relationship with the Earth's gravitational force aligning our body in motion, so that we can store the energy released through the knocking of the spirit into an ever-evolving structure. This then can enable the dismantling of our conditioned concepts of mind and body to occur in a more smooth and graceful way.

Along with this, I seek to impart how any attempt to change who we think we are, or our self-concept, in a meaningful way in relation to our natural evolutionary process by not considering the depths to which we are programed in our body computer is only a superficial exercise. This is only a redistribution of the amount of energy made available to us within the agenda of our learned behavior. What is important is to dismantle this agenda.

When I meet someone who has had an "opening experience" and has begun to sense their inner evolutionary path pulling them, there seems to be an overriding force propelling our interaction. Our conversation seems to wander from subject to subject, or better yet, many different subjects arise seemingly of their own accord. Being in this serendipitous sequence allows our paths of evolution to enliven us, behind the scenes as it were, and a larger energy exchange happens as we commune with each other.

In a similar way I have composed the story in this book by using a series of characters with different, yet similar perspectives, each one of them presenting a different way to access body consciousness. This I feel can enable us to perceive the body, our storehouse of perception, and its interconnectedness to the Earth's force in a more comprehensive and integrated way. It is my hope that you, the reader, can allow an appropriate serendipitous conversation to arise within you as you read *Chi—The Sixth Sense*, extracting what you intuit is important.

*Chi—The Sixth Sense* is set in various locations and cultural backgrounds. It has basically three sections; the sections overlay each other like spirals, with each pass going deeper. In the first section the basic concepts are introduced. I then go back through and expand upon these underlying concepts in more depth and begin to explore their applications. Here in the second section, body practices and training are detailed. And finally, in the final section, along with further reiteration of the basic concepts, I amplify and focus on the title of the book, *Chi—The Sixth Sense*: how to engage and flow with the evolutionary force that is pulling us along our specific individual path to develop deep knowingness, joy, and well-being.

Dr. Daniel Santos
Tiruvannamalai, India 2024

# SECTION 1— The Knocking of the Spirit.

Chapter 1

## FELINA—ZEN SICKNESS

I had met Felina in Phuket in a Chi Gung class she had been attending for a few years. She was of particular interest to me because she had told me that she had been a psychologist for years, and I was wondering how she was able to reconcile or meld together a physical practice like Chi Gung with psychology, which at least in my mind was a very mental practice.

We had arranged to meet, and she had invited me over to her home. Felina had a beautiful house overlooking the sea, on the other side of the village from where I was staying. As I passed through the entryway and neared her front door I took in the ambiance. I was presented with pre-Columbian South American clay artifacts, artfully placed creating beautiful patterns of light and shadow, which reminded me she was originally from Colombia. Felina surely had an artistic bent to her, I thought.

I knocked on the door and Felina greeted me very graciously, with that particularly effusive Latin American hospitality that I was very familiar with and enjoyed so much, having experienced it from my travels in Mexico and South America. This familiarity made me feel immediately comfortable and at home. I followed her to her kitchen area where she offered me some coconut water. I noticed that the inside of her house was decorated with feathered adornments from the Amazon and fine textiles from Peru and Mexico. We exchanged cordialities and I mentioned to her that it was unusual to see Latin American textiles, especially of such fine quality, in Thailand where you usually find yourself surrounded by rich silks from Southeast Asia.

We walked from the kitchen out to a lush garden area, chatting in Spanish. There is something engaging and lively about conversing in Spanish with native speakers which English lacks. The cadence and rhythms of Spanish with its big round vowel sounds and rhyming verbs provide a texture of communication that is full-bodied and quite delightful.

As we sat down at a table to enjoy our refreshments and Felina settled into herself, I noticed how her body simply exuded vitality. For some reason that I was not quite sure of yet, she began telling me the story of her life and how she finally ended up studying Chi Gung in Thailand.

She told me that when she was young, she had lived in a small town in Columbia until her family moved to the suburbs of Bogota when she was twelve years old. While living in this small town, she had close friends and her life with her family was very sweet. But when she moved to the suburbs of Bogota, everything changed. In her new environment she didn't have any friends at all. Her family life felt fragmented as her father became involved in his new work and her mother spent most of her time in her new social circles. Felina missed her old friends and the specialness that she had felt in the small town and couldn't really find any way to replace them. She told me that as she remembered it, she seemed to spend most of her time watching TV. At school she tried to relate to her new classmates, but it never worked out very well. Instead, she found herself becoming more and more withdrawn. She related that even now, when she tried to remember this time, it seemed like a blur. But in hindsight she could see that deep down inside of her there was something gestating.

When she was 16, her parents sent her away to Mexico where she began to feel good again. In this new setting she made friends easily and fell in love for the first time. When she returned to her home in the suburbs of Bogota three months later, she was devastated by having to leave her first love. She was never quite the same after that. In Mexico, an energy had been released in her that she had no way to deal with because it was so unfamiliar. After she fell in love, life energy was flowing through her in such limitless abundance that she could not control it. Back in Bogota, having had to leave her love, she found herself pacing and walking the streets with a restlessness she had never known. To her, it felt like a cat was inside of her chest scratching, looking for a way out. She walked the streets around her house incessantly. She couldn't really concentrate in school like she had been able to before. Then, before she even noticed it, she was sent off to university. At university it never really seemed like she could settle down and she continued having problems concentrating on her studies; relating to others proved to be difficult as well. During that time, she had another boyfriend or two, but the disquieting feeling she'd been carrying around never quite settled out and when she went through breakups with them, it was stirred up strongly again.

Then she tried marijuana. The first time she smoked it she had an episode during which she couldn't hear or see in the same way—everything just seemed fuzzy. She found herself telling her mother about it and crying on the phone. Her mother promptly came to help her, putting her in a hospital. There they tried medicating her, which didn't solve anything. So a day or two later, she began covertly spitting out the tranquilizing pills that were given to her, and in about a week she was able to talk the doctors into releasing her.

After she left the hospital, wave after wave of energy was still moving through her; she wasn't sure what was happening, and no one around her seemed to have any answers either. "I began to understand that there was no hope of anyone understanding what was going on with me, and that I would have to figure it out myself," she said.

Her frantic pacing in the streets continued and she found herself randomly walking, literally anywhere. Walking seemed to be the one thing that helped. She even remembered walking in the countryside for hours at a time, which provided her some temporary relief. She thanked God she had legs and feet.

Back at university she began reaching out and studying whatever she thought could help her. This took her into the fields of anthropology, psychology, and world religions. The only answers she found that seemed to make any lasting sense to her were things that had to do with the Earth and the body. This led her to studying shamanism and related healing systems. She said that during this time it started to feel as if something almost mystical was leading her on, showing her the way. And that amidst the tumult, the amount of synchronicity in her life was almost overwhelming. People would mysteriously give her pertinent information without having any way of really knowing exactly what it was that she was interested in or studying. And the most interesting people would pop into her life.

Felina kept trying to find an answer in the academic fields. Anthropology and psychology seemed to be the closest subjects where she believed she could get some answers. From anthropology she learned that older more rural societies had a niche for people that were suffering afflictions similar to what she had been going through and that they typically became healers or shamans. She found that in general the role of these "people of wisdom," as they were often called, with their knowledge and perceptions of things beyond the "normal," was to give succor and counsel to the rest of society.

Learning of this she became inspired, and she began in earnest to sniff out the truth, now feeling that she was getting somewhere. The knowledge of the existence of these "people of wisdom" in ancient societies germinated inside her, and she realized that maybe there was something she could share with those around her. It also came to her that she wanted to find a way to engage with people, because relating to and sharing with people was important. But still she wasn't quite sure what she wanted to share or how she would do it.

She then decided psychology would be the next logical step for her studies, making it her major at university. She had thought it would be the logical place to find answers. But it turned out to be a bust. She said she only found small fragments of truth here and there, and that in general they were in short supply. Overall, she found that academia was governed by people who were in their heads, who in most cases were separated from their bodies, and that in general they were merely pimping societal values. She was beginning to come to the understanding that lasting changes can be made and sustained only if they contain a strong body component. However, she had made friends with one professor who she grew close to and who was interested in her quest. With his help she was able to finish university and graduate.

She went on to tell me that after graduating she went out into the world where she kept trying to piece herself back together in a new way. She kept having bouts of disorientation, during which she would sometimes feel exhausted and as if she was falling apart. But it was also at these times when it seemed as though her world "opened up."

Felina told me that one of her biggest difficulties at this time was relating to other people, and in particular when one of these states overtook her. She said she investigated paranormal psychology a bit, space abductions, and various forms of channeling. She then went back to psychology to explore in more detail the work of Carl Jung, which initially seemed promising and partially satisfying. It seemed to offer some solutions. Jung had been at the edge of the intellectual thought of his time, and it appeared to her that his explorations had some merit. But in the end, she found his work lacking because he didn't put enough emphasis on the body and did not have enough understanding of it, at least for what she felt she needed.

So, she began exploring more body-based modalities like Rolfing, Postural Integration, and various forms of massage. At that time, she also read a book about "openings" that happened as a result of Kundalini experiences that seemed to explain some of what she was going through. She also investigated some of the teachings of Bhagwan Sri Rajneesh in India and started practicing various forms of the internal Chinese martial arts, Hatha yoga and Buddhist meditations, before finally meeting Silvio, Li Tse, and Angelique about ten years ago here in Thailand.

Felina closed her story by saying, "They taught me how to create a structure in my body within which to stabilize and enhance the Chi flow. This slowly but surely stabilized my mental and emotional ups and downs and enabled me to get a good grip on the psychic phenomenon that I had opened to."

Finally, she paused for a moment and made a sweeping gesture with her right arm to indicate her house, garden and everything around her, "And then my father died. He gifted me generously, and now I have this."

Water falling from a small cataract made of beautiful rocks and then flowing into the swimming pool created a soothing sound, mixed with the singing birds in the trees, and as I looked up a sea eagle glided in the currents of the gentle sea breeze. Although the specifics and circumstances were different, her story reminded me of a similar progression or sequence of events in my own life. I could resonate with her experiences, but it left me with a lot of questions about the process she described. There were some areas about this progression that I wanted clarified.

"I can relate to a lot of what you've told me, Felina," I said. "And it seems like you have a good overview of what actually happened to you. But I'd like to know about it in more detail so I can see how it applies to my own experience."

She replied, "One thing to look at is the power of the activation of sexual energies in the body, and how learned behavior allows these energies only a limited means of expression. It really has an investment in keeping those sexual energies under its control. I've seen similar experiences happen to many people in their adolescent years at the time that sexual energy was being activated in their bodies. The structure that learned behavior had created for them just could not contain the amount of energy passing through them. In fact, all of the people I'm close to now in my life have gone through a similar experience of having their learned behavior crushed by energies beyond "their" control. And what I've learned from Li Tse's and Silvio's teachings has helped me so much to put my experiences into perspective."

"I resonate with your experience. Do you have a name for this shock to your system that you began experiencing as a teenager?" I asked.

Felina said, "As I told you before, I found some references to it when studying works on the opening of the Kundalini, but the best descriptions I've found were in my studies of Buddhism. In Chan or Zen Buddhism, I've heard it referred to as 'Zen sickness.' What they describe is something that can happen—for example to a meditator, usually a novice—when s/he releases so much energy in her/his body arising from deep meditative states that the internal circuitry of the body cannot deal with it. In Tibetan Buddhism the resultant condition is described as 'the creation of an internal wind disease in the body that neither doctors nor medicines can treat.'"

She looked at me and smiled, then went on, "We would simply say that the continuity of one's learned behavior has been severely compromised. The size and intensity of the energy available to one's system has suddenly increased many fold and to deal with it, the definition of oneself needs to be adjusted accordingly. One's ability to function using only one's learned behavior loses its edge, becomes less concrete, and begins to wobble. Your learned behavior just can't handle the energy and craps out."

She laughed. "This break, or 'Zen sickness,' will often begin to happen during puberty, as I was saying before, when there is so much life energy released into the body—more than the established structure of learned behavior can handle."

"But doesn't everyone go through puberty?" I asked. "And does everyone go through this disorientation that you and I have both experienced? Why do some people have this break that is so hard to heal when other people seem unphased by it?"

For a moment Felina let her eyes wander to a violet orchid that was perched onto the branches of a nearby tree, then replied, "It's a combination of at least two things: one, the amount of energy being released, and two, the strength or rigidity of the individual person's learned behavior. If the structural rigidity of learned behavior is weak and a strong blast of energy is released this combination can make it very difficult for that person to become functional again."

"What happens to so-called 'well-adjusted people'?" I asked.

Felina replied, "When the release of sexual energy at puberty happens to a 'well-adjusted' person's learned behavior, s/he is able to incorporate that into items of their learned behavior that have been created for that, functioning containers created by the learned behavior of the times, socially accepted groups or fads or activities. They may even create new items if they don't contradict the underlying order of the learned behavior of the times."

"Does 'Zen sickness' only happen during puberty or in meditation?" I probed a bit further.

She looked at me as if she had anticipated my question, then said, "Perfect question! This break can also be triggered or accentuated by the loss of a loved one, a near-death experience, extreme fatigue, extreme depression, grief, ill health, hunger, hate, anger, or even drug overdose. Anything that overwhelms learned behavior can trigger it."

I responded, "OK, I think I can relate my experience to what you're saying: that there can be a break that opens us up to new vistas and when this happens the old way of operating remains only semi-functional. What kinds of problems have you seen people experience during the course of getting out of this state?"

Felina collected her thoughts for a moment, then said, "There is a process that everyone who has experienced this kind of break has to go through, a process during which we realize that we are so much more than what we had been taught to be. In this phase we feel so very frustrated and limited. From deep inside ourselves we feel that our old ways of seeing ourselves have been choking the life out of us and that we can no longer live within those constraints. But, on the other hand, we have no reference points to create a new habitation for ourselves. We are lost in the 'in between.' For some it is very dramatic, and can be dangerous, too.

"You basically get knocked out of your old home. On the one hand, the new state that you find yourself in does not allow for you to perceive or experience the world in the way you did before, but on the other hand, you don't know how to deal with those new and varied ways of perceiving or grasping the world you've been opened up to. The precision of perception of your learned behavior world that you were locked into and that was so crystal clear has been damaged. When you move beyond the grip of learned behavior you move into a new energetic world. A whole lot of energy that was previously being used to keep your rigid container place is suddenly available to you. But yet, you don't have the energy or experience to know how to handle it."

She looked around for a moment, stretched her arms, smiled then continued, "Also, many people experience illnesses caused by their learned behavior breaking down and are stuck in a no-man's land. They can't crawl back to their old, learned behavior and have nowhere else to go yet. There are many psychological as well as physical conditions that can arise from this rift, as you may well imagine, like what are called schizophrenia, psychosis, multiple personalities, and Post Traumatic Stress Disorder, to mention a few."

"You may even begin to notice, as I did in my work, that people experiencing this break, or 'Zen sickness,' may behave similarly to people who have come from war zones. Experiencing war firsthand can break down your learned behavior, too. You will see that they exhibit many of the same dysfunctions that one can observe in war veterans. And many become susceptible to physical diseases that involve the immune and nervous systems.

"Their sense of self has been fragmented and they are at a loss to put it together again, like the story of Humpty Dumpty," she said laughing. "You know Humpty Dumpty? From Alice in Wonderland? The egg man who fell down from the wall? 'All the king's horses, and all the king's men, couldn't put Humpty Dumpty back together again.'"

"I see, their sense of self has been shattered and their immune systems have become fragmented too—is that what you're trying to say, Felina?"

"Yeah, think about it. This is a very different way to see and think about health and illnesses. You know, the immune system has to do with what you choose to let in and what you reject as not being good for you or not being a part of you. The sense of self has a direct correlation to the immune system. It draws the line between what you perceive yourself to be and what you perceive you are not. So, if the sense of self is fractured, the physical immune system is weakened and susceptible to fracture too. People become predisposed to a whole raft of immunological or neurological diseases as a result, such as allergies, environmental illnesses, immune deficiency disorders, epilepsy, and others."

"OK, so we get jolted. What do we do then?" I asked, appreciating all of the information about the subject, especially this new way of looking at and understanding disease.

She continued, "Let me reiterate when your learned behavior gets jolted like this, you're in a no-man's land. Your old abode does not provide much comfort anymore. You have no reference points in the vastness you're facing. This can be very draining. Your back is against the wall and your only viable option is to figure out how to allocate your energy better so you can navigate in your new energetic environment. You'll never be able to go back to that same comfort and safety that you thought you had when your learned behavior was solidly intact."

Felina paused for a moment, swaying back and forth then relaxing. "What we're talking about is the art of expanding your perceivable world while still maintaining a grasp on your learned behavior. Sometimes it is called a 'spiritual path,'" she said, laughing to herself. "It is really a balancing act. You have to make your focus flexible and pliant. You have to create a new, ever-evolving home."

"And how do you do that?" I asked, fascinated.

"What I've found from having gone through these experiences myself is that Chi Gung, or any right body movement, can be an immense help in doing that. If you continually concentrate on getting the Chi flowing properly through your body it will open the path back to your true self, in a fully integrated way. What is vital is a focus on reorienting the body to the energetic world around you.

"OK, this helps me to see something a bit more clearly," I said reflecting on the process I went through myself, "I can now better understand how illness and accidents can occur at this time when too much energy is released and cannot be integrated. What you are essentially saying is that illness and accidents can be caused by a break in one's learned behavior? The energy that you're projecting out into the world at this time is being haphazardly sent out. And because it is much more intense and stronger than what you had previously been trained to handle, these things can occur? So, it can be a bit of a rocky road, right? And accidents and illness may happen as a result."

"That's right," she answered. "You can get hit by a big chunk of energy that you can't handle very well. But at least you have a chance."

She paused to peer at me. "At least you have a chance," she repeated. "A chance of seeing how you have been enslaved by learned behavior which 'well-adjusted' people do not have. A chance to explore and embody your true self. A chance at joining with the evolutionary forces of your being."

Chapter 2

# Silvio—Learned Behavior

It was a day in May. Chiang Mai in May is a good time. The rains are just beginning. They cool the land off after the hot season. It is still plenty hot, but the rains are refreshing, and they clean the air. The air can get quite dreadful during the hot season. There is no wind to speak of and the haze of smoke and pollution can make life miserable, as the country folk all over the north of Thailand and into Myanmar burn the chaff in the rice fields and the underbrush in the forests.

But yes, it was May. The smoke had cleared, and the tourists for the most part were back home in their cold climes, enjoying springtime.

I walked into the tea house. It was a factory outlet, dedicated to the sale of celadon ceramics. The displays, as always, were beautiful to look at—blue and green crackled ceramics. But the real treat was the backyard; a yard full of large trees, with four or five tables scattered underneath and a rock fountain over to one side, supplying a subtle background noise of splashing water. Here one could talk at ease, eat desserts and drink tea in a garden setting.

I had come to talk to two men who I had recently met: Li Tse, a Chinese man in his early sixties, a self-described student of the "living arts," and Silvio Lorenzo, who Li Tse endearingly called "the toy maker." The toy maker was a little younger than Li Tse, short and slim. He simply radiated energy. He taught Chi Gung classes here in Chiang Mai.

I had met Silvio a while back. The first time I met him, I remembered asking him about Chi Gung. What was it? He had told me that it was hard to define as there were countless forms of Chi Gung in the Chinese Tradition. He said that Chi Gung roughly meant "cultivating life energy."

He went on to say that what he taught was the work of getting the life energy to move through the body in the most efficient way to bring health and inspiration to our being. In short, to remember our natural being with all of its strength, flexibility and magical heritage. "Yep," he had said at the time, "*Life energy cultivation*—that should cover it."

I walked through the sales area of the celadon shop to the backyard and noticed that the two of them were already there, talking. As I approached, they both stood, a bit formally it seemed to me, and smiled. Li Tse then motioned for me to sit.

They were already drinking tea. So, I signaled the waiter and ordered some tea for myself.

After we had talked for a while, I remembered a question that I had for them. From our last conversation I had formulated a query to try to help me understand and encapsulate what we had spoken about then. So, at one point when the conversation ebbed, I asked them both, "How does awareness translate into energy? And how does it move through our bodies? And thirdly, how can we access more energy?"

When I put that question on the table that way they looked at each other and burst out laughing. Finally, Li Tse said, continuing to chuckle, "As my auntie would say: 'now that's a real lallapaloosa.'"

Li Tse then gestured to Silvio as if handing the stage over to the toy maker, who looked at me and smiled.

I waited expectantly, for Mr. Silvio had a way of being both disarming and charming at the same time, and somehow talking to him always stimulated new ideas within me.

"Well," he started, "It's all about how we touch the world around us and what we perceive ourselves and our bodies to be."

He then spread his hands, slightly shrugged and smiled with a sense of finality.

After a moment's silence, being a little surprised and a bit confused by his statement, I asked, "Is that all?"

"Yep," he said with a grin.

"Should I go on?" he continued good naturedly after a bit.

"Please," I replied.

"OK, today I will give you the quick version," he smiled. "And later on, if you like, we can talk about it more fully."

He took a deep breath and looked up as a squirrel moved along a rather large limb and then over to the next tree. He then looked at me and began his explanation.

"There is a sublimely subtle pulsing that is happening everywhere. This fills the world and us with awareness and life. This subtle pulsing takes form as 'us' in our mother's womb. First, as a faint almost imperceptible pulse. Then, as the heartbeat. And later on, after we are born, as the breath, and also in the way we move our bodies.

"Our bodies are endowed with a finite amount of energy that comes from an infinite source." He scratched his chin for a moment. "I think I can say that awareness—now, not 'self-awareness, but awareness—is that infinite source."

I looked over and saw Li Tse nodding and listening intently.

The toy maker went on with mock seriousness, "And that furthermore, the way we perceive ourselves is directly related to the way we focus on and move our bodies." Again, smiling and spreading his hands.

I waited in silence for a bit, then somewhat impatiently asked, "That's it?"

"Yep," Silvio replied, still grinning.

I felt stranded so I asked, "Well, please fill in the blanks if you would and make the short version a bit longer?"

He chuckled, "The longer version goes like this. We really have two bodies that are linked into one and that the connections between the two have become distorted." He finished shaking his head with a smile.

This made me even more confused.

Enjoying my look of confusion seemed to make him want to continue, "Let's go back to that burst of energy that continually pulses through us. I think a good way to look at it is that it actually forms two bodies. First there is a 'subtle' energy-body and then the so-called physical body. Now if all was well, this very, very subtle pulsing would first go into or through our subtle energy-body and then on unimpededly to the body of muscles, blood, and bones we usually think of as our physical body. Unfortunately, this free flow of energy has gotten interrupted.

"This pulsing has gotten redirected to enhance and support the patterns of our learned behavior, or the consensual patterns of the times we are born into. This not only isolates us from parts of ourselves which we should naturally have at our disposal but also keeps us from relating to the world in a full way which could give us more energy."

"What exactly is this 'learned behavior' you are talking about?" I asked.

"Well, isn't that the 64-thousand-dollar question?" he replied as he looked up into the tree overhead to see the squirrel running back along the limb from where it had come.

"Learned behavior basically is the social rules about patterns of touching oneself and others that society has pounded into us for its perceived self-perpetuation," he stated dramatically.

"And why has it done that?" I asked, seeking further explanation.

Slightly raising his hand and tapping his index finger on the table, he said with a grin, "That is another story in the Naked City. And not really pertinent to our discussion right now."

Li Tse could not suppress a chuckle.

"Let's get back on point and talk about how learned behavior gets put into our body in the first place," Silvio continued, looking for a moment over at the waterfall in the corner of the garden then back at me. "The way we learn to function in the world is taught to us at a very early age and is stored and reflected in the way in which we breathe and use the combined muscle groups of the body."

I again must have looked confused.

"Yes, really and truly, through your breathing and moving patterns you are a compilation of everyone you have been around since you were a child," he said as his smile broadened into a Cheshire-Cat grin. "And when you break it down again, learned behavior is a series of rules of touch that perpetuate society. At least in the way society thinks it should be perpetuated."

He then paused for dramatic effect, taking a breath, then continued, "Our bodies need to breathe and need to move and learned behavior has just taken over those functions—for its own ends. And this has become the base for how we think of ourselves and for what we perceive is being reflected back to us from out there," he said, opening his hands to indicate the world around us.

*"Breathing?"* I asked.

"Sure as shootin," he replied.

"Why breathing?" I asked with a perplexed look on my face.

"OK," he said, pausing for a second. "It has long been known by those that have studied the body over the years—yogis, Buddhist monks, and many types of shamans—that breathing and the mind are connected. That our thoughts and emotions follow the breath, and/or vice versa. They are intimately connected."

At that moment I recalled having read both Buddhist meditation texts and Hindu scriptures that had stated just that. I also remembered the time, not so long ago, that I had spent studying with a monk in the mountains of northern Thailand. This monk focused on the twenty-or-so possible breaths or breathing patterns that we repeat day and night and how they relate to different states of consciousness and perception.

I wanted to know more about what Silvio was talking about, so I asked, "I am still not so sure what breathing has to do with touching the world around us?"

He took a long look at me, then said, "Take a few breaths and stay aware of your breathing."

"All right," I said, focusing inwards feeling my breath.

Then he continued, "Breathing is a wave of touch within our bodies. Can you feel that?"

"OK," I said as I felt the pressure of my breath moving throughout my body. "Yes, I can feel that."

Silvio went on, "We have been trained so that the wave of the breath moves through our bodies in prescribed ways that support our learned behavior."

I was still perplexed and must have really shown it, for Silvio leaned over smiling and patted my arm, then sat back as he said, "Just think of a child lying next to his or her mother and tell me that she does not pass her wave pattern of breathing on to her child. And then as we grow older, she and the rest of the humans around us teach us how to move. And so it goes. We are taught how to breathe and then how to move and who we think we are by those around us. We learn to fit into a living pattern of breathing, moving, talking and thinking—prescribed to us by learned behavior.

"We live in a world where bodies talk to bodies. We are taught specific ways of moving muscle groups—patterns, rhythms of movement—from the bodies around us when we are young. And at the same time, our breathing wave flows and works with these patterns and movements in this ever-fluid world that we live in."

"Makes sense," I said.

"What I am saying," he continued, peering at me, "is that how we move and breathe reflects how we've been trained to be in the world. And that furthermore, our trained body movements, our self-reflection, sense of self, and our learned behavior are all directly connected."

"Now we are really getting out there," I said. "I can't quite put that all together, yet."

"Now that we have started moving into the realms beyond, let me go on," he jokingly beamed. "We are confined to patterns of motion in gravity. Maybe Li Tse will talk to you about that sometime. He is the philosopher around here. He likes to talk about gravity and this force field of the Earth within which we live," he said, nodding over into Li Tse's direction.

We were then distracted by some Thai people walking by, two beautiful women walking hand in hand.

"Thai women are beautiful, but why are they so much more beautiful here?" I wondered.

"How nice of them to come by," the toy maker said. "Here you can see a bit of learned behavior in action. Cultural moving and breathing patterns are different from each other. Different races move differently, different professions move differently. Think about how a policeman walks for example. And think about walking in crowds: some cultures do it better than others."

"And Thai women are prettier here," I continued musing to myself.

"You know yourself how much easier it is to walk in a crowded place in Thailand than it is to walk in a crowd in America," he went on.

"Somehow these people have learned how to walk together much more comfortably than we do in the West, for example. If you start looking at cultural differences and how people move in them, and express themselves in different movement patterns, you can see how learned behavior is installed a bit differently in each culture. And how the rhythms and patterns of body-to-body movement differ slightly from one culture to another."

He again scratched his chin, then continued, "But really these are only minor differences. These Thai people in their special Thai way are just as stuck in their learned behavior as Westerners are in theirs."

I took one last glance at the Thai ladies and then switched my mind back to Silvio again.

"Anyway, to get back to our splendid conversation—or should I say my monologue?" he said laughing, knowing full well that he now had my full attention.

"The basic premise is that how we move reflects how we have been trained to be in the world. And that our body movements—both internally through our breathing, and externally through our movements—are synchronized to move to the beat and rhythms of our learned behavior.

"We are also given certain predispositions even before birth from our mother and father in the water environment of the womb—especially from our mother," he said, looking at me intently. "Now follow me carefully! These patterns that are established in the womb in its fluid water environment are then transplanted into an air environment after birth where they are exposed to a different sense of gravity," he said smiling, looking over at Li Tse.

Then he turned and his stare returned to me. "Got that?" he asked, looking at me to sense if I had understood. "Especially if we grow up with the same mother and father, these predispositions are further anchored into us as we learn to move in this new world surrounded by air. And even if we don't grow up around our natal parents, learned behavior gets further instilled in us anyway by the movement and breathing patterns that the society around us lives by in our new gravitational environment.

"You can also think about it in this way: before we were floating in a water environment, and now we are forced to function in a much different gravitational field which requires a different use of our five senses. As we're learning to move our bodies, especially our arms and legs, we are very susceptible to the influences around us as we adapt in order to survive in this new air environment."

"Wow, that's a lot to absorb!" I thought to myself and looked up into the sky for a moment, seeing the movement of the clouds, then seeing the breeze moving the leaves of the trees above me. An image came to mind: of a baby leaving the womb. It started to cry and began to move, being exposed to this air environment that was new and foreign. Putting myself in the baby's place I started to understand more deeply what Silvio was saying: that in the midst of our feelings of helplessness and dependency we could be coerced into whatever was offered.

When I returned from my reverie, I looked back at Li Tse and Silvio. They were watching me sipping their tea with smiles on their faces.

Silvio continued his explanation, "Learned behavior is also reflected in the way we learn to speak and in the emotional charges behind those words. The people around us talk to us and we learn to talk back. Yep, indeed we learn to talk to other humans!" he said, laughing, "And not only that, but we also begin to create energy loops by talking to ourselves and convincing ourselves of who we are. And inbuilt in this 'communications' system there are runners or things set in place through rhythms and patterns that keep reminding us to talk to ourselves in the future.

"And every time we talk to ourselves and think of 'our story' we 'freeze the frame,'" he said, connecting his two thumbs with his index fingers in front of him as if framing a picture. "Like stopping a movie. Thus, interrupting our connection to the fluid world around us. But again, this is another story in the Naked City which we should make a date to talk about at a future time—if you'd like to continue?" he said, baiting me with his eyebrows as if he were Groucho Marx.

Li Tse interjected, seemingly enjoying Silvio's elucidation immensely, "Or, to put it in other words: there are a hundred-and-one ways that we keep the nasty system going and continue to torment ourselves on into the future."

They looked at each other appreciatively and then Silvio grabbed the moment, "So, another part of your question was how can we access more energy? To get into this we had to first look into how we lost our direct connection to our source in the first place."

He rubbed his palms together as if gathering energy, then said, "Now I can say that, for me, the key for getting our energy back and remembering the 'natural' patterns and rhythms that synchronize us with the flowing universe around us is to change the way we move our bodies."

He stopped talking for a few moments and I noticed that my mind had become very clear. I became aware of a sudden opening: birds chirping—vines climbing up trees—two cats playing on the stairs—orchids in the trees—more orchids hanging from coconut husks on some mighty branches—stag horn ferns—and the play of light and shadow on the grass through the leaves.

After sipping his tea and then slurping it a bit to grab my attention Silvio continued, "Remember now, when I talk about changing body movement, I'm also talking about breathing as well as the movement of the limbs. Breathing is the inner wave, movement is the outer wave, and they're essentially linked.

"Using Chi Gung with the objective of correcting our body movements and putting breathing into proper perspective—let's say, correctly synchronizing the inner wave and the outer wave—can lead to allowing more natural rhythms and patterns to inhabit our being. This then can give us the energy to move our awareness to other locations, away from our learned behavior. And we can learn to stabilize our awareness there. We can learn to create a reality inclusive of but not limited by our learned behavior. When you can do this your body will establish a greater connection to the world around you and you will be able to access much more energy."

He shook his head as if recollecting a forgotten thought, "So much of our energy has been used up or overused or been tired out simply from focusing awareness on the patterns of learned behavior. In a very real sense learned behavior is just one of many possible patterns, as illusory as a dream, that is maintained by learned rhythms of breathing and movement. Consciously working with the body's movements, both internally and externally, can help you to create another dream, a bigger dream than the dream of learned behavior. You can learn to live in a bigger reality.

23

"Chi Gung practice with the right focus is one practical and pragmatic way of accessing more energy and awareness, stabilizing new perceptual realities, and anchoring these new ways of moving and perceiving in our bodies. Changing the way the body habitually moves and aligns with gravity can also change the reflections that you get back from life all around you, and in this way can let more energy circulate through your being from 'outside' of yourself as well.

"So, if you want to 'live your dream' as they say, or even begin to find out what your dream can be, conscious and focused body practices can help immeasurably."

With a self-satisfied look he asked, "Does any of this help to answer your questions?"

I could only numbly nod by this time. And glancing over at the next group of Thai women walking by, I knew it was time for more tea and cookies...

Chapter 3

# Li Tse—Gravity

The next time I was to meet my friends, it was at Wat Umong on the outskirts of Chiang Mai. A wat basically is a temple complex, and in the Thai language Umong means "tunnel." Wat Umong was originally a forest temple founded in the 14th century. At this wat there are brick-lined tunnels going through and under a hill that are cave-like. This is where many shrines are situated. I like going to these shrines very much. I have found that there is something very meditative about the still air under the Earth. It seems to have a quieting effect on the body.

On the same hill, above the tunnels there is a beautiful chedi. These often-massive structures are built representing the five elements of the Buddhist-Indian tradition. These chedis, or stupas, as they are called by the Tibetans, are much revered. I was once told by a Buddhist teacher of mine that they were built to spread the teaching and to enable one who perceives them correctly to gain enlightenment just through the act of seeing them.

Wat Umong is a wonderful place much like a park, with huge grounds and beautiful big trees along with the temples; libraries, and monk quarters typical of a wat complex. It also has a small lake filled with fish and some very large turtles that can be seen sunning themselves on logs on the muddy banks.

It was on the side of this lake where there are a series of concrete tables and benches under very large old teak trees that I was to meet my friends. When I arrived, I saw Li Tse seated at one of the tables under the shade of

25

one of these old trees with their enormous leaves. Apparently, Silvio had not arrived yet.

Li Tse smiled when he saw me, and I returned his smile as I walked up and took a seat at one of the concrete benches at his side. We spoke for a bit as we waited for Mr. Silvio to make his appearance. We talked about how the Thais seemed very adept at shaping things out of concrete from dragons and *nagas*—snake-like deities—to elephants and assorted demigods. Not to mention trees and the tree-like tables and benches we were sitting on.

It felt so good to be out in this environment, looking out over the lake with a gentle breeze ruffling the leaves overhead. As if reading my thoughts, Li Tse said, "It is a wonder to be in this natural setting. It is very healing for us when we are surrounded by nature like this, because we are reminded of our 'natural' being and our 'natural' connection to all that surrounds us, and of the evolutionary force running through us.

"It reminds us of how we could flow freely with all that," he said as he made an expansive gesture with his arms trying to take in the whole world. "And of what we really are. It reminds me of a poem that I wrote once in my youth."

He took a long breath, and these words came streaming out:

*Within the vast eternity of Awareness*
  *gravity was born,*
*Deep in the folds of gravity*
  *pressure, movement, and life,*
*I can in my small way touch all this*
  *with my hands my eyes and my ears,*
*And I can taste and smell it*
  *on the breeze of life.*

The poem seemed to fit the occasion, but I was not yet sure how.

"That is very beautiful," I said. I pondered a bit more then asked, "*Gravity?*"

Li Tse looked at me and said, "Exactly. Gravity is moving and full of awareness. Gravity is this pressure all around us that we can feel, created by the Earth," he said, moving his arms once again in a slow expansive arching gesture. "Gravity and the resultant pressure it creates are the basis of the cocoon of the Earth. And the Earth is alive," he said, moving his head back and forth and smiling. "Gravity is the cohesive awareness that binds things together. It is that force that we feel pulling us down into the ground—sticking us to the Earth. And it is the source of the resultant pressures which it creates in us and around us that seemingly pulls every which way. But there is an order to it."

Li Tse scratched his chin as if collecting his thoughts, then continued, "Let me go over this again. For us, there is a feeling, a sense of gravity, that we feel as a force, which pulls us into the ground, and then as a result creates pressurized movements all around us. What I am getting at is that it is a feeling. Not specifically what Newton talked about or what Einstein worked with or whatever scientific ideas have evolved since the—but what we feel under and around us."

I noticed the reflected light shining off of his prominent cheekbones as he looked over at the water before he continued, "I like to use systems that have been around for a long time as a base for describing what is around me, probably because they are time-tested. Some of those folks long ago who studied the body, gravity, life and the beyond knew something about what they were doing—Indians, Chinese, Egyptians, and shamans throughout the world. They were not just sitting around, although I am sure that they sat around quite nicely, just waiting for science to come along to 'clarify the world,' but they were avid explorers of the mysteries of life. And the body was their instrument of choice."

He stopped again for a minute to reflect, then went on, "We are pushed into learning, we are pushed into becoming more aware! We are pushed by some inexplicable force to evolve, to find out what we really are! Don't know why or how but it is there and I can feel it pushing."

He then peered at me, laughed and said, "You have to really notice what you feel around you, dude."

27

Li Tse paused again and looked out over the lake, pointing out a huge turtle swimming at its far end. We watched for a bit as the turtle moved slowly through the water until it reached a log, then slowly eased itself up to bask in the sun.

He cleared his throat, and continued, "Gravity not only pushes us down, but it pushes everything else down too. Just feel the pull on your sit bones now.

"So here we are in the midst of this gravity-filled awareness that permeates everything, both 'inside' and 'outside' our bodies. And we perceive this gravity/awareness inside and outside our bodies via our senses. Through combinations of our senses, we create a sense of a body and of a self. We do this within our personal cocoon in the midst of this vast awareness," he said spreading out his arms.

"Are you saying that through our five senses we make choices of how to perceive gravity and the pressure around us?" I asked, a little perplexed. "Very good," he replied. "Gravity/pressure is the pervading force around us, and we use our five senses to organize what we choose to perceive and thus how we choose to see ourselves and the world.

"There is more to it," he went on. "Gravity is not a static thing; it creates pressurized movement and through that it essentially creates the space and time we choose to be in. Gravity also has within it a memory bank that is created and held within the rhythms of the flows of the pressure it creates.

"The Earth remembers things. It helps us to remember who we really are," he said nodding.

"The human body is structurally organized to bear the pressure of gravity. It is able to balance the downward pull as well as the resultant upward push and the pressure and movement all around us. The bones of the body form a physical framework within which the life-force and Chi can flow. This structure is maintained in conjunction with our tendon- and muscle-systems. These support the patterns and rhythms of contraction and expansion that then define the alignment of our tissues and create the song, as it were, of our being. This is how you might see the body system' from a purely physical point of view, but as you will learn later on there is really an 'energetic structure', or should we say a 'pressure structure,' that holds it all together."

He stopped, looked over at me, then pointed to a statue of the Buddha and said, "The Earth is a powerful living being that supports all we can perceive with our senses. Each different posture we adopt lets gravity pull the body in different ways, to place our organs into different configurations. You see that statue over there—the Buddha is seated with his left hand resting below his abdomen and the middle finger of his right hand is touching the Earth.

"The story of this posture goes something like this: at one point in the Buddha's life he was challenged. In a way it was a challenge, but it could also be looked at as a very insightful question. This occurred when someone asked him, 'You sit here and talk to us as if you know everything. You say you are the Buddha. How do we know it is true?'"

"And you know what the Buddha said in reply?" Li Tse said, gently scratching his chin, looking at me.

I gestured for him to continue.

"The Buddha smiled and responded by tenderly touching the Earth with the middle finger of his right hand and saying, 'I am the Buddha. The Earth is my witness.' And thus, this posture is called the 'Earth Witness Posture.' It is the most common Buddha image you will see and is not only a testament to the Buddha's attainment, but at the same time a statement that attests to the power of the Earth. The Earth is a powerful creature," he said, smiling.

I remembered seeing Buddha images in various positions but usually sitting. Other than that, the most common one seemed to be the Buddha in a lying posture: lying on his right side which was reputedly the posture that his body was in when he left this Earth.

I looked over at Li Tse and he gestured with a wave of his hand for me to share my thoughts.

"Ah yes—the lying posture," he said. "The lying posture is very important. There are five postures, you know? Four for the actual body—lying, sitting, standing and moving. The Earth is a powerful force, and its pressures affect us in many different ways. And these effects have to do with what position or posture we are in.

"In the 'Earth Witness Posture,' the Buddha is in the sitting posture. In the sitting position notice that the torso is upright but the extremities, the arms and legs, are passive. This allows for deep inner contemplation,

29

but it is not well suited for interaction with the outside world.

"The standing posture: I am sure you have seen statues of the Buddha standing. There are some around. This is a posture where the energies of the body are activated. The arms and legs are engaged, as are the wrists and ankles. Maximal gravitational alignment when in the standing posture increases the energy flow coming up from the Earth through your feet. Standing is about lining up and facing the world directly. So, thus it is often spoken of as a 'posture of power.'

"Then movement," he said as he moved his arms and circled his wrists. "Moving is the one posture that is the most interactive, the least static, and in many ways the most vital and alive of the postures. It is through this posture that we actively engage the world—how we bring the world to us, as in eating or pushing things out of the way as we move forward. Sometimes you will notice this posture depicted here in Asia as a being or god dancing with many arms and sometimes many legs.

"And then as you mentioned there is lying," he said looking at me. "Relax," he smiled, "What do you naturally want to do when you don't feel well? You just lie down. Or what do you do every night to recharge yourself? You lie down. You do this to allow the body to benefit from the unimpeded healing power of gravity. Lying is a passive way of aligning gravitationally with the Earth. In this posture your muscle or bone structure is not being used to support you. Thus, in many ways you bypass the structural alignment that you have adopted via your learned behavior. There are less hindrances for your energy-body to connect naturally with your healing-body template. Understand that it is in the lying posture that your personal cocoon of energy is naturally aligned gravitationally without much interference to the great cocoon of energy of this Earth," he said, patting the bench he was sitting on.

"In a way of speaking, when you are in a lying posture, through the pull of gravity you are getting a relatively unimpeded nonspecific energizing bath of the Earth's energy. This natural alignment with gravity allows for a passive circulation of Chi or life-force to move throughout your body. Thus, energy can move more efficiently, and you are able to align more intimately with the subtle pulse of your being."

" One thing though: the lying posture is the most difficult in which to concentrate or focus because our spine is not aligned perpendicularly."

We sat in silence for a moment, then we both looked over at a big spider web suspended in a nearby tree and watched a huge blue butterfly fluttering close by it. I could only imagine what the resident spider was feeling.

"I really like this big cocoon," Li Tse said chuckling, slowly moving his head from side to side expansively, taking in as much as he could of the world around him. "The real key is to align one's personal cocoon with the energy of the Earth's cocoon through all of the postures and while mixing this energy with your focused purpose."

"What exactly do you mean?" I asked. "Aligning cocoons?"

"I call what we live in a 'cocoon' because it is a good image for me—gauzy and enclosing, yet permeable and very much alive. To get a feel for it, you can direct your attention to the feeling you get when you are just waking from sleep."

I looked at him rather strangely, not having the slightest idea where he was going with this.

He bulged his eyes a bit and beamed a smile at me. "Do you ever become conscious as you are waking and know that if you move your body you will wake up?" he asked. "You know it is hard to explain, but it is like you are in a subtle-static-electric-gauzy-like feeling suit. A fuzzy feeling like being inside of a cocoon."

"I have had that experience, yeh," I responded, nodding pensively. "When that happens, I am not sure if I am awake or asleep. But I enjoy being in that state a lot."

Li Tse replied, "The reason you enjoy it is because you are experiencing your energy-body a little and its healing effects without the total encumbrances of your learned behavior."

"No wonder scientists are touting the benefits of sleep these days as a key to longevity," I thought. "I remember reading recently a study that came to the conclusion that one of the keys to longevity was a good night's sleep."

Incidentally, this can be a doorway into your dreaming," he continued. "Because it is usually while we are lying that we let go of our idea, or better yet, our learned behavior idea of our body. Because, as I told you before, it is in the lying posture where you are somewhat gravitationally liberated from learned behavior's patterns aligning with gravity. You may be unaware what options are available to you and drift around, but you are actually freer to experience different combinations of sensual activity.

"What I am saying is that the freedom from the gravitationally-imposed structure of learned behavior that your body experiences in the lying posture, is what allows the energy-body to infuse your healing-body with energy.

"But again—one of the drawbacks of this posture is that it is much more difficult to maintain the same quality of focus or concentration as compared to sitting or standing."

He gazed back over at the spider weaving a web-like cocoon around her latest meal. He looked intently at this alive and resilient pattern. It felt as though he were listening to the trembling movement of the web.

Li Tse then returned his attention to our conversation. "And just as we wake, before we move, the learned behavior is not yet totally engaged. It has not totally inhabited your muscle structure and we can better sense that feeling of Chi all over our body—that gauzy, cocoon-like feeling.

"One way of looking at what we are trying to do here with our Chi Gung is to transfer this gauzy feeling of Chi that you feel while in the passive posture of lying into the active posture of movement. Or relating to the world through this fuzzy feeling of Chi, but also adding the focus and concentration that are easier to achieve in the upright postures. When standing and moving you can learn to move this same Chi-feeling through the body to reach the fullest possibilities of integration on this Earth platform. We are learning to fuse Chi with our internal concentration or focus. How and why we do this is the center of our study."

He looked around and giggled like a giddy little child as if he had just given me the secrets of the universe. Then he looked over the lake, took a breath and continued in a jovial mood.

"One way that I like to look at our Chi Gung is that it is about taking the recuperative energy and deep knowledge of oneself naturally available in the lying posture and translating it into movement or into the ways in which we touch the world. I tease Silvio about this by telling him our Chi Gung is a 'sleeping exercise'. He laughs with me when I say this because he knows that our Chi Gung actually is about aligning and relaxing the body in motion and filling it with the sensation of Chi fused with focus. And in addition to that he also recommends to his students to wake very slowly in the morning so that the process of 'physicalizing' can be studied. He tells them that this is a time when there can be a different and a fuller kind of contact with the energy-body."

I thought to myself that Thailand was a perfect place to practice sleeping. The Thais seem to be masters of it. They can seemingly sleep anywhere. Any part of vacation or a day off for a Thai seems to be mostly devoted to eating and sleeping.

This made me remember one of the things that my first Buddhist teacher had said when asked, "What is there to do in this life?" She had replied only half joking—but only half joking, "sleep until you are hungry and eat until you are sleepy."

As I popped out of my musing, 1 Li Tse began talking once again, "Is all this talking of sleep making you drowsy?" he asked good naturedly, having noticed my reverie.

He then continued by reiterating, "You can learn to move this cocoon of sleep or the kind of fuzzy feeling that envelopes you, that feeling that you sense as you wake, into and through the movements of the body. By becoming aware of and using the very subtle vibrational feeling of Chi and applying it throughout various essential movements you can also move this fuzzy Chi-feeling to activate the important energy centers of the body. These are locations in the energy-body where Chi naturally gathers and radiates. And it is from these centers that the energy-body connects with the physical body," he said as he slowly waved his right hand in front of his face with a chuckle. "Or we can do the reverse and just go back to sleep."

He thought this was very funny and his chuckles changed into laughter before he went on, "We can teach ourselves to create a new dream in motion, thus destabilizing the dream of our learned behavior. We can allow more fluidity to enter our system so we can move more freely through the folds of gravity—which is our birthright. We can also move the awareness and perspective of waking consciousness developed through Chi Gung practice back into sleeping consciousness. You see it really is about a fusing of the natural Chi around and within us with our 'internal' focus or intention."

He then held an imaginary remote control in his right hand and proceeded to press this thumb into his palm as if he was changing channels. "At least we can have a whole series of dreams to choose from," he then said, chuckling.

"It is by moving our focus in gravity through the different postures that we can allow the force of evolution to push us on, or light ourselves up," he said, laughing at himself and beaming even more.

He once again pointed to the Buddha statue. "This man really knew a lot," he said appreciatively. "The Buddha also said something else that is very important to us when a disciple sincerely inquired, 'Where do I look for enlightenment?'

"And the Buddha had responded, 'Look in your fathom-long body.'

"Remember that!" he said emphatically, "Look into your body and let it speak to you."

I noticed the morning light reflecting on Li Tse's forehead, nose and face and accentuating the sparkle in his eyes as he turned the index finger of his right hand to point to his body.

I nodded and smiled in understanding.

Then I felt like our discussion about postures was not complete, and I asked him, "You mentioned that there were five postures...but you have only told me about four. Am I missing something?"

"I thought you would never get around to asking," he said as he raised his index finger. "The fifth posture is perception. Perception is the way we choose or have been taught to put together the five senses."

"Perception? Is perception really a posture?" I asked even more perplexed.

Li Tse responded, "It is in the sense that the postures are ways of putting together the five senses. Do you remember how previously we discussed how each of the postures aligns our organs in different ways to gravity? And the organs are linked to the senses."

He paused for a moment, then went on, "So in some ways perception is like the moving posture in that it permeates all the other postures—but even more so. But there is more to us."

I interrupted, "But how would it be possible to be without perception through the five senses?"

"Think on this, my friend," Li Tse replied. "This is the crux of it all. There is more to us than the five senses. It is the study of the posture of perception that begins to open the whole ball of wax. We exist before perception," he said gently, looking straight at me.

"When you look at it carefully you realize that you are more than what you perceive. Something has to be perceiving through the five senses, no?"

That stopped me in my tracks, and I looked confused. But he continued. "Then consider this—are 'you' perceiving or holding any other posture when 'you' are in deep sleep? Or are 'you' perceiving or holding any other posture when 'you' lose your sense of self in deep meditation? Or are 'you' perceiving or holding any other posture when 'you' are strobing between action and inaction? And what about the place where awareness meets Chi?"

He paused for a moment to let that sink in. "Learning about gravity, the force of the Earth, is a great thing. Learning that what we think we are is actually patterns of touch, and that these patterns shape and combine into these five postures, is also a good thing to know." He grinned.

"So, you're saying that gravity is one of the keys to a total body experience?" I asked. "Are there other keys?"

He replied, "There is one other important key that we have not touched on. We will talk about it later, in detail: the power within us that knows."

Then we sat there enjoying the play of light on the trees and the water for a while.

I finally got around to asking him a question that had been on my mind for some time. "Why do you call Silvio 'the toy maker'? Does he make toys?"

That got a big smile and brought out a burst of laughter from Li Tse. Then he said, "It's not so much that Silvio makes toys. But it is how he uses them as aids to help people understand about themselves and their bodies. Many of his toys he does not make at all. In fact, he always has his eye out for new ones, but if he cannot find what he wants he makes them himself. He knows that they are very descriptive of the way we carry ourselves, and that they can be used as physicalized images for understanding the body mechanics, which can be used to help unlock the energies contained in the body."

He smiled inwardly and chuckled. He could not conceal his affection for his friend Silvio.

Chapter 4

# Silvio—Circle the Wagons, "We're Surrounded"

As if on cue, there was Mr. Silvio walking towards us with a toy in his hands. He had one of those toys—"friction toys," I call them—a small car with wheels that you brush across the ground a few times, then place on the ground and let go. It then goes forward on its own, while showering sparks everywhere.

He unceremoniously sat down and started playing with his toy on the table. As he did this, he started talking about charging up energy and how to move it throughout the body. With a sly grin on his face, he turned around to look back from where he had come. He then turned back around to face us and asked mischievously what we had been talking about behind his back.

"Gravity!" I said.

"So, Li Tse is talking to you about gravity, is he?" he said with a laugh. "Gravity is always behind your back, you know?" He turned around again then he spun to face me and said grinning, "Has he told you about the 'truth-body' already? That is one of his favorite subjects too."

"Not exactly," I replied.

And sensing an opportunity to ask a question about a growing confusion in my mind, I voiced it, "What is this 'truth-body,' anyway? You guys are talking about 'truth-bodies,' 'energy-bodies,' 'healing-body templates,' and even 'subtle-bodies? What's with all of these bodies?" I asked with a perplexed look on my face.

They both burst out in laughter at my apparent frustration.

Then Silvio, beaming, said, "They are really all just facets of the same thing. We want to know the truth, we want energy, we want health, and we want to be able to move around in a bigger dream.

"And if we go one step further and focus on these different 'bodies,' we may even begin to understand that there is something that is directing us along our path. How about that?" he said, spreading his palms out to me, then revving up his toy again.

When the sparks cleared, he continued, "The next step is that we start to ask: what is our connection to this thing we really are? What is that thing, anyway? How does it work?"

He looked at me with a piercing gaze. "Truth, energy, health: it all amounts to the same thing. This is our 'natural being' wanting to evolve itself."

"But tell me more about this truth aspect," I said, a bit overwhelmed and somewhat confused.

Silvio chuckled, "Getting more energy enables you to align all the truth that you have come across in your life. This can become a doorway, a direct connection to the truth of who you really are. It fills you with true information about your true self and opens up the path of return to your true essence.

"Can you see the truth of what I am saying?" he continued, smiling with a chuckle.

"OK," I replied, "Then how is this related to the energy-body or getting more energy?"

Silvio replied, "In a way we are always sending out energy and it is being reflected back to us by circumstances and events in our lives. For example, we seemingly live out the same dramas over and over again because we relate to people in the same way we have been trained to.

"Now if we increase our energy or make a more efficient connection to our other body or bodies," he said with a grin, "We get more knowledge of who we really are. When this happens, we are able to put together more truth about ourselves—whether it be linking together things that have rung true for us in the past or opening ourselves up to receive more truth." The more times he said the word "truth," the broader his grin.

He laughed as he continued, "For in a way, truth is compacted energy. When we find more truth, we are gathering together previously dispersed energy. We feel like we have gathered more energy, but in truth our energy was there all along. We are just remembering it," he said, holding onto his arm.

"And allowing it to reorganize itself in its 'natural' way. We are moving beyond the bonds of our learned behavior and instead letting our energy flow as it should."

Silvio then paused to see what effect his rambling had on me. I thought he was checking to see if anything had sunk in at all.

Again, he went on, "This process of finding the truth is like a more-inclusive and ever-expanding spiral. And because you are getting more energy into your truth-body—the essence that knows who you really are—not only will answers come to you internally through memory or your internal voice, but they will come to you from the outside too—through synchronistic interaction with the world around you. Increasing the connection with your energy-body will make you more whole. It gives you more energy. The truth-body teaches you the truth. Helps you to recognize the truth, leads you to the truth and helps you to remember the truth."

"Had enough truth yet?" he asked as he beamed and again revved up his toy car on the tabletop. Then, after enjoying the sparking, he continued, "Deep within we know who we could be or who we really are, and we want to be that. You know," he said, "the end result of life, liberty and the pursuit of happiness." Silvio really seemed as though he could not contain himself as he beamed me another smile.

He then paused for a moment, seemingly to let the burst of energy that he had brought to our table settle before continuing. "And Chi Gung is what I use to rev up the engines of the other body."

I looked up at him and asked, "Silvio, explain to me a bit more how learned behavior works? How do we get trapped into using only part of the energy that is available to us, and how does the way we have been taught to move and breathe affect our access to our 'natural' energy that you talk about?"

Silvio put his car down, put his elbows on the table, rested his chin in the palms of his hands, bulged his eyes out grinning at me, then began, "What holds learned behavior together are the rules that it thinks it needs to perpetuate itself. These are the patterns of touching and moving and perceiving that we are taught as babes, as well as the patterns and rhythms of interrelating with others throughout our lives."

He paused for a minute then said with emphasis, "Be sure to remember this: learned behavior is about its own self-perpetuation. It cares little for the individual. The dictates of learned behavior determine the basic touch patterns that we are allowed and those that we are not allowed to experience. And these touch patterns are gravitationally imprinted into us via breathing and moving when we are young. And the core of this imprinting is based on learned behaviors' rules about sex and touch and the sexual act. Because if learned behavior can control that, it's got us by the 'short and curlies,'" he said, chuckling once again.

I must've looked a bit confused again because he burst out laughing, but I was not so sure that he was laughing at me or just laughing for the sheer joy of his expression.

"OK, OK," Silvio said, "I'll go a little slower and be a bit more precise. Learned behavior is predicated upon how we touch ourselves and the people around us. These touching patterns are coming from learned behavior trying to control our life-force, our sexuality. So, societies, or the learned behavior of the times we live in, tell us how to be and act with each other, sexually. This then becomes the underlying basis for the basic touch patterns that are allowed and those that are not. From here, all of our breathing and moving patterns radiate. Basically, it defines what I call the male/female agreement, or all of the ways we are supposed to deal with the men and women in our lives."

He laughed and added, "Notice that these are topics that we are trained to avoid talking about in depth. While at the same time they fill us with the utmost fascination.

"You following me now?" he said, beaming out another infectious smile. "Learned behavior is concerned with perpetuating itself. Life is 'created' through the sexual act. Therefore, learned behavior is very concerned with the way in which we view sexuality and perform the sexual act.

40

"One more time in a different way so you don't forget," he went on. "The touch patterns spiraling out from our sexual habits are the linchpin to the touch patterns that are imprinted into us when we are young. And these rhythms and patterns are held within our moving and breathing patterns. These then create the foundation for our sense of self and the way we relate to others."

"But who controls learned behavior?" I blurted out, "I can see what you're saying: that individuals come and go in the service of learned behavior—but who controls it?"

"Still waiting for that story from the Naked City are you?" he said, laughing. "Well, really and truly it is best not to focus very much on that because if you think about that—and the real word to focus on here is 'think'—that will lead you right back into the clutches of learned behavior. And believe me, many people are stuck right there. This is a slippery slope.

"For right now you've got enough on your plate to think about. The pieces of that puzzle will come together, and you will understand that better as you gather more energy by learning the exercises of our Chi Gung."

He paused to take in the scene of the lake, then put his attention back on me and started up again, "Let's take a look at how it works. Think about the brightness of youth and the enthusiasm with which the young go about grabbing onto the learned behavior of the times and culture that they are born into. Then watch as people get older and see how they get suffocated and constricted by the overuse of these repetitive patterns. What you will observe is that after their early years, people begin to lose their dynamism and elasticity and their energy wanes."

After this last statement he then looked up at the sky through the huge leaves of the teak tree spread above us. We listened to the sound of the splashing made by some fish being fed breadcrumbs from the nearby bridge.

Silvio looked at me and slowly took up his toy car, deliberately revved it up, then continued, "What happens is that your seemingly concrete needs begin to eat up all of your energy and it appears that there is no way out. This creates a desperate situation. It may not seem desperate for those

stuck in it, because they find themselves in a situation full of boring repetition. Stuck in the same rhythm of repetitive movement patterns, unable
to conceive anything else. And they don't really know it. In terms of the
spirit this is a desperate situation. Their energy is slowly being leached
out of them.

"Learned behavior has a great strategy. We are taught to endlessly
repeat our thoughts, breathing and movement patterns. At the same time
these are supported by those around us who do exactly the same thing.
This makes all parties involved feel accepted and wanted. As a result, we
end up inadvertently pinned down by mutual consent to a limited way of
being in the world."

"Li Tse, isn't that what you would call 'boring,'" Silvio said, looking
over at Li Tse.

Li Tse chuckled and nodded his approval.

I was a little stunned by the magnitude of what Silvio had just revealed.
It seemed like an impossible situation. I sat with that for a moment, then I
asked, "What makes us forget who we are?"

"It's simple, can't you see it?" he said. "We are numbed by the effects
of the ordinary concerns brought about by everyday life. Let's call it the
trance of everyday life. We are caught in the shuffle of body movements
and breathing patterns of those around us. These patterns and rhythms
suffocate and control us to the point that we have very little time or
energy left to really settle down and examine ourselves. In order to affect
a cure, we have to examine the disease first, right, doctor?" he said, jutting
out his chin and looking over in Li Tse's direction.

Li Tse, on cue with a serious voice, raising his index finger, said after
clearing his throat, "Yes indeed—how do we get so trapped into using
only part of the energy that is available to us? Why are we touching the
world in such a limited way?"

I raised my hand in front of me in a stopping motion, "Stop! Halt!" I
said. "Wait a minute, you guys, wait a minute. Slow down. This is a lot
to take in. You are saying that we are supporting our learned behavior on
the inside by how we move and breathe? And on the outside these patterns are being sustained and perpetuated by our interactions with those
around us? Sounds like we are surrounded! What are we supposed to do,
avoid contact with all humans?"

"Circle the wagons!!!" Silvio yelled out wide-eyed, circling his right hand above his head, then scrambling his arms around as if looking for a gun, whereupon Li Tse doubled over in laughter.

Silvio beamed and after a bit said, "I just wanted to show you the magnitude of it. How learned behavior makes it seem like it is the only game in town. I just wanted to show you how learned behavior manages to make its control invisible and seem so innocuous. I wanted you to see how we are being pushed around by learned behavior. How learned behavior overlays the primary pulse of life with its own rhythms and patterns without us realizing it.

"We have been set up to lose by default. We don't realize that there are other options. All we can see is what learned behavior has trained us to see. At this point it doesn't matter who controls the learned behavior— because it is in control," he said, rubbing his palms together. "In fact, thinking about who controls learned behavior can really become a terrible distraction. What we need to do is to use our energy to focus on how to release ourselves from it."

"That's right, Boss," Li Tse interjected, chuckling.

Silvio smiled then said, "The way we align ourselves in the world is by continuously renewing our sense of self. Learned behavior is a very solidified dream or creation, and it takes energy to see that we are more than that, that we have other options. When you are stuck in learned behavior and don't have enough energy you cannot even see it as your predicament, much less do anything about it.

"So, the question is, how can we access more of who we really are?" he emphatically asked. "You probably have an indefinable feeling that there is more going on out there," he said as he waved his hands in front of him as if trying to look through a fog, then stopped and peered at me. "But you are really stuck because you don't have the energy to do anything about it. It takes a certain amount of tension to keep the lines of perception of our learned behavior in place. And this takes up almost all of our energy. Couple that with the fact that our ability to perceive in any other way has become atrophied through time, and then you can begin to see how stuck we really are."

"So, yah, circle the wagons!" He smiled looking at me with a glint in

43

his eyes, rolling his shoulders, then peering at me again to judge the effect of his statements. "We have to learn to delicately loosen the iron grip of learned behavior," he said, making a fist, then repeatedly opening and closing his hand in smooth and gentle but powerful motions.

I interrupted asking, "So you've talked about how our breathing and moving keeps the habitual patterns of learned behavior in place. Is there any other way that learned behavior sustains itself?"

Once again Silvio slowly and thoughtfully picked up the toy car, and then deliberately and ever so slowly, began revving it up again on the table where we were sitting. "Now we're getting somewhere!" he said, lightening up, and this time letting the car go, then catching it just as it rolled off the table.

Then Silvio took a breath and then answered my question. "Language—and the emotional charges that it carries with it! When we're young we are told who we are by those around us, and then when we begin to think in language ourselves, we sustain this sense of self through a story that unfolds with that self as the central hero.

"This story that we're given when we're young is really what keeps our sense of self together. It is the centerpiece of all of our dramas and the way we have learned to deal with others. And we perpetuate it day and night by talking to ourselves. We do this by continually repeating, updating, and amplifying it. And that's only what's happening on the inside. Concomitantly, on the outside, family and friends are reinforcing that. When you interact with them you collude and perpetuate each other's story within the limited agenda given to you by learned behavior."

Then Li Tse piped in, "We do it all the time. We make tape loops inside with our thinking and outside when we engage with others." He raised his hands, looked from one to the other, repeatedly opening and closing them so they mimicked two talking heads.

Silvio smiled and nodded approvingly, then continued, "You are making tape loops. Yep, you are. You're looping your repetitive story into other people's story and recharging it. And strangely enough, when you do this, you feel as though you get a reprieve from your own internal talking. And you do, indeed.

"But in the long run, this only strengthens your tape loops. And it makes you want to continue to reach outside of yourself even more to get a break from your own internal machinations. However, this really only functions as a distraction from your internal tapes. This external talking just makes your loops more complex and even more 'interesting.' But this only increases the stranglehold of learned behavior—though in more complex and 'interesting' ways," he said, snickering. "In the end it only strengthens your looping ability and your dependency upon it.

"This internal dialogue also creates specific sets of dramas in our world that need to be repeated in order to keep our sense of self going. The constant repetition of the same dramas unfolding helps us to maintain a rigidity that holds our perception in its properly learned behavior place and does not allow us to grow into our true potential and to spread our wings.

"You stimulate your learned behavior by running through your story and pitting it against your friends' stories. This is an extraordinary act of collusion. And through it you are kept very busy and have very little time to settle down to examine yourself."

He stopped talking for a moment to focus on his hand that was slowly revving up the toy car on the table. I was starting to appreciate his use of props. He noticed that I was looking at him and sent the car in my direction.

We sat in silence for a bit, and as we did this, I took the time to reflect on what he had just said. And I realized that in my life, when I focused on myself for very long periods of time, I would become somewhat bored and "paralyzed." I then saw how I would look for a release outside of myself, and what I usually chose was talking to my friends. When I did this, it seemed to help—but not really. I remembered that when I did this, I felt that there was something amiss. Slowly I began to sense what Silvio was talking about. I related my thoughts to him.

He smiled and said, "Yes, it is true that when you focus on your learned-behavior self for very long you will feel constricted. On the other hand, when you shift your attention to exchanging tape loops with other people you may get a sense of relief, but if you look closely, you will sense that there is something false about it. And you will find yourself in the same predicament as before. This is exactly what I was talking about, and it is a prime example of how the collusion works. Because in the end you are only reinforcing your tape loops and thus perpetuating learned behavior."

Li Tse leaned forward and interjected, "Learned behavior can work in seemingly devious ways for the unsuspecting," he said wrinkling his brow. "For a specific example, let's get back to your question about who or what is behind learned behavior?"

He chuckled. "Most people who look at this just end up making new 'exalted' tape loops and weaving them back into their very own stories. Anything that will keep them from bringing the energy back down into their bodies to be stored," he said, pinching the skin of his hand. "These people are just fooling themselves. They truly feel that there is something out there manipulating the scene. And we would agree with them. But then they make the fatal attempt of trying to find an answer to this feeling by using the rules and frames of learned behavior to do so. They are trying to figure out something that is beyond the realm of learned behavior while staying on the agenda and using the terms of learned behavior. What nonsense!" he shrugged.

"It is just another twisted variation of the same pattern. One of the seemingly endless variations of the same theme of keeping people focused on learned behavior. Once you gather enough energy you will learn to see it for what it is: a quite simple strategy repeated over and over again that learned behavior uses to keep attention focused on itself. What I just described is just a little bit more sophisticated technique of co-opting, which I am sure you will hear more about later."

Silvio put his left fist under his chin for a moment, then raised his right index finger as if another idea had just come to him, "Here's another example: have you ever come home tired and turned on your TV set and felt the great relief of not having to think of your problems? Only to find out that after looking at the TV set for three hours you feel more exhausted than when you turned it on?"

I nodded and told Silvio that I could relate to what he was saying because at one point in my life I was so addicted to watching TV that in order to break this habit I had to lock my TV set in the closet.

Silvio and Li Tse snorted and chuckled at the thought of me closeting my TV.

Li Tse finally said, winking at me, "Well, that's a good solution. But how do you tell someone that your TV has to 'come out of the closet?'"

He then slapped his thigh and they both laughed, and I joined in at the thought of my TV "coming out of the closet."

Li Tse then said in the midst of his laughter, "The rhythms and patterns of learned behavior have an inertia behind them, as they have been going on for a long, long time gathering momentum. It takes a while to derail them. Locking them up in the closet for a while seems like it might help."

Silvio chimed in, "Come to think of it, the result of the way learned behavior ensnares us when we are young is like watching a TV with only a fraction of its channels working. You can see how this would put a dent in your potential viewing pleasure and would only give you a limited view of the world." He grinned mischievously.

Chapter 5

# Li Tse—Pressure

There I was once again in Chiang Mai, walking beside the Ping River through the flower stalls of Wararot Market. I was on my way to meet Li Tse on the far bank of the river. I had started out in the Old City of Chiang Mai, a walled city surrounded by a moat, built over 700 years ago. It was a center for Buddhism, and even to this day contains over 300 temples. It was the thriving hub for this part of the world, full of monks in their orange robes, elephants, and markets with goods from China and Burma (Myanmar), as well as the surrounding hills.

Although many times rebuilt, the buildings of this part of Chiang Mai had an ancient flavor to them. I am not sure if it was due to the plethora of wats, temples, and old chedis, its revered status as a center of learning and culture, or just something that oozed up from the ground into the walls, but there is a presence to be felt here. I had felt something similar in other places like Oaxaca City in Mexico, or the jungle city of Iquitos in Peru. It was a kind of palpable magic as if a spell had been cast that steadfastly fought against the constant onslaughts of time and globalization. It manifested here in Chiang Mai as a sense of ancient connectedness—from the mirrored animal statues of mythical creatures and chedis of the temples, to the smell of the leaves and the flowers from the trees.

That sense of ancient connectedness trailed a few blocks eastward of the Old City to Wararot market along the Ping River, where the whole north of Thailand still came to trade. The market is in the midst of Chiang Mai's small Chinatown, surrounded by shops of all kinds.

Inhabited by Northern Thais, settled-in Chinese, a myriad of hill tribe peoples, and a few Burmese who were lucky enough to make a living here. There is a feeling to this market. A dance to it. To walk in it is a joy. The folks here knew how to walk together. If you happened to bump into someone— which was not often, especially considering how many people were around—it was barely a glancing touch. This was much different than what I had experienced in the suffocating crowded streets of Shanghai, or walking in crowds of Westerners, who were so used to moving about in cars and relatively physically isolated from each other.

I had reached the flower market after going through the main two three-story buildings. The bottom floors were filled with food stuffs, and the upper ones were the home of clothing stalls, seamstresses, low-cost restaurants, beauty supply shops, and beauty parlors. I always liked the aliveness of the market and enjoyed it once again as I walked through. After passing though the flower stalls, I soon found myself walking across the Ping River and looking down from the bridge. Down below, at the water's edge, I saw Li Tse sitting, gazing out over the water.

I meandered down and joined him on his mat by the river. Li Tse liked to bring tea with him to our meetings. He poured a cup of tea for me from his thermos in greeting as I sat down. We sat for a while watching the activities around us. We noticed the people on the opposite shore fishing. A few long tail boats passed by. We saw a few paddle boats here and there, and even watched a tourist boat go by, all while enjoying the fresh breeze coming off the river.

I liked listening to the rich sound of Li Tse's voice as we talked and enjoyed the scene. But I had a burning question to ask him from our last encounter that I felt Silvio had not really answered to my satisfaction. So, I diverted our conversation to talking about Silvio then finally asked, "From what Silvio said about learned behavior, it sounds like we are surrounded. We are surrounded by humans who move and breathe to the tune of learned behavior. It seems so overwhelming. Do we have anything working in our favor?"

Li Tse peered at me for a moment, then turned his head to gaze at the river and answered, "Although we are surrounded by learned behavior, both internally and through the people around us, there are indeed things working in our favor. We are surrounded and supported by the Earth's cocoon and our connection to it," he said, patting the Earth with his right hand.

"Sense what's all around you," he said, opening his palms upward. He then sat back, relaxed, picked up his cup and took a sip of tea, exhaling a sound of satisfaction, "Ahhhh...!"

He then continued, "Not only do we have the Earth's cocoon to rely on, we also have that within which knows what and who we really are, and which is seeking expression. The body knows about its connection to the Earth and is always listening to this feeling within us that knows and is always trying to correct itself and its relationship to gravity and pressure. We just have to let it talk to us and learn to listen carefully. We must give the body a chance, then the essence within us that knows can speak to us through it. Buddhists speak of the body as 'The Precious Human Form,' because through it and in it we can realize who or what we really are."

"Does learned behavior have any value at all?" I asked, slightly changing the subject.

"In a way, learned behavior serves a purpose, even with all of its draw backs," Li Tse responded. "It's quite necessary because it gives us a way to relate to other people. It has a function. It is the home base that we are given until we can disentangle enough energy from it. Once we gather enough energy, we can use it to relate to the world of people without the cumbersome side effects of its exclusivity.

"To learn to live with and without it at the same time is important, because we need to eat, nourish our bodies, and communicate and interact with our fellow humans," he said motioning with his hand to all the human activity around us. "We need know how to talk the body-to-body talk of learned behavior and the body movements and breathing patterns that support it. But at the same time, when we gather enough energy back, we can also expand beyond its limits to move along the path of who we really are. We can do this by maintaining our awareness of the Earth's cocoon around us and by listening to the essence within us."

I had another question for Li Tse that I had brought with me, "You know Li Tse, I listened to Silvio talk about all these bodies, but I'm still not sure I'm clear about this."

His eyes rolled upward and a big grin appeared on Li Tse's face when I mentioned Silvio's name.

"That does not surprise me," he responded, "because we're somewhat bound by language and its limitations. Some things are not so easy to talk about. These concepts of the different bodies are an attempt to describe, within the limitations of language, a force that exists beyond its realm. There is a force that is trying to put us back together again. But being beyond the realm of language, this force can only be alluded to—thus the 'bodies.'

"And then of course there's Silvio," he grinned, "who is more of a doer than a talker. He likes to ride on these big currents of energy, so sometimes it's hard to keep up with him," he said, pausing.

"Let me see if I can clear this up for you a little bit. When describing this force that is trying to reintegrate us, we don't know how to talk about it, so we talk about it in terms of certain aspects that can be envisioned and expressed through language. And we call these aspects the 'energy-body,' the 'truth-body,' the 'body of focus,' and the 'healing-body template.'"

"Well, why do we even call them bodies?" I inquired.

"Because this body," he said, pinching the skin of his forearm, "with its five senses and all its movements is the crucible within which our evolutionary transformation is taking place. This body is the center of the cocoon of our transformation, surrounded and supported by the cocoon of the Earth. You can use this concept of various bodies existing simultaneously, interacting with each other, and feeding each other, to begin to understand the force that is trying to integrate our wholeness.

"Like Silvio said, the truth about this force is that it will help you to know yourself, give you better health, more energy, and, I would add, help you evolve to something greater.

"It is hard to tell which aspect of this force is more important because these aspects all interrelate and feed each other, but in general the idea of the energy-body encompasses them all. Let me try to give you a linear example; when you begin to free up energy from your learned behavior, knowledge rains down upon you in terms of understanding who or what you are," he smiled. "This is the 'truth-body.'

"You also gain a greater ability to focus because you access energy more efficiently. This is the 'body of focus.'

"And when you move this energy through the 'healing-body template' you gain more energy in general and better health as a result.

"This is just one example of how energy can flow through the various bodies. But it can flow in any number of other ways and in any number of directions. You can begin to understand who you really are more clearly if you think of yourself as being a summation of all of these aspects. It's not as if you actually have these separate bodies. This is just a way of talking about and understanding the dynamics of what's taking place in your cocoon. These concepts are just touchstones that can help anchor us outside the purview of learned behavior."

He relaxed for a moment, letting his eyes move over the water, turned and looked at me, "Knowledge is one aspect, but it is fleeting if not fused into the other aspects. So, you need the energy aspect to help transform this knowledge, the body of focus to focus it and the healing-body template to ground it down.

"This is a lot to digest, so just sit with this for a while, but next time you see Silvio ask him about teaching you fourth-dimensional chess," Li Tse chuckled.

"This explanation makes things a little clearer", I said, beginning to feel the gist of what he was talking about.

"Before we move off of this topic, think of this," Li Tse continued, raising his index finger to accentuate what he was going to say. "The body knows what it is doing. When we break a bone there is an intrinsic force that knows how to knit that bone. When we cut ourselves, there is a template that gives our body a pattern of how to mend that wound. Reflecting upon where this power comes from will give you a key to understanding how the other aspects I mentioned interrelate. And even where we came from and where we are going."

As we stopped to watch an egret fly by, a fisherman on the other side of the river reeling in his catch, and continued to enjoy the fresh breeze from the water, his last statement triggered off a memory. I remembered a time once, sitting in a forest looking down at my feet and seeing my toe-nails, and then reaching up and running my hands through my hair and wondering, "Who or what is the me that is growing these."

We sipped some tea for a bit, then Li Tse looked over at me and began, "What I really wanted to talk to you about today is pressure. Inherent in the folds of gravity are layers of pressure, and this creates the flowing and moving world around us. The entire world is made up of movements of pressure. We are really just balls of pressure moving in a world of pressure."

He laughed, then went on to say, "We live within a cocoon of pressure in the midst of the cocoon of pressure of the Earth. Look at the rain, the clouds, the wind, the waves, and currents in the sea to begin to understand how pressure works in the cocoon of the Earth. We have similar pressures working inside our body. In fact, in the medicines of the ancients, the internal functions of the body were described in terms of elements whose interrelating created certain types of pressure. And diseases were often described as climatological occurrences that corresponded with what we observe out in the cocoon of the Earth.

"To understand this a little bit more fully you can also look at the Chinese art of Feng Shui, which literally means 'wind and water.' Feng Shui is the art of placement, and the study of how physical and energetic forces interact and influence each other and us. If you go along with me here and see that inside our cocoon there are climates created by friction between elements, and that these climates are reflective of the elements and climates in the Earth's cocoon, you can surmise that Feng Shui is really the art of balancing the two. You can see that Feng Shui is the study of balancing the pressures inside and outside of us, or the art of watching and working with the flows of the world.

"We live in a world of pressure," Li Tse said, opening his arms to embrace all around him. He smiled and continued, "We move, pulled by the strings of gravitational forces. And all movement is basically based on pressure. You see, perceiving the world as pressure is a very practical way of understanding it. We can choose to perceive the world as a series of pressures which are the active aspects of gravity. You can feel it in your body, you can feel it in the downward pressure of gravity where your body touches the Earth and the resultant pressures that then create movement. You can even think of the pressures created by digestion and the internal workings of the body, like the pressure created by the circulation of blood and fluids."

"I see!" I said, nodding in agreement, feeling my body relaxing as the realization and knowledge about what he was talking about sunk in.

Li Tse continued his elucidations, "You can learn to sense the pressures around you with total body presence. The rhythms and patterns in pressure can be sensed with the whole body. We are just one pressurized ball of mud, sloshing around in a world of pressure," he said with a laugh. "It's a very visceral way of understanding and interacting with the world, whether it's sensing the current weather or the people around us."

This was something! This conversation seemed to change my idea of what my body was and how it worked with the world around me even as he spoke. I had a glimpse at seeing my body as being in perpetual motion aligned with movements and pressures around me. I was glad Li Tse had explained this to me the way he did. What he said felt right and made me realize that I actually had always felt this pressure. It really did change my idea of my body to think of the world around me as currents and waves of pressure.

I was also slowly coming to the realization what a refined person Li Tse was. To put these concepts into words required a great deal of concentration. It took a lot more directed energy to convey a real feeling like pressure through words and concepts than just experiencing it.

Li Tse observed the look on my face and started to laugh. "I think you are beginning to get it," he said. And then, responding to the startled expression on my face of feeling as though I had had my thoughts read, he exclaimed, "Yes! Even thoughts have a pressure!"

He leaned over, took a sip of tea, put down his cup, and rested his elbows on his knees. He then steepled his hands under his chin, took a deep breath and said, "There are folds in the Earth's gravity and also folds in our own gravitational fields. We're living in a big ocean of currents and waves of pressure. But to put it into proper perspective we are even more than that."

He paused, then said, "I want you to ponder on this for a moment—where does the pressure of the body begin and end?"

We sat for a bit, then got up. Li Tse took up his thermos and cups and put them into his bag. He waved to the "mat man" whom he'd already paid for the pleasure of using the mat we'd been sitting on. In Thailand, often at parks or beaches, places where people go to relax, there are locals who conveniently rent out mats so you don't have to bring your own.

We crossed the river and meandered back through the small lanes of an old section of Chiang Mai until Li Tse took me into a wat. These temple complexes are usually quiet places. They are one of the few places in downtown Chiang Mai where you can have sanctuary from the noise and traffic of the city. We walked through the grounds of the wat, which was full of mirrored and gilded facades and statues of mythical creatures, until we found a bench in the shade of a huge tree whose trunk was wrapped in bands of varying colored cloth. In Thailand, an old tree such as this is believed to contain powerful spirits and a deep connection to the Earth. The multi-colored silks tied around it often signify the Thai belief that heavenly beings reside within. In the countryside a tree such as this may even be a place where people deposit broken statues, shrines, or spirit houses because they believe when something is broken it can bring bad luck if they keep it around. So, they bring them to these trees to ask the spirits that inhabit them to ward off and absorb any bad luck that may be associated with the objects.

We took a seat next to each other under this living being. "Can you feel the pressure of the presence of this tree and all the life it engenders around it?" Li Tse said, pointing with his chin to a bird singing in the tree.

"We also have a presence and a pressure. People can be seen as pressure bubbles in the Earth's pressurized cocoon. We live and move in a pressurized sac within its field. And you can learn to feel this pressure around you with your total body awareness."

He looked at me knowingly as a small red and black dragonfly flew around us, stopping to stare at us through its bulging eyes.

"Life is about the energetic movement of nature. For example, if our bodies do not move, life does not flow through us. And pressure is another way to talk about movement, about life. Also, when you begin perceiving the world in terms of pressure, the predominance of perceiving with the eyes diminishes. It's like the difference between looking at an image on a TV screen and walking around in life. Perceiving the world as pressure is a fuller body experience.

"We can exchange pressure too. People exchange pressure with each other all the time," he said, slowly leaning his shoulder into me. "We relate to each other through patterns of pressure and touch. The way we perceive or even pressure ourselves and the world around us is intimately connected to the way we focus and move our bodies. We are individual sacs of pressure, but there is also a huge human sac of pressure that occurs when people get together in mass. And it can pressurize us in many different ways when we interact with it."

Li Tse got up and gestured for me to follow saying, "We are now going to go to a market to feel the presence or pressure of bodies, the pressures of moving in a crowd." We continued walking towards the old walled city. We walked for a few blocks, gradually gathering with the people who were slowly streaming into the "Walking Street" market that happens every Sunday here in Chiang Mai.

We soon found ourselves amidst the booths of swirling silks, clothes, indigenous earrings, colorful purses and bags from the hill tribes, carved antiques, opium pipes, jewelry, and the colors of famous lacquered umbrellas from outlying villages displayed throughout the market. We walked through the sounds of children playing various instruments in the middle of the street, mixed with those of a troupe of blind young boys singing and playing their arrangements. These sounds were layered with the murmurs of the crowd. And, as an overlay, we sometimes heard the music of ensembles of elders playing lyrical traditional tunes and instruments. All these drifted in and out of range as we slowly walked, feeling the market around us.

Li Tse came close to me and gently nudged me with his elbow and said, "Can you feel the pressures in the crowd?"

That triggered off my awareness of pressure. I began to sense the world around me in terms of pressure. I could feel the pressure of the people walking toward me. I could feel the pressure of walking behind someone, having to slow down because they were moving more slowly than I was. Then I could feel the pressure of having to weave my way between people like a fish swimming in currents of pressure. I began to sense the people in the market as blobs of pressure, each one with a different quality. I could not only just feel them in front of me, I could feel them all around me, creating currents of pushing and pulling. I got a feeling for how these individual blobs of pressure were interacting not only with each other but as a unit.

I then noticed that different groups of people had their own flavor of pressure: a cluster of schoolgirls, a group of foreign men, intimate couples, even the vendors who were stationary and not moving in the flow with the crowd—each of them had their own quality of pressure. And I could feel these groups of pressure rubbing up against each other.

Li Tse nudged me again and pointed over to the right with his chin. I noticed a lanky Thai man dressed in blue cotton work clothes with a wispy gray beard. He looked like a Thai from the village and seemed to have a lot of energy for his age. He had a sparkle in his eyes and radiance in his face. There was something else to him that I could sense. Something exuding from him that I couldn't put my finger on. I felt attracted to him somehow. His way of being contrasted sharply with the people around him. He had a presence to him. Then it came to me very strongly that "presence" has a pressure and that each of us, maybe not as strikingly as others, emanates a special kind of pressure.

As we observed him, he quickly turned to look back at us with a smile and I realized he had sensed the pressure of our gaze, which made me remember the many times I'd felt the pressure of someone looking at me, whether I was facing them directly or even if they were behind me or to the side. I especially remembered the sensation of driving a car and quickly turning my head to the side to sense the pressure of a person in a passing car staring at me.

And as we walked on, it coalesced in me that attention is a special type of pressure too. And that the pressure created by the focused attention of a crowd can be a very intense one. I could remember the rush of energy I had felt when I was a young teenager playing guitar in front of an audience. I could also remember times of feeling very uncomfortable having to speak before a group of people in a class.

We moved along and once again found ourselves wandering into a wat. In this wat I noticed a group of Buddha statues off in the corner. There were eight statues, one for each day of the week, with Wednesday having two. Some of these statues were lying, others were standing or sitting, and they were holding different mudra gestures with their hands. I suddenly realized that even postures have a pressure, and I got a sense of how postures direct the pressure contained in the body in distinct ways.

The yard of this wat was filled with food stalls—sushi, all kinds of Thai foods wrapped in banana leaves, deep fried and stir-fried foods, sausages, grilled fish, squid, and chicken. We meandered our way through and picked out some small fish casseroles wrapped in banana leaves and sat down at a table for a snack.

When we finished, we got up and walked towards another wat, to an area where people were doing massage, and the next thing I knew Li Tse and I were sitting alongside each other in a long line of chairs getting foot massages, watching the people in the market walking by.

Li Tse leaned over and began talking, "It's easy to under-stand that massage is a kind of pressure. Creating and moving pressure in the body in this way can be very beneficial."

I looked over to the side of the massage area and saw there was a small shrine with lit candles to either side, two glasses of red colored water, flowers, and small fruit offerings. It was a shrine to the sage Shivago Komarapaj. He sat cross legged, with a long white beard and piercing gaze. He is said to have been the founder of Thai massage and medicine. You can see a shrine to him in many places where massage is practiced and taught. He was purported to have been the physician of the Buddha over 2,500 years ago. The history of Thai massage is closely interlinked with Buddhist monastic tradition, being originally preserved and disseminated by monks to the people. It is just in the last few decades that this art has become more secularized, being taught and propagated by lay people who want to do massage for foreigners without much oversight by monks.

As I sat there enjoying the massage, feeling the pressures on my feet brought me closer to a total body experience, and enabled me to sense the moving pressures around me more keenly. This triggered memories of previous experiences with Thai massage. There are different massage lineages, different massage masters. Some of the lineages and teachings have even been propagated by mediums—channeling information about massage from ancient Buddhist and other spiritual sources. In Thailand I have experienced styles of Thai massage where the medium practitioner is taken over by his/her spirit as the practitioner performs the massage in a trance-like state. Nuances in techniques are often developed from such a teacher who is given knowledge by calling in one of his spirit friends. This activity adds another facet to Thai massage that invigorates and keeps it alive by bringing in information "from beyond the realm of learned behavior," as Silvio would put it.

When I came back from my reverie, Li Tse continued, "Massage is actually a very specialized form of pressure. Massage is applying pressure to one part of the body to equalize a pressure in another part of the body, with the goal of balancing the overall pressure in the body sac. It is an attempt to create an equilibrium between the pressures in the body sac and those coming from outside, so that the body can function better."

Suddenly I winced and recoiled as I felt the pressure of a teak wood massage stick go into my foot a little too hard. The woman working on my feet smiled up at me and asked, "*Jep mai?* Does it hurt?" I nodded my head and grunted.

"Is pain a kind of pressure?" I asked Li Tse facetiously.

Li Tse chuckled and said, "You got it! Pain occurs when the pressure is too much. Pain is too much sensation or touch, too much pressure. And in a real way pain defines the limits of our so-called physical body."

After our massage I felt a little more spring in my step as we walked back, out of the wat into the crowd. I chuckled to myself thinking about how the pressure of my body had just been readjusted.

Then we were back into the pressure of the crowd. We continued moving through the currents of pressure around us, when suddenly everyone stopped as the Thai National Anthem, "The King's Song," was played. It was stunning to sense how the pressure changed dramatically and settled when all movement stopped as everyone listened to the music. We waited and watched. When the anthem finished, I saw the carousel of pressure and movement explode back into life again, as I sensed the sounds of the cosmic calliope starting up again around us.

We took a left turn into one of the side streets, leaving the "Walking Street" market and continuing into the depths of the Old City, and entered another wat on our right. I thought to myself, "These wats are literally everywhere." As the daylight waned we walked into the compound of Wat Chedi Luang, and eventually found ourselves sitting on a bench on the northern side of the huge old chedi under a plumeria tree with large pink flowers.

I reflected on the wat's history. Wat Chedi Luang is one of the oldest temples in Chiang Mai. The construction of the temple began in the 14th century. It took until the mid-15th century to be finished. At that time it was the largest building of the kingdom of Lanna. In 1468 a statue of the Emerald Buddha was housed there until it was moved to Luang Prabang in Laos in the middle of the 16th century, and eventually found its way to Bangkok, where it is now. The massive main chedi is adorned by 16 huge elephant figures all the way around its base, and there is a station on either side where you can find a pulley system for raising water to pour on the top of the chedi as a prayer offering.

"I think you were able to sense the rhythms and patterns of pressure in the interactions in the crowd out there in the streets," Li Tse began. "Did you notice that the attractions and repulsions between people you observed are a type of pressure? And the feelings you were having observing those interactions are a type of pressure too. I can go as far as to say that emotions are a kind of pressure within us. Even thoughts create a pressure.

"You see, we live in a world of pressure," he continued. "Can you feel that the pressure now in the late afternoon is different from what it was this morning? Even at different times of day, light changes and pressure changes and we feel differently. On a grand scale, the pressure of the moon affects the tides of the oceans. Even the pressures of the planets have an effect on us.

"This wat is an old, old place. When this wat was constructed back in those times, and in times before that, people thought of the body quite differently. They perceived the body as a pressurized sac with bones supporting it—really a bag of bones!" He laughed.

"Furthermore, they perceived that inside the bones is a gelatinous marrow, which in a physical sense embodies our essence. It flows out to the rest of our body and the body processes in turn nourish it. First the pressure emanating from the marrow stabilizes and pressurizes the bones from within. This then builds the bones and makes them strong. Then it flows out to feed the blood. After that it moves even further outward from the blood to feed the muscles and then moves out to nourish the skin. It then radiates outwards beyond the skin, which you can perceive as the sensation of Chi which actually is like a subtle substance that forms this cocoon that surrounds us," he said, spreading his hands in an arc around him.

"This structure of the bones is organized to stabilize the continuous downward pressure of the Earth's gravity on our body sac. The body's skeletal and muscular systems play a primary role in maintaining the structural integrity of the body by organizing the pressures of the forces exerted upon it. There is also an energetic structure in the body around which Chi can flow. If this structure is optimally operational, the Chi flow is maximized and the essence in the marrow can be recharged. When the balance of pressures in our body is intact, the whole body can reciprocate and maintain and recharge the essence in the marrow. But when there is not enough pressure in the body sac, then the essence seeps out and is depleted."

Li Tse stopped for a moment then went on to say, "In my experience, correct postural alignment is a natural result of focusing on increasing the flow of Chi. When we keep Chi flow as the core of our practice, we have something around which to build and sustain it. This is the way we correct our posture from the inside. Not only do we get correct posture this way, but at the same time the pressure that results from maximizing Chi-flow then allows us to align our cocoon with the cocoon of the Earth. The force of gravity then can maintain and sustain the correct pressure within the body sac."

He then said with a sense of finality, "This then invigorates the healing-body template. Health can really be defined as the free flow of Chi and pressure in the body. Maintaining optimal pressure within the body sac and distributing this pressure throughout the body is the key to good health and longevity."

"I think I'm beginning to get this, Li Tse. But I'm wondering what happens to this pressure when we lose it? Where does it go, and can we get it back?" I wanted to know.

"Great question, young man!" He chortled. "I think you understand enough now that I can begin to address your query. Although you'll really learn about it more fully when you get into our practice of Chi Gung.

"The answer is really in what Silvio has been talking to you about—your moving and breathing patterns. Pressure is lost due to our lack of proper movement and breathing. It atrophies and solidifies as a type of energetic mass in the form of energetic crusts and cobwebs that encapsulate our body cocoon. If we start to properly adjust our moving and breathing patterns, we can begin to regain our pressure."

"I can somewhat follow you, but it still is not totally clear," I responded, feeling a bit overwhelmed.

"It may help if I describe the process that goes on as we regain our pressure," he said. "We begin to repressurize our bodies by creating more Chi flow. By repressurizing our bones and strengthening our blood in this manner, we will reinvigorate our whole skeletal structure, directly helping to avert diseases such as osteoporosis or fragile bones and many other maladies. Incidentally, the biggest bone in our body is the femur, the upper leg bone. By pressurizing and strengthening the muscles over this area we can replenish the 'sea of blood' and further compact and strengthen the bones. The right kind of Chi Gung can be highly effective for strengthening this area, building the muscles of the upper thigh, and revitalizing the essence in the bone. In fact, I have heard this upper thigh area referred to as our 'second heart', because if it is strong every time we extend and contract it, it helps to pump the blood and fluids through our body, thus enhancing the body's circulation."

He laughed, slapping his thighs, "You could even say that our thighs are the pillars of our health."

He rubbed his chin to catch a thought, "You understand that this is just a more corporal way of describing the integration of the physical body with the various 'bodies' we spoke of earlier."

"I'm a little frustrated," I said, scratching my jaw. "I can follow what you are saying, but it all seems a little bit abstract to me just now. Can you tell me your personal experience?" I asked.

Li Tse leaned back stretching his arms and took in the glow of the setting sun. "What I have experienced is that the more that I balance the pressures in my body and allow more Chi to flow, the pressures from the world of people impinge less upon me. The pressure in my body is maintained at a higher level by my body's direct interaction with the gravity of the Earth. I need to rely less upon the pressures that come to me from the outside, i.e., through relating to other people, to function in the world. And I feel more complete within myself. Thus, I have less need for the prescribed ways of learned behavior in order to sustain a sense of self. I'm being nourished by the Great Mother herself," he said with a lighthearted laugh.

"This has given me an overview from which to look even more closely at the effects of pressure and the flow of Chi in and on my body and in that of others. As I started to get my energy back by repressurizing my body and relying less on those around me, I started to get a perspective and sense as to what degree people are colluding to maintain learned behavior and how it influences them. Perhaps you noticed while we were observing the rhythms and patterns of pressure in the market that we have been taught to depend on the pressure of others to sustain ourselves, rather than relying on the pressure of our own natural beingness and its connection with the Earth's cocoon. You probably can't see the extent to which this affects us yet, but I think you can get a sense of what I'm talking about."

I nodded, impressed by his elucidation but also a bit alarmed by its implications.

Li Tse continued, "What would be optimal would be for people to relate with the Earth from a place of internal integrity. Then a very natural way of interacting could emerge. But as it is now, instead people leave a pressure imprint on us, an impression. We're pressing each other all the time," he said, pressing his thumb into his ribcage and letting out a yelp as if it was hurting him.

"What practical value does all of this have?" I wanted to know. "To me this still seems so abstract. What kind of advantage can balancing and increasing the pressures in our body give us?"

Li Tse raised his eyebrows a couple of times, looking at me, then winking and said, "What you're really asking is what kind of advantage would this have for me?"

He suddenly leaned over and pressed my chest with his finger. "Fair question!" he said. "Be patient," he went on, raising his hand and showing me his palm in a gesture telling me to slow down. "Because honestly the answer to your question is: you won't know until you get there," he grinned.

"You will learn later through practice how your body can be aligned by balancing and moving the pressures through your body. As you do this you will gain perspective from having distanced yourself somewhat from learned behavior. You will also be able to see what learned behavior has done to other people. If you look back at the wake of where you've come from, you will be able to see how the people around you have not really changed and are still so very susceptible to the patterns of learned behavior. This then will give you even more impetus to continue to gather energy.

"To the extent that you've put yourself back together, you also will be able to see how physical conditions or diseases arise from people's inefficient way of moving Chi in their bodies. Then you will be able to make the conclusion of how this is caused by their unconscious repetitive movements and their collusion with learned behavior."

"Cut to the chase," I said, laughing, "what can it actually do for my body? How can it make me free?"

He looked down pensively for a moment then back at me candidly. "Well, for me these practices have made me healthier, gradually dissolving physical and emotional problems that have dogged me all my life. I've watched them slowly dissolve and slip away. The effects are that I'll be walking along, or one day I wake up and suddenly notice a problem is no longer there, and that if it should happen to return it is much less intense."

Li Tse paused for a moment, looking up at the huge chedi being held up by massive elephants and the pink light of the fading evening sun engulfing the ancient structure. He then said, "Even more importantly—it has given me a direction in life, something to pull my life together around, and it gives me solace when I falter."

Chapter 6

# Silvio—Silvio's Chi Gung

I was walking with my friends Li Tse, and Silvio, the toy maker, to a waterfall in the mountains above Chiang Mai. We were on a trail next to a large stream meandering through a forest of bamboo and deciduous trees, occasionally having to make our way through piles of huge teak leaves lying on the path. As I walked alongside, I noticed a buoyancy about them. They both had a bounce to their step and a joyful exuberance to their being. It was exhilarating just to walk in their aura of vitality.

We passed one small cataract in the stream on our way up the trail. We walked a little further and stopped at the base of a larger one and found our way to a grassy area alongside it. They liked it there, so we chose a place to sit and arrange ourselves. Here the cool, fresh scent of the waterfall mingled with the smells of the forest vegetation.

Li Tse had his water bottle, a small camping stove, tea, teapot, cups, and woven bamboo mat in his backpack. With his stove, teacups and a few little tea snacks, Li Tse set the scene. He spread out the mat and made all to his liking. He then lit the stove and began to set water to boil. Silvio was off into the forest and when he returned, he hung an origami-like grasshopper he'd assembled from bamboo leaves in a branch that hung over our spot.

In the history of tea in China there is a tradition of going off to special places in nature to have a kind of "inspirational picnic," to celebrate our connection with life with tea as the central element. When you drink good tea it elicits a certain kind of camaraderie that allows for deep communication with a clarified mind. Puer tea in particular, Li Tse's favorite, was traditionally the tea of choice for old sages and scholars, because it produces a unique crystalline clarity of mind.

The old Puer tea plants in Hunan province are trees now. Some are 1,700 years old. Puer tea is packed into cakes and set aside to ferment. The longer it ferments the more its qualities and flavors are enhanced, to the point that the older tea can sustain as many as twenty infusions. Puer is graded and priced accordingly, with the older cakes of compacted tea going for exorbitant amounts of money.

Li Tse had brought some Puer for this occasion and broke up a bit of a thirty-year-old tea cake. He put it into a small teapot and watched the action as the water began to boil on the small stove, the size of the bubbles increasing from "shrimp eyes" to "crab eyes" and finally to "fish eyes", until it reached perfect boiling point. Puer tea is infused at slightly hotter temperature than oolong or green tea, so the bubbles in the heated water are allowed to reach the size of fish eyes before infusion. Li Tse poured the water into the small teapot to quickly rinse the tea. After he'd poured this out, he then poured water into the teapot for the first infusion and let it sit. Silvio sat down to join us at the point when the tea was poured, and the stage was set for our conversation.

"We've come here today so I can finish my explanation about learned behavior," Silvio began. "As I have told you, our energy, or our capacity to create energy from a complete interaction with the world around us, has been co-opted by learned behavior. It has set an iron net over and throughout our bodies, confining us to very restricted moving and breathing patterns. Thus, our energetic pathways have become clogged with limited fixations. They are glued together like pasta that has not been stirred and prepared properly." Silvio raised his right hand with his fingers and thumb held together and made an emphatic gesture of trying to pull his fingers apart with his other hand.

His hand gestures reminded me of my difficulty in untying the rubber bands on every bag of food one buys at the food stalls here in Thailand,

I thought whimsically to myself. The way they spin and twist those rubber bands around is still a mystery to me. "Maybe if I gather enough energy, it'll increase my knowledge to the point that it will reveal the secret to taking these rubber bands off more quickly!" I mused. "There has to be an esoteric method to this."

Silvio brought me back from my reverie as he continued, "We somehow feel that we are not all here, that we need more energy. And these feelings ring true. We need more energy for healing and the pursuit of our innermost desires. Where are we going to get it?" he then asked rhetorically.

"The only place we can get it is by taking energy back from the way learned behavior has twisted, diverted, and corrupted it for its own ends. We have the energy in us, but we have to untangle the mess that the dictatorial power of learned behavior has put us in. We need to separate bound-up energy currents and get the energy circulating in its proper natural ways again. What we are dealing with is reclaiming our bottled-up energy back from learned behavior. And as I have told you before, this learned behavior is kept in place by our repetitive acts and motions."

"Where do you get the spark to initiate this process of reclaiming your energy?" I asked.

Silvio looked at me and grinned approvingly as if I had asked the right question. "We must dig deeply into ourselves to contact the evolutionary force within us that knows who we are, a blueprint of our potential. Also, we can use our connection with the natural world that surrounds us to help inspire us to learn about ourselves."

He then paused, this time for dramatic effect, looking around and then refocusing on me before he continued, "We need to allow that within us which knows our inherent beingness to come alive again. We have to develop a new continuity based on this. If you engender the process of gathering your energy back, this will create an inertia of its own. The body can fix itself as more energy is released from learned behavior in a natural progression that builds upon itself. This unleashed energy can then be transformed into health and well-being, as well as serving as a base for new perceptions."

He looked up, then played with the origami grasshopper above his head for a moment, and went on, "Remember, learned behavior is not a fixed thing. It is a movement, a series of movements through time that has tone, rhythm, and pattern. Don't think about it as something static—it is moving and changing, always moving. There is also continuity to this movement that manifests in our cultural underpinnings around us, and it has grown in us since we were born. We need to stop our absorption in the ways of learned behavior so something else can happen.

"Break up the rhythm! Create a dissonance! So other energies can enter and a new natural order can be reestablished."

He smiled, rocked back and forth a few times, then said, "Staying away from learned behavior beckons a solution. One has to slowly be weaned off learned behavior as one builds up the energy-body. The way learned behavior is established is through habitual patterns. The first thing we must do is to detach our awareness from our own personal story that learned behavior has instilled in us, and reclaim the freedom to focus on something else."

"Okay, Okay, OKAY!!!—but how do you actually do it?" I asked, a bit desperate.

He smiled, bent down, took a sip of tea and put his teacup down. He then suddenly bulged his eyes out and loudly clapped his hands in front of his face, then cupped them around his mouth and yelled, "BREAK TIME! BREAK TIME! TIME OUT!"

This startled me. Stopped me in my tracks!

"To allow something else to happen! To break-up the continuity!" Li Tse chimed in, chuckling. Silvio continued, "Even our most famous cultural role models took a break: Buddha, Christ, and Moses—they all spent time alone to allow their own beingness to seep into them, to permeate their bodies."

This reminded me of "the diet" that the shamans of the Amazon recommended for gaining knowledge. In addition to eating very bland foods, it is required that one spends long lapses of time alone in the jungle—a withdrawal from human interaction.

Silvio looked at the jungle around us, moved his head from side to side, then said, "You like to travel, don't you? Traveling is something we like doing because we can begin to move just a little beyond the collusion of our own culture. It gives us a little reprieve. Traveling disrupts the rhythm of our established movement patterns—the way we relate to those around us. Although many times we like to bring reminders of our learned behavior with us, such as friends and travel companions."

This made me think about how living in Thailand had turned into a break for me. It had been a silent retreat of sorts. It broke up my usual way of relating to others. The language and customs here in Thailand were so vastly different. I could see a bit of how their patterns of walking on the Earth, as an expression of their learned behavior, were different from mine. Being in this "difference" created an enjoyable dissonance for me. And this allowed an unusual rhythm of new energy to rise up in me. I could now, after having listened to Silvio, see that this breakup of my cultural training was really one of the reasons that I liked traveling. It made me feel freer and somehow, I could flow better.

Li Tse then spoke up, "I also know you've been traveling the world, exploring remnants of ancient cultures. Why do you think you do that? I think it's because brushing up against these ancient cultures gives you a glimpse of a way of being that's different from the learned behavior you were brought up in. And you like the taste of that freedom that seeps in through this juxtaposition."

"That sounds about right," I said in agreement.

We paused to enjoy our tea and snacks, taking in the scene around us, the chirping of the birds, the constant murmuring of the waterfall and the freshness of the cool air coming from it. I idly watched a line of ants crawl along a log a few feet away, and this made me wonder about how they perceive the world.

Thinking about what Silvio and Li Tse had said brought a question to mind, "So, are you saying that it is better to travel alone than with friends and others that you meet along the way?"

"No, not at all," Silvio replied. "In fact, we are humans and social interaction is important. I'm just giving you a perspective to look at traveling from and to look at the way you relate to others, because you may want to allow a new way of relating to evolve. It might actually be useful to keep friends and acquaintances around for a while because they can provide a buffer and lessen the shock of disengaging the charges from your learned behavior. It is better to give up learned behavior gradually. To disengage from it in a sustained way—step by step, until you accumulate enough freed up energy to become completely independent of it. Otherwise, it could be quite dangerous."

He paused for a second, then went on, "Although an occasional shock or two can't hurt, especially in the beginning when it often takes a good jolt to give us a breather," he said, striking the side of his head with a laugh.

"When you look at it closely you see that we use a tremendous amount of focused energy to maintain our learned behavior. But this sustained focus on what is only a small part of our true potential eventually drains us and actually prevents access to other, more vital sources of energy. And to compound the problem, access to those other energy sources has atrophied from lack of use.

"What I am talking about is getting energy back from learned behavior so you can re-deploy your focus. It takes a supreme effort to break the bonds of learned behavior. And to incorporate the energy released once those bonds have been broken takes even more energy. Because we need more energy to realign ourselves and stabilize a new, ever evolving perceptual platform to operate from. We need to create a place where energy can be stored, energy that we access from other sources beyond the domain of learned behavior. You see, we need to exercise our atrophied abilities. It's like building up a muscle."

"Huh?" I said, shaking my head in confusion.

Silvio smiled. "I get your confusion," he said. "Sometimes a little movement helps. So, I'll move a little for you."

He then stood up and began to walk back and forth in front of us, animatedly.

"It seems paradoxical," he said. "You would think that by loosening the grip of learned behavior you would experience more energy. You do— and at the same time you don't," he stated, as he stopped for a moment and faced me.

"It takes a lot of energy to keep the habits of learned behavior functional so we can deal with the world around us. But this is constantly draining because we are not playing with a full deck. We need energy to break down those old circuits. After we have broken out of those circuits, we then have access to other sources of energy available to us. True, but at the same time the ability to use and store the energy from these sources has atrophied, due to lack of usage. Although we have access to new realms of freedom initially, we may not experience this, but instead a sense of depletion and confusion."

He started his walking back and forth again.

"So, we need even more energy to re-enliven those 'lost' connections that have atrophied. The fact is that we are not used to handling more energy. The paradox is resolved when you see that first, a lot of energy is needed to break down the circuits of learned behavior, and secondly even more energy is needed to handle and direct this new energy once it is released. So, you see, we are talking about the need for two bursts of energy. Ultimately you will end up with more energy, but it is a balancing process—on the one hand breaking down the boundaries of your learned behavior, and on the other hand using the energy which is then made available to adjust to your new energetic habitat. You need to learn the process of actually incorporating and using the energy that is released after you have broken down your old patterns."

Silvio continued his animated pacing, then stated, "If too much energy is released too quickly from your learned behavior patterns without you being able to incorporate it, this can cause some real difficulties in terms of psychological and/or physical problems. The breaking down of old patterns and the emergence of powerful new energies may lead to truly disruptive situations. Because you are beginning to emanate energies that you are not yet familiar with and not yet able to handle skillfully—which may open you up to things—like accidents," he said somewhat amused.

*"Accidents?"* I asked.

Silvio replied, grinning, "The way the world out there will respond to the new energies you are emanating is not totally predictable during this initial process, because the quality and quantity of the energy you are emitting can be erratic. So, it is best to understand this progression of releasing and redeploying and go on about it in a gradual and systematic way. What I am really talking about is becoming accustomed to the way that holding patterns break down and get reformed as they release new energy flows in the body."

"Boy, it sounds like a big adventure," I intervened. "But it also seems this could lead into a real 'identity crisis.' How would you deal with that?" I inquired.

"Suavely and with great ingenuity," Li Tse interjected chuckling, then sitting back, he raised his cup and sipped his Puer tea, appreciatively. Silvio laughed, then continued, "From the rigid view of learned behavior that you've been taught, this indeed can look like a constant identity crisis. You must learn and train to become comfortable being in a state of shifting and ever-evolving identity. No longer associating as strongly with your old story, your old view of yourself and the world that you've believed in up to now. When you're able to do this consistently, the burden of carrying around your old ideas will dissolve and make room for new circulations of energy in your body and in your life. This newly-released energy needs to be directed and this can be done through focus and movement."

He paused for emphasis, then looked at me and said, "What we are trying to accomplish is to create a more flexible and pliant learned behavior, devoid of emotional charges."

Li Tse tapped his teacup against the teapot a couple of times until he had my attention, "Hopefully you will retain a sense of self, but it will be expanded. And more energy will seep into your life around the edges and through the seams of who you think you are. But this takes sustained, consistent practice."

He paused then restated with a smile, "Yep, I like that: a gradual seeping process."

"Won't 'undoing' one's learned behavior change the way you think of family and friends?" I asked.

"Damn well, sure it will," Li Tse went on. "Your relating will be transformed. In effect, the truer and deeper links will be allowed to come through and the more superfluous stuff or ways of relating will pass away. You'll inhabit a bigger spectrum of perception and activities. If you choose to continue to relate to those people close to you, you probably will have to do so within the range of their perception and activities.

"Hopefully without any judgments," he added, laughing.

"But don't kid yourself—everyone is wearing a uniform of one sort or another," Silvio said, chuckling.

As I tried to digest what they were saying, Li Tse continued, "By learning to listen to and trust the body you can learn to walk the tight rope on the edge of learned behavior, creating a new life full of magic and mystery."

Silvio squatted down in front of us, took a sip of tea, then began talking, "Conscious and focused body practices can help you immeasurably. Talking and working with the body can give you a practical and pragmatic way of accessing other sources of energy available while stabilizing and storing them. We can rebalance our energy flow by spreading it throughout the body in new and different ways. Thus, we can create a new living structure based on the intuitive knowledge that the body holds, expanding our range of movements beyond the range of the former habitual movement patterns dictated by learned behavior. A new way of moving can turn into a way of storing energy, away from the perceptual bias and body memory of learned behavior."

Silvio stopped for a moment and started walking back and forth again and said, "Remember, what we are really talking about are moving living systems. Let me illustrate.

"Each time we hit the ground with our feet, it sends a pattern of vibration up through our body."

He slowed his pace to bring my attention to the way he was placing his feet on the ground, then continued, "As this pattern of vibration is repeated again and again, it develops its own specific rhythm. When this rhythm resonates through time it permeates our physical or gravitational energetic structure. It is repeated muscle functioning that holds this pattern together," he paused to look at me.

"Imagine a pattern in motion. By moving in different patterns, other than our established habitual ones, we can begin to tune in to the larger rhythms and natural patterns evolving through us and in the universe around us."

He put his right hand to his chin as if catching a thought, then went on, "Breaking up our habitual rhythms creates a dissonance which saturates and short-circuits learned behavior so that other rhythms can enter the system. You could say, you are learning and perpetuating a method of cognitive derangement repeatedly breaking the continuity of learned behavior."

He looked at me, chuckling at his own ingenuity and said, "In some ways, it is very simple. Our natural integrity will express itself if given a chance. There is something seeking expression through us as aware beings. All we are doing is studying this process and allowing it to flower. By bypassing learned behavior, the body is allowed to relax into itself, and this naturally creates a welling up of the innate knowledge of who we are."

"You see—simple!" Li Tse echoed, with a broad smile.

Silvio continued, "We have to somehow pull away from our learned behavior to get a glimpse of something else. This is where Chi Gung comes in. Our Chi Gung is about changing the habitual ways the body moves and enhancing the feeling of Chi. This then can be used as a springboard for engaging life around you and transforming the reflections that you receive back from life out there," he said as he stopped for a moment and took in the scene around us.

Then after a deep breath, he went on, "Chi Gung is a way of taking a break, a movement break. If we focus on staying with the feeling of Chi, we can begin to break the trance of learned behavior. Chi Gung, or 'right exercise,' can give us the energy to move our awareness to a different level, beyond the realm of learned behavior. Chi Gung, if done with the right focus and intention, is a practice that can gradually release us from learned behavior and enhance the balancing process involved in establishing a new energetic foundation. It can also assist in buffering us from the physical and psychological problems that can arise in this transition that we discussed earlier. This is a lot of what our Chi Gung is about.

"Most healing systems or movement systems want to help people become more balanced within the confines of learned behavior that they already inhabit. They are not interested in accessing more energy, but only seek to balance the energy within the frame of a person's learned behavior. In contrast, our Chi Gung is focused mainly on the process of disengaging from learned behavior and the freeing up of our natural energy so we can reclaim our birth right and re-integrate with the evolutionary forces seeking to flow through us."

He continued walking, absorbed in his explanation, "Rightly done, our Chi Gung not only provides a break from the movements of learned behavior, but also beckons a solution to the yearnings of the Spirit.

"The conscious intention of calling in awareness is an important element that makes our Chi Gung unique. Using the body as a vehicle for grounding and balancing awareness enables us in a pragmatic and sustained way to increase our energy spectrum. It also provides a vital platform for stabilizing new awareness within our body structure."

Silvio was really on a roll, "The Chi Gung we teach is focused on activating our energy-body and particularly its connection to the healing-body template. But what makes our Chi Gung especially different is its internal focus and goals: our Chi Gung is focused on perceiving with the totality of our bodily senses, and learning to ride on the waves of pulsating moving pressures all around us.

"We are involved with reclaiming our physical as well as our living energetic structure that can accommodate our true nature, as opposed to the limited structures of learned behavior. Through our practice we are remembering energetically and gravitationally the proper structure within which we reside and through which Chi can flow freely," he paused with his head tilted downwards, stroking his chin with his thumb and index finger as he continued slowly walking back and forth.

"Creating a moving, evolving structure within our body through time and space can accelerate the movement of Chi. You need energy to develop a new structure, and then even more energy to maintain and sustain it," he smiled, looking at me.

"So, first it takes energy to break away from our learned behavior. Then, secondly, it takes even more energy to stabilize the new flexible structure so that you can keep the Chi flowing at a higher, fuller, and more integrated energy level. You have to keep exercising that muscle. This is what we focus on."

Silvio finally sat down and looked up at the sky for a moment. My gaze followed and this opened me up to the sounds around me, the sparkling air, and the damp smell of the lush vegetation. It was truly a joy to be out in nature with the two of them.

After a pause and a few sips of tea Silvio continued, "As I have told you, learned behavior is transmitted from body to body. In juxtaposition, so is our Chi Gung—but what we focus on in our Chi Gung is transferring a direct knowledge which maintains an evolving sense of wellbeing, body to body."

"Why do you focus so much on learned behavior?" I asked.

"That's the best question yet, right to the point." He went on, "The reason that I was forced to deal with learned behavior is that I found it to be the biggest impediment to our wellbeing. And that basically the way we have been physically taught to walk around in the world by our learned behavior is the root cause for many of the diseases we experience. That's the reason it's so important to deal with it.

"Learned behavior changes the rhythm and patterns of our body in motion. Getting our energy-flow back from learned behavior is the way to reestablish proper Chi-flow in the body once again, which then translates into optimal health."

He stood up and said, "If you stay with the sensation of Chi consistently and over sustained periods of time, this allows the right way of walking on the Earth to seep into you."

He got up and started walking again, "Yep, you can learn to walk a new way in the world. When this is initiated from the inside by focusing on enhancing the quality and quantity of Chi flow, the placement of your feet then aligns the body properly in its relation to gravity. And this then optimizes the balance of pressures in the body."

He kept pacing slowly back and forth, and after a moment continued, "We also focus on the essence of breathing in our Chi Gung. As I have told you, breathing and our emotional environment are intimately linked. Breathing is a moving internal touch pattern. Learned behavior impinges upon this natural pattern and limits it by impressing upon it its own prescribed ways. Our natural breathing wave can be reestablished if we can maintain contact with the essence of breathing. As we do this, we then can bypass the learned behavior patterns."

He stopped in his tracks and turned to look at me, grinning, "The thoughts and emotions of learned behavior are like a foreign import that we unwittingly accept as our reality. Like a parasite we want to disentangle ourselves from."

His statement made me ponder for a bit, "Silvio, are you saying Chi Gung functions like a kind of pest control?"

That made us all laugh together.

Li Tse chimed in, chuckling, "It will help dissolve 'you,' your sense of self."

He then continued, "Our Chi Gung will help to break up your learned behavior's thought patterns and erode their understructure. It will free you up from learned behavior's habitual body movements and breathing patterns and give you true choice once again. New patterns can then be allowed to form based on strengthening and affiliating with the evolutionary forces that are moving through you.

"If you keep up with the Chi Gung practice, you can build up the energy to detach and witness the comings and goings of your learned behavior without grabbing on. As the established patterns of your learned behavior get de-charged, what you will observe is that the comings and goings of familiar moods, feelings, and states of mind will pass by less frequently than they used to. And when they do, they will be less intense, less captivating. They will become less compelling as gradually they will be eroded away by the greater flow of Chi in the body. As you cut the rhythms and patterns of learned behavior you return to the fluid currents of life that are flowing through you. You begin to open to your total body awareness, your link to everything," Li Tse said, beaming.

"So, to sum it up," Silvio said, taking over, "First, we cultivate our awareness of Chi. Then, through our practice we build a balanced energetic body structure to maximize its flow. And finally, we learn how to stabilize and maintain this enhanced Chi flow and the awareness that goes with it.

"We are interested in building a structure from the internal knowledge of Chi flow, as opposed to trying to put together a posture based on a hodgepodge of non-integrated approaches from the outside. We are not so interested in the external forms of movement, but in teaching and embodying structure and internal principles. What we are interested in can be introduced and incorporated into many forms, even and especially while just walking down the street."

Silvio stopped, faced us and opened his hands to his sides, taking a slight bow as if looking for applause and Li Tse obliged him by starting to clap his hands, then began laughing.

Chapter 7

# Li Tse—Chi, the Sixth Sense

I remember that morning vividly. It had rained the night before, the air was fresh and clear, and there was a gentle breeze blowing once again along the Ping River, or Mae Nam Ping. The literal translation would be "Mother Water Ping." Living in this land of rain and rice, water was noticeably the mother of all.

I was walking with my friends Li Tse and a wonderful self-taught musician who referred to himself as Hollow Bamboo. We had walked over the Ping River from the area of Warorot market on a small, dilapidated bridge. We had to go around a diversion because this particular foot bridge was blocked off with wire and wood. But the barricade had a hole in it, created by those that used it. It seemed that the city bureaucracy needed to block it off as unsafe for insurance purposes, but those that needed to just kept using it and the public officials did not seem to mind.

We crossed the narrow bridge and on the other side there was another wat. There are so many wats in Chiang Mai that none of us even knew the name of this one. The grounds were quiet and peaceful with a beautiful chedi and flittering sounds from numerous small bells high up on the eaves of the buildings. Mr. Hollow Bamboo liked tea as did Li Tse, who as usual had a thermos of tea with him, and when we sat at a bench, he pulled out some small cups and served us. After enjoying each other's company for a while Mr. Bamboo went off to a bench nearby to play his *shakuhachi* flute.

While we sat there in the gentle breeze and with the sounds of the flute around us, I asked Li Tse a question, "I have been thinking a lot about what Silvio talked about. I am overwhelmed by thoughts of how I am surrounded by learned behavior—by the way people move and breathe around me. So, if we're surrounded by movers and breathers and in a sense, everything is predetermined by learned behavior, that makes me wonder if I have any free will? It seems to me that I make my own decisions all the time. Isn't this exercising my free will?"

Li Tse took stock of me for a moment and then began speaking, "It appears to 'you' that you do have free will, but don't forget," he said, raising his index finger in the air in front of him and shaking it in my direction, "that learned behavior sets the agenda. And thus, the decisions that you make are made within a small, predetermined window of options.

"The impression that you're making your own decisions is compelling, but really, you're just making decisions within the choices given to you by the learned behavior of the time. The bigger decisions are left to the institutions of society, the pimps of learned behavior. And believe me—those decisions are made for you and yes, you are surrounded by them," he said, with a gleam in his eye.

That triggered memories of a time when I had been the chairman of a state-governing body, where I learned the power of making the agenda. I would make the agenda and everyone would give their opinions. Heated discussions would happen over those topics on the agenda, and everyone thought that they were making a significant difference. But no one seemed to realize that everything not on the agenda was not discussed at all, and that their attention was being directed by the agenda itself—similar to what we see in the mass media these days.

"To take it a step further," Li Tse continued, "Take a look at that small window of options that we are talking about. Most of the decisions made by 'you' are made in the context of your 'sense of self.' And that very sense of self that you experience is, as Silvio has illustrated for you, a product of your learned breathing and moving patterns that surround you.

"So, your real essence is encircled by both the people around you and by your sense of self, which is sustained by the moving and breathing patterns 'inside' you."

He then took a dramatic pause before saying, "I hope you can see that really there is only one choice you have. And that is, whether you want to free yourself from the iron grip of your learned behavior or not."

I was a little stunned by the implications of what Li Tse had just explained and it must have shown because he began to chuckle. This relaxed me, and I then was caught up in the soothing sound coming from Hollow Bamboo playing his flute, and this relaxed me even more. Then I began to feel the gentle breeze on my cheeks.

Li Tse watched me, and enjoyed himself before going on, "What I really wanted to talk to you about today is touch," he said, touching his right index finger to his thumb, looking at me. "Touch is our primary sense. If you think about it—people can live without sight, without being able to hear, taste or smell, but have you ever heard of anyone being able to function without touch? Really think about it. The other senses would not work without touch. We could not even think if we would be unable to touch; language would not exist. We could not say a word." He chuckled.

I wrinkled my brow, pondering his statements.

But he just went on, "The tactile level is almost impossible to speak about. The complexity of our bodies is really beyond our intellectual capacity to understand—and touch is the linchpin that keeps our sense of body together.

"We live in a sea of feelings, a sea of sensations, an ocean of Chi," he paused. "It is through touch that we feel," he paused again. "And at the subtle edge of touch is the sensation of Chi. And Chi creates a webbing throughout our body and senses that seemingly holds our world together," he stated with his eyes growing wide in mock awe and surprise, then playfully continued in a singsong manner:

*Breathing, touching*
*Smooth touch, smooth mind.*
*Jerky movements, jerky mind.*
*Smooth breathing, smooth movements.*
*Gross breathing, gross mind*
*Smooth being*
*Aaaaaaaah—Yes*

As he looked at me, the afternoon light reflected off his eyes, and I once again became aware of the penetrating but gentle sound of the flute that Hollow Bamboo was playing off to my left.

After pausing for a moment, Li Tse continued, "From gravity and touch the senses flower. The senses are dependent on gravity and touch to function. And through gravity and touch and their extensions to the other four senses, we create the world we perceive around us. We perceive through the sensations of sight, sound, smell, taste, and touch. But touch is the link to the living force field of gravity around us."

My mind wandered to recall as best I could that much of physics was based on the speed of light—at least before the advent of quantum physics—because it was thought to be a constant and the fastest there was. But now modern science is beginning to acknowledge that in subatomic space there is movement faster than the speed of light.

I voiced these thoughts to Li Tse.

"Bravo!" he said, "but that is as far as they have gotten. Think of this: awareness is faster than light. It is the fastest thing around," he said, nodding his head. He then snapped his fingers and laughed, "It is instantaneous!

"Maybe light is the fastest we can grasp with our five senses, but we are more than our senses. And the world of our senses, which some scientists may not like to admit, or at least try to forget, is the basis of language and mathematics and thus the basis of our human 'physics.' Science is based on reflective thought, or in a more basic sense the subject/object duality which we use to define our sense of self. The merging of the subject/object is the doorway to pure Awareness.

"Pure Awareness is beyond the realm of self reflection. It is the ultimate truth that by definition cannot be grasped by the sense of self, and again, by 'definition,' must be faster than light," he said, with his smile ever broadening. "Science keeps trying to get closer, but it will never get there. Science is like the salmon in our seas, rivers, and streams. It is trying to get closer and closer to the source, but even when it gets there it will find that the only answer is to surrender to the force and merge with the feeling of life all around us. Life is all around us, just waiting," he said with a grin, allowing his eyes to take in the world.

Then, taking a breath, he continued, "When we study perception and our senses—using the ultimate machine, our bodies—it is much the same: we can get close to awareness and even go quickly back and forth from pure Awareness to a subtle awareness of self, like a strobe light, but we cannot really merge with Awareness until we surrender and let go of our sense of self. I can mumble on and on about this, as Silvio constantly reminds me," he laughed at himself. "But the telling of it fills me, so I keep doing it."

He beamed at me, saying, "The point that I am trying to make here is that really, we are more than our senses. And more than our sense of self, at least in the way we are talking about it now, which is a pattern based on those self-same senses created by learned behavior."

This brought up memories for me of people who I had known who had experimented with sensory deprivation tanks, where they floated in darkness in salt water, which altered their sense of gravity and perception to the point that they were experiencing something very similar to a womb-like state, and like being on an edge of something "beyond".

"So, let's focus on our senses," he said bringing me back. "We live in a sensual rainbow—a spectrum of sensory experience. It is a spectrum, to be sure, for one sense blends into the other just like what you see looking at a rainbow. On face value, sight is on the fast high vibrational end of this spectrum and touch is at the slower end. In this way of looking at it there is a spectrum to our senses, from slowest to fastest, beginning with touch and ending with light."

He paused, looking around for a moment, then went on, "Light is seemingly the fastest thing we can grasp with our senses. But we are more than our senses. Don't forget that," he reiterated, raising his index finger for emphasis.

"Now that we have talked about the spectrum of the senses, what I want to focus on is the progression of the senses. I want you to learn to see the senses as an ever-repeating pattern that we call 'the sequence.' This 'sequence' has physical, psychological, and perceptual ramifications or permutations. And its centerpiece is touch.

"Touch is the touchstone of the senses," he said with a laugh before continuing, "To understand perception more clearly, we will rely on 'the sequence.' I think about it and use it as the 'golden mean of perception.' I like to call it the 'golden mean of perception' for its pervasiveness, usefulness, and adaptability. You know about the 'golden mean' or 'Phi, the Golden Ratio,' right?" he looked up at me with a question mark in his eyes.

I actually did know a little about it. Although used at least as far back as the people who made the pyramids in Western culture, it was used by Euclid and others in Greek times, and then its use grew in importance once again at the time of the Renaissance. The golden mean, or Phi, is a mathematical proportion used to mathematically understand and describe beauty, harmony, and proportion in the natural world—the shape of the nautilus shell, or even the construction of a leaf as seen by the human senses. It can also be used in describing the physical proportions of the human body as well as many other facets of life and the universe. It pervades the patterns, rhythms, harmonies, and melodies of music. It is a very adaptable and useful concept that has a variety of applications. In effect it permeates and, in many ways, defines our view of the natural world.

I related what I knew about Phi and the Golden Ratio to Li Tse. He smiled, nodding his head and then went on, "Here is an idea I want you to hold in mind while I talk. Bind this concept of the 'sequence' together with the image of a flower—the image of a water lily or lotus floating on the water, with its origins in the muck at the bottom of the pond. It opens during the day and closes again at night. It opens for a few days, is pollinated, and then moves on to the next stage of its evolutionary pattern. Life continues to flow through it even as it transforms to seed. Got the picture?" he said, looking at me but smiling inwardly and chuckling.

He then went on, "Much like the flower, we begin from a spark of life in the muck beyond perception. We grow and flower, then open and close for a series of days, and then transform into something else.

"When we are conceived, the sperm penetrates the egg and our growth begins. During this stage, our awareness of ourselves is all touch. As we proceed a little further in our growth in the womb, the senses of sight and sound appear to help us define ourselves. Then when we are born and we begin to breathe and eat, taste and smell are thrown into the mix. When we follow this sequence or progression, we see that first we experience the primary sense of touch. Then in the womb-water world, we develop sight and sound. And smelling and tasting only occur when we move into the air world after birth.

"OK, got that?" he asked.

"Now, let's look at this a little more carefully," he went on. "Before what we commonly experience as touch, there is a very subtle touch, a very subtle electric-like vibration which is the sensation of Chi or *prana*, as the adepts of the subcontinent call it. It is the outer edge of touch, the most subtle thing we can sense. This sensation of Chi is where the flow/feeling of life meets touch.

"Then at some point this subtle pulse of Chi initiates the flowering of the heartbeat, where we begin to identify ourselves with the senses of sight and sound as we grow in the world of the womb. It is here that we clothe touch with sight and sound. Here we begin to dream.

"Eventually, we transition from the water realm of the womb into the realm of air and are born into the world here as we know it. Here we begin to breathe and become aware of fragrance and taste. As this sequence of the senses proceeds, Chi spreads like a delicate net, permeating all the senses at a subtle level, forming a fine web.

"Can you see that picture in your mind's eye? Eh?" he asked, raising his eyebrows a couple of times.

I grunted, "Uh," and then said I could and that I liked it.

With that he continued, "Now, we can apply this sequential pattern of sense evolution and its devolution to our diurnal and nocturnal rhythms. Every night when we go to sleep, we slowly close the flower of perception, closing our senses. We perceptually go through the same process that I just described, but in reverse order so that we go through the full spectrum of our senses, withdrawing back to our essence, to get recharged much as the lotus," he said, moving his right hand in front of him, palm up and drawing his fingers gently together and releasing them over and over.

He then stopped to listen to the sound of the flute drifting through temple grounds and watched as a huge leaf slowly fell from the towering trees above us.

He continued, "When we go to sleep, we first leave the level of the breath, smell, and taste. Those senses become very subtle. Then we retreat to the area of the heartbeat where light and sound predominate—back to where dreams occur, similar to our experience in the water world of the womb. Then we recede one step further into deep sleep, to deep touch and beyond. After recharging ourselves there, we come back out from the blackness of the world of touch to the world of dreams once again, light and sound, and then again to our everyday awareness in the world of breathing, with added taste and smell."

I wanted to be clear on what he was saying, so I made a statement, implicitly asking to be corrected if I was wrong, "So in the formation of the embryo the sense of touch occurs first, then sight and sound, then lastly taste and smell because they are dependent on air to function. Do I have that so far?" I asked, looking at him.

He nodded, and so I went on, "And in fact, every time we go to sleep, or go from our waking state to deep sleep, we go through this same perceptual sequence in reverse and then back through the original sequence again as we awaken. Is that correct?"

"It seems you got it!" Li Tse said, smiled approvingly and continued, "We also follow this same pattern as we engage the image of our physicality. When we sleep, we go deep into our core and beyond, becoming recharged by that original pulse of life that we are. Then as we come back to waking consciousness, we re-engage with the template of the human form that was nurtured through the womb experience, and perceptually begin to relate to our physicality through dreaming. Lastly, we awaken to our idea of physicalness.

"So, you can then begin to see the process of how we engage this physicalness we call the body when we come from deep sleep, and how we then disengage from it when we return to the original pulse of life."

He paused and took a deep breath.

"Do you recognize the same sequence in all these processes? Can you feel how 'you' recreate 'yourself' every time you go to sleep and wake up? Can you sense how as you wake up your idea of physicality becomes more concrete?

"We do this in the same way the lotus flower opens and closes every day before moving through to its next stage of transformation, turning to seed. This process is repeated in us, too. First, we grow through our sense of self, and it then disengages as we move on to the next stage of transformation that awaits us. Unless we are interrupted," he laughed.

"It is interesting to note, and you can see it easily in the flower. Its essence is neither its form nor its opening and closing, but something else. Yet, truly, it is also its form and its opening and closing. But more than that it is something that moves through it and beyond. Can you sense this?"

What he was telling me was a lot to grasp, so again I asked for clarification, "Let me make sure I follow this sequence," I said. "First, we start with the sense of touch, then overlaying that comes light and sound, and then finally taste and smell. But isn't being born and physicalizing basically touch again?" I asked with a furrowed brow.

He then looked at me, put his hands together and bowed his head, looking back up at me with a smile. "Very good! It all begins and ends with touch, and more essentially with the sensation of Chi. That's how the snake bites its own tail to complete the circuit," he said, making an infinity sign with his fingers by touching his two thumbs and index fingers together and joining them in front of his chest.

He continued, "Let's look at it in a slightly different way. You can now see that the senses of seeing and hearing stemming from our water realm experience in the womb overlay touch, and these in turn are overlaid by smelling and the sense of taste stemming from the air realm once we are born.

"If we look closely at our sensual spectrum, Chi exists before touch, and then sight, and after that it moves throughout all our senses like a fine webbing. The feeling of life surrounds and saturates us. The closest we can get through our subject/object perspective is through subtle touch. Chi-touch is at once the most subtle and most gross of the senses. It permeates and at the same time is just on the edge of them all. So, you can see how Chi is in everything and all pervading. As a practice, if you stay with the sensation of Chi, you are right on the edge of connecting with the force of life and your true essence."

"Aaah, so that's the sequence, I got it," I said.

Li Tse paused for a minute, chuckled at himself and went on, "Consciousness of self should be able to develop naturally and to grow in an unimpeded, flowing manner, and take us to our next stage of development. You can see by this sequence, there's a natural rhythm to it all," he said, smiling.

Tilting his head to the side and then straightening it up, Li Tse said, "If there is a 'we,' 'we' have to perceive! The energy of necessity has to flow through us! It is THE LAW!" he said, energetically tapping his index finger onto the bench.

"Thou shalt perceive!" he went on, chuckling.

"But what and how and in what mixture of the sequence is the question? As our awareness moves from the Chi-touch level to the eye/ear level, like in the womb, and on to the smell/taste level, like in the waking world, we are taught to cluster or sequence together our senses in certain specific ways.

"Here's where the problem arises," he went on. "We have to let the energy flow through our spectrum of perception, but it is our choice how and in what sequence it flows, and how we identify with it, or how we choose to grab onto it. However, most of us don't even realize we have that choice.

"And here is where learned behavior intervenes," he exclaimed. "Our awareness is manipulated and monopolized by learned behavior. It accentuates certain combinations of sensual perception for its own self perpetuation, leaving out so many other potential ways of mixing and matching our perceptual data."

"How does it do that?" I asked.

Li Tse responded, "Learned behavior dictates, controls, and selects the way that the senses are used in concert. We are not just the combinations of perceptions that we have been taught to perceive. We are more than that. But learned behavior assembles sensorial data in a certain way and teaches us to identify ourselves with that. Learned behavior is the glue that puts together and binds us to 'the story of who it has taught us to be.' This is instilled in us through the moving and breathing patterns of those around us, and then it is stored in the moving and breathing patterns of our body.

"Try thinking about it in this way: energy is flowing through us. It flows through our perceptual spectrum triggering the patterns of what we perceive. Learned behavior steps in to set the agenda that severely limits our options of perception by dictating the way in which we cluster together our perceptual inputs. In this way it creates almost insurmountable barriers to our understanding of who we really are. It is a big impediment to our self-knowledge. This not only has ramifications for how we perceive, but also to our health, sense of self and general well-being."

He peered at me, then rubbed his hands together and continued, "So you got that? Then let's look at how this applies to our view of our physical body.

"What we perceive and experience as the physical body is another limited concept given to us by learned behavior. Learned behavior twists and molds the dance of perception away from its original connection with the life-force to suit itself instead."

This made me recall that in my studies of Chinese medicine, I had been able to see how the image we hold of the body has changed over the centuries. Over a thousand years ago, the body was described very poetically and lyrically by its relationship to the five elements and our relation to the world of spirits around us. This has changed in our modern times. I was able to see how a body view that merged much more with the flowing world around us through time turned gradually into a model more separated and solidified. The body today is seen increasingly as an "object" that begins and ends at the level of our skin.

Li Tse brought me back from my musings, saying, "Learned behavior is a corruption of the original feeling of life. Not only are we lured into thinking that we are solely what we perceive through our senses, which creates our sense of self, but also this sense of self affects our perception of the world around us. Learned behavior keeps us blinded by the patterns of its sole interpretation, which plays out through our sense organs. We are bound by the limits of the mixture of the five senses that our learned behavior allows us to perceive. Do you see now that learned behavior creates only a limited view? And how this also affects the rules of touch we've been accustomed to living by? Learned behavior really creates its own tacto-visual reality."

Li Tse stopped his elucidation to listen to the meandering tones coming from Mr. Hollow Bamboo's *shakuhachi* flute. This allowed me to shift my attention to the breeze moving through the leaves in the trees above. A question arose in my mind, and I asked, "Don't we need a sense of self—language and culture—to exist in this world?"

"I would not use the term 'to exist,'" Li Tse replied. "We need them to be able to function at a certain level, yes. But we don't need them to define the essence of who we are. We don't need learned behavior to define us to the point that we cannot maintain our connection with the feelings of life and awareness around us."

He took his index fingers and rubbed behind his two ears, then pulled on his ear lobes. He absorbed once again the scene around him, then looked up at me and continued, "To get a feeling for how learned behavior works and to see a way out, let's look more closely at this. There are charges—I would say emotional charges—that glue our sense of self, language, and culture together. If we can de-charge this emotional glue that permeates our learned behavior, then we will have much better access to a whole perceptual experience."

"Interesting," I said, going over my lips with my tongue, the aftertaste of the tea still lingering in my mouth.

Li Tse went on, "If we do this, then on the one hand we can relax through our strategic 'what will I do next' mentality in order to allow more of our total self to surface. On the other hand, we can still maintain a toehold in the world of learned behavior, keeping it available to help us survive, but without its encumbering emotional charges. We can learn to exist without these emotional charges and not be bound by them," he said. "We then can swim like a duck in water without getting wet!"

"How do we do that?" I asked.

"By developing a total body awareness, an awareness of Chi flowing through the five senses," he answered expansively. "You can start by bringing your focus to the level of touch and beyond as often and consistently as possible, learning to stay present with the sensation of Chi. Cultivate that awareness so that it can become stronger and seep throughout your body. Then you can begin to store Chi awareness throughout your being. In this way, you merge the five senses and begin to feel with the whole body, developing a Chi-touch body, so to speak. You can collect it in your being-bank," he said, laughing, beginning to move and stretch. I liked it when he did that. It loosened up my body just watching him.

Li Tse went on, "With the right focus, you can use Chi Gung to get a sense for Chi-touch and develop a system for unfolding all of your possibilities," he said, repeatedly poking his chest and belly with his right index finger, which brought a grin to his face. "When you gain enough energy, you can then witness with your whole body."

"Gain enough energy? What do you mean? Here we are with energy again. How do I gain energy?" I asked.

Li Tse replied, "By regularly doing your Chi Gung practice with the right frame of mind and the right focus and thus cultivating the sense of Chi throughout your body."

A big, scarred tomcat walked up and peered at us. It was rare to see a cat in Buddhist temples because the monks have a habit of feeding and adopting stray dogs, which chase the cats away. Juxtaposed to this you see a lot of cats and very few dogs in the Muslim areas of Thailand. It is said that Mohammed had a cat.

"Synchronize the touch of breathing with the touch of movement and your body may even start purring. I know it does for some people," Li Tse said with a knowing smile and a twinkle in his eye, as he pointed with his chin over at Mr. Hollow Bamboo and bent over to rub the cat under its chin.

He looked at me intently, smiled and said, "When you cultivate the sense of Chi then you can touch the world lightly with your breathing, movement, and other senses. And you can even extend this to your social interactions. This is how you can learn to interact with people without being caught in the trappings of the emotional charges inherent in their learned behavior. In this way you can be in the midst of the world without being of it."

"Here he is with the duck in the water again," I smiled to myself.

Li Tse continued, "Learned behavior breeds a deep-rooted fear of touch. And as Silvio told you before, learned behavior comes down to rules of touch—how we are allowed to touch ourselves and each other. As you rekindle your connection to Chi-touch, the feeling of Chi will move deeper and deeper into your body, helping you to touch yourself and the world around you in a more vital and joyful way."

He sat back and relaxed, waving his hands back and forth in front of his chest as if he were stretching out fibers of energy. And once again the sound of the flute and the tingling of the tiny temple bells in the balmy breeze softly held my attention.

I voiced, "Li Tse, when I am with you or Silvio, my sense of time seems to change. Does awareness of Chi-touch change your sense of time?"

"In theory, and in my experience, it does," he said. "You certainly don't feel the charged presence of learned behavior as much, and this loosens up the particular sense of time that comes with it," he smiled.

"But I think that what you are noticing when you are around us is how we have compacted our bodies. When we compact the body, we are compacting time and space too. It is like being in the pressurized eye of a hurricane. The present becomes brighter, and past and future recede. When we connect and compact the body, the subtle body is reconnected more strongly with the physical body, and our sense of self and our story becomes more fluid. When your cocoon, my friend, interacts with our cocoons, your body senses this and connects and compacts a bit, and your sense of self and sense of time changes too."

"*Connecting and compacting the body?*" I inquired, feeling intrigued.

Li Tse raised his palm to stop me and said, "You will learn about that later. For now, just try staying with awareness of Chi. Chi definitely has a timelessness to it. Give yourself an infusion of Chi. Let the world of Chi open you to the feeling of life."

He paused to drink in the beautiful tones of the flute floating our way, then said, "As you stay focused on the sensation of Chi, you are focusing on the edges of your sense spectrum. So, in a sense you are on the edge of time. You are right on the edge. And from this edge you will be ready for direct access to Awareness itself. And in this way Chi can become a bridge to the knowledge of that which we really are."

"I'm finally starting to get this," I thought, "and it is really interesting to me." I wanted to know more! So I went on to ask another question, "I want to know more about breathing," I said.

Li Tse looked at me, bulging his eyes out, and moved his eyebrows up and down, then chuckled. "That's a good one," he said, "breathing is a way of touching. Breathing is a way of touching the whole body. This touching is like a wave undulating through us.

"Now it's time for you to learn about the practice," Li Tse said as he flicked his eyes over to the right and pointed with his chin over at Mr. Hollow Bamboo, who was still playing his flute on a bench underneath an enormous tree. He then, with a gentle underhanded wave, indicated for me to go over to him. Without further ado he gathered his tea utensils and wandered away with a bouncing step.

Chapter 8

# Hollow Bamboo—Breath

After Li Tse got up and strolled away, I walked over to where Bamboo was sitting. Surprisingly, the purring cat followed me. I sat down next to Bamboo. The cat settled down at his feet. He bent over and rubbed the cat's head and then stroked it under the chin a few times.

"My old friend," Bamboo said as he looked down at the cat. "I come here often and usually I see him."

I looked around the temple grounds for a bit, then I asked Bamboo, "Why do sometimes your friends like to call you 'Hollow Bamboo?'"

"To have fun with me," he said. "But also, because they know I like to be called that. When I play the flute, I like to think of myself as a hollow reed that connects Heaven and Earth. Wind—the music of the earth and the voice of heaven...movement...life," he said as he leaned over once again to stroke the cat under its chin. It apparently liked it, because when he stopped it remained blissfully frozen in that position.

He then added, straightening up, "And I also enjoy doing Chi Gung with the boys."

"Li Tse said that you knew all about breath. He told me to ask you about it," I stated.

"Ah yes...breathing," he said with a guffaw and a smile. "Listen," he said. And with that he picked up his *shakuhachi* flute and began to play.

I closed my eyes. It was a sweet sound that reminded me of watching a gentle breeze moving over a grassy plain. Off and on I could hear the sounds of the temple wind chimes and when I opened my eyes, I could see small gusts of wind gently moving the leaves overhead. He played on for a while, the tones becoming softer and softer until he finally stopped. I looked over at him to see him raise his eyes and smile.

"I play the flute with my whole body, you see," he said, blowing slowly into his flute and moving his fingers over the holes. "I synchronize the winds in my body with the wind that is coming in through my nose and out from my mouth through to this hollow bamboo. I breathe in and out. From the outside, it may look like I am not moving my body in co-ordination with my breath as you see my fingers going up and down and sliding this way and that. But though it may not look like it, they are moving in the same rhythm and flow as the breath—the quality is the same. The breathing wave and the movement wave are merged as one. At the same time as air is coming in and out of my nose and mouth, my fingers are moving to the same deep rhythm. It is in the same stream."

"*Stream?*" I asked

"Yes. Some people say that this special breath created when breathing and movement synchronize is like breathing in the essence of a cool mountain stream," Bamboo continued, grinning enigmatically. "And on the other hand, all we are is a stream."

"I still don't quite understand," I said.

"OK, stand up," he said, stroking the cat once again before getting to his feet. "I will show you. I will show you how to breathe while you are doing Chi Gung—as it is the same thing as becoming a hollow reed and playing the flute," he smiled. "And then later how to connect to the stream of Chi all around us."

He began, "Get into a stance, balancing your weight evenly between the heels and the balls of your feet." He showed me by moving his body into a martial arts stance that he wanted me to imitate. His feet were shoulder width apart.

"What do you mean exactly?" I asked, as I tried to copy him.

"Good question," he said. "So often the most basic things are overlooked and never taught. Let's explore. Move your feet a bit wider apart," he said as he spread his feet out beyond his original shoulder width position. "Keep the outsides of your feet parallel. Bend your knees and sink into that posture," he said, looking at me.

I did as he directed.

"Do you feel how most of your weight is on the balls, the front part of your feet?" he asked.

I nodded.

"Good, then let's go on. Now I want you to put your ankles close together," he instructed. "Relax your shoulders and allow your whole body to sink down into this posture and you will feel that now most of your weight is on your heels.

"What we are after here is balance," he went on. "So now place your feet once again in the original position, keeping the outside of your feet parallel, and you will discover that in this position your weight is equally balanced between the balls and the heels of your feet. This just happens to be about shoulder width apart—which is the way this position of placing the feet is usually referred to, but the why of it is rarely explained," he said with a self-satisfied grin.

"Next," he continued, "put your hands straight out in front of you."

He held his hands comfortably in front of himself at chest height, about eight inches apart.

"I am going to teach you about movement. I am going to show you how to synchronize breath and movement—but not through ups and downs, ins and outs, but through quality of feeling."

Bamboo looked at me quizzically, then motioned for me to put my hands up in front of me at chest height as he was doing.

"Can you feel a sensation in your hands, a tingly fuzzy feeling, like stretching a living cocoon? Or you may detect it as a pressure," he grinned. I felt a tingling in my hands and nodded in agreement.

"This is the feeling of Chi," he stated. "Some people will feel it as a tingling, some as heat, and even others as a sense of pressure. Now start moving your hands slowly, keeping the awareness of this sensation in them," he said, as he began moving from side to side, turning at the waist, as he waved the palms of his hands back and forth in front of his face.

"Don't move them too fast or you will probably lose the awareness of that sensation. At this point it does not really matter how you move them. Just keep moving them and stay with the awareness of that sensation."

As Bamboo moved, he looked up to see the leaves on the top of the trees slowly moving in the wind. He brought his gaze back down and rested it on me.

"OK, now continue to move slowly so you can keep that fuzzy feeling, the feeling of Chi, in your hands, and also in your belly, especially in your belly, if you can. The more you do this, the more you will be able to feel this sensation throughout your whole body. Be sure to relax your belly," he said, gently patting his lower abdomen. "The belly is very important.

"Now, move and breathe with the same sensation that you feel in your hands."

He continued turning his waist from side to side and waving his hands.

"What we want to do here is to get the feeling of Chi in our hands and body synchronized with the feeling of Chi at the entrance to our nostrils. Breathe with that same sensation of Chi while at the time same feeling it in your hands and body," he said. "It's like breathing the essence of a cool mountain stream."

I stopped moving and furrowed my brow and looked at him with a confused look on my face.

"OK, OK, I am going too fast," Bamboo said. "It takes a while to learn how to play the flute," he chortled.

"Sense the same sensation that you feel in your hands on the inner ring of your nostrils where the air comes in and out. That same fuzzy feeling. Or even better yet, feel it at a point in the middle of your nostril holes. Focus on this sensation of Chi. Don't get distracted by the in and out of the breath, but focus on the continuous sense of pressure, the velvet-like sensation of Chi as the air touches the edge of your inner nostrils or that point in the middle of your nostrils where the air is coming in or out, a very subtle continuous tingly feeling."

He continued slowly, "OK, now breathe and move synchronizing your awareness to this sensation. Do not focus on the up and down or side-to-side movement of your hands, or the in-and-out movement of your breath. Focus instead on a continuous consistent feeling, a fluid fuzzy feeling in both your hands and at the entrance to your nostrils. It should not matter if your breath is moving in or out, or your hands moving left or right, up or down. What matters is keeping the awareness of Chi continuous. We just want to synchronize the feeling in your nose with the sensation in your hands and body."

As he kept moving, he said, "The breath, as my friends probably have told you, creates a touching on the inside of your body which moves waves of sensation that we can feel. So in a way, we are synchronizing the way we touch the air inside our bodies with the way we touch the air outside our bodies. You can even say, 'the inner and outer winds' of our bodies. The air is moving inside your body, making a wave and you are touching the air out here," he said, indicating his moving hands with his chin, "with the outside through your skin."

He looked at me to see if I was following, liked what he saw, nodded approvingly, then continued in a somewhat hypnotic voice, "Whether you are breathing in or out it does not matter.

"What matters is keeping the awareness of Chi on the inside, all around the inside of your nostrils, and on the outside, in your hands, and even in your belly if you can. You will feel a sensation like tiny fibers moving right at the edge of your perception.

"Again, at this point the movement or form does not matter. It does not matter in what pattern you move your hands. Right now, all we are dealing with is synchronizing breath with movement," he said, mesmerizing me with his voice as he moved his hands slowly from side to side.

"Remember to keep your belly full and relaxed. When you learn this well, your belly will not seem to move at all. It will stay round and full. Take long thin breaths, all the way from the trunk of your body out to your wrists and ankles, hands, and feet.

"Chuang Tsu, an ancient Chinese sage, teaches us that the wise man breathes from his heels, while the ordinary man breathes from his throat. We want to take long breaths, not deep big breaths, taking the breathing wave all the way down from our nose to our ankles and back up again. Let's call them long, thin breaths, like breathing in the essence of a cool mountain stream. Keep moving with the same feeling in your hands as in your nose," he said with a twinkle in his eye and a shy grin on his face.

We continued for a while and then he started speaking once again, "You are swimming in a sea of Chi, both inside and outside your body, like a fish in the sea. It may feel like different rhythms to you as you notice the sensation of Chi in your nose and on your hands, but it has the same quality of touch. One's body movements and one's breathing can unite in this way. Let the feeling of this kind of breathing flow through your motions."

His words brought a picture to mind of the tiny multi-colored mosquito fish which you see all over Thailand, swimming in huge clay pots full of water lilies, darting from under one lily pad to another.

"This sensation of Chi is like the velvet of a candle flame or water pouring over smooth stone," Bamboo went on. "A very living, alive feeling. Just keep focused on this feeling. This is the feeling of life," he said as our arms moved and swayed.

We kept moving a bit longer, then stopped and opened to our surroundings. We went back and sat down on our bench under the huge tree. The cat was still there waiting for Bamboo to rub its chin, which he did. He seemed to enjoy it as much as the cat did.

After they finished their communication, he looked up at me and said, "So this is what I do when I play the flute. I don't feel air going in or out, but I keep in touch with the subtle velvet feeling where the air is coming in or out, in my nose or my lips. Then I put that same subtle, velvety Chi-feeling through my body to my hands and fingers. This is my practice when I play the flute. This is the way I blow into the bamboo and the way I touch the world through my breath. This is the same sensation that moves through my body and out through my fingers. This then creates a sound continually, synchronizing itself with the world out there. This is my music," he said, rolling his eyes around a couple of times and grinning.

"And what you just learned is how to play the instrument of the body from the inside and out," he said with a laugh.

Bamboo looked up again at the leaves fluttering in the trees above us. Then looked up at me as he bent down to stroke the cat once again, and said with a mischievous smile, "At some point your body may literally start purring like our friend over here. By touching the world in this way, we begin to enliven our subtle energy-body. Our subtle body is very benign; virtuous by nature. If people would just synchronize their breathing with their movements, we would live in a much better world."

"But is it not true that breathing and movements are synchronized to the rhythms and tunes of our learned behavior?" I countered, remembering what Silvio and Li Tse had told me.

"Right you are, my friend," Bamboo said, leaning over and patting me affectionately on the shoulder. I looked up and was caught again by his seemingly ever-present smile. "This is very tricky business," he continued as he rubbed his hands together. "Learned behavior has captured the rhythm of our true nature and made us play its own tune."

He then tilted his head to the side and said, "Oh, I forgot something. In my musings I left out a most important part. Something Li Tse would say, 'Our breath and our movements need to be synchronized with the awareness of the cocoon of the Earth around us and with that within us that knows. When we stay with the feeling of Chi, this then allows the energy within our bodies to match the Chi-flow of the Earth around us.'

"Breathing and movement with awareness—focused awareness. That is what brings about the awareness of Chi."

He then looked at me and said, "The important thing for you at this point is uniting the feeling of Chi in movement with the feeling of Chi in the breath. A learning to breathe with your whole body, a touching on the inside through breathing, and a touching with the outside through movement, skin touching air, creating a synchronized more total breath to enliven your body."

A question came to my mind, and I asked, "What happens if while you are practicing this technique you just taught me, your mind fills with thoughts?"

Bamboo looked around for a moment, made a humming sound, then nodded his head, "Oh, those things," he said, grasping the air in front of him as if he were trying to catch a pesky fly.

He continued, "If that happens, gently go back to focusing on the Chi sensation in your hands, nostrils, and if you can, in your belly," he said, leaning over once again to scratch the cat's ears. "Let smooth-touch-smooth breathing hook in the mind and you might even start to feel the Chi at the edges of your thoughts.

"Let's look at this a bit more closely. In a certain way there is a battle going on. There is a very, very subtle pulse to the primordial life-force. As you develop in the womb this gets overlaid by your heartbeat and then by your breathing. It has its natural rhythm and tunes. We want to regain our contact with that.

"But what has happened is that learned behavior has subtly inserted its own rhythms and patterns into the mix and then absconded with your natural breathing, heartbeat, and body movements, and instead redirected this energy to its own tune," he said, rocking back and forth and smiling.

"One of the reasons you want to focus on synchronizing your breathing wave and body movements with the sensation of Chi is because when you do this, you begin to erode the emotional circuits that keep your learned behavior intact."

Bamboo picked up his flute and quickly tooted on it, rolling his eyes around a few times. He then put it down again and continued, "By focusing on the subtle force of Chi we can teach our body to refocus on its original song. We can allow ourselves to realign our breathing, heartbeat and moving patterns to a more primary pulse, to the rhythm of life.

"So, essentially, instead of focusing our awareness on the in-and-out breathing patterns and movements of our learned behavior, we redirect it to focus on the sensation of Chi in our nostrils and in our body. And by synchronizing these two Chi-flows, we begin to neutralize learned behavior's rhythms and habits. We learn to focus on the feeling of energetic fibers inside the nostrils and throughout the body."

"OK," I said. "But what's this about *fibers*?" I asked. "You all seem to talk about fibers a lot."

Bamboo's smile broadened, he tilted his head to the right and said, "Because it feels like fibers when you sense the sensation in your nostrils and in your palms. And when you can see them, they look like fibers too. We live in a gauzy cocoon-like structure. We all wear a gauzy cocoon around us," he laughed.

"If you keep practicing, your senses will unite more and more, and you will get closer and closer to whole body awareness. As you do this you will begin to sense this fibrousness. Maybe you will call it something else, but for me I experience it like strands or fibers. Some healers I know who "see' this sensation call it feeling the strands of mother of pearl. It is beautiful and smooth like silk," he said with a laugh.

"Oh, those silkworms and their cocoons again," I mused to myself.

Bamboo paused, listening to the gentle breeze, and then gazed upwards at the small bells tingling from the edges of the temple's rooftops.

"We live in a sea of Chi," he said, looking at his hands. Then looking at me, he continued in a poetic kind of jingle:

*Like waves. Like water.*
*We are like the fishes in an ocean of Chi.*
*Water and waves have a pulse.*
*Chi has a pulse too.*

He beamed and went on,

*The air inside and outside of us is moving and pulsing.*
*We live in a sea of Chi.*

"It is through breathing that we can stabilize the relationship between the so-called inner and outer worlds, which can be a doorway to the realization that we are everything."

He stopped, smiled, and looked at me while bending over to stroke the cat once again.

"Yep," he said. "For sure, purring is the life-force moving through the body."

# SECTION 3— The Four Women of Phuket

Chapter 9

# NOI—MEMORY

I left Chiang Mai after having gotten the address of Noi from Silvio and Li Tse, after telling them I was on my way to the beautiful island of Phuket.

Phuket is the largest island in Thailand. Only a bridge separates it from the mainland, but it is still an island on the Andaman Sea. It is one of many islands that trail down to the straits of Malacca where the ancient Indians and then Arabs and Chinese came through to trade. The Chinese, of course, came from the East to reach the Indian subcontinent and perhaps beyond, whereas the Indians and Arabs passed by on their way to the East Indies. They were later followed by the Portuguese, Dutch, and English. These islands are quite beautiful when seen from the air, and because of their strategic importance as commercial water routes, back then they were also home to many pirates. The water is much cleaner here on the Andaman side of the peninsula than on the gulf of Thailand side. This clear water and the sunny beaches make Phuket the number one vacation destination in Southeast Asia.

I had arranged to meet Noi on a secluded beach. As I approached a small beach structure made of poles and palm fronds with beach chairs facing the sea, I noticed a beautiful Thai woman waving and beckoning me to join her. Noi was in her mid-thirties, shockingly beautiful in her Thai way, and stunning in her black and white bikini. She sported a small waist and hips, and her breasts were small but ample, and of course she had that silky thin long black hair that the Chinese claim is the essence of yin.

109

She was sitting at a table underneath a thatched roof which was a bit away from its related beach-bar-restaurant. I was a little shy and taken aback when I neared her. I had not expected her to look like this. But she immediately disarmed me with her smile, showing off a perfect set of teeth in that special way that Thai women can. There is just something about the way a Thai can smile that can make your day. So, I was immediately put at ease even before she began speaking.

"My name is Noi," she said as she stood up and *wai*-ed. This is the gesture of putting the two palms together in front of the torso that the Thais use to say "hello" and "goodbye"—done with the hands placed in front of the forehead for monks, at throat level for respect and at heart level for equals.

As I sat down, I waved the waiter over and ordered a fresh coconut to complement hers. I began thinking about her name. Thai people all have nicknames, one syllable or sometimes two short syllables. These are usually the nicknames bestowed on them when they were young, or a syllable of their real name which are often quite long. Noi means "small" in Thai. As we talked, I found out that her older sister's name was Nit, which means "little." The two words together, nit noi, mean "just a little" or "just a little bit." "How Thai," I thought. I could just see two small girls running around the village named "tiny" and "tinier."

Noi was now working freelance as a software writer for a computer company. I found out that she also did Chi Gung with a group here in Phuket, and in that way, she had become friends with Silvio and Li Tse. This combination of a computer person who did Chi Gung amused me. It seemed strange to me because I had thought that computers and body movement were the antithesis of each other.

When I told her she laughed. She then said, "You know, the body is actually like a computer."

"I don't get it," I said, looking a little bewildered. "How's that?"

She slowly got up, and said, "You see, the body is like a computer. The torso is the main body of the computer," she said, stroking her torso along her sides from her shoulders to her hips with a wiggle and a smile. She then put her hands on either side of her face and said with a gleam in her eyes, "The head is the screen." Then she nimbly touched her legs and arms and said, "The arms and the legs are what plug us into the world. More specifically, the legs bring the energy up from the earth, and the arms are the way we relate to the world outside," she said, waving her arms and dawning that disarming smile again.

"So, you can see it is especially important to get the energy moving from the torso to the wrists and ankles and back, to get the energy in your body moving in the best possible way." She then sat down, hardly able to contain herself.

Noi had finished her coconut water, and she began to spoon out the juicy white coconut meat. After a few mouthfuls she continued, "To describe it in Chinese medical terms," she said smiling again. "The 'mainframe' of the computer is the torso and relates to the internal organs. The face is where these organs express themselves and thus would correspond to the screen of the computer. It is where information comes together to be perceived.

"And each organ system in the 'mainframe' corresponds to one of the senses. Look at my face," she said, which I was all too happy to do. "Sight corresponds to the eyes," she said pointing to her eyes. "Hearing corresponds to our ears. These two holes of the nose correspond to the sense of smell, and the mouth," she said, covering a grin with her hand, "relates to taste."

"But I would think that the brain would correspond to the 'mainframe' of the computer?" I said, questioningly putting my hand on my head.

"That is the Western world view. Up to now, that's the best that it has come up with in their system of how things are supposed to work. But it ain't necessarily so!" she said.

"In the East, the 'mainframe' of the computer is here—in the heart," she continued, putting her right hand over the center of her chest. "Look at it this way. Embryologically, the head grows out of the body after it starts to take form in the same way that the other four senses grow out of the sense of touch—very much like the screen of the computer doesn't light up until it has instructions from the mainframe.

"But let's get back to the holes," she said with a laugh. "You know the body has nine openings or holes? In the vernacular of the ancient yogis and Taoists there are nine holes through which the body interacts with the so-called external world.

"The story in some traditions goes like this: God grabbed a lump of clay and rolled it into a ball and then stuck his finger in that ball of clay nine times making nine holes. Then God blew into the holes and gave man life. The seven holes in the face have to do with seeing, hearing, smelling, and tasting—but all these senses grow out of the sense of touch," she said, coming closer and massaging my shoulder, "Touch comes first!"

All of a sudden, a bulge started forming down in my swimming trunks. She looked down at the bulge and said, smiling, "See! Your body knows all about touch!"

She leaned over, patted me on the forearm, laughed and said, "You can tell your little brother to calm down now. We are not going to spend too much time talking about the two holes down below until later. Those lower two openings relate to defecation, urination and of course, as your body reminded us—procreation," she laughed.

"Let's take a break. Why don't we go for a swim and let your little brother calm down a bit and see if you can make it down to the sea without showing," she said, laughing at my discomfort.

She then grabbed my hand, stood me up, and we walked down to the water.

The water felt good. The temperature of the sea in Phuket is warm. There is no shock to the body walking into it. Actually, it felt wonderful, and to have such beautiful company made it even more so.

After we swam for a bit, we got out and walked back out to our table. At that point I asked Noi to tell me a bit more about this body/computer analogy she had been making.

"Oh my god, you want more," she said delighted. "The boys up in Chiang Mai warned me about you."

She leaned over, putting her elbows on the table to cradle her head, and of course smiled, then said, "Did you know that the body retains information or data?"

"You don't say," I responded.

She sat back, assessing me for a moment then began, "Awareness is stored in the body, but 'stored' actually is not really the proper word. 'Stored' is too static a word. The body actually stores knowledge as flow and movement. And if we allow the body to liberate itself, it can relearn to naturally allow awareness to flow through it more efficiently. And the more unimpededly it flows, the more storage space is created, and then we have more space for memory."

"More memory storage space?" I asked surprised.

"Yes," she said, "We store memories and realizations in our body much in the same way that a computer stores data. And when we have more storage space, we can efficiently store more data."

"And now we are moving onto memory, are we?" I said. "But as people get older, they lose their memory, *chai mai*, 'isn't that so?' What about that?"

She looked at me smiling. "What happens is that their storage space is limited and continues to be progressively overloaded and limited by the repetitions of their learned behavior. What is usually referred to as memory is just the story of our story, which is just learned behavior based on perceptual sequences created by that very conditioning. The storage space gets overused, clogged, and ceases to function efficiently. But if those 'old ones' are able to expand the energy flows in their bodies then they can learn to remember much more. And much more not only from the point of view of their story, which becomes more pliable, but also in terms of remembering who they really are beyond their learned story. They will be remembering in a different way or in a different sequence and not be affected by their conventional memories"

I thought about that for a second as I watched the waves breaking on the beach. "In a different way? In a different sequence?" I asked.

"Yes," she said. Then she stopped for a moment to devote herself once again to eating her coconut. Then, licking her lips, she continued, "When we get more energy flowing, we start to remember who we really are and from this perspective we can allow ourselves to expand and remember even more. It is a process. Let's look at it even more closely and say that not only are we talking about the quantity of energy or Chi-flow but also the quality of that flow. And when this flow increases, at the same time our capacity for storing data or memory also increases. But the funny thing is that there is really nothing to remember. We already are THAT." She paused giggling.

I looked back at her with a puzzled look on my face, not quite catching her drift.

"This is how the body/computer analogy can help us," she said smiling and went on, "Do you understand a little bit about how computers work?"

"A bit but not too much," I responded.

"Do you know what fragmentation is?" she asked.

I replied, "I think so. Isn't that when normally-usable parts of the hard drive get locked away and blocked from being able to access other parts by the repetitive use and processing activity of the computer?"

"You got it," she said, running her fingers through her hair and then shaking it out. "Yes," she said, starting to sound business-like, which brought a smile to my face.

"So, as you understand that then look at it this way: the hard drive of your body/computer becomes fragmented by being stuck in learned behavior. And I am sure you learned a lot about learned behavior being around Li Tse and Silvio up there in Chiang Mai," she smiled knowingly.

I nodded.

"In the same way that your learned behavior limits the flow of energy in your body, by controlling its movement and breathing, rhythms and patterns, this fragmenting process begins to limit the usable hard drive space in the computer," Noi went on. "For example, while you could be functioning with one gigabyte capacity while there was no fragmentation, you're now only functioning at ten-megabyte capacity due to being unable to access the fragmented portions of the drive. So, you're cut off from the rest of the energy-space that might be available to you and from the inherent capacity that your body and being possesses to store memory.

"How about that," she said, again with one of those disarming smiles of hers. It seemed like there was no stopping her once she got going.

"Certain energetic pathways in the body that have been overused by the repetition of learned behavior are not allowed to replenish themselves through a full spectrum of interaction with other energy pathways. They become cut off from the potential of the whole usable hard drive of the body/computer. Then those pathways progressively become increasingly stuck together and crusty," she smiled and put her hands in front of her, intertwining her fingers, then wiggling her wrists as if she were trying to unstick her hands. "And eventually they wear out, disabling access to the vitality of the whole organism."

"OK, I kind of get that," I said.

"You can also look at it this way," she went on. "It is as if you're using only one window on your computer screen instead of the, let's say ten that might be otherwise available to you.

"As you have probably noticed by now, I do like talking about this stuff. It gets me very excited," she said, smiling at me once again, her eyes sparkling. "If you don't defragment your hard drive, the otherwise useful space becomes unavailable, causing the computer to operate increasingly slowly and inefficiently, to the point where it's running at less than half of its inherent speed and capacity. And eventually it will run so slowly and inefficiently as to be no longer useful."

Noi paused for a moment to look out at the sea. "Making your learned behavior more flexible and less draconian helps not only in psychological ways, but in physical ways also. This is actually what we're doing with our Chi Gung. This is similar to defragmenting your computer's hard drive."

"Can you tell me more about how I can defragment my body?" I asked.

She stretched her hands over her head, then settled back down into her chair and went on, "For starters, in body terms, articulating your joints differently, or changing your body movements from those of your normal learned behavior helps a lot. You can amplify your movements to include a larger spectrum of motion, which will have the effect of allowing you to access more of your innate potential.

"And more importantly, if you focus on the internal interconnectedness of your body, you can begin to re-connect your body from the inside. In this way you can increase your memory space and the quality of your memory in an efficient way by training your learned behavior to be more flexible and pliant. It doesn't need to control you or act like a dictator taking up all the energy. It can co-exist with other avenues of energy-flow, which all together then can be allowed to find their own natural rhythm. You can learn to let it flow by without grabbing onto it."

"So, what you are saying is that having a personal body practice like Chi Gung can be a real help in enabling your body to access more energy to work with. But tell me more about memory," I said.

Noi looked at me smiling once again. "If you allow your natural or more encompassing rhythms to emerge from within, then more room is made for your real memory, and with it the ability to remember your deepest Beingness. Remembering ourselves in this way can create a core around which a new sense of memory can be built. And using this more encompassing foundation will not only clear up more memory space but will realign that memory, and your conditioned memory will become less important. It can operate by itself without you getting in the way, which then will create a much more substantial base from which to remember things in general. This is evolving defragmentation in action!" she said with a grin.

Wiping her brow in mock fashion she then said, "I think that is enough talking for now. Let's go enjoy ourselves."

We spent the next couple of hours swimming, talking, and resting. After that, at her suggestion, we got on our motorbikes and headed to her house.

Upon arriving at her house, she left me sitting in her yard in a chair under a beautiful flowering tree and went in to take a shower and change. Noi came out a few minutes later dressed in some vertically striped, black-and-white, tie-around loose pants that here in Thailand are called fisherman's pants. Again, she looked quite stunning, especially in her loose white shirt.

She then offered me a pair of fisherman's pants and I went off to take a shower and change too.

When I came back, she was putting a white flower in her hair and looked over and flashed me that smile. We then went over to a roofed pavilion where she said she did her Chi Gung every day.

"Let's take a little journey into the body," she said as an opening, then went on to ask, "What have you learned so far from the boys up in Chiang Mai?"

I recounted my talks with Silvio and Li Tse and my experience with Bamboo in the temple where he had shown me how to play my body like a wood wind by synchronizing my breathing and movements. Then I demonstrated for her what I had learned, moving my body as Hollow Bamboo had shown me.

After I had finished Noi asked, "How is Mr. Hollow these days? As empty as ever?" she laughed, looking upward slightly as if remembering him affectionately.

"I bet he did not teach you about evolving defragmentation!" she added.

"No," I said, shaking my head and rolling my eyes.

"So, let's go back to the movements he showed you," she paused for a breath. "You know, what he taught you is a variation of a Tai Chi Chuan movement called 'Wave Hands like Clouds.' You get that Chi feeling in your hands and move them back and forth in front of your face."

We both got into our stances and began moving. Noi began to speak as we swayed from side to side. "You were asking earlier about memory, right? Doing Chi Gung, the way we practice, makes more energy available to us, and with this you can begin to realign your memory. You can allow yourself to learn to remember who you really are and allow your memory to put itself back together in a new way. And as this process frees up even more energy, you then can even go back through your life and remember yourself differently, realizing that those so-called memories are not that important, setting up new co-ordinates for your memory.

"So, now, using this same movement, we are going to begin to reconnect the body. Or to remember the body—pun intended," she said, giggling.

She stopped moving and then said, "Come over here," waving at me, palm downwards, as they do here in Thailand when they beckon you or even wish to stop a taxi or a bus. "Let me give you a taste of what you are getting into."

"At the beach we talked about the seven holes or openings in the face and now, as promised," she said with a mischievous grin on her face, "We are going to talk about the two bottom openings."

115

She got into a stance and said, "Come closer." She beckoned me to her side, then took my right hand and gently pressed the tip of my index finger to the base of her skull where the vertebrae of the neck connect to the skull.

"Feel that? Feel that faint pumping?" she asked.

"Yeah," I said. "It is faint, but I can clearly feel it."

Noi then led me over to a chair at the side of the pavilion where she sat down, then rested her left ankle on her right knee. Then she took my finger and again gently placed it on the sole of her foot in the space below the pads under the toes. Here I detected that same pumping pulsing sensation once again.

"This point is called the 'Bubbling Spring' in acupuncture," she said. "It is from here that the energy of the Earth rises up into the body."

"Where did that pumping sensation come from?" I asked, for the pumping had stopped.

She held her hand up, smiled, and said, "In a minute."

We repeated the same procedure as I felt the pumping sensation in the middle of her palm, a point she called the "Labor Palace," and then also on the top of her head on a point she said was called "One Hundred Meetings." But as I felt these two points, the pulsing stopped and started intermittently.

She had asked me if I could feel the pulsing. After I had answered affirmatively, she said, "That's good. That you can feel this through my body is a telltale sign that you are starting to develop your sense of Chi. On the outside this pulsing is more subtle and for some people hard to detect, but from the inside it feels much stronger. I think that is why they call some of these practices 'internal,'" she said grinning.

She then stood up and asked, "You know how I do that?"

"No idea," I responded.

She giggled and said, "By pumping my perineum. That point between the two lower holes. When I initiate the pumping action in my perineum and at the same time connect up my body, it can be felt in these other specific areas of my body because my body is 'connected.' It's a work in progress. The more 'connected' you are the more you can feel it.

"And right now, I feel a little shy about having you feel my perineum so you will have to take my word for it," she added, batting her eyelashes, with a twinkle in her eye.

"This point on the perineum is called 'Meeting of Yin.'" In Hatha Yoga it more or less corresponds to the Mula Banda. She then looked me in the eye and continued, "It is from here that we can close the two lower openings and start connecting up the body. In the beginning this can be learned by tightening up the muscles around the anus. Then later on, as one learns to differentiate the muscles in that area, it is done by ever so slightly contracting the perineum and bringing the sensation of Chi there," she said, grinning again.

Noi then picked up a wooden toy that was on the table at the edge of her workout space.

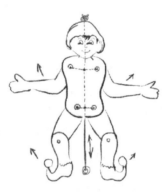

"This is one of Silvio's toys that he uses to help us learn how to reconnect the body. Look what happens when I pull the string."

She began pulling and releasing it. "Pull down on the string and the legs, arms, and head connect. Let go of the string and the toy loses its dynamic tension. When you close off the two lower holes at the perineum, and you start reconnecting the body and getting your dynamic tension back—just like pulling on the string," she said as she playfully pulled on the string a few times before putting it down.

"Come over here," Noi said, waving at me as before, palm downwards, then getting into her stance again. "OK, I want to start by going over proper body alignment in a very general way so that you can begin to get an idea of what we want to teach you "To connect up the body, the first thing to do is to begin to study right posture. So I want you to feel my body. 'Body memory' is very strong, you know. When you feel something

117

through touch, body-to-body, you don't forget very easily. It lingers on in your memory," she said with that Thai smile.

Then she went on, "Now, the first thing we want to do is to begin to properly open up the connection between our hips and sacrum and our feet and the Earth. So first, sink down into your legs and open your pelvis gently, as if it were a flower. This helps to activate the 'Meeting of Yin' point at the perineum and allows the energy from the trunk of your body to flow downwards.

"Now, feel my lower back," she said, placing my hand on her lower spine. "Feel how this posture elongates the spine. Can you sense how my lower vertebrae stretch out? Next, we want to connect to sky above. So, I will pull up on the back of my skull, or the "jade pillow area," as if there is an attachment that is pulling it upwards. This opens the vertebrae of my neck and upper back," she said, putting my hand high on her upper back just where her neck connected into her torso. "And next, relax like this: drop your shoulders, which will open your mid back, and you will be all set.

"When you align this way, you begin to open up the great 'Tai Chi Pole' that runs from the perineum point, 'Meeting of Yin,' through the *Dan Tien* in your belly, to the 'One Hundred Meetings' point at the top of your head." Noi then picked up the toy and pulled on the string again to show the connection.

"What does 'Dan Tien' mean anyway?" I asked

She radiated a smile, and replied, "It means 'place where energy gathers and from where it can be directed,'" she said. "There are three major ones, which I am sure you will learn about later, but right now we are talking about the lower one in the belly.

"OK, let's move on. Let's do that variation of 'Wave Hands like Clouds' that Mr. Hollow taught you," she said, getting into a stance opposite me and starting to move, turning her waist from side to side, the rest of her body following, then motioning for me to join her.

"Now practice what you learned from Mr. Hollow up there in

Chiang Mai. Feel the Chi in your hands. To begin to become aware of the sensation of Chi, the hands are one of the best places to start. After you can feel it there, then bring that awareness to the air passing in and out of your nostrils and then try to sense it in your relaxed belly. But don't forget to check internally if you are in the right posture. And as we move become aware of the sensation of Chi in your perineum, tightening it ever so slightly. This closes the two lower openings and, in this way, you can begin to connect up the Tai Chi Pole by sealing its lower end.

"And in the same way that you experienced the pulsing while I was pumping my perineum point," she said smiling, "This will further activate the points in the palms of your hands and the soles of your feet, and also the 'One Hundred Meetings' point on the top of your head.

"Can you do all of that? And one more thing, if you are sensitive enough you may begin to feel a slight cupping sensation when you activate the points on the soles of your feet and on the palms of your hands," she giggled.

"It seems like a lot to remember to do all at once, but I'll try," I replied.

Internally my attention kept running around trying to do all that she instructed.

We kept slowly moving, turning our waists, and waving our hands in front of our faces like moving them through clouds.

After a couple of minutes, she began speaking softly, "Now close your eyes and turn your hearing inward. When you do this, you may hear a high-pitched sound—but even if you don't, try to direct your hearing inwards. Focus also on that fuzzy feeling in the nose that Mr. Hollow taught you about. And if you can, keep your mouth shut," she giggled again, "And let your tongue rest on the pallet above your upper teeth, feeling the Chi sensation there too. That way we've successfully closed the seven upper holes. So basically, we closed the outflows of energy through the upper seven holes, and by slightly tightening the perineum we sealed the lower two holes. The ancients would say, "Restraining the outflows."

"Now, how does it feel to be one connected sac of tissue?" she asked, chuckling.

"All of this will start to allow the energy to flow back to its root in the lower abdomen, which the Taoists call the lower Dan Tien and the

Tibetans call the 'Secret Place,' instead of letting it flow outward through the perceptual preferences of our learned behavior.

"Now keep the Tai Chi Pole straight and focus on the points on your palms and the bottoms of your feet," Noi reminded me.

I was getting a little overwhelmed and stopped moving and complained, "Isn't that a lot to focus on all at once?"

She laughed, "Yes, I'm sure you are overwhelmed. I am just at first trying to give you a generalized overview. And I am certain it seems like too much. But what I am teaching you has an inward progression. Meaning, we start from the outside and move in. From the moving patterns that we've been taught by learned behavior to the natural way of Chi-flows in the body. And this makes it easier as we go along, as one practice will overlap the next. After all, we are just going back to the natural order of things, just remembering who we really are, remembering the natural co-ordinates for our memory," she laughed. "Trust me, there is a unity to it. Just be patient and do the best you can.

"OK, start moving again and listen while I talk," Noi began synchronizing her breathing with her words, speaking slowly on long out breaths.

"Let me say it again. Two things. First, all these points of focus are overlapping, so that it is not as hard as it sounds because you are just focusing on the natural lines of interconnectedness that are already there. Second, since they are all inherently connected, even if you only focus on two or three of these aspects, the effect is that that focus is radiating incrementally out to all of them."

We continued moving for a while as she continued speaking in a slow voice, "Our memories are not only stored in different areas of our movement body, but also in the quality of these movements and how they synchronize with our breathing patterns. Memories with emotional charges that are stored in the breathing and movement patterns of our learned behavior can clog our energy field, fragmenting our body computers. These movements and breathing patterns become repetitious through habit, leaving our being brittle and not very open to the feelings of life around us."

Noi paused for a moment, then started up again in the same slow tone of voice, "It's not really about getting more energy, but making the system more efficient. Then you will feel like you actually have more energy. Also, the quality of the energy flows will become more concentrated. You are defragmenting the body, reconnecting, remembering, putting yourself back together. Reorganizing and restructuring the body from the inside."

"Let's stop moving for a moment and look at it another way," she said as she went to the doorway of her small pavilion, signaling me to come sit on the nearby steps with her. After we had settled in, she continued, "The physical body is the repository of our past memories and actions, and the tendencies that are attached to those.

"You're taught a story of who you are by the people around you. This story is the glue that holds your learned behavior together. If this story is rigid and inflexible, it creates imbalances in your system.

"Patterns of memory are stamped together by emotional charges. Until we begin to de-charge our story, its sequences of memories are held and stored in our limited movements. The end result is," Noi continued, shaking her head back and forth, "That the self-reflection that your story engenders is redundant and energetically exhausting. And this leaves you only with only a limited connection to the subtle energy-body that your learned behavior allows you, and then life can get boring," she grinned mischievously.

"I'm a little confused about where you're going with this. It seems to me that we need memory, right?" I asked. "If our learned-behavior way of remembering only binds us, what can we replace it with and still have a functioning sense of self? Or, otherwise, without a memory—who are we?"

When I looked at her and I saw a gleam in her eye and a flash of that disarming smile. Noi paused a moment, then raised her shoulders, moved her palms up in front of her and shook her hands in a dramatic gesture. "Exactly," she said, "You hit the nail on the head. We can allow for a new story to rise from within us, with a different sequence of memories, realizing that those so called memories are not that important. A 'new story,'" she went on, "That is based on remembering the truth about ourselves. We then line up our memories in a new way, remembering the truth about who we really are and the path we have taken to remember it."

I felt my face contort into a confused expression, which made her laugh.

After she settled down, she then explained, "Our most important memory is remembering the truth about who we are, that unfathomable thing that we know but cannot explain. So, since you can't explain it, you begin by remembering what you can of the times you've experienced truth in your life. You begin to put together your own personal sequence of awakening. This is based on your remembrance of experiences when knowledge and truth came to you at various times in your life. You begin to remember and construct a new self around this progression. In this way you set your memory in line with your own innate path of knowing and evolving, and this then becomes the basis of your new story.

"Remembering who you really are, remembering your magical heritage, uniting with that spark of illumination that's always been you. And at some point, you may even let this new remembering go," Noi said as she turned to look at me.

"Firstly, your memory and sense of self can then begin to rest on the bedrock of the story of your liberation from learned behavior and the journey back to your natural self. As you let go of your old, programmed story, its order, rhythms, and patterns fade, and a new song emerges to take its place. We replace it with a new song of remembrance."

I looked over at her and she winked at me with a sparkle in her eye. "Self-discovery is about a new identity," she continued. "You start to remember in terms of a new ever-evolving you. You start to remember your total self and realign with the fluid story of how you freed yourself from learned behavior," she said, smiling. "Your memories will then start to line up around your path of self-discovery. Old experiences will be called up in new ways and seen in a new light when needed, without the emotional charges that linked them to your learned behavior."

"Oh, now I get it," I said, "So you don't really lose your memory of past experiences, they're just re-aligned in a different way without the emotional charges that formerly linked them together."

"I think now you are getting it. And at some point, you may even let this new remembering go," Noi said, wrapping her arms around her knees and pulling them to her chest.

"Now can you see how you can defragment the body bound by the sense of self given by your learned behavior? And how can the resultant new story give you more energy and more storage space? As you loosen up more energy, more space becomes available, and more memory can be accessed more efficiently and coherently. You then begin to realize how, by de-charging your past experiences that held your old story together, you can allow a new story to surface, an ever-evolving tale about your journey back to your true self," she stopped for a moment, beaming at me with a smile.

Noi continued, "Let's get practical by supplying the physical component. By doing Chi Gung with the right focus, you can get the energy flowing to loosen up your memory and provide the space so it can be reformatted. You can create a moving structure within which you can more store Chi flow, and this the re-activates the memory of how you know you could be."

"Well, I'm beginning to understand. And now this computer analogy of yours is starting to make sense," I said, laughing.

Just then a squirrel began chattering in a tree above. I wasn't sure if it was searching for food or warning off a potential rival, but we both looked up and watched it scurry from branch to branch, then scurry off on telephone wires to another tree.

Noi raised her chin in the direction of the squirrel, then looked at me and continued, "This new kind of memory is more efficient because it is centered around your journey to your very core. Instead of being like that squirrel which remembers a tree as the pathways it covered jumping from branch to branch, you become more like the tree trunk itself, remembering yourself as the trunk and roots from which the whole tree emanate. The trunk is directly linked to and aware of its branches, and its 'tree memory' is very interconnected and intact. Very different from the hodgepodge tree that the squirrel remembers. So instead of using all your energy jumping around like a squirrel, trying to remember one twig or leaf, you can be like the trunk of a tree, well rooted and with easy access to all your parts. Defragmented!

"Thank God for squirrels," she said grinning. "Got it now?"

"OK, I got that," I replied. "But how exactly does Chi Gung fit in? I don't quite get that connection."

She winked at me and continued, "What getting more memory and making a new story is about is creating an internal body structure that enhances the quantity and quality of Chi flow in your body. This new flow creates more storage space. Not a fixed storage space like a storage locker," she said, laughing. "But more like a moving, living environment that engenders more life. Your new memory will become stored in the quality and quantity of the free flow of Chi in your body. What we are trying to do with our Chi Gung is to sculpt a storage space in motion that maximizes the space within which energy can flow. Then, with more Chi flow you have at your fingertips, the energy needed to create a base for a new story with a new sequence of memories."

She paused for a moment to let that sink in. "Really, what is our purpose here in this world?" she then went on. "We are here to remember ourselves. And our personal story should not be static and encumbering; instead, it should be flexible and pliable and not get in our way."

She looked around her garden, taking in the world around her, then she looked up into the trees and smiled again before continuing, "We can develop a strong connection to the feeling of life around us by learning to walk and move on this Earth in a more complete way. This then will begin opening us up to remembering. Somewhere we have a flowing memory of who we could be, of what we really are. We only have to make space for it to surface.

"In a strange way your story is also what creates your sense of time and space. Your story should become so flexible that for long moments it does not seem to exist at all. The thoughts needed to sustain it are called upon less frequently, and you become more of a flow on the edge. Your self-concept or the idea of who you are may just keep dissolving until you become just a flow," Noi said laughing. "Our story should be a flow. For now, try to see your story and that of those around you in terms of quality of flow. You want to sustain a smooth and supple quality of flow.

"To sum it up in terms of our body computer: activating the sense of Chi and its flow stimulates your sense of wholeness, connecting you with your fundamental essence and your subtle energy-body with your physical body. This then can jumpstart the reordering of your memory which will turn into your new story until you won't need that anymore either."

Noi stood up and stretched, "I'm starting to get hungry. But before we eat, we should go over the exercises that you learned today. You remember our exercises, right?" she asked, leaning over and then hitting me with that mischievous smile of hers.

"First, you feel the sense of Chi in your nose and then in your belly," she said, touching her nose with one hand and rubbing her lower abdomen with the other. "Then you activate the sensation of Chi in the palms of your hands and soles of your feet," she added cupping her hands and feet. "This stimulates the Tai Chi Pole, connecting your body from the perineum to the 'One Hundred Meetings' point on the top of your head." She smiled, then said, "And as you do this practice, you'll soon discover that the spaces in between will slowly start to fill with Chi."

She paused then went on as if finishing a dissertation, "Do you remember how closing the nine holes in the body can imbue the five senses with the feeling of Chi? This disengages the five senses from their trained learned behavior sequence and its rhythms and patterns of perception. Your senses can then connect back to their source and redeploy themselves in terms of a new story or song," she said, singing the last few words and breaking out into a giggle.

She then looked at me, retreating back into her dissertational tone, "Learned behavior really is a drag on the flow. The combinations of sensual inputs are potentially endless, but learned behavior chooses to accentuate only a few. The self-perpetuation of learned behavior is only one tangent or one aspect of our possible ways of perceiving. And because it takes all our energy, we are unable to access so many other ways that are innately available to us.

"Memory should not be based on a heavily encumbered past, or on the weight of tedious repetition. It should be based on an ever-expanding present that can include the 'past' and the 'future' when needed, and it may get to the point that Now ceases to exist because you realize that Now is based on the fact of not having a past or a future. What you really have to ask yourself is: are you programming your computer? Or is your computer programming you? Is the memory that your learned behavior taught you controlling you, or is your real sense of self at the helm?"

Noi paused, waving her hand through her hair, then continued, mockingly shaking her index finger at me, "Our body is a great storehouse of knowledge and awareness. We can tap into this. As we learn more about our wholeness, information can be stored more efficiently in new pathways created by new movements and can then be accessed efficiently by operating from new ways of remembering.

"But beyond all this, the more you begin to trust who you really are, and connect with your true Self, which is beyond your little learned self and your idea of the body, the whole idea of memory changes. Instead of needing to remember everything, as your so-called inner world predicates, you begin to merge more and more with the so-called other world of perceived reality. Then the greater Self takes care of more and more and you need to rely on what you are calling memory less and less.

She then hit me with a self-satisfied smile and leaned over, grabbing my hand and, pulling me up from my seat, and said, "I'm starving, let's go eat!"

Chapter 10

# ANGELIQUE—CO-OPTION

Noi had related to me that she was part of a group of people who practiced Chi Gung together here in Phuket and suggested that I attend some of their classes. She told me that these classes were now being held at the home of a French woman named Angelique. Noi also mentioned that a few years previously Silvio and Li Tse had taught and inspired Angelique and some others in Phuket with their ever-evolving Chi Gung forms. And that they, Silvio and/or Li Tse, visited from time to time, and the folks who lived here in Phuket often went to Chiang Mai. In this way they were all able to practice together and share their discoveries.

As I approached Angelique's house, I was lost in thoughts about gravity that Li Tse had introduced to me some time ago. I had noticed signs here in Phuket for special excursions and activities from snorkeling, scuba diving, jet skiing, surfing, windsurfing, being pulled over the water in parachutes, and riding banana boats. These were large, inflated banana shaped raft-like things that a group of people could get on and be pulled behind a speedboat so that they bounced and sloshed around to the squealing delight of the participants. The Thais in particular enjoyed these.

I realized one thing that all these activities had in common: they redirected the body's sense of gravity, essentially giving one a break from one's learned behavior patterns or the orientation one had become accustomed to in relating to gravity. "So, that is what 'taking a vacation' really was," I thought. "People are instinctively looking for ways of taking a break from their learned behavior by changing their gravitational underpinnings."

Then, in addition, I remembered what tourists did in Chiang Mai for "fun": zip lines, hanging in harnesses, rafting, tubing, and elephant riding. My thoughts then took me to roller coasters, skiing, snowboarding—"Boy, did people ever want to take a break away from their learned behavior!"

I even remembered seeing a TV show about the effects of weightlessness on the astronauts in the International Space Station. The pressure in their body seemed to change and they even gained height. And then I remembered the feeling of freedom from dangling my legs over a suspension bridge in Mexico, the water some 300 feet below. And the unique sensation of lying in or even making love in a hammock. I could see that instinctively something in us craves to move outside of the way we have been trained to experience gravity.

I thought, "Indeed it must have been quite a shock to us: the difference between being in the womb's water world, and then having to learn to function in an air environment. Our whole muscle and bone structure needed to be taught to line up differently. And in the process, this made us incredibly susceptible to the training of the learned behavior around us."

When the impact of these ideas hit me, I began to understand why we might want to take a vacation from the rhythms and movement patterns of learned behavior.

When I arrived at Angelique's home, I followed the sound of voices into the grounds where I was welcomed by two beautiful Queen Anne palms and many-colored flowering bougainvillea bushes. Today there was a luxurious breeze from the sea. The air played with bamboo wind chimes, and I could hear the clucking of chickens and the occasional crowing of a rooster from a neighbor's yard.

Then I saw the sala where they did their Chi Gung practice. An open structure: eight teakwood pillars supporting a high-pitched roof. As I moved closer, I noticed that the floor was also of teak, providing a wonderful surface on which to place one's feet. Off to one side there was a

Buddha image sitting in the "ward-off posture," with incense and candles that stayed lit even in the gusts of the light breeze.

I introduced myself to Angelique and the others, and was happy to see that Noi was there too. Angelique came over to me and mentioned that we should spend some time together after the class. Angelique told me that the movements they practiced were designed to give each person an opportunity to practice internally at whatever level they were at. During the class I followed along as best I could.

Everyone glowed after class. You could just feel it in their bodies. I certainly could feel it in mine. I thought, "There might be something to this body-to-body thing they keep talking about."

As the class broke up, I stayed to spend time with Angelique, and I mentioned to her the feelings I had experienced after class. She then proceeded to tell me about the power of doing movements as a group.

"Much of learned behavior is a system of touching stored in our breathing and moving patterns that we are doing all the time and that is being reinforced by the way that others move with and around us. But if as a group we start moving and touching the Earth in a different way, together and at the same time, this establishes a new way of moving and breathing while being with people. This new way of moving can then be juxtaposed to the training that learned behavior has imposed upon on us. Not only are we moving differently, but this new movement is also being further reinforced by those people around us who are moving in this fresh way too. Doing movements like this in a group grounds this new sequence of actions into the memory of the Earth even further, which can make the effect even more substantial than doing them alone."

All of a sudden, an image surfaced in my mind...I remembered being in the main plaza of Taos Pueblo in New Mexico. I was surrounded by two-story mud adobe buildings that had been there for hundreds of years, with the clear turquoise blue sky above. And in the background was the silhouette of the nearby mountain peak that towers over them, where Blue Lake is nestled, the source of water and sustenance for the pueblo. I could see and smell smoke rising from the fires burning around the pueblo. There was a clear, crisp quality to the air. Before me, all the people of the pueblo were dancing together. From small children to the ancient ones who could barely walk. They all danced the same steps. Some were wearing animal skin attire to embody the spirits of animals. And others with painted faces wore colorful feathers, corn husks, and shells. They were all chanting and stepping in unison to the beat of the big drums.

I remembered that being there had given me the feeling of being in a dream, and now I was getting a sense of why. I realized that when I was there, I had been caught in the no-man's land between the learned behavior of my culture and theirs. It was a wonderful feeling of displacement.

And secondly, I realized and appreciated how they kept the continuity of their culture intact through their dancing, their collective movement, even while being surrounded by "white men." I now began to understand how moving together on the Earth at the same time, and with the same steps, to the same beat, can create a deep unity amongst the participants through their collective connection to gravity and the Earth.

When I came back, a little stunned by the depth of my reverie, I looked up and found Angelique looking at me smiling. She waited for a moment, then went on talking, "To make the effect even stronger, if the focus of the group is to activate one's internal knowledge and one's memory of who one really is, it tends to further reinforce and stabilize the separation from learned behavior and give a new sense of direction in the midst of the breaking away from it."

I looked at her, scrunching up my face with a quizzical look and shrugged my shoulders to indicate that I didn't quite understand.

"Look at it this way," she said smiling. "I don't know how old you are, but do you remember rock'n'roll? The twist? Or even ages ago, the jitterbug? Or even more recently, the rave craze?

Each in their own time was seen by society or the learned behavior of that time as being risqué, non-compliant, and detrimental to the morals of society—basically, uncontrollable. These new movements were viewed as threats to the perpetuation of established social order."

She paused to look at me to see if I was following, then continued, "I'm only pointing this out to show you that movements done collectively that seemingly differ radically from the patterns of touch prescribed by society are seen as threats and challenges to learned behavior.

People are only moving their bodies collectively in a different way—and it causes such a panic!" She laughed.

"But then, when you look at these phenomena more closely, you can see how they were eventually co-opted by learned behavior and have become an integral part of our great 'cultural' history and deemed 'safe.'

Because they lacked a greater focus or intention, these 'dance crazes' became easy prey for learned behavior, which is constantly seeking to maintain control. They had no grounding in anything very deep but were just rebellious expressions of youth that were then absorbed into the learned behavior of the times.

These new ways of movement gave the participants a very temporary feeling of freedom, a feeling that somehow, they had changed something, when in the end they really hadn't."

This made me think about astronauts again, about the very first astronauts, how transformed they were by their experiences when they had returned to the Earth. Through weightlessness and seeing the Earth from space they really had had "super-normal" experiences, especially judging by what they got into when they returned. But as I thought about it, I could understand how that really doesn't happen anymore to those who go up there, or at least not to the same extent.

Then upon thinking about what Angelique just said about the co-optive powers of learned behavior, I could see that even the exposure to new perceptual inputs, such as weightlessness, have become co-opted by the learned behavior of our time; it had lost the edge of newness and resultant inspiration.

But it still does amaze me the way some of those first few astronauts were profoundly changed by their experiences. So, I wanted to know more about why these new dance movements did not sustain themselves. And I put this to Angelique.

Angelique looked at me and said, "This co-option happens because the participants aren't conscious of from where the impetus for their rebellion arises. Deep inside there is really something more, a profound longing to be free, to transform. The energy of youth is forever looking to expand into its true potential," she said. "But as these people grew older and their energy waned, they could no longer sustain that impulse."

She paused for a moment, then went on, "On the one hand, we have a rebellion against prescribed movements which are enforced on us by learned behavior. And this rebellious spirit is liberating and frees up energy. But because it lacks an abstract focus or an intention that is beyond the range of learned behavior to sustain it, it eventually gets absorbed back into the continuum of learned behavior."

She looked at me mischievously, then said, "It is even interesting to see what is happening these days with computers and smart phones. Yes, it is exciting and there is somewhat of a reprieve from learned behavior but look at what it is doing to the movements of the body by putting it into tense or listless postures. I am sure that learned behavior will adapt easily to this. And from what I see it already has!" she said, laughing.

"Let's go sit in my gazebo and have some tea," Angelique said as she gestured to me to go over to the gazebo alongside the sala while she wandered off towards her house. In a bit she returned with a tea pot, tea, cups, and a kettle of hot water. We settled into the small gazebo on cushions with a low table and made ourselves comfortable.

As we talked, she opened up about her life and interest in healing. "I was a sickly young girl," she told me. "My constitution had never been strong, and I was extremely uncomfortable in the social milieu I grew up in. At one point my association with the world became intolerable and in my teenage years, as puberty took hold of my body, a literal explosion took place which saw me going around seeing images of Jesus Christ and going into churches and talking to the Virgin Mary. No rock'n'roll or jitterbug for me," she joked.

"To put it simply, my learned behavior was fairly non-functional to begin with, and when the sexual energy started moving through my body, my social conditioning couldn't handle it. I really didn't know what to do. I didn't know who to ask. Who to talk to?

"I really needed to understand what was going on with me. After a few years of searching, and in a very natural way, I was drawn to the healing arts. I began to feel a movement, a force that was leading me to find out more about myself, and this eventually led me also to shamanism. I began to study whatever I could find about shamanism, which took me to studying the beliefs and cultures of the North and South American indigenous people. Eventually I understood that shamanism had permeated all cultures, and at one time encircled and connected the whole globe, even reaching to the far northern lands of Siberia and the Inuit.

"In the West, our links with this worldwide shamanistic tradition were severely compromised and broken, especially with the advent of Christianity, then with the Renaissance and the subsequent rational thinking and scientific method that developed as a result. And they were compromised even more by the interaction and friction between Christianity and the scientific approach which developed into a system of beliefs that isolated the physical aspects of our existence from that of the Spirit even more."

When she paused for a moment, I noticed her French origins: the delicacy of her ear lobes and high cheek bones, and I was further drawn to the refinement of her hands and fingers.

"Shamanism was originally handed down as an oral tradition, mouth-to-mouth and body-to-body," she continued. "When I encountered Chinese Medicine, I could see that it was really a codified shamanistic tradition. I saw that how it differed from the other shamanistic traditions was that it had been written down. It was the recorded history of shamanism in China in a medical context. By studying this system, I was able to examine a very sophisticated medical model of the human body in which the arts and sciences of acupuncture, moxibustion and herbology, as well as the movement arts, were encapsulated. This was extremely exciting to me, as I could immerse myself in it because a lot of specific information about shamanistic thought was available. With that sense of discovery and excitement, I began to investigate and research acupuncture.

"I met a woman who became my best friend, who was engrossed in this study. The first time she placed a needle in my body it was a profound experience, and in some new way I was reconnected with my body. It was this reconnection which was of so much interest to me. It made me feel like I was in the midst of some traditional shamanic ritual.

"From this experience I became even more interested in the Chinese medical model. I decided to devote myself to studying acupuncture and its application in curing disease. I began to seek out teachers to learn the practical applications of this medicine. I studied individually with three different teachers and finally received my certificate to practice. Shortly thereafter I was appointed to the recently established governing body of acupuncture where I lived, where acupuncture had only recently been accepted as a legal medical practice.

"Oooouuuiii!" she said in French. "I have completely forgotten to serve you, my friend. May I offer you some tea," Angelique said as she poured hot water into the small tea pot. We waited for a minute for it to brew. We then sat back with our tea, and she continued, "I had studied Chinese Medicine with much inspiration and feeling, and since acupuncture was just arriving from China to the West, I there was a sense of magic for both me and my clients in my practice. They had not been exposed to acupuncture at all, and so it was a new experience for them.

"But slowly I watched this sense of awe and magic disappear. I watched my clients get a so-called 'knowledge' of acupuncture, and an expectation of what acupuncture was going to do for them, and what an acupuncturist was supposed to be. This seemed to put everything into boxes and to inhibit the magic and sense of awe from happening.

"Being on the governing board I also watched acupuncture becoming institutionalized into the medical establishment. The premise for this was that we were protecting the public from malpractice. But the underlying assumption was that people didn't know enough to take care of their own health. I also witnessed Chinese Medicine being institutionalized into the Western way of categorizing and viewing disease. I now see that overall, it was a superb co-option by learned behavior," she laughed.

"Western Medicine is highly consensualized and uniform, and the learned behavior of our times was doing the same with Chinese Medicine, which has thousands of years of written history behind it. It was the fact that Chinese Medicine was written down was one of its advantages, and what had helped me so much left it susceptible to be taken over by learned behavior. By writing it down, it had grown away from its oral and thus body-to-body tactile roots and contexts, and learned behavior was able to easily co-opt it—the information had lost its spirit! Never write anything down," she exclaimed, laughing.

She then stopped to ask me if her story was boring me, and I told her she had my rapt attention. So, she continued, "This entire process of co-option, on the surface at least, was being pushed by what I'll call 'the medical industrial complex,'" she chuckled. "This was due mostly to the vested interests of insurance companies, pharmaceutical companies, and the greed of the newly formed acupuncture 'schools.'"

"So, I watched acupuncture and Chinese Medicine, which had imbued me with inspiration and a sense of putting my life back together in a new way, lose its magic. I felt like a part of me was being dragged back into the learned behavior in which I had grown up, and that had proved so inadequate for my needs. This was a very confusing time for me. I walked around in a daze for a few years until I met Silvio and Li Tse, and they introduced me to their Chi Gung. It was a relief when they taught me that what I had seen happening to acupuncture was just a good example of co-option. A good example for how learned behavior keeps us held within its grasp by incorporating something 'new' to make us believe that we are 'progressing,' but does actually not change how we talk body to body. So what I saw happen to acupuncture was much the same co-opting process which happened to the jitterbug and rock'n'roll." She laughed again.

"Before I had met Silvio and Li Tse, I felt so bad because I had personally invested so much into thinking that acupuncture and Chinese Medicine was a doorway to a new paradigm. Then I felt acupuncture had sold its soul to I-was-not-sure-what. But Li Tse and Silvio helped disassociate me from that emotional reaction to my supposed loss and showed me that this is just what learned behavior does. One of the techniques of learned behavior is that through time it co-opts and incorporates into itself new things that are initially threatening to it," she paused. "It just keeps expanding, and like 'Ole Man River,' it 'just keeps rolling along,'" she said giggling and enjoying herself, swinging her fingers from side to side as if conducting.

"Learned behavior is big!" she said continuing, "I really want you to see here that learned behavior is not a static thing. And even though it is evolving and moving and changing, it still maintains its control. Not only are the people around you colluding to keep your attention fixed there, but social institutions, including the medicine of the times, are colluding to keep you in its grasp. It distorts the subtle pulsing awareness that comes into our being to support its own ends, its self-perpetuation. And it leaves us with only a small portion of what we really could embody."

She paused to look at me. "At first, because we are so much a part of it, its control and tactics to maintain that control are difficult to spot. Later on, it can become easier to see. Learned behavior is always evolving and moving and absorbing new things, reforming itself. This aspect of learned behavior can be very alluring and seductive, and may make you believe you are evolving and changing—but be careful! Often, what really happens is that you are merely involved in that ever-changing evolution of learned behavior.

"It's really just smoke and mirrors. Learned behavior just keeps rolling along," she said smiling, moving her fingers in the conducting motion once again. "The true test would be to see if it really changes the energy flow in your body and thus changes the ways you relate to others, body-to-body. Instead, what normally happens is that it's just changing its clothes at your expense, and that's all," she laughed. "Tricky fellow, that learned behavior," she said with an eye roll. "Remember, if it looks like a duck, quacks like a duck, walks like a duck—it ain't necessarily a duck!" she chuckled.

"Acupuncture, instead of being used to help one create a new life based on one's 'natural' potential, has become just another pimp for keeping people stuck in the movement patterns of learned behavior."

She paused then said, "However, acupuncture throughout its history has been used by some people, with the right focus, to help incorporate their knowledge of who they truly are. Chinese Medicine has inherent within itself a system that incorporates the connection of our physical body to its source and then back out again into the world. Acupuncture, with its system of meridians, points and energy flows, innately contains within itself the template of how life energy should flow through our bodies unimpededly.

"What is happening now is that learned behavior is funneling off the energy that is not being used to support its view of the world. In effect, learned behavior is using acupuncture as another way of turning people into robotons that work for it and help it perpetuate itself through its prescribed moving and breathing patterns. Learned behavior has isolated ancient Chinese Medicine, bending and distorting it to support its own limited view of the body."

"To look at this from an 'acupuncture-point perspective,' in terms of energy flows, the way it works is that learned behavior selects patterns of acupuncture points throughout your body and repeatedly stimulates only those, while deselecting others. This co-option is not static but is a movement through time with a cadence and a rhythm to it. The ruthless part of this is that this constant repetition of patterns and associated distorted rhythms can spawn a whole raft of diseases and misalignments in the body, both on the psychological and physical levels. Their cause simply arises from the way that learned behavior has taught us to move and breathe.

"Just one more thing," Angelique went on with her captivating French accent, "Most healing systems we encounter want to help people become balanced and functioning—but only within the system of learned behavior. Their idea of health is based on functioning well within learned behavior—both psychologically and physically.

"These prevalent systems are not about getting more energy to understand who or what you really are, but are only interested in balancing the accessible energy within the realm of learned behavior to help it to perpetuate itself. It is so insidious!" she winced and reflected for a moment, then stated empathically, "Real healing is helping people reconnect to their evolutionary path."

Angelique leaned over and looked at me. "Can you see the result of learned behavior creating its own incomplete view of the physical body and its functions, and how that impacts us as individuals? It's like being in a big room full of windows and having one's face pressed and glued against just one of them and not being able to move, not really knowing that there are other windows available. It's only one limited view. We have within us an uncomfortable feeling that something is wrong, but unfortunately at the same time we don't have the energy available to explore this because learned behavior has taken all of our energy."

"But should we not use acupuncture to cure people's diseases?" I asked, a bit overwhelmed by the implications of what she was telling me.

She sipped some tea, licked her lips, and then continued, "First of all, you need to understand that learned behavior uses 'disease' as a way of telling you that you are not behaving within its parameters. This is the way learned behavior bends 'disease' for its own means. It is not telling you how it is helping to create this 'disease,' nor is it telling you that there are other options for getting well. The learned behavior kitchen is serving you one dish—that you are not performing according to its rules, and it wants you to get it together and toe the line."

She paused, then smiled, "But, yes of course, acupuncture should be used to cure diseases. But using it for this purpose should not obscure the bigger picture of its quintessential usefulness for the journey of self-remembrance. Instead of only being used to cure diseases within the framework of learned behavior, acupuncture could be used to create a new life based on one's 'natural' potential."

"I've mostly been able to follow you up to here...but what's next?" I asked. "How do you get out of the clutches of learned behavior? How can redirecting energy through acupuncture help us to remember and embody our potential? And how did meeting Silvio and Li Tse help you to realize and understand these things about learned behavior and the need to break away from it?"

"Oui, I'm so glad you asked!" Angelique said as her face lit up. "The answers to your questions are quite simple. I met Silvio and Li Tse and began practicing their style of Chi Gung, and it was not long before I found out for myself. My true nature began to open, and answers began pouring in.

"Studying with Silvio and Li Tse allowed me to see acupuncture in a new light, in the context of movement. They showed me how acupuncture meridians are tactile flows of energy that can actually be felt with a sense of touch and Chi. And that these flows are continuously being activated through movement and breathing. And that they are not just things that you visualize and see on charts.

"This has allowed me to see the entire system of points and meridians as a wonderful template of health for the whole body. When I do Silvio's Chi Gung and synchronize my movement with my breathing in various postures, the energy builds within me until the learned behavior is overridden and new information about what I really am comes tumbling out.

"Finally, after studying with Silvio and Li Tse, I understood that acupuncture was in effect a living, moving diagram of the connection between the subtle energy-body and the physical body, and that one of the great uses of acupuncture is to reconnect the two bodies in an efficient and fluid way."

"Wait one second: What two bodies?" I interrupted. "You all keep talking about all these bodies: an 'energy-body,' a 'knowledge body,' a 'body of focus,' and now you come up with 'subtle-energy-body'... and what is this 'healing-body template' anyway? That sounds like still another body? At one point Silvio and Li Tse tried to explain it to me, but I'm still not clear what you all are talking about with all of these bodies?"

"Fair enough," she said, chuckling amused. "It's funny to me because I once had the same confusions and questions. Let me put it this way. There is a force out there—in here," she said, pointing to the space in front of her with her index finger, then reversing her hand and pointing to her body. "This force connects our physical body to the life-force and to the infinite. It is subtle, or can be called subtle, because it cannot be seen by our day-to-day vision. We have noticed that this force has certain attributes so, in order to understand it better we have somewhat arbitrarily decided to refer to it by a series of descriptions of its effects. We know that our connection to it powers the body and gives us a feeling of energy or lack of. So, we call it the 'energy-body.'

"A very broad stroke to this painting," she said, holding her hand in front of her chest, moving her hand slowly back and forth. "Do you paint?" she asked.

"I've never painted myself, but I've had many friends who did, and I often enjoyed being around them and connecting with their energy as they worked," I responded. "So, I'm a little familiar with it, at a distance."

"I get the picture," she said, smiling, amused. "So, think of what I am describing in terms of 'painting in broad strokes' or preliminary work. First, we outline what we are going to do with broad strokes, then we fill in the details later as we go along."

"OK," I said.

Angelique went on, "So, we mentioned the energy aspect. But we also notice that this force gives us knowledge about who or what we really are. This force teaches us how the so-called 'world' operates, and from its deep inner recesses can give us a sense of direction. Thus the 'truth-body,' or the 'knowledge-body.'

"And then we notice that in this force there exists something like a moving, living template of health, part of it being an energetic replica of our physical body that knows what well-being is. It innately knows what sickness is and can stimulate processes in the physical body that enable it to heal itself. This we call the 'healing-body template.'"

She rolled her shoulders a bit and then continued, "In a practical way this is how to think about the healing-body template: you cut yourself. What knows how to fix it? You feel pain. What defines it as pain and tells you that something is wrong or that you have pushed beyond your limits? This aspect has a form which helps you to define what your body is and how it can function optimally. Thus, we call it the 'healing-body.'

"It's really all the same thing. We are just overlaying words and images to get a feeling for it. And we keep using the word 'body' because this force we're talking about seems to cover and concentrate on, or be grounded down by, our physical body. So then, body-body-somebody-anybody-no body," she laughed. "Is that any clearer for you now?"

"Uggggh," I nodded.

Angelique laughed, seemingly delighted by my response, and went on, "Well, these bodies are all one thing and they are all happening at once, but for our poor little intellects to be able to begin to grasp this, and for us to get a feeling for this greater force, we cut it down into these ideas of different bodies and a healing-body template."

She paused, leaning over and drinking the rest of her tea, then said, "Too much talking, and not enough moving spoils the broth. Why don't we go back to the sala and move some Chi."

She continued talking as we walked back over to the sala, "I talked to Noi, and she told me what you went over with her. I really like Noi, what do you think of her?" she asked.

"I think she's beautiful and knows a lot too, a good combination, eh?" I replied.

Angelique smiled knowingly as we continued walking towards the sala. When we arrived, she said, "What we want to do today is to show you how to re-connect the body and to begin to create a proper structure to align yourself with the Earth's gravity."

She got into her stance, her feet parallel, shoulder distance apart, knees slightly bent, and began doing the variation of the "Waving Hands like Clouds" form that I had practiced with both Bamboo and Noi.

As she moved, she began talking, "I am going to show you the next practical step in learning to connect up your body. First, focus on the sensation of Chi where the air enters and exits your nostrils. Then, follow the two air channels back to where they meet way inside your head to move your focus beyond your learned patterns of breathing. Focus your vision inwards. Then, direct your hearing sense inward and put your tongue lightly on your palate, feeling a sense of Chi. So now we have closed the seven upper holes of the face.

"Next, relax your stomach and detect that same sensation of Chi that you're feeling at your nostrils but now in your belly. Finally, extend your awareness of Chi to that gauzy feeling, or a sensation of pressure, into your hands and feet. OK, are you with me?" she asked as she continued slowly moving her body.

I nodded my head and uttered "uhnnung" in acknowledgement.

"OK, now engage the Tai Chi Pole from the perineum up to the top of your head."

"Wait a minute," I said. "You need to slow down a little for me. I know I learned this from Noi and Bamboo, but I have not embodied it all yet. And I have a question: how does breathing in this new way I am learning bypass the breathing patterns of learned behavior?"

"Good question!" she said, pausing. "Let's sit for a minute for this one," she said, moving to sit on the steps of the sala and gesturing to me to follow. After we were settled, she began speaking, "I like to use this model to explain the effect of breathing on the body."

She went on, "In the ancient texts, particularly of the Buddhist/ Hindu milieu, they talk about the three primary channels of energy in the body. One beginning at each nostril, then proceeding to wrap around the mid line of the body," she said as she moved her index fingers in two descending "S-curves," starting from her head to the bottom of her torso. "Until one ends at the tip of the sexual organ and the other at the anus. The third channel is located on the central line of our body over which these two other lines cross," she said as she moved her left hand up and down the center line of her body. "Where the two outer channels wrap around the central channel, they form what is called a knot or chakra, which inhibits the free flow of energy, thereby creating 'duality.' And these constrictions of energy are reflected in our breathing patterns."

"How does the central channel breathe if the other two channels are breathing through the two nostrils?" I asked inquisitively.

"That's pretty quick thinking," she said, chuckling. "The breath of the third channel is all pervasive, even to the point of coming and going through the pores of your skin. It can be felt when you concentrate on the sensation of Chi in your nostrils and follow the breath back up to where the two streams meet. Because it is all pervasive, it is there in both nostrils, and it is both in the in breath and in the out breath. Uniting your awareness with it is the trick. By noting the sensation of Chi in your nostrils, and leading your awareness back to the point where the sensation of breath from the two nostrils meet, is a way to find it.

"And by focusing on this third breath you can then bring your attention to the central channel, and begin to loosen the knots that are created when awareness flows through the two outer breathing channels that create duality.

"This then allows your true nature to begin to permeate your being. So you see that by focusing on the breath of the central channel, we concentrate our awareness there. It no longer flows out into the world of duality where learned behavior reigns.

"And so, to bring this back around—generally, the longer we stay with the sensation of Chi in the breath and throughout our body the freer we become. *Kao jai mai?*" she said in Thai. "Do you understand?"

She then got up and we walked back into the sala where she took her stance again and began moving. "I think we've covered what you've learned up to now. But now we're going to add something. We will work on re-connecting the joints."

She stopped and said, "Wait a minute." She then looked up and smiled. "I think we need a Silvio prop here." After she said that she went over to a cabinet at one edge of the sala and pulled out two toys. "Here, have a look. This first one here is what I call a 'pop-up toy' which will show you the overriding principle involved."

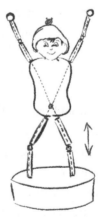

It was a wooden human figure interconnected with elastic strings, set on a stand that collapsed when you pushed up from underneath, and sprang back to life when the pressure was released.

Angelique said, "When you push up, he collapses—which is pretty much the state we have all been reduced to by our learned behavior. When you relax the pressure he springs back to life—and we have an interconnected vibrant body.

"By slightly stimulating the perineum you begin the reconnecting process that Noi showed you. Then, as we reconnect, it feels as if elastic connections throughout our joints are engaged," she explained, collapsing and reconnecting the toy a few times, laughing.

"Now have a look at this second toy I think Silvio created himself. He really likes his gadgets and I've been around them for so long that I am starting to like them too," she smiled. "This one can help you to visualize the body mechanics that I am about to show you."

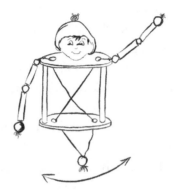

"The first toy demonstrates how we can re-connect our whole body by starting with bringing our attention to the sensation of Chi at the perineum. And this second one demonstrates how movement in the body, once it is connected, can be initiated by the wrists, elbows, and shoulders, and ultimately from the Dan Tien in the lower abdomen."

Angelique moved the bead below the toy from side to side and thus made its arms go alternately up and down. She then put down the toy, looked at me and started moving again. "Now watch and see if you can detect the toys in my movements."

I was able to see exactly what she had described: first, how she connected her body. It was like elastically elongating the joints, and then after she was connected, how she was able to initiate the movement of her whole body from different joints. First from her wrists, then elbows, then shoulders, and then lastly from her lower Dan Tien. I was not sure how I was able to see it, but I could make it out. I figured it was partly due to suggestion because she had just explained it, and also because of the accumulated body knowledge that I had gained by being around these people. Maybe I was starting to understand, this body-to-body stuff, I mused.

"Let's go on. I want to cover a lot with you today," Angelique said. She then walked over to a pillar in the sala, leaned back against it and slid down into a sitting position. She took a deep breath and then said, "Let's look a bit more into the mechanics of movement and the central role of the lower Dan Tien. I want you to walk around a little bit."

"Walk around?" I asked.

"Yeah, walk over to the edge of the sala there, then walk back over here. Walk back and forth as I explain something to you," she said.

I began walking, not knowing what this was all about. But thinking about what Angelique might do to me, and so I became more self-conscious of my walking.

She caught my attention when she said, "Feel your ankles as you walk. Can you feel how your normal walking motion flexes your ankles? Notice how when you step, your ankles flex forward, and then as you put your weight on them, they flex back. I want you to note that." She motioned for me to stop and sit down.

Then as she got up, she said, "But this is not the only motion that your ankles can make." I then watched as she began walking in a novel way, twisting her ankles outwards and inwards as she shuffled along in a way that somehow reminded me of a bear ambling in the woods.

She asked, "Do you see how my ankles are moving differently now than the way that yours were moving when you were walking?"

I nodded in reply.

She went on, "They're twisting inwards and outwards, moving from side to side instead of flexing forward and back. This is what can happen when we initiate the movement from the two sides of the lower Dan Tien and allow the energy to move down to our ankles."

She smiled at me as she continued moving. "Our ankles then begin to twist instead of flexing. This twisting action is really the result of initiating the movement from the two sides of the lower Dan Tien, torquing the energy into a natural outflow through the feet. You should be able to deduce from this that when we usually walk, flexing our feet forward and back, that this is only a limited version of the possible ways we could move our ankles or even walk." She laughed.

"As opposed to flexing, what I am doing now is called 'twisting,'" Angelique said as she continued moving. "Using this twisting motion that originates from the lower Dan Tien and then torquing it down to the ankles, we can open the legs and torso to new flows of energy. We connect to the Earth in a new way. This movement opens up new combinations of energy currents from our legs to our torso that we don't usually use. This series of movements is so profound that one of Li Tse's teachers from China based his cancer Chi Gung on it. Twisting like this invigorates the lower part of our torso and our connection to our major physical energy center, the lower Dan Tien, thus giving our healing-body template new energies to reconstitute itself.

"You can combine this walk with various arm and wrist postures to further direct the energy," she went on as she continued this novel way of walking while she showed me different ways of positioning her arms.

"Is there a name for that way of walking?" I asked. "It reminds me of watching a bear ambling along."

Angelique stopped and replied, *"Geng mak,* very astute," she said, speaking Thai. "That's exactly what we call it, the 'bear walk.'"

Then she gave me an eye roll as she laughed and said, "If it looks like a bear, ambles like a bear," she paused for effect, "and smells like a bear, probably it is a bear."

She then went on to say that in our normal movements we don't habitually use twisting motions, not to mention taking them all the way to their extremes the way she had just done. Angelique further explained that moving to the extreme range of the twisting motions activates meridians that are little used in our normal day-to-day movements.

"You should understand by now how moving like this, you would release new energies that flow into your torso, thus giving new life to your bowels and organs," she said. "You should also begin to realize why this would be good for curing cancer. In general, cancer occurs because there's not enough energy in a particular area of the body to direct the cells to function normally. When the healing-body template has more energy, the body can heal itself.

"Remember," she said, raising and shaking her right index finger. "Giving more energy to an area in the body that is weak, the healing-body template will know what to do with it. Healing is about 'helping' the body to heal itself. Because it innately knows what health is."

I nodded in agreement, beginning to get a feel for what she was telling me and maybe a sense of where she was going.

She went on, "In addition, you soon will become aware of how the postures and movements that we do with our upper body can be used to direct that energy to different organs and bowel systems in our torso. You'll understand this better once I begin to show you the mechanisms of our 'Eight-Point Chi Gung.'

"But first I want to point out some more energetic principles. I want to give you a description of the healing-body template in fluid motion. Many of the major acupuncture points that are used to regulate the energy in the body are located around the joints. So, specifically, the movement of the joints when the body is in motion is what activates these points and stimulates the flows of energy. And when the body is connected back up the way I was showing you before, the joints can do their job properly. The energy activated from the movement of our joints, once initiated, then flows to the torso and back creating a dynamic tension. Once you understand these energy flows, you will be able to grasp that by moving your joints in specific ways you can activate specifically-related points and meridians that move energy to particular organs and bowels. By using this information, conclusions can be made as to which exercises or movements are most effective for dealing with particular illnesses or imbalances. So, you can begin to see from this example how both acupuncture and Chi Gung use the same underlying principles, "

But then Angelique started raising her index finger in the air and flashing a Cheshire grin, "We must learn to deal with the elephant in the room. What for us is the great paradox. How do we work with the so called 'body-mind,' while at the same time knowing from the depths of who we really are that neither of these really exist.

"That's enough for now," she said laughing, then looking up at the sky and seeing that there might be some rain coming. "Let's go to get a bite to eat before it rains!"

Chapter 11

# ANGELIQUE—HEALING

We returned to Angelique's home in the fresh air after the rain, sated after our meal. As we entered her land, she told me how she had learned over time not to put trees too close to her house.

"You have to learn about a different set of trees here in this climate," she said. "Some trees have roots that will affect the foundations of a house and others have leaves that will clog the gutters."

The result was that her plot of land was airy and surrounded by trees. Her house was built in an "H" shape with a kitchen, living room/dining room in the crossing line of the "H," with a bedroom and bath in each arm. One of those was now used as a study and another as a treatment room. There was a big swimming pool off to one side with water cascading down a rock fountain feeding it. On the other side of the house was her fishpond, gazebo, and the sala for practicing Chi Gung.

On the way through her house Angelique stopped by the study and picked up a human anatomy atlas that showed a skeleton with three or four overlaying transparencies showing the bowels and organs. Also, there were illustrations displaying the circulatory and nervous systems overlaying a picture of the entire body in layers. We continued out to the gazebo with the book, and she put some water on for tea. I leafed through the volume as she prepared the tea.

When it was ready, she brought it over and sat down, "Here try this, my friend. This tea is called 'silver tips.' Lately it is my favorite. It's the single buds from the white tea plant. These days it is touted as the healthiest of the teas. You might have to get used to it though, the taste is very delicate. But it has a definite clearing effect on the mind." She smiled.

I took a sip. I told her that it produced a nice flow of saliva.

She said, smiling and raising her right index finger, "Did you know that saliva was our first food?" She then went on without waiting for a response, "Saliva was the first substance we ingested as babies and what coats our food and initiates digestion. That is one of the great benefits of drinking tea! And the quality of saliva formed by tea is a particular indicator of a tea's quality."

I nodded in appreciation. I could see now how Angelique, although sweet on the outside, was very precise and I imagined she could be a very demanding teacher. She looked very alive, though I could not be sure of her age, but I wouldn't have expected a person with her youngish appearance to embody so much knowledge.

After pausing for a moment, she continued, "I want to talk to you about healing today. And some of the better road maps of the healing-body template are these acupuncture meridian pictures," Angelique said, pointing to a set of three charts on the wall behind us. I looked to where she was pointing and for the first time, I noticed that there were three acupuncture charts on the fixed walls of her small pavilion.

"Although not comprehensive enough to show the energy centers in the body, these maps do give an idea of the body's energy flows, particularly the way the energy flows around the joints and through the arms and legs. The energy pathways get much more complicated in the trunk, where the organs, bowels and deeper energy centers are located.

"A map with this arrangement of points and how they connect to each other can be used as a model for understanding how the more outer energy flows in the arms and legs connect to the deeper layers within the body. It was based on this type of model that the efficacy of the different acupuncture treatments and Chi Gung movements was theoretically divined.

"Do you remember? I referred to this before, when I told you that by looking at postures and movements through the views of the body, that these maps of energy flows provide conclusions can be made as to which exercises are most effective for dealing with particular illnesses or imbalances."

Angelique paused to ponder for a moment before going on, "There are three ways that we can affect our healing-body template. One, via the outer skin with techniques that are specific forms of pressure applied to the body from the outside. For example, the Asian technique of acupuncture, which is a complex discipline, and also various forms of massage, which are specialized forms of touching.

"A second way is through the manipulation of joints, tendons, muscles, and tissues through exercise and movement. With systems like Chi Gung, Hatha yoga, and even dance, you can very directly contact and stimulate the healing-body template from within. But in this case, you will be working with the dough of the donut.

"Just whetting your appetite," she said as she chuckled with a mischievous smile. "I think you will find out more about this dough later."

"Did you know that the body is really like a donut?" Angelique went on, smiling, "We have this skin on the outside," she said rubbing the skin on her arms. "Then the dough that we just talked about in between, and then we have this skin on the inside," she said, first pointing to her mouth with one hand and then tracing the digestive tract with the other.

"So, you can see that it is through the skin that we deal with the world—whether it is inner or outer. Through the outer skin we interact with the world out there," she said, opening her arms wide as if embracing all the surroundings. "And we interact with that same outside world in a different way with our inner skin, through the foods and liquids or anything else we may ingest.

"This leads us to the third way, alimentation. What you take in orally is processed and then releases energy that creates specific types of pressure and resultant movements on the inside skin of the donut body. This internal process is a complicated affair shrouded in mystery. Because of the intricacies of the digestive tract and all its functions, it is the most difficult and complex way to influence the healing-body template," she said, smiling while rubbing her tummy.

"In general, it is much less complicated and more forgiving to use outside stimulation, or movement and breathing, to affect the healing-body template than having to deal with the digestive tract. Incidentally, one thing that I have noticed in my acupuncture practice is that people who have a regimen of body movement and breathing like Chi Gung or Hatha yoga are the easiest people to treat. They respond much better to both interior and/or exterior stimulation, because they have a stronger base and connection with the healing-body template than those who do not have such a practice." She smiled.

"Hmmm," I pondered, then pulled up a question I had been waiting to ask, "Speaking of practice. I am wondering what is a good amount of time to spend each day practicing integrating into my body this knowledge you all have been teaching me? Is there a certain minimal amount of time each day that allows one to establish a new energy flow in the body that is practical amid conducting everyday life?"

"You are a practical one, aren't you?" she said with a wide grin and a twinkle in her eye. "Well, here's a rule of thumb. In the Chinese classics they say that the energy or Chi completes a circuit through all the meridians of the body 55 times a day. So, you see, about every half hour the energy cycles through the entire meridian system. If you want to make an impact on your whole body and lay the foundation for a new series of actions and awarenesses in your life, you should practice at least one cycle or about one-half hour a day. And if you double that it would be only one hour," she beamed. "But one-half hour out of a whole twenty-four-hour cycle is a workable amount of time for anyone to start with."

•

Angelique stopped for a minute to look up and noticed, as I did, that the rainclouds were still trying to come in over the southwestern hills. "Let's walk over to the sala before it starts raining," she said. "There's something else I want to show you today."

After we arrived at her sala, Angelique moved to one of its eight supporting poles and leaned her back against it, then slid down into a sitting position. "Sit like this over there against that post," she directed.

"I want to begin to talk to you about our Eight Point Chi Gung. It was Li Tse who helped develop this Chi Gung. He once mentioned to me that this Chi Gung and its applications were initially taught to him by two

'Sky Beings.'" she said, chuckling and rolling her shoulders and moving back and forth against the post massaging her spine. "Ask him about it some time."

She then continued, "I think this image over there will help you," as she pointed to a framed picture that was attached to another post across from us in the sala. I got up and walked over to look at the picture she had just drawn my attention to. It was a drawing of a person with eight highlighted points on it—four around the hands and wrists and another four around the feet and ankles.

When I looked at it even more closely, I saw that there were two points on the inner side of each wrist and hand and two points on the outside. This same pattern was repeated on the ankles and feet, with two points on the inner side and two on the outer side.

I then noticed the two enlarged drawings next to the main figure, which showed close-ups of the hands/wrists and feet/ankles, with highlighted "X" and "O" marks on the selected points.

Angelique told me that each one of these points corresponded to one of the eight Ba Gua. I remembered this term from my study of the I Ching.

I turned away from the picture, faced Angelique, and asked her, "I have had a question in my mind for a long time that I think you may have an answer to. What actually is a 'Gua'? It seems like it is important to understand."

She motioned for me to come back and sit against the pillar. After I had settled, she collected her thoughts for a moment and then began to explain, "A Gua usually refers to one of the primary eight divinatory symbols used in the I Ching. Together they are called the Ba Gua, or 'Eight Trigrams.' You know what the I Ching is?" she asked.

I nodded; having used it for a long time. It was the text used for divination in China for thousands of years. It was based on images created by different combinations of solid or broken lines representing the eight primary forces of nature. One of the most popular current representations of these Gua can be seen in the Korean flag, where four of these trigrams are prominent.

"The Chinese use them to help describe 'primary' relationships between things," she continued. "And now we're going to begin to put together how the actions of the twisting and flexing motions in the body are ruled by these eight points and their corresponding Gua."

She pointed across the sala to the picture and said, "You will also soon experience how these points are connected to meridians or the lines of energy flow that you can actually feel in your body."

Angelique rubbed her hands together. "Now watch what I do and follow me as best you can," she said, extending her legs in front of her. She then started twisting her ankles inwards and outwards. I did the same, sitting with my back against my post, stretching out my legs and twisting my ankles from side to side.

"You are now experiencing the possible range of motion for twisting your ankles. Can you notice how those two points on the inside and outside of the foot and ankle marked with 'X's are the extreme points that are activated when we twist our ankles to the farthest end of their range of motion?" she asked, while pointing at the pictures. "It is important to move to either extreme to fully stimulate and activate these points," she added, continuing to twist her ankles in and out, like windshield wipers.

She moved on, "Next, we'll flex our feet by stretching our ankles straight and moving our toes as far away from our torso as possible. Then we'll bring them up and stretch them backwards towards our face, thus stretching the Achilles tendons and ham-strings as far as we can. These are the extremes for flexing the feet and ankles. And these stimulate the two points you see, one on the inside and one on the outside of the feet/

ankles marked with 'O's. You got that: 'X's are for twisting and 'O's are for flexing?" She grinned.

"Yeah, I got that," I replied relieved, convinced that at last I was possibly faced with something a bit easier to understand.

"Are you ready to move on?" Angelique asked, and then without waiting for an answer continued, "Watch me, and you can see that a similar thing happens at the level of our wrists and hands."

She raised her arms straight in front of her and began twisting her wrists and arms all the way inwards, then all the way outwards.

She motioned to me, "OK, now you try it."

As I copied her movements Angelique said, "Can you feel how this stimulates those two points in the picture at either extreme of the twisting range of motion, one on the outside and one on the inside of the hands/wrists marked with the 'X's?"

"Now, next we'll flex the hands/wrists." Angelique put her hands in front of her, pushing her wrists upwards with palms turned up as if holding two trays. She then turned the palms over, pushing downwards until they rested on the floor.

"Do you recognize the two points, one on the inside and one on the outside right above the wrist, marked with 'O's? The one on the inside corresponds to the upward-flexing motion, and then the one on the outside corresponds to the downward-flexing motion."

"The stimulation of these eight points through movement is the basis of our Eight Point Chi Gung. They represent the limits of possible motion that can be stimulated for getting our energy to move from the trunk of our bodies to our extremities and back," she explained.

She then stood up and said, "Why don't you get up now and we'll apply some of these exercises moving our energy through our arms and wrists while doing the 'bear walk.'"

I stood up and positioned myself behind her so I could best watch and emulate the movements of her feet as she began walking.

"Do you notice how we twist our ankles outwards and inwards through their extreme range of twisting as we walk this way?" she said, as we began walking, directing my attention down to my feet. "We are stimulating the two points on the feet that we were just working with while studying the twisting motion, though we were sitting."

She stopped and said, "And as I showed you before, while we are doing the 'bear walk,' we're also opening and closing the two sides of the lower Dan Tien, releasing energy into our torso. We can then direct the energy out from our torso in specific ways by twisting or flexing our wrists and hands into the various postures we just studied."

We then for a few minutes went through the various postures of our wrists and hands as we continued the "bear walk," until Angelique took a deep breath and stopped, saying, "I think that's enough new movement for today. As you practice these movements your feeling and understanding of what they're doing will grow within you. But be sure to practice," she chuckled.

"And don't forget that the way that we perceive the world is intimately connected to the way we focus on and move our bodies. You are involved in a reconstruction and reclamation project allowing your body to teach you to understand its innate potential."

•

Angelique went to the entryway of the sala and took a seat there, motioning for me to come and join her on the steps. She rubbed her hands together energetically and said, "So let's go over what we did this morning and just now to make sure you've got it all straight in your mind.

"First, we went over how to connect the body. Initially we reconnected the body the way Noi taught you, by activating the energy in the perineum and the Tai Chi Pole up to the top of your head. Then, we studied and experienced connecting the wrists, elbows, shoulders, the chest, and the two sides of your lower abdomen. And how by regaining the elasticity of those connec-tions they help reconnect us to the center of the body, the lower Dan Tien.

"You should have been able to feel and understand that when your body is re-connected in this way, you can initiate movement in your whole body, from your wrists or your shoulders, for example. This is done with a feeling that is produced by reconnecting your body, which creates a sensation as if you've tightened the elasticity of your tendons—like the 'elastic man,' you remember?" She chuckled. "You begin to pull your body back into its natural alignment from within, and this allows our joints to assume their proper function in creating and distributing the energy throughout the body."

Leaning back and rubbing her belly she continued, "Remember, energetically everything that we have studied so far leads us back to this place: the lower Dan Tien, the seat of our physicality. At this point what we're really doing is cleaning up the connections that inherently exist, by remembering our body. Just like that guy," she said, gaily pointing to a statue standing on a shelf in her cabinet, depicting a fat laughing Buddha with his hands held over his head.

I wiped my forehead with the back of my right hand, feigning physical tiredness, then smiled and said, "Oh-lala, Angelique, you taught me a lot this morning. I'm a bit over-whelmed."

She replied, "I know, it may seem overwhelming in the beginning, but what we're actually learning are just overlays."

She held her hands in front of her and illustrated her point by making the motions of peeling off the layers of an imaginary onion.

Continuing to do these motions, she said, "One principle overlays another, and we're working our way from the outside in. In the beginning this appears more complicated, but with practice you will understand.

"We do it this way because in the beginning all that learned behavior allows you to perceive is the 'outside.' But things get simpler as you go along, as more and more the outer layers dissolve into the inner ones. Then there's less to learn and more to experience because you are developing a new sense of awareness for the feeling of life and its movement in your body. Until at last you may become the awareness itself"

"Let's have a little bit of fun," she said.

"By compacting and connecting the body as we have just learned you increase pressure in it, thus creating more Chi-flow. This can be felt for example in your hands. When you connect your whole body in this way, you're creating more pressure by uniformly squeezing your body sac tighter from within, and this increases the flow of Chi, making more of it available. The feeling is like squeezing toothpaste out of a tube.

"You can even feel it sitting down! Let's try it.

"Connect up your body, relax your hands, and become aware of the sensation of Chi there. Now create a base for containing the Chi flow by closing the lower two doors. Gently squeeze and stimulate the perineum point. Can you feel that extra amount of Chi flowing through your hands as you do this?"

"Yep, that's good," I said laughing.

"I am glad that you can feel it already," she said. "It normally takes a bit of training to be able to feel those sensations."

•

I enjoyed being there in the sala with Angelique. It was relaxing in an energetic way just sitting with her. I looked over at her for a moment, a little awed by all her knowledge. It made me wonder how she had become involved in all these practices. So, I then asked her, "What happened in your life to push you into becoming a healer?"

Her eyes wandered across the sala as if looking for a clue. She replied with a gentle smile, "Well, to make it short: I've been driven to explore healing for reasons of my own health. And because I've been through this adversity myself that qualifies me to be a healer."

"How does that work? Does being sick help?" I asked.

Angelique reflected then said, "You are beginning to understand how illness can provide an opening for one's inner path to surface. Now you are learning how to consciously stimulate a conversation with your body. And bodies do talk to bodies."

She paused for a moment to let that sink in. "When a healer has personally been through the pain and transformation that illness can produce, it is easier for patients to open up and trust her or him. Intuitively, other people can sense what you have been through. And so, at a very deep level, at a body-to-body level, people trust you. And this more than any other thing qualifies one to be a healer."

She then continued with emphasis, "Deep down, people's bodies can sense the depths to which another has traveled and the pain that they have struggled through. This then can allow for the creation of an environment within which people can freely share their problems, and their spirit can get renewed direction."

She then said in conclusion, "So, because I was sick, I studied healing to help myself. And when I started treating people, they could feel that from a deep place. I could understand their plight. And by exploring this connection, healing became my art."

I smiled and nodded.

"A struggle seems to happen in the interplay between the subtle energy-body and the physical body," she continued, slightly changing the subject. "I would say that health is... properly connecting the subtle body with the physical body and correctly aligning the links between the two. Disease occurs when energy is entangled and does not flow in the most efficient manner between these two bodies. The more effectively you can improve this connection, the more energy you will feel.

"But you see the problem, don't you?" Angelique inquired reflectively, "Our learned behavior is parasitic in nature. It wants to keep its host alive, but at the same time it wants to siphon off as much energy as it can without killing it. The end result is that learned behavior diverts away much of the Chi-flow from the subtle body before it can make its way to the healing-body template."

She stopped to look at the trees and plants around us then went on, "I think by now you can begin to see the depths to which learned behavior reaches and how it tires out and exhausts our natural energy.

"To disentangle ourselves from learned behavior is a process, a process that is in flux and requires constant evolving. We need to maintain a focus on something which is beyond the scope of learned behavior. The concept and feeling of Chi are just such a thing. It is beyond its reach. Also, the more Chi we have access to, the more we can begin to store the needed energy to move awareness to other locations, away from our learned behavior. So you see, as we gain more of a sense of this flow, we can not only stabilize our awareness away from learned behavior, but at the same time our body can access more energy to focus on its own health and well-being."

Angelique smiled and continued, "Through practices of energy cultivation such as Chi Gung, we can stabilize the process of breaking up our old patterns and storing this freed-up energy in the healing-body template. So, you can see that in terms of reconnecting the subtle-body and the physical body, doing Chi Gung with the right focus can be a valuable tool."

"But there are so many healing systems out there," I said, feeling a bit frustrated. "How can you tell one from another?"

She looked at me and responded, "You have to have a fluid concept of healing or learned behavior will co-opt it. But as a rule of thumb, just remember that healing comes from the free flow of Chi in the body. And that if we keep the concept of the body as efficient and fluid as possible, this can greatly help us to dissolve into our True Self."

She hesitated, then went on, "There are those who think that balancing the limited energy at your disposal given to us by learned behavior is what healing is about. But this is not real healing. This is simply treating patients to allow them to keep functioning within the limitations of learned behavior. This even includes most practitioners of the so called 'holistic movement,' who have been subtly co-opted by learned behavior and conventional Western medicine.

"I have been around the block a few times and have the internal scars to prove it," she said laughing. "And still there is much I do not know. But there is one thing that I'm sure of: that real healing is about gathering more energy back from the clutches of learned behavior to explore who or what we really are, and to reconnect to our path of evolution."

She paused, looked at me and continued, "This is why it is said that the Buddha is the greatest physician who ever lived." She then smiled as she moved her hand slowly, pointing out some of the Buddha images she had placed around her grounds.

I smiled and nodded with appreciation, as many things fell into place.

She leaned over and punched me lightly on the shoulder, beaming, "Voila, there you have it! You see what heals all ills is the knowledge of one's essence!"

I looked about and at the same time heard the gentle splashing of water from a fountain in the distance. Once again, I relished in the feeling of being here in Thailand. Taking a breath of the lush air, and feeling the breeze on my skin, and watching it caress the leaves of the trees filled me. And it took me back to what my teacher in the Peruvian Amazon had taught me: that we come from plants.

He would say, "Plants are what we are. They created and now sustain us. To worship the plants is to worship life."

I drifted back and told Angelique my remembrances.

She smiled appreciatively and then said, "Our energy-body has a deep relationship with the Earth's cocoon and the plant world. And our energy-body is what keeps the physical body alive.

"And as our energy-body charges us up and we begin to reconnect our bodies, we naturally become aware of release points that want to be stimulated, as the energy-body begins to accentuate them. And this takes us back to acupuncture and Chi Gung!" She beamed.

This led me to ask, "I still don't understand completely how the Chi Gung you're teaching me can help me heal? Talk to me in a practical way. Give me an example."

Angelique paused for a moment, then replied, "OK, let's say you have a bad knee. Your knee does not function properly. So, you do one of the variations of our style of Eight Point Chi Gung, directing Chi-flow into that area. This triggers a healing process on many levels. By moving Chi into that area, you activate the corresponding healing-body template there. And just the act of keeping your awareness there can help you to heal your knee directly.

"But at the same time, by focusing Chi onto the pain in your knee, you send out a message to the world around you that is reflected back. The increased Chi flow in this area produces a charge of synchronicity."

She smiled and looked over at me, "Remember: what we put out gets reflected back. Don't forget that what we perceive as the world around us is how we have been trained to see the world, so there is a very intimate connection there.

"By focusing Chi into an area, a whole progression of 'healing steps' are set in motion." Sweeping her hand around in front of her, she continued, "From the world out there, an answer to resolving the pain in your knee may come back to you in many different ways: such as a friend recommending a practitioner for you to go to, or noticing a right healing salve in a shop, or striking up a conversation with a stranger on the street who comes up with some surprising helpful advice; or you may even get a part of your healing from a direction given to you in a dream. But regardless—the healing process is set in motion."

"Can you expand on that, Angelique?" I asked

"I have been waiting to paint this picture for you," she replied, laughing. "Here is a visual analogy that I can give you to understand the phenomenon of synchronicity and connectedness.

"Let's call it 'the projector, the slide, and the screen,'" Angelique continued. "Sometimes healing of the physical body does not take place as directly as we have just spoken about. Nonetheless, simply by focusing the Chi of the energy-body on a diseased or painful area in your physical body can cause answers and solutions to come from the 'outside' world— via a conversation, a glimpse of something, or even a firefly going up your nose," she said, laughing and rubbing her nose a few times, having fun with me.

"Let's look at this more closely. I think you might like this explanation.

"There is a light within us—our essence—that functions as a projector. This light shines through a 360° living slide: an amalgamation of our belief systems that emanate from our sense of self which is stored in our breathing and movement patterns. You remember that connection, right? Our essence illuminates this slide like a projector and the energy pattern in the slide is sent out into the world. So, then what comes back at us from the world out there originates from the impressions on this slide. What we observe on the screen of perception around us is a reflection of our belief system, which is based on our sense of self. Got is so far?" she asked, checking with me.

I nodded.

"But this is not merely a visual slide," she went on. "This is a multisensual slide which has become filled with the perceptual preferences given to us by learned behavior. Because as we know, our learned behavior warps the connections between our subtle energy-body and our physical body for its own ends. So, when we increase the circulation of light between these two bodies by increasing our Chi flow, thus bypassing learned behavior, a much cleaner slide is created, and the energy sends out changes.

"The stronger the connection and coherency that exists between the aspects of the subtle body and the physical body becomes, less residues are left on the slide and more of our own essence can be reflected back to us from life around us. And as a result, we end up more connected to the world around us. The outcome being more Chi-flow and better health.

"Let's go back to your knee," she said. "By directing Chi into that bothersome area, this has the effect of changing the slide there and a different projection goes out through the slide into the world. You follow, right?

"You see, your body really has a reflection/connection with the world around you. So, by increasing the Chi in this area you will 'mysteriously,'" Angelique raised her eyebrows, "attract answers from synchronistic events in the living matrix around you. You are giving the healing-body template more energy to work with, and it knows innately how to work with it in its many ways.

"Any more questions?" she asked, pausing to take in the scene of the trees, flowers, and breezes flowing around us.

She stretched her arms out over her head. "When you do our Chi Gung consistently you are continually training your body to get used to moving a greater quantity and quality of Chi through it. This engenders a continual focus outside of learned behavior which enhances the light in the projector and the circulation of light between the projector, the slide, and the screen. This then increases the clarity of the slide, which brings more of a sense of connectedness or synchronicity into your life.

"And when you are continually increasing the movement of Chi-flow in your body, this builds on itself, creating a 'healing lifestyle.' Once old patterns are broken down in this progressive manner, the released energy is incorporated and stored as new flows of energy, and both your inner life and outer life, become richer. Your connection to the feeling of life becomes more constant as 'you' start to dissolve into the flow of life that is everywhere around you."

We stopped talking and watched a lizard move slowly, ever so slowly, around the edge of the fishpond. It stopped to do some lizard push-ups for a moment, and then when a frog suddenly jumped into the pond it scurried off.

"So, tell me, Angelique. I'm curious about what makes Silvio and Li Tse's Chi Gung so special for you?"

She rubbed her chin for a moment, lost in thought. "There are lots of reasons," she began. "But I think that in the most practical and enduring sense, doing their Chi Gung has made me stronger, healthier, and more grounded.

"It was not long after practicing their Chi Gung consistently that the flood gates of knowledge about my true nature began to open. And I was glad that Silvio and Li Tse were around to help me understand and incorporate all that was coming in, and the way in which it was changing me. They helped me put it all into a useful context. They taught me a focus that lasts through time. The continual focus of becoming your True Self."

She paused to reflect then said, "They truly are my friends. They realize they don't have all the answers—in fact they don't even like the idea of being teachers and try not to set themselves up that way. They prefer to conceive themselves as evolving guides or signposts along the path.

"Also, they helped me integrate the many things that I'd already learned—in a new and vital context. And I have always liked their emphasis on connecting the energy or healing-body to the physical body, and the wide range of internal practices they teach that focus on this."

Angelique reflected for a bit more, then looked at me and added, "The ancient peoples were much more into using the body directly as an instrument to assess and explore the world than we are today. I like how Silvio and Li-Tse relate their Eight Point Chi Gung and other things they show us to the I Ching and Feng Shui, for instance, because for me it is important to connect to those ancient ones and their views of the world.

"I also like their combined approach, which is good: stretching, Chi Gung, meditation, acupuncture, cupping, sexual yoga—'anything that works,' as they say. They stress that all these techniques should not be used to support the physical body as a pawn of learned behavior, but instead to enhance and explore the knowledge of one's True Self and connect to the path of evolution.

"But what I appreciate about them the most is that they are constantly exploring and following their own paths and encouraging others to do the same. They have an attitude of 'not-having-anything-to-lose' that I also find very appealing. I appreciate how the dispersion of their knowledge is predicated on the principle of knowing oneself, and that it is not based on self-aggrandizement. If you trust them there are no 'secrets,' and they present their information in a straightforward and methodical way. New principles and practices are given to you when they feel you can absorb them best—not trying to withhold information, but giving it to you at the most appropriate time.

"But indeed, the jewel of their teaching is their intense focus on finding out who or what we really are." She smiled and then said with sparkling eyes, "In this way they transmit the contagious disease of freedom."

•

We paused for a moment, and I tried to absorb all she had told me.

Then I asked, changing the subject a bit, "Where did you study acupuncture, Angelique?"

She replied, "In many places. And now that you mention it—that's another reason which makes Silvio's and Li Tse's teachings so appealing to me. They themselves had been practicing acupuncturists in the past. And this helped me to expand and enhance my knowledge of that art. Since we shared that common background, they were in a position to answer some deeper questions about acupuncture to my satisfaction. For example, they taught me how to effectively combine Chi Gung and acupuncture. They showed me what points to stimulate while doing Chi Gung.

"I don't know if you've seen Silvio doing Chi Gung with acupuncture needles in his body?" she said, laughing at the image.

"No, I haven't. I didn't even think you were supposed to move while you have needles in your body."

"Well, it is possible to do, and actually is a good technique. Triggering a specific meridian by using related moving forms is good. Then focusing the energy specifically by needling can accentuate the curative effect even more. Usually, this needling is not done in the affected area but in a corresponding area far away. Moving the part of your body that's painful or afflicted through positions where the pain resides, while the needles are in place, directs energy into the healing-body template in that area, and into that range of the meridian flows where it's most needed."

She looked at me then continued, "And then I appreciate the movements they have shown me; some of which concentrate on the eight basic meridians of the body, which have always interested me."

"Angelique, you've been doing this for a long time—overall, what's the most important principle of healing that you've discovered in all this time?" I asked.

She clapped her hands and smiled. "Healing should be defined by the amount and quality of Chi flowing in the body, and not by how well the body can serve the aims of learned behavior."

She pondered for a bit. "And practically, what I've found is that staying with the sensation of Chi is the best way of accumulating energy. Although subtle to understand, increasing the Chi-flow in the body can produce a direct effect on bodily health because activating Chi-flow stimulates the energy-body through which the physical body is strengthened.

"But this needs to be done from the inside. Once you know about Chi-flow then you can for example adjust your posture to enable more complete gravitational alignment—thus getting more energy from contacting the Earth."

She reflected for a moment before she went on, "What you have to ask yourself is, why does the body want to be more gravitationally aligned? When you do this, you will discover that the more aligned the body is with gravity, the better the flow of Chi. With proper alignment you will have a better connection to, and thus more circuitry engaged with your healing-body template. This then gives it more energy to work with and therefore improves your health."

She paused for a moment, resting her chin on her folded hands, and smiling mischievously. Then, suddenly, she peered at me, her eyes bulged, then lit up as she leaned back and she slapped her thighs and said, "But really the secret is—GET YOURSELF OUT OF THE WAY!

"Let the body heal itself!!! All that healing ever is, is helping the evolutionary process along. Help to expedite the body's wisdom."

Chapter 12

# Felina—Your story

The next day I found myself again walking to Felina's house. I looked up and there was a beehive in the tree above me; I salivated thinking of the wonderful honey that must be in it. It was made by those little black forest bees who would gather the nectar from the jungle flowers, which is much more refined, delicate, and multi-flavored than the honey made by the imported and domesticated bees from Europe.

Walking over to her house brought back memories from our first meeting there when she had told me her personal story and her descriptions of "Zen sickness." I thought that I had understood her as well as I could at that time. But I was curious to hear more from her about what she had hinted at as "rewriting one's story."

Once again, we settled down in her garden close to the soothing sound of the beautiful cataract flowing into her swimming pool with the luxurious trees all around. As we sat down, I first wanted to understand more about how her experiences at university had shaped her ideas on learned behavior.

So, I asked, "Felina, last time we met you mentioned that you consider academia 'pimping' learned behavior. What do you exactly mean by that?"

Felina smiled, unable to contain herself, and said, "Universities are institutions, and all institutions by definition pimp the learned behavior of the times. That is their function as pillars of society—no matter how much they talk about free thinking. They are either into rigidly maintaining learned behavior, or in the process of co-opting new ideas into learned behavior. Universities are masters of integrating new thought into the entanglements of learned behavior. I guess Angelique went over the principles of how this works when she talked to you about co-opting," she said, chuckling knowingly.

"They can really fool you. These institutions are dedicated to keeping the underpinnings of society intact. Because of this, either overtly or covertly, whatever is taught there is laced with the goals of learned behavior."

"So, what about psychology and psychotherapy?" I asked.

She smiled in delight before answering. "In reality psychology and its offshoot psychotherapy are co-opters extraordinaire!"

She was clearly enjoying herself now.

"For starters, most of the time, their concepts are only based on thinking, on the mental aspects of ourselves, and not grounded down in body movement. And most importantly, don't forget, psychology is taught in universities, so it is laced with learned behavior to begin with. And by and large its main goal is trying to make people fit 'back in.' It is not very concerned with creating a life that can exist outside of the learned behavior of the times.

"You see what I am saying?" she said, grinning. "When you work with psychology, yes, energy can be released, but two interrelated things happen: one, the energy gets quickly co-opted back into one's story again as there is no storage capacity to house the released energy properly, and, two, the energetic memory gets lost in the shuffle because there isn't an energetic structure to maintain and remember it.

"Furthermore, when you look closely at the workings of psychology in practice you will find that underneath its veneer the questions being asked are: Why are you not fitting into learned behavior? How can you fit in better? Or how can you improve your learned behavior to better match the learned behavior around you? Don't forget," she said with a laugh, "being well-adjusted to a sick society is not necessarily a good thing

"You see, these folks are not dealing with a full deck. Mere thinking does not affect the healing template at all. Thinking will usually let you down. You can play with your story, but any new story you may create is always put back together in terms of learned behavior, just stealthily shifted around.

"Tricky proposition this," Felina said, pondering for a moment. "Concentrating too much on the problem and then, when energy gets released, not having an energetic structure to store it. So, you just keep concentrating back on the problem; and this all loops back into self-involvement and thinking even more about oneself. So in essence, issues seem to get resolved, but no more energy is added because whatever was gained is directed back into focusing on oneself and one's learned behavior story. It becomes an endless cycle because it lacks the right focus of reclaiming our energy and storing it in our body."

"OK, so then why don't psychology people deal with building up the energy in the body?" I wondered aloud.

"The concept is simply foreign to them," she replied. "They don't have any idea nor even a frame of reference for how to do that. It's just not an option. They may sense it at a deep level, but they really are not given the means."

She paused before continuing, "We've got to take a break from our own learned behavior to let the atrophied parts of ourselves come back to life again. And not focus on it even more the way psychologists usually do! The point is, psychotherapy is not encouraging people to embody their full potential. This is due to lack of techniques that have to do with changing the moving and breathing patterns of the body and releasing and storing Chi-flow. And psychology lacks any motivation to do this because it is laced with the aims of the status quo."

She looked at me and said, "Incidentally, knowledge can and does exist without words and without thoughts. Our body-sense can help us realize this. Our body really does have a deep memory of our evolutionary path and we can learn to tap into this."

"So, what about the disciplines in the West that exist on the cutting edge of accepted thought?" I asked.

She laughed. "You mean those new ideas that are in the process of being co-opted? Those are usually only indirectly concerned with creating a free flow of Chi in the body. Thus, their information will be fragmentary until backed up by a knowledge of or a focus on proper Chi-flow. And even when they create a release of energy, they often do not include a component for stabilizing and maintaining this increased Chi-flow.

"So, tread carefully with the latest fad. You simply may be attracted to it because it seems to somehow have broken free from established ideas.

169

But in reality, it is usually in the process of being quickly co-opted back into the mainstream. One thing that you should ask yourself about these so-called 'new therapies' is this litmus test—do they create and sustain changes in our breathing and moving patterns?

And do they create and sustain changes in how our bodies talk to each other?"

I was getting confused as some new thoughts had entered my mind wanting clarification, so I asked, "Let me get personal, Felina. What's the difference between what you have gone through, and this co-opting that Angelique had told me about? Weren't you co-opted?"

"I wasn't swallowed up in co-option," Felina laughed, "Because I was always one step ahead of that process. I was so shattered that learned behavior couldn't get a good foothold, and by the time it finally did I had moved on to something else. As a result, the pieces of my shattered learned behavior became the steppingstones to my new story and new memory. I was using this process not to solidify learned behavior but to make it more pliable and flexible and with more spaces in between. And perhaps most importantly, I kept finding ways of moving more energy through my body and storing it there. It started inadvertently, out of necessity. I had to do this. The problem that I had was that although I was able to stay one step ahead of learned behavior, my way of doing it was very exhausting. So, it was quite a relief when I ran into the Chi Gung of Silvio and Li Tse, where I found a codified way of doing it.

"I think this is the way of our 'natural' evolution away from learned behavior. It first happens unconsciously, arising from a deep body memory, and then the process becomes clearer as the pattern of gathering and storing energy repeats itself and becomes more conscious. In a minute, I'll show you one of the practices that I learned early on that helped me keep myself together."

She then laughed at herself and said upon reflection, "Boy, that was a mouth full. But here's one more thing," Felina said raising her index finger and playfully shaking it at me, "As one's story begins to unravel and dissolve it becomes harder and harder to relate to other people's stories in the same way. We are still in the day-to-day world, but we don't share the same co-ordinates of focus or the same day-to-day reality of those around us. We become energetically more self-sufficient and in a real way we don't belong anymore. We just don't care about the same things that others do. We live in a bigger world. We are in their world but not of it."

She went on, "I realize that this is something that many people experience to some degree, and that it could even well be part of the 'human condition.' But the problem is that these people have no sense of focus to give them direction and no body component to rely on. They are just being blown about by the wind," she said laughing.

"That was a lot of talking, eh?" she said wiping her brow. "Now let me show you some things about the body."

She pointed to a lush grassy spot over to her right. "Let's go over to that shady spot under that big tree you can see over there. It's a good friend of mine. It will help us now."

After we were settled there under her tree friend, Felina said, "I think I can show you something that the others have not shown you yet—shaking. It is something that I stumbled into before I made their acquaintance. This particular technique helped me a lot to begin to heal myself, and it is especially good for psychological and nervous disorders. It was actually the key I used to get over my 'depression.' And doing this technique was instrumental in pointing out to me the primary role of the body in maintaining our learned behavior, and what can happen when we begin to change our habitual muscle movement patterns and make more space for the flow of Chi in the body."

She directed me to get into a stance. "You know the routine by now. Remember to keep the outsides of your feet parallel, shoulder width apart, because this automatically evenly balances the pressure on the front pads and the heels of your feet. Then bend your knees slightly and straighten your back as if there is a string holding you up from the crown of your head.

"OK now, look," she said. "Put up your arms up like this, as if you are holding or embracing the tree.

It's like you are hugging a tree, right?" She laughed. "Have you hugged a tree lately?" She then chuckled a bit more before going on.

"If you hold this posture long enough, inevitably you will begin to shake, because your old way of aligning with gravity will tire out because it cannot take the strain. But that takes a while. You can short-circuit this process by shifting your awareness to feel the vibration from the Earth coming up through your feet and through your body. In this way you can begin to shake from the get-go," she grinned.

As we stood there holding this posture and slowly beginning to shake, she began explaining, "I've discovered that shaking happens when learned behavior's alignment with gravity becomes saturated or overstressed, which for example happens when you hold this 'embracing the tree' posture too long. This saturation level of our learned behavior's moving patterns can also be attained while being involved in exhaustive physical practices. This happens to runners, for example, when they run a long enough distance that they get into a state when they feel as if they have merged with the world around them. The problem being that they need to run farther and farther to attain this state, which can exhaust and even injure the body. But if you are able feel the vibration of gravity coming up through you as you begin to shake, you can short-circuit the need to saturate the moving patterns of learned behavior through exhausting forms of physical exertion.

"You might also notice that you can think while doing this shaking exercise, but your thinking will not have the same emotional 'charges.' There will be a type of clarity amidst your thoughts."

She chuckled. "By shaking in this way, we create a kind of 'cognitive derangement.'"

We continued shaking.

"Now listen," she said, as she began speaking slowly and rhythmically in a hypnotic voice,

"If energy is flowing smoothly through your system, your life will become much more fluid and vital, and more synchronized and merged with the world around you. Not only your sense of self but also your perception of the world around you will become more alive.

"We live in a pulsating, vibrating world. We are taught only a limited way of moving through our learned behavior. We are taught that we live in a world of objects when we really live in a world of flowing vibrating energy. If we allow this vibrating force to move through us, we can begin to vibrate with it. We can contact this pulsating world and let it heal us. Shaking saturates our learned muscle structure or learned behavior structure of our body and allows energy to move through to other areas. Shaking in this way puts us in a position to learn directly from the Earth's vibrations that come from its gravitational pull and the forces that are created from the resultant pressures around us."

"Now keep shaking, but keep your eyes closed, and I will tell you a little about me," she said. She once again began speaking in a slightly hypnotic tone of voice:

"When I first started shaking on my own, I was frightened when my body began to spontaneously vibrate. However, as I began to study, I read some ancient Chinese and Japanese texts that related people's experiences of being in meditation and spontaneously beginning to vibrate and move their limbs as great quantities of energy circulated through their bodies. This was one of the positive manifestations of the 'Zen sickness' I mentioned to you earlier.

"I also learned about people in religious ecstasy who shook and vibrated because the force that they engaged with was too strong for their body concept or learned behavior to handle. I noted that mediums trembled and shook when spirits entered their bodies and that there were many religious people who took shaking for granted as part of the religious process, such as the Shakers and Quakers.

"From all of this I realized that trembling or shaking was OK, that it was the body's way of processing more energy than it was normally taught to handle. I saw that shaking could be used as a way of digesting energy, especially when I learned how to maintain my internal energetic structure. I understood that if I wanted to embody more energy, I could accomplish that by opening my body to it through shaking."

She paused, then spoke a little slower, moving me even deeper into

173

that trance-like state.

"We are intimately connected to a vast unbroken harmony existing within the eternal matrix of the Earth and beyond. The entire human body is suffused with energy from the environment, which is converted and exchanged within the human organism through vibration.

"Our health and well-being stems from the active patterns of cellular vibration within our tissues. The body's cells are constantly vibrating in patterns and rhythms that enhance the flow of the Chi in the body.

"There is a vibrational resonance that keeps us intact and interacting. Shaking begins making new pathways or a new webbing throughout our bodies through which Chi can flow.

"Shaking can help you to stay in touch with touching. It saturates your old way of being with gravity and thus engages new pathways of energy. As your feeling of touch becomes saturated you will begin to open to Chi, at the edge of touching—the Chi sensation, from where you can create a new base.

She paused. "OK," she said softly. "Open your eyes and relax."

As I stood there, she continued speaking slowly and rhythmically. "If connecting up better is combined with shaking this stimulates the healing-body template. I know this from experience. The first time I tried shaking on my own, after having learned this way of doing it from a friend, I was lying on my couch depressed. I forced myself to get up and start shaking. After just ten minutes the depression lifted. I really could not believe it!

"Now I understand the process more and I can see what had happened. I had simply saturated and thus by-passed my learned behavior's way of being in gravity, thus initiating a freer flow of Chi to happen throughout my body. This allowed for new energetic pathways to open, giving me more energy by saturating the patterns of my depression and moving beyond them. And this made me feel good. I then started doing the practice every day for at least twenty minutes, sometimes twice a day, and this definitely helped cure my bouts of depression.

"I think you can understand how shaking could help many psychological and nervous disorders by giving the energy or Chi in the body new pathways within which to flow, and thus making more points of contact with the flow of the world around us."

"I can see that," I replied.

She continued, "Shaking can provide an opening for becoming aware of and beginning to embody our natural self. It not only loosens the grip of learned behavior, but also opens up new avenues for storing it. Shaking can be immensely powerful, especially when mixed with focus and the other principles you are learning. It can help the Chi-flow in the body and can be a jumping off point to realizing who we really are since the sensation of Chi permeates all the other five senses—and at the same time is beyond them."

Felina smiled. "By staying with the sensation of Chi, the conditioned grasping that goes on to keep your story intact is transcended."

She then stopped for a moment to reflect then went on, "Specifically, I'm convinced that the tactile vibration initiated through shaking practice loosens up the sacrum—the linchpin of our bone structure and the location where the corresponding nerve pathways to our sexual energy reside.

"I think Angelique may have already talked to you about the sacrum. I am not sure," she said. "But the two of us have discussed this at length and came to the conclusion that in many ways our learned behavior and the way we channel sexual energy through our bodies is directly related to the manner in which the vertebrae of the sacrum fuse. And that one of the keys to getting in touch with our innate vitality and strength is to keep loosening up our sacrum!"

She went on to tell me how the vertebrae of the sacrum fuses between the ages of sixteen to thirty-four.

This resonated deeply inside of me, especially when I thought about her trials and tribulations during puberty as well as my own, and so I asked, "What do you recommend about sexuality?"

She looked at me and laughed, "You really want to grab the bull by the horns, don't you? In general, the answer is quite simple. Sexual energy has to be important: it powers our physical body. It is our life and blood energy. Used to enhance the Chi-flow in your body, it can become an incredible energy source.

So, use it.

"But go cautiously because it is very personal, complicated, and subjective, and in many ways operates well beyond the realm of words. There are so many variables—men are different from women and then each man and woman is different, a planet unto themselves. Our sexual nature is really a morass of individual subjective complexity, and contained within it are the deepest agreements of our learned behavior.

"Learned behavior has very deep roots that go into the sexual act. And so many of our normal interactions are based on a complex code of sexual conduct that learned behavior has implanted in us. The sexual act is really a deep dance of collusion with each other's learned behavior. So studying sexuality can take us to the core of our quest to become free from learned behavior."

*"Sexuality—a deep dance of collusion?"* I asked a bit surprised. "Can you explain this a bit more?"

Felina replied, obviously delighted by my question, "Ultimately, you must understand that learned behavior is really centered on its own self-perpetuation and is based on the rules we learn of how we can touch ourselves and others. The sexual act is the ultimate act of touching that we're capable of as physical human beings, and thus it is heavily impregnated with those rules. As you begin to touch sexually, you start to exchange learned behavior patterns held in muscles and breathing patterns. We even play learned-behavior sexual games in order to get 'close,'" she laughed. "And then, once we are 'close,' the interaction and collusion happen so rapidly and intimately, and the information being exchanged body-to-body is so enormous that it is overwhelming!

"Let me give you an example: the biggest problem of working with sexuality and another person is that routines are set quickly. Learned behavior takes over and rapidly begins to set the agenda. The minute agreements in our moving and breathing patterns are quickly readjusted on the surface. And because these agreements reach very deeply, it is difficult to move beyond or evolve through them.

This is one of the reasons we like to change partners or to 'get a fresh start,'" she grinned mischievously and chuckled.

I really wanted to know more about this, so I asked, "But how about all these studies that are done about sexuality? Do they have any relevance?"

"Sex in this day and age," Felina said, "Is never studied as an energetic phenomenon. Instead, it seems always to be studied with the strong agendas and overlays of learned behavior. Learned behavior wants to keep the lid on sexuality in just the right way. Learned behavior, as we have seen, has so much invested in sexuality that you can expect the results of these so-called studies to be skewed. These studies are conducted by folks at universities or by people who have been heavily influenced by them and, of course, trained by them. Couple that with the fact that these studies are created to be viewed by learned behavior, then it is not difficult to see how the agendas of learned behavior are laced into them."

She paused.

"If you do a study of sexuality where everyone, all the participants and even the researchers, have the same learned behavior, then the agenda is set and there is little room for anything else."

I reflected for a moment how the sexual fluctuations in my life had unbalanced me. This was something that I felt strongly but could not quite put into words, and I asked her about it, "How do you think sexual fluctuations affect our mental balance, Felina? Because in my case I suspect that they have a big effect. I can remember time and time again when I felt I needed a sexual release but could not find one, and it seemed like the energy then internalized and drove me crazy, made me unfocused and at times even depressed. Can you see what I am trying to ask?"

She looked at me and smiled understandingly. "If we go back and look at my story, we can see what it did to me. It rocked my world," she said, grinning.

"Sexual energy, when it comes up against our learned behavior, exerts a strong pressure. When there is too much pressure, the structure of learned behavior gets pushed to its limits. The crusts that learned behavior has created around us begin to crack. This affects our mental balance.

"Sexual energy has a lot to do with mental focus, creativity, and health. If learned behavior keeps too strong a lid on it, this then can easily result in real depression and even violence. We see this around us all the time."

Felina went on, "The question becomes, 'How much energy or pressure can learned behavior handle before it cracks, and energy starts leaking out?' I can remember so vividly how I felt compelled to walk the streets in Bogota when sexual energy became overpowering. I had to try to move it through my body—somehow to let it move through me.

"There is a unique aliveness to sexuality. Sexual energy wants to move throughout our whole body.

One reason sex feels so good is because once again the energetic interaction gets so intense that it saturates and overwhelms learned behavior. In fact, one of the reasons people enjoy sex so much is because somewhere during the act there is a small break from learned behavior or one's own story.

"This I believe is the real cause of so-called 'sex addiction.' It just feels so good to get away from our monotonous boring suffocating story—one's connection to the learned behavior of the times. In fact, the psychological component of most addictions is the same—at some level we all yearn to experience more of our total beingness. We want a break. We want to experience more than our learned behavior allows us to. The means for accomplishing this can certainly be put into question, but the impulse to want to learn more about oneself and how one could be evolving is, at least from my point of view, perfectly understandable."

As she smiled and looked up into the trees, this allowed me a moment to remember some of the addicts that I had worked with in my clinic years before, and how I had so easily gotten close to them. I could now understand why I felt the connection. I could see how at a deep level I had appreciated the fact that at least they had tried to loosen the bonds of learned behavior, and that because of this I had felt a real affinity for their struggles.

Felina pulled me back as she started talking about sexuality again.

"When sexual energy gets strongly activated, learned behavior gets overwhelmed and marginalized because of the vast flows of energy in the body. So even with all its pitfalls, the exploratory potential that this state can produce in terms of freeing ourselves from the clutches of learned behavior is great. The core of most sexual yoga is based on just that—studying what can be attained in this state. These practices revolve around staying on the edge of or in the state of orgasm when the energy is the strongest, to the point that deep realizations can occur."

"OK," I said. "I can see that. But what about the expansion of foreplay and sexual prolongation in the public domain that we've seen happening recently? And what about pornography? Doesn't this help people loosen the grip of learned behavior too?"

"Ah," she said with a smile, "A perfect example of learned behavior's co-option and its way of keeping a lid on sexual energy. Don't forget now about the minute touching agreements that we share when we touch each other sexually. Learned behavior wants to be in control of the build-up to orgasm and also the coming down from it. What a good idea to prolong it in order to make the co-option even longer, while at the same time making it feel like some kind of liberation. Make it 'weird and interesting' so that new diversions are created and learned behavior can keep its hold on the populace. In this way people get hooked on focusing on the act and become blind to what lies beyond and within it."

She paused, and then went on, "Learned behavior uses pornography to institutionalize new norms. You have to understand that you are going directly against the interests of learned behavior if you attempt to leave it out of the sexual mix. So, it has come up with its own forms of prolonging it, as you so well have pointed out. Thus, we have a 'ritualized learned behavior' way to prolong our learned behavior patterns in the sexual act."

She laughed again.

"Remember, learned behavior's ideas about sex are just one way to look at this creative act to the exclusion of other ways and whatever health benefits they may have to offer. If learned behavior can stay in control, it really does not care about the means. Also remember that staying within the limited container that learned behavior allows Chi to flow in allows its agenda to be set. If this container does not change, nothing really changes. Things just get shifted around in the same energetic pathways in the body, even in sexual activity. So in the end learned behavior still controls the agenda and thus the range of energetic expression.

"Learned behavior makes people think that they are breaking away and doing something new. This is exciting, but most of the time they are just being co-opted into an expanded agenda of learned behavior.

"The real question is not, how can you do sex differently, but how can you use sex to understand and get more energy? How can you use it to create and maintain increased pressure in the body? To increase the Chi-flow in the body. To empower a new structure for Chi-flow. To create a vehicle where you can store realization."

"Does sexuality affect your story?" I asked.

"Yep, it is the basis of it," Felina said, smiling.

She then peered at me and asked, "How do I act to get approval or to compete to get sexually received and relieved within the matrix of learned behavior? And more than that—how do I feel sorry for myself when it does not work out?"

I shook my head, confused as to how she had gotten from talking about sex to feeling sorry for oneself.

She looked at me and chuckled, before going on, "Let's look at your story, the story you have been taught. What is your story really? The lines you feed yourself. The repetitive patterns you use to hook into and identify with the people around you, and the way we collude with each other in our movement and breathing patterns.

"So, think about it," she went on. "After we are trained in learned behavior from the people around us—what do we do with it? Repeat it repeatedly and practice it with each other," she continued, chuckling.

She then started waving her hands in front of her face as if she were trying to bat away mosquitoes.

"Just as a song becomes stuck in your head and you can't get rid of it," she laughed. "We endlessly repeat these rhythms and patterns in our thoughts and movements, and these are supported by those around us who are doing the same thing."

She kept waving her hands grabbing at imaginary mosquitos, chuckling.

"This is how our habitual movement patterns get placed and moved gravitationally through space and time. Making each other feel wanted—but inadvertently pinned down by mutual consent to only a limited way of being in the world."

180

She continued swatting imaginary mosquitoes, then said, "It just will not stop. How do you get rid of it?"

Her antics made me laugh too. Her antics not only reminded of those crazy songs that sometimes I could not get out of my head, but also of the suffocating feeling of heat and irritation that mosquitoes could produce in me, especially in these subtropical climates.

Felina kept grabbing at mosquitos, while saying, "The learned behavior of our time creates a heavy and ponderous internal structure, and the personal stories of the people who are affected by it become very thick and heavy accordingly. We need to de-charge the words and images of the old story, the emotionally charged thoughts that keep us self-involved."

"Wait a minute. Wait a minute," I said, laughing and waving my hands and swatting away at my own internal mosquitoes. "Before you get started," I said, "This does not sound so practical to me, your idea of creating a new story. It sounds like a form of denial of one's past experiences."

"To the contrary," she stated emphatically, grabbing the air in front of her one last time, then changing the tone of our conversation by stopping to look intently at me. "It is the essence of practicality. Create a story with lots of holes in it, so to speak, to pit against all the learned behavior that tells you about feeling sorry for yourself, being weak, getting old, and not being able to take care of yourself. To buffer yourself against the idea of losing your friends and having your idea of family betray you. You need to create a story that regenerates itself, an ever-evolving story that continually invigorates your health and leads you back to your essence."

She paused, was pensive for a moment then went on, "A pliable and flexible story that connects you with the feeling of life, revitalizing you, instead of taking your energy away with dull repetition: that is what we are looking for. A story that can buffer you from the debilitating onslaughts of learned behavior, from both your internal repetitive discourse and the collusion that you come up against while relating to others. Replace the fractured incomplete story given to you by learned behavior with a dynamic, flexible, brilliant one, one whose progressions become steppingstones to your evolution, one that you can even pit against your own idea of death."

She stopped to take a breath, and then started playing at grabbing mosquitoes again, and then we both broke out laughing.

"The more resilient people are those whose story is more fluid and varied," she continued. "It can keep your memory intact by making the way you remember or order events more efficient. You don't really lose your memories, but reshuffle them and look at them in a different light. Actually, you allow them to reshuffle themselves because you cease to grab on to them. Enjoy them and let them go."

"I really want to get this down. What does our story have to do with our movements and breathing?" I asked.

Felina replied after pausing for a moment, "That is how one's learned behavior and one's story is held in place. Our story is held in place and perpetuated by the rhythms and patterns of moving and breathing and their supportive charged thinking patterns. This is another reason why having a body practice to ground down new energy is so important, because you are surrounded by learned behavior. You are surrounded by one big dance—the way you and all those around you breathe and move.

"And we want to replace it with the 'Real Big Dance,'" she went on, grinning. "The dance of reconnecting to the cocoon of the Earth!"

She stopped for a moment to look around, "The Earth is just waiting. You know. It holds the memories for your next step. You must replace a story based on self-pity with one based on your ever-evolving life."

"There you go again jumping off to something else," I said, laughing and waving my hands in front of my face. "What do you mean...based on self-pity?"

"Look at it carefully," Felina said. "The core of the story we have been taught is sure to be self-pity. It is self-pity which brings up superiority and inferiority, or how we judge ourselves in relation to others. If you did not feel insecure or inferior and feel bad about yourself, why would you be involved in wanting to be superior? You want to feel superior, so you don't feel sorry for yourself. Why do you want to feel better off than others unless your story at a deep level makes you feel inferior, and you pity yourself?"

She steepled her hands under her chin, studied me, then said, "Can you see how self-pity or feeling sorry for yourself is the root of those feelings of inferiority and superiority? If you eliminate self-pity, the charges that hold learned behavior together will collapse like a house of cards."

She stopped for a moment to reflect before she went on, "Why do we focus on our story? Really the only reason is that it is a habit. The ultimate addiction. Getting more energy means being less attached to your special kind of self-pity. People are attached to their self-pity and will defend it to the end, but when you have more energy, you simply have no time for it.

"The point is that you don't want to spend time massaging or manipulating your story at all. You need to look at it, de-charge it and 'get away' from it. Letting your de-charged story run on automatic pilot."

Felina then went on to elaborate, "Also, if you don't do something about your story, it will wear out your body. Accept it and go beyond it. Don't worry about your story. You just don't have time for it."

I raised up my hand to stop her again, or at least slow her down, so I could assimilate what she was saying. Then I asked, "So actually, how do you create a new story?"

She laughed, "It is simplicity itself. You don't. You increase the Chi-flow in your body and the ability to sustain it, and this allows you to become more identified with the deep strata of your beingness, and your story just follows along to help you navigate through the world.

"Really, what is your story good for anyway? It is just a means to give and get energy from the people around you. Normally this creates a dance of dependent relationships—people leaning on each other in specialized ways. And as you now understand, that type of dependency also has a strong physical component.

"From a practical point of view, if you can produce and sustain Chi-flow from your own connection to the Earth's cocoon, you do not need to rely so heavily on the energetic exchange with others. Or, in other words, you don't need to pay attention to your story in your relating to yourself and others. Leave your story behind, step outside of it like a snake shedding its skin, or like discarding a set of dirty clothes. Leave behind the way you relate and the motives you have been trained to relate from. Your story will become less important to you and those that try to grab onto those parts that are de-charged will not be able to touch you."

She then leaned over and lightly touched my body with a slight electric charge that sent shivers all through me, grinned and said, "And then you can begin to touch the world lightly."

Felina looked around and after a moment went on, "You just marginalize your old story and its corresponding sequences of memories, and instead surrender to the stream of life around you. This is how you allow your memories to reorder themselves. Instead of straining to create a new narrative within the same structure of energetic flow, you just transcend or go beyond your story for your evolving energetic needs. The more we get into the vastness of who or what we really are, the less important the story becomes.

"Then your memory will not wear out as you get old, and it will not impinge on your ability to concentrate. As you now understand, the ordering of our memory is the basis of how we keep our story together. And memory is stored in the quality, as well as in the quantity, of energy flow in the body. When you create a flexible story it revitalizes your memory. It gives it more life."

"I like that," I said. "So this is one way you can feel healthier as you get older. More balanced Chi-flow in your body will allow you to remember, to feel healthier."

Felina smiled and continued, "When we reconnect directly with the energetic memory of how Chi was meant to flow unimpededly through our bodies, we enable more space for storing energy. The inefficient dead ends of our old story are eroded away by more Chi-flow. When you have a fluid and pliable story, and you nurture Chi-flow, a new silence and spaciousness will pervade your being.

"The urge we feel for grabbing for and identifying with prescribed sensual perception lessens, and we find ourselves in a world that is much more fluid and not as sticky. And when you gather enough energy, you can even begin to dream beyond your story—just like moving beyond the dramas in your dreams where you can start to act in unimaginable ways. You then have gained the capacity to act outside of your story.

"This can all become quite confusing, because as Li Tse must have gone over with you, there are two forces at work here. One is the force of gravity or the Earth that is trying to synchronize the so called 'inner world' we experience with the 'outer world we perceive, so that we become one with the flow of life. And secondly, there is a force that is pulling us toward our true self, which transcends and encompasses all that."

"This all sounds good." I said, "But in a practical way: what do you do with your thoughts?" I then asked.

"Study the Chi of the mind," Felina continued without a pause. "Thoughts have a pressure. You can learn to sense Chi on the edges of your thoughts. Find the flow of Chi in the midst of your thoughts. Stay on the edge of your thoughts, dramas, and emotions. Remain aware of what is beyond your story. Don't forget—your story is a movement pattern. And as you enliven the flow of Chi, your story will slowly clean itself out. The emotional charges will erode away."

She paused for a moment of recollection, then continued, "The problem is we all think we are so important, and love our self-involvement so much, that we turn even the smallest things into huge boulders in the stream of awareness. We keep concentrating on them instead of on the flow of Chi. If you learn to change your focus to the stream of Chi, you will flow over, around and through them. And if you stay with this flow, they will erode and be swept away."

"But what happens when the energy runs low? When you get tired? When your Chi flow lessens? Will the rocks on the bottom expose themselves again?" I said, grabbing onto her metaphor.

"Good question," she chuckled. "You are talking about the garbage heap of learned behavior, those deep roots of your story that have not been de-charged. What you will find is that many of the smaller ones have been washed away and that others have been worn down. And as you build up the muscle of energy flow the bigger ones will affect you less and less.

"We need to physicalize new breathing and moving patterns that arise from within and stabilize them into a new pliable story grounded in the

185

body. Let the flow of life move freely through your story. Just allow this stream to flow and it will take care of most everything."

Felina paused, then said, "Your old story provided you with a great service. It got you this far. The proof is you are alive here in front of me," she laughed wholeheartedly. "So, say thanks. Appreciate it, then learn to let it go.

"Wave 'bye-bye,'" she said as she chortled and waved her hand back and forth at me.

"OK, OK, but what you are saying sounds so much like what people do when they don't want to face something. They feel challenged by some big problem and they merely change some unrelated activities—have sex, go to the movies, or go to the gym," I reflected.

"Ah, once again the perfect question," she beamed.

"The impulse to change the focus of one's activities during an unwelcome experience is the correct and natural one. But what you just described is usually just another kind of co-opting. Because the new activity that is chosen is usually based on the moving and breathing patterns of one's learned behavior instead of on increasing and storing Chi-flow in the body. So, a person just diverts their attention from one aspect of their learned behavior to another, instead of using their challenging circumstance as a steppingstone, as an opportunity to move beyond it. They go to the gym or have sex, just re-engaging their story and its dramas by using the same old muscle and breathing patterns. It is not enough, just changing the object of focus: change it to something beyond the realm of learned behavior.

"Watch it! Learned behavior can get a bit tricky," she said.

Felina then looked up, grinning, as she peered at the rain clouds starting to gather in the southwest.

Then her grin turned into a chuckle as she sat back and looked down at my crotch saying, "Just don't forget, the root of your story rests down in your sacrum."

And her chuckle turned into a laugh as she raised her index finger and said, "And especially don't forget—Freud is everywhere!"

Chapter 13

# ANGELIQUE—EMBRYOLOGY AND MERIDIANS

I found myself, once again, at Angelique's house in the Chi Gung class. I was expectantly waiting for class to end, specifically because Angelique had asked to meet me afterwards. She had told me she wanted to talk to me in depth, that she was going to show me how one can feel the meridians of the body through the sense of touch.

As usual after class everyone was parading around in the afterglow of renewed energy. I was feeling it too, and it seemed that I experienced it even more, every time I practiced with them. Everyone wandered off to go on with their days, until only Angelique and I remained, drinking water and relaxing a bit.

"I want to teach you today how to feel meridians," she said suddenly. Then she went off into her house and returned with a tight-fitting black top to go along with the fisherman pants she had worn in the Chi Gung class.

"OK, now I am ready," Angelique said, radiating a smile as she sat down next to me drinking from her water bottle.

After a moment she began, "At first, I thought that the meridians that I saw on acupuncture charts were energy flows that people who went into deep meditation in China and India had perceived once—and that may well be true. But after meeting Silvio and Li Tse, I found out that these meridians can also be felt with the sense of touch and manipulated through body movement. If you move your body in an appropriate way, you can feel them. So, let me begin to show you how we can do just that," she said.

We put our water down and walked into the middle of the sala.

Angelique said, "Do you remember the last time we were together I showed you how to twist your hands and wrists all the way in and all the way out?"

She stopped and said, "Wait a minute, wait a minute," and walked over to a bookcase in the sala, grabbed an illustrated volume of acupuncture meridians, and said, "I think seeing these illustrations will help you to visualize what you will be feeling."

I started to say something.

"Hold that thought, whatever it is," she said, as she playfully raised the palm of her hand. She then opened the meridian book to a page that had a diagram of a meridian called the "Governor Vessel" on it.

She placed the opened book at my feet so I could see it as I looked down. The illustration I saw was a meridian that ran from the tip of the coccyx, up the spine over the top of the head, then down through the middle of the nose, ending at the upper lip.

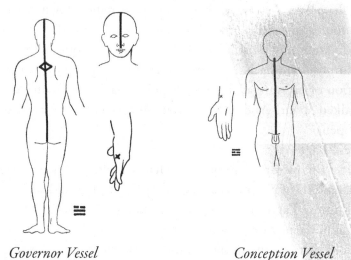

Governor Vessel                         Conception Vessel

"Now, I want you to remember the point marked with an 'X' on the hand, between your wrist and the beginning of your little finger. You can see it here in this book," she said.

She then pointed to the picture across the sala with the eight points on the wrists and ankles we had studied last time I had been with her. "It is one of the same points we talked about before. It is stimulated, you'll remember, by twisting your wrist all the way inward."

She continued, "This point is called a master point because it is used for opening the Governor Vessel meridian. It can be stimulated by using different techniques such as acupuncture, Chi Gung or even massage. In acupuncture for example, this is the point where you place a needle when you want to open the Governor meridian. Pretty interesting, don't you think, that the point that opens when you maximally twist your wrist in this way is the very same point used in acupuncture for opening this meridian?

"Stay aware of that as we go on. I think you're going to appreciate the ingenuity of the way Li Tse put together this Eight Point Chi Gung."

Angelique concentrated her gaze to peer at me and said, "Do you remember what we did last time?

"We're going to build on that today.

"Get in your stance and re-connect yourself. Become aware of the sensation of Chi at your perineum; this should initiate you getting into the right posture. Now, while keeping your hands down at your sides, twist your arms and shoulders all the way in, with the backs of your hands at your hips, twisting until the little fingers point to the front and the thumbs point back. Now that you're in this position, can you feel a sensation of pressure at this master point marked with an 'X' that we just talked about? And feel how your shoulders roll forward and your back opens?"

"Yes," I agreed.

"Does this picture correspond to what you felt, and allow you to better understand the way your back opened up?" Angelique asked.

"Hmmm," I agreed, feeling the meridian in my body exactly as I was seeing it in the picture in front of me.

"Hold that posture until we move to the next one," Angelique said, bending down and turning to the next page in the book, to a diagram of an energy channel called the 'Conception Vessel' or meridian, which ran from the perineum, up the mid-line of the front of the trunk of the body, to the bottom of the lower lip.

"Now, I want you to twist your wrists 180 degrees the opposite way, outwards, like shown in this picture. Be aware of the point marked with an 'X' in this diagram, just up the crease of your wrist. Do you feel how twisting your wrists outwards in this way activates these points? And can you detect how this then spreads out your shoulders, pushes out your chest, and opens up the front of your body?"

"Yeah, I do," I said, becoming even more interested.

Angelique said, "This is the master point that opens the 'Conception Vessel' meridian."

She then pointed to the picture asking, "Now, does this picture help you to detect the sensation of this meridian that is generated by holding this posture?"

"Oh yeah, that's pretty good!" I replied. "Now I can see it and feel it. It's like combining the feeling of touch with an inner vision of sorts. Hmmm? Interesting," I pondered.

"Okay, that takes care of twisting motions in the upper part of our body. Now you know how to activate two of the eight points," Angelique said. "And you're beginning to learn how to feel the meridians in your body. Let's direct that feeling/inner vision and see what happens when we twist our legs and ankles."

She bent down again and turned the page to display another meridian labeled the *Dai* or "Belt Vessel."

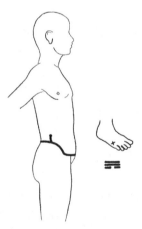

*Dai or Belt Vessel*

"To activate this meridian, we begin by turning our feet inwards—pigeon-toed, toes pointing toward each other—then dropping the sacrum and sinking down until we feel our knees being strongly pulled towards each other."

I followed her instructions, moving into this new posture.

"Hmm, yes, again I can feel that. This is fascinating, Angelique," I said.

She smiled then asked, "Do you notice how this posture activates the points near the outsides of your feet, which are marked with 'X' in the picture? This is the point of the Eight Point Chi Gung system which opens the Belt Vessel. It is activated by twisting the ankles inwards. The Belt Vessel is the only meridian whose pathway runs horizontally across the body. This vessel cinches and loosens the bundles of meridians that are flowing vertically through the body—thus the name 'Girdle' or 'Belt' Vessel. When it functions properly it ensures a good energetic connection between the upper and lower parts of the body.

"Let's go on," she said energetically.

She squatted down for a moment and flipped through the book on the floor until she found another page with the diagram of the *Chong* or "Penetrating Vessel."

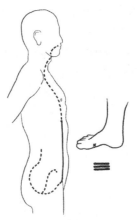

*Chong or Penetrating Vessel*

Angelique then said, "Now I want you to rotate your legs and ankles outwards until you can feel this point just a little behind the ball of the big toe in the arch of your foot, marked with an 'X' in this diagram. You felt this point the last time you were here when we were sitting against the posts, twisting our legs outwards, you remember? And now we're activating the same point while standing."

I moved as she directed.

"Can you feel how stimulating this point through this posture opens the whole front of the body? This posture opens the meridian channels on either side of the mid line, like you can see in the drawing."

"Hmm. This is really something," I said amazed at how this worked and beginning to sense the implications of what Angelique was showing me.

"So, think about this," she went on. "The first two meridians we studied were activated by the twisting of the wrists inwards and outwards, and the second two meridians were activated by twisting the ankles inwards and outwards. We marked them with 'X' on our drawing over there," she said, pointing across the sala to the pictures I had studied the last time I was here.

"Twisting is an important form of movement, and we can see this exemplified here. These four meridians activated by twisting our wrists and ankles to their extremes are the four most primary and important meridians in the body."

She paused, and then changed the subject slightly, "Remember last time when I asked you to walk normally, you observed that in our normal movement patterns one hardly ever twists at all? So, in a way, these are movements we rarely use. Just think on this: if there are eight main points, and four of these are rarely activated by our habitual way of moving, then 50% of the energy that would innately be available to us through movement is not being utilized. By activating these points and their associated meridians that I've just shown you we can begin to recover this energy."

"Now, let's get into the flexing motions, taking a look at how we stimulate the other four meridians," she said as she bent down once again, flipping pages in the book on the floor.

"Look at the pictures of these next two meridians and you'll see diagrams that correspond to two more points of the Eight Point Chi Gung. Points that get stimulated when we flex our wrists."

Angelique got up and moved into her stance. She connected up her body the way she had taught me previously, then waved me over to her side and directed me to put one hand on her back over one kidney at the level of the diaphragm, and the other over her solar plexus area in the front. She then pushed down with her wrists and hands until they were at about her waist level and said, "This activates the points on my forearm just above my wrists. You can see them marked with an 'O' in the picture. This posture is often called 'Lilies on the Water' because it is as if your hands are like lily pads floating on the water. This pushing down motion activates the 'Yang Connecting Vessel' and the kidneys. When I do this, you can feel the pressure increase in my back over the kidneys."

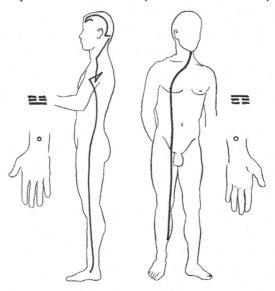

*Yang and Yin Connecting Vessels*

She then reversed her wrists so they were facing upwards and raised them to about chest level, as if she were holding two trays, and then said, "And this pushing up motion activates the 'Yin Connecting Vessel', and it can be felt in the front of the torso when you connect up your body. Once again, you can see the point activated in this picture marked with an 'O' just above the inside of the wrist, right? And it comes with a corresponding pressure activated on the front side of my diaphragm where my liver and spleen reside. Can you feel that?"

"Uh huh," I responded affirmatively, having been able to feel and see the pressures moving in her body that she had described in both postures. Now I was getting the idea why she had chosen to put on her tight-fitting top.

Angelique continued, "Do you understand that by activating these different points while keeping my body connected, I can direct the energetic pressure to different areas in my body? This way I can increase the Chi-flow in a specific area, and that activates the healing-body template there."

She lifted her hand, placed it on my chest, smiled and gently pushed me away. She then put her hands down, resting them on her hips.

"And now: how can we use this knowledge?" she asked. And not waiting for a response she went on,

"Well, it should be obvious to you by now that if you increase the Chi in an area, it will activate the corresponding aspect of the healing-body template. So, for example, by increasing pressure in the kidney area, one would be able to influence the kidneys and all their related functions.

"This is another example of how this knowledge was used by practitioners when devising precise healing movements and postures for certain maladies. By moving the body in specific ways, specific organs can be isolated and stimulated in a more exact manner. I think by now you can also understand how it works that by stimulating certain meridians through motion you can treat corresponding ailments."

I was about ready to ask something when again she stopped me, raising up her right hand again with her palm facing me and said, laughing, "Don't get impatient with me now. We're almost finished."

She then bent over and turned some pages to another illustration that showed two more meridians.

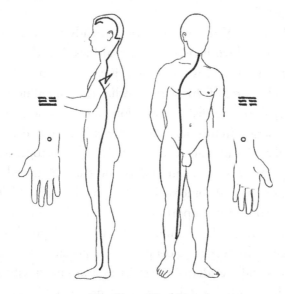

*Yin Yang Heel Vessels*

"These are the last two meridians I will introduce to you. They are a little more recondite," she said, while relaxing back into an upright posture. "They operate more internally and are called the 'Yin Heel Vessel' and the 'Yang Heel Vessel.' Their activating points are located just below the ankles on the inside and outside of the foot.

"Do you see how the Yang Heel Vessels flow up the body and to the head through the area between the eyes? And how the Yin Heel Vessels also flow up from the two ankles through the front of the body but terminate in the area between the eyes?

"Now let's see if you can feel these meridians," she said.

"Connect your body up, put your heels close together and be aware of them, and at the same time of the area between your eyes."

I did as she said.

Angelique instructed, "Now close your eyes to help your concentration. Raise your heels slightly and then let them drop to the floor. Do that two or three times while you keep your body connected and your awareness concentrated."

As my heels hit the ground, I felt the energy rise to that place between my eyes.

"Did you feel anything?" Angelique asked.

I replied, "When my heels hit the ground, I could feel a little jolt between my eyes."

"Good," she said. "You may have heard already that the ancient sages said 'the true man's breath rises from his ankles. But the breath of the ordinary man arises from his throat, so it is easy for him to be consumed by the lusts and desires of this world'. What they are alluding to is that when the energies of your feet are well joined to the energetic centers of the head, the energy circuits of the body are enlivened and connected."

She clapped her hands once, then rubbed her palms together. Then she said, grinning, "So, now you can understand that the meridians indeed are alive and flowing and come with sensations that can be felt.

"OK, there is one more important thing that I forgot to mention: that in acupuncture theory the meridians and the corresponding points of the Eight Point Chi Gung are coupled in a special way. When activating these points and meridians, the twisting movements of the feet and ankles are paired with the flexing movements of the hands and wrists, and the flexing movements of the feet and ankles are paired with the twisting movements of the hands and wrists.

"But enough of this for this. I don't know about you, but all this talking made me hungry. Let's go somewhere and eat before that rain gets here," she said, glancing at a sea eagle that was soaring above us and the clouds forming behind it just above the green hills.

A couple of hours later we once again found ourselves in the little pavilion close to the sala, drinking her favorite "silver tips" tea.

After chatting with her a bit, I finally posed a question, "Angelique, why are these eight meridians of your Chi Gung the most primary?"

She replied, "Well, you have felt their importance. And you conceptually understand how variations of twisting and flexing are the building blocks of our movements. Now we can fill in the picture with some theoretical information.

"Let's look at it from an embryology point of view," she said as she walked over to the sala and got another book from the bookshelf.

"You know how Silvio likes his toys? Well, I like my picture books," Angelique said as she returned.

She sat down, then opened the book to a brightly-colored plate which showed a human embryo in various stages of development.

"Look at this," she said. "We start as a fertilized egg. After being fertilized that egg then splits into two, then into four, then into eight, then on and on through time until eventually a body is formed the way we know it."

She went on, "When the egg splits and divides into two, there is an energy line that connects the two cells. This energy line corresponds to the Governor Vessel and the Conception Vessel meridians making a ring around the original cell."

She peered at me, then continued, "Those were the first two meridians we worked with earlier today. The formation of these two channels is what divides our original cell into two halves, which correspond to the left and hand right sides of the body we now inhabit.

"Now imagine how the two cells then divide into four," Angelique said, pointing to the next picture on the page, "and remember the Chong or Penetrating Vessel and the Dai or Belt Vessel as you do this. Now we have the four meridians, you see, that relate to the twisting movements we studied, the four major energy channels of the body.

"Are you following?" she checked.

I nodded in approval.

"Good," she went on. "Next then, the cells divide again, into eight this time. The four new meridians created by these divisions correspond to the meridians stimulated by the flexing motions of the body. You should remember that these are called the Yin and Yang Connecting Vessels, relating to the hands and wrists, and the Yin and Yang Heel Vessels, relating to the ankles and feet.

"The development of these last four meridians gives us the eight most primary meridian channels of the body, its most basic energetic template. These meridians become the first energy channels or pathways of the life-force in the organism. They are the foundation for all the later evolving patterns. After that, the other meridians develop as the organism continues to unfold.

"Not only do we evolve from these energetic pathways, but these meridians and their interrelated patterns continue to remain operative even as we grow older. They are part of an unconscious organic memory in our being, and a template through which energy continues to radiate and spread within our bodies."

She paused for a moment, then said, "Can you see now why these first eight meridians are primary? Does this make sense to you now?"

"Yes, now it makes a lot more sense to me," I acknowledged.

Angelique then pointed again to the first few pictures of the embryology series shown in her book.

"Do you see how this development progresses," she said in her precise

French English, pointing to the pictures, then continuing, "The rest of the meridian pathways form prior to the formation of the bone structure, organs, tendons, and muscles that make up the body that we know. So, essentially, whether in acupuncture or body movement, when we talk about meridians, and specifically the eight primary meridians, we are talking about the original primary pathways of energy flow in the body."

"So, if I understand you correctly," I pondered, "When we're working with these meridians, we're working with the basic roots of the life-force that flows through our body. The first eight meridians are the most primary because they formed before all the others."

"Magnifique, Mr. Practico! So, now keep your eyes on these pictures as I continue," she said pointing to the book again.

"As these meridians continue to evolve, they develop into the meridian matrix of the fetus. The body continues to grow in the womb, and bones and organs form. Here we see the development of the torso and the head," she said, pointing once again at the illustrations. "And the last things to develop are the arms and legs. So, when the body comes out of the womb, some of the most rapidly developing parts of our body are these arms and the legs, which we'll need to rely on to function in the new gravitational environment that we are born into.

"You can see that at this point," she said, grinning and pointing to a picture of a woman holding a baby. "After we are born, we have moved away from the water world of the placenta to the air world on our mother's lap."

That turned a light on inside of me and I said, "Yes, I can now understand this better! We're moving from the way gravity affected us in a water environment, the womb, to the way it will affect us in the world of an air and earth environment, where we will really need our arms and our legs to be able to function."

"You're following right along," Angelique said with a smile. "Now listen carefully. We leave the placenta behind, the bubble we lived in the water world. But when we move on, out into this air/earth world, we grow into a new 'placenta', one that is defined by our new range of motions."

"Just a moment," she said, excitedly dashing off once again to the bookshelf in the sala.

She returned with a book on renaissance art and opened it to a drawing of human proportion by Leonardo DaVinci called "Vitruvian Man," showing a man with legs and arms outstretched, the fingers and heels touching the perimeter of a circle surrounding him.

"You mean Leonardo DaVinci was into this stuff we're talking about, Angelique?" I asked.

"Well, he was none too shabby," she said, laughing. "He was into a lot of amazing things way before his time.

"Getting back to our discussion though, this new placenta of the air/earth world that we're born into creates something that we call the 'movement body,' which I am sure you will hear more about later when you head back to Chiang Mai. It's one of the things Li Tse loves to talk about.

"And while we are growing in this new gravitational field of the air/earth world, the learned behavior of our times is simultaneously being introduced into our being by our interactions with the rhythmic patterns of the breathers and movers around us. This happens just as our arms and legs begin to plug us into this new world and we are just learning to use them."

"Wow," I said, "Now I am beginning to see what you guys are talking about—how learned behavior gets instilled into us at such an early age. We're dependent on the people around us to help us and teach us how to move. We have no choice at this point and are utterly helpless without their support. I even get a feeling for how and why people learn to make their movements fit together and, in a sense, hold each other up."

Angelique smiled, then went on, "Once we have begun to walk and are moving about in this air/earth world, our legs and feet draw energy up from the Earth, and our arms and hands become the primary way we interact and exchange energy with the world and the people around us. For example, we eat and drink with our hands," she said, smiling, lifting her teacup to her lips to take a sip.

"What I want you to reflect on here is the outward movement that we're describing—the way the life-force develops first through the cell, then through the meridians, and later through the organs and bones, the torso, and head, and finally through the limbs. I want you to see how we've moved from the cell all the way out to the formation of the arms and legs."

"Okay, I see that, but what is the next transformation after that?" I asked, anticipating the train of our conversation.

"Isn't that the question?" she radiated with a wide grin. "What happens to us in our next stage of development beyond this life? What are we doing here?"

"Well, what are we doing here?" I inquired.

Angelique replied, "Perhaps by looking back in the rear view mirror, at our physical evolutionary process, we may find some insight and help to figure that one out, or at least get a feeling for it. We very well may have an energetic future that goes beyond our body that we inhabit in the Earth's gravity. Just as a child in the womb has no idea s/he would be thrown out into the Earth's gravity, we have no idea where we might end up next," she laughed. "Although we may have an intuition or two about it."

She smiled, looked around then said. "But we can certainly state that we have something within us, like a pressure, that is seeking to express itself out into and through the world we perceive out there. To become our True Self and take us to the living realization that we not only are our small, learned selves, but everything we create and perceive." She paused and smiled.

"It's too big of a question for us to grasp in language, but we can begin to intuit the answer. Let's continue to follow this evolutionary line of thought and see where it could lead us," she said, rocking back and forth.

"The maturation of our appendages and their articulations, our wrists, ankles, elbows, knees, hips, shoulders, is the next stage in our personal evolutionary development when we leave the womb and will determine the range of our interactions with the world. The natural growth and blossoming of the movement of our articulations is what allows us to merge and interact totally with the world to our full capacity and on towards our next stage of development. If we're able to free up our energy—remembering who we really are, diffusing the charges of the overlays of learned behavior which are impinging upon our 'natural' growth—we then can become free to participate in and explore our evolutionary pattern. We can go back to what we always were. What we were before so-called birth and what we will be beyond so-called death. Like the snake biting its tail?"

We took a momentary break as both Angelique and I took another sip of tea and took in the luxurious air around us, enjoying a moment of equipoise.

She then continued by saying, "We humans don't have it quite so easy as the migratory creatures in nature that seem to have an innate sense of where they're going, because our learned behavior has hijacked a lot of our natural ability to feel the patterns of life all around us."

"I want to show you something," Angelique said as she got up and stretched, knuckling her back, waving for me to follow. The shadows weren't long yet, and there was still a lot of time left in the day. We walked over to the pond she had on her land and watched the colorful koi moving in the water.

"They're beautiful, the way they move," I said.

"How nice of you to notice," she exclaimed "It's an art form that I like to practice, mixing certain koi together to watch their colors blend and merge as they swim. In this pond I play with a gold motif. Notice that all the fish here have gold in them, some gold and black, some gold and red, and I even found some that were gold and orange, see that one over there?" she said pointing to a small fish off to the side.

"I also played with the sizes to create a glittering, living, moving collage that gives me great pleasure. I can sit and watch them for a long time. Do you see those two small ones over there that are totally gold? Right now, they're my favorites."

After observing the play of moving colors in the pond for a while, Angelique went into her house to change her attire once again. This time she emerged with a multi-colored tight-fitting top. I then followed her to the sala where she began showing me the next steps of her instruction.

Angelique started, "Now we're going to work on the next level of connecting the body. This next stage of connecting is about 'segmenting the torso' and 'compacting the body'."

"Look at these," she said, laughing, going over to her cabinet, and pulling out three toys. She dangled the toys in front of me playfully. She then went to a line that stretched between two of the posts in the sala and hung them there.

"I don't know if he found them or made them himself, but this is what Silvio came up with to help show the workings of the principles of segmenting and compacting the body."

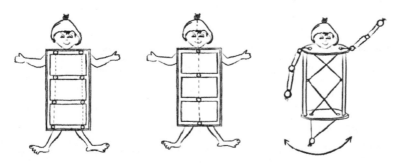

She looked at me and said, "With the help of these three guys I will now show you the next levels of segmenting and compacting the same way that Silvio and Li Tse showed me.

"Take a look at this one," she said, holding the first one up and pushing on the three different segments of the doll's torso. "Keep this toy in mind," she reminded me.

*Segmenting One*

"Watch," she said, "While I reconnect my body along the Tai Chi Pole as I showed you before, and then begin moving these three segments in my body independently. I want you to see these segments distinctly and separately as I move.

"See that!" she said as she moved her body. "Lower, middle, upper. Lower, middle, upper. Lower, middle, upper."

As I watched her, I could see that she was slightly pushing out each of the different body segments shown in the toy, activating them separately. She did this slowly, one at a time, so I could follow.

Angelique repeated, "Lower, middle, upper. Lower, middle, upper." Then she said, "You can only do this if you keep the body connected. This is a subtle movement. To be able to see the separation of the segments from the outside can be a bit difficult."

For some reason I could see it. I hadn't realized that the body was capable of moving this way. I also really appreciated that she had donned her latest tight top, as this helped me to see what she was doing more clearly.

She continued, "I just want you to see that there's a horizontal segmentation happening in the torso. It will become clearer as we go on."

Angelique then went over to the line with the toys and playfully grabbed the second one, which also had three segments in the torso with one central shaft around which the three segments could rotate.

*Segmenting Two*

"Look at this guy," she said. "After we have segmented the torso, we can learn to move each of the individual segments backwards and forwards, side to side." Angelique made this clear to me by separately pushing the left and the right sides of each of the segments of the toy's torso.

She pointed to the central shaft and said, "This is like the Tai Chi Pole."

She got into her stance again, connected herself up, and I watched as she was able to move each of the three segments backward and forward, independent of each other.

"Pretty cool, huh?" she said. "What do you think about that?"

Before I could say anything, she went over to the line again and pulled down the third toy and began playing with it.

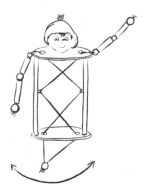

*Connecting Joints*

She pulled the bead at the bottom of the toy, first to one side and then to the other, which had the effect of raising and lowering the opposite arm of the doll accordingly.

Angelique put the toy back and turned to face me, then got into her stance, and said beaming, "You can do this with your body too."

Then as she began to move, she continued, "You see, you can move the energy in your body in a zigzag pattern, starting from the lower right segment up to the middle left and zig-zagging to the upper right and moving the energy out through the right arm."

Not only could I literally see the energy moving along that pattern as depicted in the toy, but after she did this movement a few times it also opened my mind to be able to experience or see/feel movements I hadn't been able to even conceive before.

I suddenly understood what these people kept bringing up. It was dawning on me how this body-to-body teaching worked. There was an aspect of actually touching the body to key into body memory, but there was also the fact that once your body was trained in the see/feel way of perceiving, you would be able to experience even more.

I watched in amazement. She saw my look and laughed.

She then became very excited, saying, "We're almost there," as she moved over to the cabinet. She reached inside and took out a turtle shell and animatedly glided back, holding it up in front of me saying,

"Look at this", pointing out the symbols of the Ba Gua that were inscribed on the bottom of the shell.

"The Ba Gua—again! Are they everywhere?" I wondered aloud.

"You see," she said, "the Chinese superimposed their divinatory symbols not only the on the eight primary meridians and their functions in the body, but also to regions on the torso. The six areas I just showed you while moving, plus a lower one above the pelvis, and an upper one at the center of the collar bone make eight—voila! The eight Ba Gua of the torso!"

She went over to the cabinet again, reached in, pulling out another toy. "Another present from Silvio," she said, holding it up for me to see.

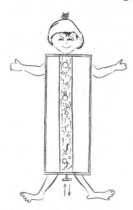

*Activated Tai Chi Pole*

"Watch this," she said, laughing, as she repeatedly pushed in on the button at the bottom of the toy, lighting it up with flashing, colored lights. "It's like the Tai Chi Pole."

Angelique said, "But let's continue."

She put the toy down with a final giggle and got into her stance, saying,

"You need to practice some before you can do this, but it's good to know where you are heading and to get an idea of the possibilities that are available to you.

"Watch my body," she said as she started moving. "I can move through the Gua in a clockwise pattern."

I watched as she activated one Gua after another, as they were depicted on the turtle shell. Once again I was glad she had changed into her tight colorful top so I could see and experience moving energy better.

"Or counterclockwise," she said and went through the same movement pattern in reverse.

"Or you can mix them all up," Angelique stated with a wide smile. "I want you to begin to understand how these Ba Gua work together and how they influence each other."

I then witnessed her body undulating from one side to the other, reminding me of some kind of snake or dragon. As I watched more closely, I saw her move the energy up from her feet to her torso and out to her arms and wrists by activating the individual Gua in a myriad of patterns. Her movements, combined with the rippling of the colors of her top as her body moved, were an inspiring, remarkable sight, and one I knew I was not likely to forget.

The show continued for a few minutes as Angelique moved through a variety of postures and forms, enjoying herself immensely.

At last, she stopped and relaxed her body and said beaming, "Glad you got that. I felt I needed to go through a lot today quickly as I don't have much time right now. I'm leaving tonight on that trip up to Bangkok that I told you about.

"And now that I've got that out of my system, let's recap today's lessons," she said, hardly being able to contain her energy. "First, I introduced you to Li Tse's Eight Point Chi Gung. Then I showed you how the eight primary meridians are related to the eight basic twisting and flexing motions of the body, and how this twisting and flexing radiates throughout the torso. I explained to you the importance of the eight primary meridians in the tissue formation of the embryo. We then moved on to the possible segmenting of the torso, and to exercises and postures for opening and closing the eight Gua of the trunk of the body.

And just now I finally showed you the fun part, some applications of opening and closing the Gua in different patterns," she ended with a radiant smile.

She peered at me as she liked to do, and then said, "First we connect, then we segment, hitting learned behavior with a one-two punch," she said, making two forceful jabs in the air in front of her. "When you hit it from two directions at once, it won't be able to grasp what is happening," she laughed.

This made me laugh, especially hearing it with a French accent.

Angelique went on, "As you continue to link your body up, understanding and embodying these mechanics of body motion, you give your being a new energetic platform where you can store more energy flow. You can begin to create a new container or structure within which you can stabilize a new way of being in the world without the fetters of learned behavior."

It was too bad she was leaving that evening on her trip because I'd actually grown quite attached to her after our time together.

As a farewell she said, "You can come here in a couple of days and talk to Veronica. If you've liked this, I'm sure you'll like to hear what she has to say. She is an engineer, you know."

As I wandered away from Angelique's house, I could not help wondering about some of the things that were coming up in relation to these people.

*What is my evolutionary path?*
*How do I attune myself to it more?*
*Who or what am I anyway?*
*What is this push that I feel every day when I wake*
　　*that makes me get up and do things?*
*How lost am I really?*

I chewed on these thoughts and hoped that these people, as they had highlighted these questions within me, could help resolve them. They certainly had made these questions come forth with emphasis after having spent time with them.

As I continued walking the questions kept coming.

*What am I doing here?*
*What should I do next to find out?*
*What is this body-to-body language that they keep constantly referring to?*

Then more questions.

*How could I connect with my body better and learn from it?*
*Even as I walk here, placing one foot in front of the other—what makes me take the next step?*

Then I found myself "in the back seat" watching my body move on, in its own predetermined patterns.

Watching thoughts and sensations moving through as if on their own.

There was no me pulling the strings!

Then suddenly from somewhere inside I heard, "What the Hell is going on around here?"

And then inexplicably I began to laugh uncontrollably, wobbling down the road, watching the body move on its own.

Chapter 14:

## VERONICA—RIGHT STRUCTURE: THE DOUGH BOY

The day was partially cloudy when I met with Veronica at Angelique's place. The cicadas were out with their high-pitched, electric-sounding rhythm, and an occasional butterfly balanced on the puffs of air in the multi-green-colored jungle backdrop. I could only marvel at the variety and intensity of the tumultuous shades of green that presented themselves in this subtropical paradise.

Veronica had been a good friend of Felina's for a long time. She was an energetic woman that I had talked to briefly at the Chi Gung class. Earlier in her life she had studied engineering at the university level but had to return home before her studies were completed to help run the family hardware store and plumbing business after her father had succumbed to a debilitating illness.

Although she had to leave her studies early, she still had the innate engineer's ability to understand things schematically. She was the perfect person to work in a hardware store because of her mechanical sense for things. People could tell her what they wanted to fix or build, and she would come up with a solution in no time. She was someone you would seek out if you didn't understand the assembly directions on a purchase. You wouldn't understand the instructions and she wouldn't need them. She would suss out the problem in no time and you would be on your way. Veronica was that kind of person.

As we walked over to Angelique's sala, she began talking about body electricity. She started by telling me about how the entire human body is permeated with energy, and how this is maintained and sustained by relating electrically to the environment. She went on to explain how matter and energy transform into each other within and around the body's cells, and that this had a cadence and rhythm to it that created sympathetic resonances throughout the body.

Veronica fascinated me when she spoke of electricity being everywhere. She brought to life the idea of how we live in a huge vibrating electric current. She said that there is a ceaseless thrum of electric energy within and all around us, and that our very movements and perceptions could be seen as being electrical. Veronica even went as far as to say that our very experience of life was a play of movement in one vast energetic electric-like field.

As we got to the sala, she got more specific and started relating her electrical metaphors to the practices all of them were teaching me.

"What Noi and Angelique have been teaching you is how to begin to bring your energy back by creating the right structure in your body or the right container. This can maximize the quality and quantity of Chi-flow, or living electricity, in your body. Those movements they taught you were designed to start breaking up the crusts that have settled on your body, that have accumulated as a result of the repetitive movements of your learned behavior."

Veronica went on, "Now that you have begun to incorporate these principles, your body is now open to sustain right structure more easily. Once you start to embody that, you can begin to create right posture from the inside, so to speak," she said, grinning.

"So, that's what we will be looking at, and hopefully experience, firsthand."

Then she caught me by surprise saying, "The essence of right structure is the Tai Chi Pole and the four bows."

She then went over to Angelique's cabinet, took up a piece of paper and started to sketch a human figure. When she finished, she smiled and showed me her drawing.

*Right Structure*

"Here we have a picture of right structure," she said. "You can see the Tai Chi Pole running up and down the trunk of the body. This is an energetic line that can be felt internally. It runs from the perineum to the crown of the head and is situated just a little bit in front of the spine. The aspect that we use to create right structure is connected to the back side of the Tai Chi Pole, closer to the spine," she said pointing to her drawing.

"There are other aspects of the Tai Chi Pole that you will learn about later, but right now we are concerned with the part that has to do with structure—right structure.

"OK," she went on, "Do you see the lower bows that come out roughly from the sacrum area and flow down the front of the two legs along the outside of the thighs? They proceed down the lower legs, then down to the outside of the feet." She laughed, looking at the rather confused look on my face but went on, "When activated properly, they open the soles of the feet, creating a cupping sensation. I am sure somebody somewhere along the line must have mentioned this to you," she said, grinning. "Springing these bows also opens the 'Bubbling Spring' points at the bottom of the feet, which then allows energy to rise or bubble up into the body from our connection to the Earth's gravity.

"Now look at these other bows," she said, pointing to the upper part of the figure she had drawn.

"They emanate out from the Tai Chi Pole at roughly the scapular level, go out through the shoulder joints, down the outside of the mid line of

211

the upper arms, then continue to the forearms where they cross over to the outside of the hands to the 'karate chop' area of the palm. Once the energy gets there, it helps to spring open the middle of the palms, creating cupping sensations there, too. This opens the 'Labor Palace' points in the palms of the hands."

She then said, laughing, "Gecko suction—hands and feet."

"Why do you call them bows?" I asked, trying to put together all she was saying.

"Because they are springy, curved outward, and in many ways when engaged they give one the sensation of stretching a bow," she replied.

Veronica looked at me and said, "You know I think that most all mechanical inventions come from observing some body mechanism. It would not surprise me if the bow and arrow were 'discovered' all around the world because those people first felt it inside their bodies. What do you think about that?" she asked, nodding and smiling.

"Interesting, I can see what you are getting at," I responded.

But I wanted to redirect our conversation to something I was trying to comprehend a bit better, and so I said, "You all are teaching me so many things from so many angles it is hard to keep track. At the moment I am more interested in what this right structure that you are talking about has to do with what Felina was telling me when she spoke about making more space for Chi-flow—and how this space makes one's story more pliable and malleable."

"You still don't get it yet, do you?" Veronica chuckled. "In order to stabilize and sustain more Chi-flow, you need to create an appropriate container. This is what we are talking about here: right structure, creating a more appropriate container. You can try to change your story as much as you want, but if you cannot stabilize more Chi-flow then your 'new' story is basically, energetically just a rewrite of your old one, with learned behavior just as much in charge. You need to deal with the way your story is sustained gravitationally through your breathing and moving patterns.

"The way you can crawl out from under your story is by creating and housing more Chi," Veronica said, laughing. "You must have just forgotten all Felina told you. I'm sure she told you that the way to solidify your evolving story is by, first of all, creating more space for Chi-flow and then, secondly, by stabilizing it through regular practice. Perhaps in all her talk about memory you missed hearing that."

"That sounds familiar," I said, "I really liked what she had to say about our story, but now that you mention it, I can remember her talking about body practice. But I still have some doubts in my mind because I have heard so many people talk about changing one's story. I have often heard it talked about in terms of addictions of one kind or another. And a lot of people have addictions—including sexual addictions."

She grinned and said, "Oh, the big one again."

She then went on, "OK, I think you have understood that in order to stabilize more Chi-flow, you need a physical practice. You need a practice that will both create and store more Chi. If you are not creating and storing more energy you are just fiddling around the outside the situation—changing a thing here and there, but not really creating a new structure for energy flow. In the overall picture of things, a healthy, evolving body creates a vehicle that can provide us not only with the storage capacity to handle more energy, but also a stable platform from which we can build up a storage bank of concentration so we can explore and discover who we really are."

Veronica continued, "And speaking of addictions, I think you have begun to see that when there is an addiction, there is an opportunity to create something new because the person, the so-called addict, has often already tasted a little freedom and is looking for more, something beyond learned behavior."

"OK," I said. "So, that is how you can address changing your story—by creating more Chi-flow with a sustained body practice. I think I can see that. But how does right posture or right structure relate to all this? I asked. "You said that one starts creating right posture from the inside. What did you mean?"

Veronica said, still grinning, "If you really want to have right posture you need to go about building it from the inside out and in a sustained way. You need a core. And that core is correct Chi-flow. You begin to generate good Chi-flow by creating right energetic structure.

"When you have this focus then all the exercises and forms and practices that people recommend for correcting your posture will then make sense. You will have a conceptual framework through which you can use, sustain, and understand them. If you don't work on your posture from the inside out, you will just be working on it piecemeal, fiddling around. You will quit after you have corrected some painful condition, or just quit because the methods you were trying became tedious, boring and did not really produce much effect at all.

"But if you focus on creating better Chi-flow, you will have a focus from which to create better posture from the inside out and the impetus to keep improving your body's relationship to gravity. And in addition to changing your story, this will also put more energy at your disposal and have the effect of revitalizing you." Veronica smiled.

And as she paused for a moment, I took the opportunity to ask another question, "OK, then, only one more question, I think?" I said, laughing at myself.

"What is that little thing in your picture?" I said, pointing to the little object in the lower abdomen of the drawing.

"Oh that!" Veronica said, putting her hands on her hips with a self-satisfied engineer's grin. "Thanks for admiring my artwork. That is a 'pulley'," she said.

"There are a lot of ways you can learn to help yourself engage right structure, but this is the best and most efficient way. You can begin to tighten and engage your whole structure by energetically tightening the link between the perineum and the lower Dan Tien."

"OK, I'll try to remember that. But Veronica: go over this again for me, what is a Dan Tien?" I asked, still not quite sure of the term.

"The Dan Tiens are places where energy gathers. This lower Dan Tien is the center of the physical body energy. It is normally referred to as *the* Dan Tien because of its importance," she said pointing to the lower abdomen area of her drawing. "It's right there, close to our original scar."

I looked even more confused than before. "Original scar?" I asked, shaking my head.

Laughing at my confusion she went on, "Yeah, the naval is our very first scar. The belly button, where it all started and from where we connected to the 'outside' world in the womb. The Dan Tien is inside the body and spatially just below it. But energetically it is very much connected to it."

"Never have thought of the belly button as our first scar. But you are right," I said pensively.

"Anyway," she went on, "This pulley idea may help to clarify all the things that up to now people have been telling you about the perineum point. Engaging the perineum point is not about tightening muscles, but about bringing the sensation of Chi to the 'Meeting of Yin' point located there, so as to reconnect this point to the center of the physical body—the Dan Tien. And when you tighten the link between the two it can feel/look like tightening a pulley. I also can relate the sensation to engaging a hydraulic valve. These are close descriptions of the feeling involved. In fact, all along the lines of right structure there are series of pulleys or valves that you can tighten up, but this is the main one."

"What do you mean by 'feel/look like a pulley or a valve'? Can you actually see it?" I asked.

"Oh my God—another question!" Veronica said with a mock look of surprise. "They should have warned me."

She shook her head and laughed understandingly, then continued, "Yes, you can see it. As the quality and quantity of Chi-flow increases, so does your concentration and then the senses will tend to merge, and you will begin to see/feel things. You begin to go back to the origins of sensation where the five senses were all the same. The closer you get back to that source the more they blend together. Remember, the Chi flows through and connects them all.

"To make it clearer we could use an electrical analogy. Electricity, like Chi, can be used to do many things. It can power a light, a cellphone, warm you up, or give you a shock, and any combination of the above," she laughed.

"So, to answer your question, the senses will naturally begin to merge as we become more aware of our Chi-flow and the stream of awareness that permeates all. And one of the results is that you can see/feel things."

I nodded, "I like that."

"So, yes: you can see/feel this pulley/valve. And I guess if you were musically inclined you might prefer to hear it," she said, grinning.

"Really these are energetic phenomena—bows, pulleys, and the Tai Chi Pole. They have no 'objective' physicality. Meaning that if you cut the body open you would not find them. You would not be able to see, hear, or touch them. Yet internally you can feel them. Internally they can be touched, seen, and sometimes heard," she added, smiling. "When the life-force inhabits your body, it creates all kinds of sensations. We are a living reality."

"But to get back to our bows," she said as she rolled her shoulders and pointed at her picture once again. "I think that learning to feel and engage this link between the perineum and the Dan Tien is very helpful in activating right structure in your body. When you link up this way the Tai Chi Pole and the connected bows spring to life. It is like 'click', and the whole system engages," she beamed.

Veronica looked at me, and then put her finger up in the air between us to prevent any new questions.

She then chuckled, stretched, and kneaded her back, before going on, "Initially, we need to internally refine and build this new structure like a muscle," she said, twisting her body from side to side. "After it is stabilized and continually refined, this new more efficient structure will get the Chi to flow better and with practice create even more Chi.

"Well, now you have the basics," she said, rubbing her hands together.

"OK, now, let's try it. Get into your stance," she instructed.

"First, activate the Tai Chi Pole. Put your focus on your perineum. Activate the lower Dan Tien. Now pull them together. This initiates the energy flow down your legs. You can feel the energy springing out of those lower bows. Right!" she said, pointing once again to her drawing. "Now direct your attention up the Tai Chi Pole and out through the scapula to activate the upper bow. And finally let the energy flow on up through your neck to the crown of your head. As you do this, I want you to sense how both your hands and feet feel as though they have suction cups in them," she laughed.

We held that posture for a bit before she said, "OK, that's just a quick run through of the basic exercise to develop right structure. Now relax while I go on," she said, laughing at herself.

Veronica then summed up what she was teaching me, "Right structure will help you to build a new container for your energy that will supersede the old structure given to you by learned behavior. As you begin to build right structure from the inside, you will then be able to store more Chi-flow in your body, in new and different ways."

I wanted to slow her down a bit to have a moment to integrate what she was imparting to me, so I formed another question, "Can you tell me more about the Tai Chi Pole. It fascinates me."

She paused to look at me and get her bearings before saying, "The Tai Chi Pole is the energetic pillar that is at the very core of our being. In the midst of our body, it is this physically invisible column which, as best we can fathom, is our most direct connection to the Spirit. And getting our Chi to flow properly from the extremities and back to it is the essence of our practice. And as you might guess, getting Chi to flow properly in this way can also cure a myriad of diseases."

She paused to let that sink in before continuing, "You could define learned behavior as probably the biggest impediment to that flow. What we are trying to do in our Chi Gung is to get that flow going again, by reclaiming the energy that has been sidelined, frayed, or clogged by learned behavior. We are trying to reclaim our energetic inheritance."

Then she took another tack, "There are so many aspects to moving beyond learned behavior. And I really like what Felina has to say about this reclamation project, and the way it relates back to our story. From the perspective of our story, you can understand what she calls 'Zen sickness,' when the flow of life-force which has been habitually trained and restrained by learned behavior becomes overwhelmed.

"As she has must have told you, this can be caused through intense meditation, a life changing occurrence, or even a strong sexual awakening. The resultant pressure that is moving with the Chi from the Tai Chi Pole to the extremities and back becomes so strong that learned behavior can no longer control and contain it. And once this breach has been made, learned behavior struggles to patch it up and then we are caught in the crossfire. At that point, the only option we have is to seek to expand into a greater sense of self."

As she paused to collect her thoughts, I got the feeling that she had talked to Felina about this in depth.

"There are other aspects of our story that can be seen in this light. We create a series of dramas in order to create a tension within us through which energy flows and interfaces with the outside world.

"These dramas allow excess energy to be released in prescribed ways through the energy lines provided to us by learned behavior. We become addicted to this, repeating them over and over. But when the pressure builds beyond the capacity of learned behavior to control these dramas, they no longer function well and 'holes' are created in our story. This is another way to look at 'Zen sickness'. We are then put into a position where in order to plug these holes we need to circulate more energy. But this is more energy than our given story and its inherent dramas can handle. So, to maintain a way of relating to the world of people, as Felina would say, 'We have to find a new pad'," she said laughing.

"Like with our precious dramas," Veronica said, "We can also see illness in this light. Illness can serve as a kind of opening or 'Zen sickness.' Through illness we create a crisis that demands more Chi-flow. The energy that we are allowed within the restrictions given to us by learned behavior is no longer enough, and we are placed in a position where we need to look for a new way to create and sustain more Chi-flow. So, in this light, you can see how illness can also be used as a doorway to self-exploration."

Veronica really had me reeling now with all the information she was giving me. But she kept going, "And we can even see it in the realm of 'the big one'," she said laughing. "You know the elephant in the room? When the pressure builds up it can seek release though sexual expression."

"How's that?" I asked with keen interest.

She looked at me knowingly and said, "A good example is when we reach puberty, a lot of energy gets released in the Tai Chi Pole. This can easily spill over the banks of the channels that learned behavior has allowed for the Chi to flow in. And even after the energy is reined in by the co-optive forces of learned behavior, subconsciously people still remember that sense of freedom, and may seek sexual release to free themselves from this pressure."

She laughed, paused for a moment, before saying, "What we are doing with our practices is building something beyond the concepts of learned behavior. We are giving ourselves another option."

It began raining softly and we stopped for a moment to watch the raindrops playing on the leaves and to breathe in the ionized air. I could see how one could get used to these patterns of rain and sunshine, and the ever-changing colors they produced here in Phuket. I was truly enjoying them.

I again felt as if I needed some clarification and a break from her long explanations, so I asked, "I really need to go back to square one. You all are talking about Chi-this and Chi-that. What do you think Chi really is?"

She grinned, pointing her right index finger up in the air, and said, "You really want an answer. I will give you one—one that you can ponder on for some time."

She continued grinning, then took a long breath, "As our old friend Li Tse would say, 'Chi is like perceptual rain, defining the edges of self-consciousness and the absolute'. He would go on to say that it is the closest "we" can come perceptually to experiencing our whole self, and maybe even merging with Awareness itself. I can hear him saying this even as I speak," she said.

"Had enough?" She beamed.

"I'll ponder on that as you suggested," I said, laughing, remembering my times with Li Tse.

"Let me give you another tangent," she offered, "A mechanical tangent that can help you to understand and to feel Chi better. Let's look at Chi in terms of electricity and the body as a generating engine."

"OK?" I said.

"The trunk of the body is like a battery," she went on. "It stores energy in its 'yin' or 'solid organs' housed in the chest," Veronica said, rubbing a hand over her rib cage. "Like our heart, liver, and kidneys.

These organs send energetic lines down, communicating with the 'yang' or 'hollow organs', like the intestines, stomach, and bladder in the abdomen," she said, moving her hand down to rub her belly. "These 'yang' organs directly interface with the 'outside' world through the food and drink we ingest. They then send the energy extracted to be stored in the 'yin' organs in the chest region. From these organs energetic lines rise to connect to the head and face—the screen from which we perceive the world," she said as she pressed the edge of her left eye with her index finger. "The arms and legs circulate Chi, pumping Chi into and out of it, distributing and recharging it.

"Chi is a type of living electricity that connects it all together. It moves through these lines, living fibers, flowing inside your body and outside it into your cocoon, and then finally through it to connect you to the Earth's cocoon."

She looked at me and said excitedly, "It's all about electricity, you know. You may not feel terribly electrical, but you really are. The food you eat and the oxygen you breathe contain energy that is converted into a kind of electricity. The electrical interchange in our bodies is even happening on a minute scale—in our cells. The condition of the body's overall health stems from the quality and quantity of Chi, which is creating active movements of cellular vibration within the tissues."

She leaned over and patted my shoulder, smiling, "We have a lot of latent energy in our body, a lot of energy resources. This body electricity idea is being investigated for practical purposes even by Western engineers. I just read an article the other day about human power generation. It talked about how our own bodies might be the sustainable energy of the future. They discussed how electricity from our own body heat, physical movement and vibration could power our cellphones, watches, and maybe even thermal underwear!" She laughed.

A thought arose in my mind, "All of these people that I was playing with here in Phuket and before that in Chiang Mai had such a good time—hopefully it will rub off on me, too."

"What we're doing with our Chi Gung," Veronica went on after a small break, "Is trying to maximize the creation and flow of energy in the body by creating right structure and then moving pressure through the body. Chi is created on the edges of pressure—just like rain and wind are created when high and low pressure systems meet up there," she said, pointing up into the gently falling rain.

"Now she is changing from an engineer to a weather woman," I chuckled to myself.

"OK," she said, loosening up her shoulders and standing, "Let's get back to our practice and learn what we can do with this right structure we are creating. So far you have learned how to allow Chi to flow through your body by defining and refining your structure. Now I will teach you how to play with the pressure within this structure to generate even more Chi-flow."

She then paused for a moment, raised her hands in front of her, palms facing each other and said, "I'm sure by now you have experienced this fuzzy feeling or sensation of pressure in your hands. The touch of Chi, right?"

I nodded in agreement.

She went on, "Movement stimulates the subtle electric currents to flow through the body. And you have already started to learn how to generate and move subtle energy in the body through the articulation of your joints," she said as she began moving her arms. "The joints function like little electrical stations, generators and transformers that create and mobilize Chi. And if you can sustain right structure, you can not only stabilize new currents of Chi-flow, but you can generate more Chi to keep things flowing."

Veronica began twisting her arms in various patterns as she continued, "Movement helps the subtle electric currents flow through the body. If you can create a current in your body through right structure and then direct it through your range of movements—or through all the possible postures of your physical being—then you will create a good full charge of energy."

I had to stop her as I was once again getting overwhelmed, and I felt like I needed to slow her down so I could better digest what she was saying, "You seem to keep equating electricity with Chi. Are they the same thing?" I asked.

Veronica responded, "Very similar, but Chi in addition to its electric-like qualities carries 'life-force'.

"But I like using the electricity metaphor to give you a conceptual feeling for Chi."

"OK, I think," I said. Still not quite sure that I quite understood the connection.

After that she paused briefly to ponder. She raised her index finger, as an idea had come to her, then began speaking, "But here is something interesting. To become more subtle, we have to build energy. The more energy we have at our disposal, the more subtle we become.

"A strange paradox when you think about it," she said, getting on a roll.

"It takes more energy to become less solid. You might think that it would take more energy to be more solid. But just the opposite is true. It takes more energy to become less static. As we are able to transform the energy being held latent in our tissues by learned behavior, we become less 'physicalized'.

"As the charge in the energy-body gets stronger, there is a unifying action that takes place between the subtle body and the physical body. At the same time this pulls us away from the 'physical body', as we have been taught to perceive it. So, the world becomes less 'stable', more fluid, at least in the way we were normally taught to think about it." She smiled, liking what she had just said.

"As a result, when you begin to become unglued from the 'body of learned behavior' and its concomitant way of perceiving, certain 'other' realities begin to unfold. This occurs because of the new ways that you are able to move energy through your body, and the resultant ways in which you are then able to perceive. Engendering this process is another way to think about what we are trying to do with our Chi Gung."

Veronica smiled again, really enjoying herself.

She then continued, "This process should be increased and stabilized progressively. Not in the haphazard way in which otherworldly new perceptions and realizations may have previously come to you, but instead in a directed, sustained way."

From the lively expression on her face, I could see she was liking what she heard. And as if on cue, she reflected, "I enjoy talking to you about this. Going over it makes it clearer for me too."

"All that talking, and what I really wanted to do is show you is the *dough boy*," she said, smiling mischievously while rolling her shoulders. "So, we'd better get on with it. I'm going to show you about 'waking the beast', or 'the double dragon', and all about 'bread dough'.

"I'm sure you're excited about that, right?" she said, looking at my confused expression and laughing as she rubbed her hands together.

I then nodded, as if agreeing but really wondering what she was talking about. But I was glad that we were about to do some movement that perhaps would help put together some of what she had told me.

"You have to develop a little round belly," she said, protruding her stomach a little bit before patting it, which caught me a little off guard. "You know, a little round belly like this."

She chuckled to herself. "What we are going to talk about next is not so good for the 'perfect-six-pack' mentality," she said as she continued rubbing her belly.

Then she added impishly, "Women sometimes have a hard time learning this because these days they're so programmed to have that flat belly, even more so than men. But really nothing could be better than a slightly supple, rounded belly."

She then beamed at me before continuing, "I remember when I first learned this, I was pretty skinny and had a really flat hard abdomen. And how after I learned to soften up my belly, by breaking up some of the adhesions and crusts in there, that this 'flat-hard-belly tightness' went away, and I felt much better."

"I can begin to get the picture," I said, grinning

"We're going to learn to make a ball of fluid down here," Veronica went on, putting both her hands on her lower abdomen. "We humans are seventy percent water—making us more liquid than solid by a large margin of more than two to one. Water is everywhere," she said, laughing. "Think about it. A fertilized egg is ninety percent liquid. Even a potato is eighty percent water,"

She then grabbed the side of her torso, saying, "So really, when you look at it, we're just a sac of liquid with some bones for a skeleton. And even your penis and testicles are a part of your old sac."

Then she raised her hand to forestall any questions and then added, grinning, "I'll get to that a bit later."

"Now, remember the practice of right structure and that pulley we talked about," she said, pointing once again to her drawing. "Bringing the awareness of Chi to the perineum closes the body container. This seals the bottom of your body sac. When you energize this area with Chi, you can then direct it up to the lower Dan Tien by slightly tightening the pulley."

She looked around to take in the scene of Angelique's sala and grounds before going on, "Angelique told me about what she has taught you so far—about connecting and compacting the body, and how this helps to break down the crusts that have built up there. And so far, today I have shown you how connecting and compacting the body can help to create right structure," she said, tilting her head and pointing with her chin at her drawing of the Tai Chi Pole and the two bows.

"The next step is to learn how to create more water pressure in the body sac. We start in the same way by sealing the bottom of the body sac at the perineum. Thus, we keep the water pressure in and intact. This then puts us in a position to create even more pressure," Veronica said, with an anticipatory smile.

"Before we talked about how the joints are like electric power and transfer stations. Now you will see that they also can act like pumps and hydroelectric power plants," she added excitedly.

"I'm going to teach you a different way to energize this body sac and the Chi flowing through it by mobilizing the fluids in your body. Instead of just moving your body through the muscle patterning that was taught to you by learned behavior, you now will learn to activate the body by moving fluids through it."

"What we are really talking about here is water pressure," she went on, "Waves of water. And how waves of water pressure can move through muscles, organs, and bowels to permeate your whole body to the point that you can end up moving your body with them."

Veronica then went on with the tone of a self-satisfied engineer, "Pressure moves through the body via a very delicate web of interconnectedness, very much like what in anatomy is called fascia. It is a webbing that weaves its way throughout the body, through muscles, transforming into tendons, ligaments, veins, organs, and then back again,"

She then looked at me to verify that she still had my attention. "We establish right structure to get the most efficient alignment for allowing the power of gravity to flow through us. Now we want to relax into our belly so that gravity is pulling down on the fluids in our body, creating the most pressure possible in a basic static condition."

These were new and exciting concepts for me. Even though I had been studying the body for many years, I had not come across them put in this way before, I thought to myself.

"Veronica," I said, "I find this really fascinating." Then after a brief pause, I added, "But how do these new techniques relate to the compacting, segmenting, and loosening up of the lower abdomen that Angelique showed me?"

"Exactly!" Veronica replied excitedly. "Segments and areas of the torso are glued together by our learned behavior. And until these blocks or crusts are broken up, we are unable to allow the fluids and Chi to flow unimpeded through our body sac. This is what those exercises that Angelique showed you were all about. And what we're going to study today is the next step: how you can control pressure and move it through your body."

"I want you to think about the pressure of moving water. A fluid pressure moving in waves through your body, through muscle tissue, through veins, and through organs. And even if you cannot follow all I am going to tell you," she said, smiling, "Just go along with me and we will see what sinks in.

"Okay, now let's get into a stance," she went on, "You know the drill, right? But now we will add in right structure."

Veronica continued, "It is in the standing and moving postures that our feet meet the Earth." She then walked over to the cabinet, pulled out one of Silvio's toy cars, and revved it up on her palm as she returned.

"Where the rubber meets the road—so to speak," she said laughing. "So, it is from within these postures that we can maximally charge our system through its gravitational alignment to the Earth."

"OK, seal the perineum. Don't forget about that pulley," she continued, getting back into her stance and dawning a serious expression, playfully looking like a drill sergeant. "It is not just about bringing the sensation of Chi to this area, but connecting it upwards to the Dan Tien. And from there you can begin to create right structure, aligning the Tai Chi Pole and springing the bows we have been talking about.

"Now relax. Let all the fluid in your body flow down into your belly and your legs, like turning off the engine in your car and letting the oil settle. Relaxing like this will allow for a more natural flow of currents of fluid in your body. This downward settling also takes excess pressure off your organ systems, which in turn relaxes your mind."

Veronica raised a finger in the air remembering something. She then went to the cabinet and pulled out a small doll. Imprinted on it were a kind of webbing, radiating out from the Dan Tien area.

"Look at this," she said. "This is one of Silvio's."

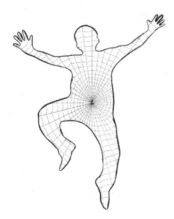

"Kind of like Spider Man," she laughed. "See the webbing? You see how the middle of the web is the Dan Tien?" she stated as she looked at the doll approvingly.

She put the doll down and went back to her explanation, "Once you have sealed the container at the perineum, what you have is liquid in a confined space. It can then be moved around by applying pressure to that container. When you do this, you can feel this fluid pressure move through most everything in the body."

"Going back to what you must have learned before, breathing patterns are part of your learned behavior that we need to learn to skillfully disassemble," she said, looking over at me to see if I remembered.

"Okay, now focus on your breathing. Can you feel how the breath moves through your body like a wave?"

Veronica continued, "Do you remember how at the very beginning of our teachings you learned to focus on the sensation of Chi in your nostrils and in your belly? Do that now—but be sure to keep your belly relaxed and let all the fluids settle. Notice that as you do this you can breathe without having to move your belly, which normally would rise and fall with the breath. This is what we are going to focus on: first, how to keep that rounded, relaxed belly at all times," she said rubbing her belly. "And then, how to move it," she added excitedly.

"I'm beginning to understand the importance of the lower Dan Tien and how so many different functions and aspects are centered there. It's the real powerhouse?" I probed.

"Yep, seems like you're getting it," she smiled. "Layer after layer of information, right?"

"But let's get back to our practice," Veronica went on, "I am going to talk to you about 'creating the ball.' This is the beginning of 'awakening the beast' that I referred to earlier," she said continuing to rub her little rounded belly.

"What we're doing now is building pressure in the body naturally by allowing the fluids to settle, by relaxing the belly to create a ball." Then she said, chuckling, "See, no six packs allowed around here. Just a ball, full of Chi."

She kept talking, remaining in her stance, "Now we want to break through more of the adhesions that learned behavior has created. I will first outline what we are going to do," she said as she demonstrated the procedure for me.

"First you will pay attention to your stance with right structure. Let your hands hang down by your sides. Let your belly relax. Let it get nice and round. And then as you breathe in, you will raise your arms up above your head and then hold your breath, keeping your hands there as long as you can, let's say for twenty-six heartbeats.

"Then exhale through your open mouth very slowly and softly as you let your arms come down to their original position by your sides. When you get to the bottom of that arc allow yourself to inhale naturally—but keep your belly ball relaxed and intact.

"Breath in and out to stabilize your breathing, again without moving the belly ball, keeping it full. The idea is to keep the ball intact and round irrespective of your breathing pattern, to keep your body pressurized through connecting, compacting, and right structure even when you run out of air," she said, grinning.

"Let's try it."

We began doing what she had outlined, raising our arms above our heads, and holding to a long count of twenty-six heartbeats. Then, we lowered our arms slowly, exhaling all our breath. I started panting. I looked at Veronica and saw she was breathing hard, but her rounded belly wasn't moving in and out like mine was. Hers was round and still.

"How do you do that?" I asked, perplexed.

"Right now, all I want to show you are the effects that can be achieved," she replied. "There are specialized exercises to learn how to do this, and maybe when you go back up to Chiang Mai, Silvio and Li Tse will show them to you. I know you are pressed for time, so all I will show you now are the possibilities. I just want to get these principles into you so you can understand and see/feel the possibilities. Just like planting a seed, I want you to realize that it is possible to separate your breathing from your belly movement.

"It takes some time to learn. For some people it takes months. In my case, I had been practicing every day for two or three months, and then one day I was climbing a steep hill and noticed that although I was breathing hard, my belly wasn't moving at all. I got really excited, especially when afterward I found out that if I concentrated on it and remembered to relax my belly, I could do this same thing while playing tennis, and even while swimming or snorkeling.

"It sounds very easy, but you'll find it's not. It requires a skill developed through persistence and practice. And," she said, grinning, pointing her index finger at me with a laugh, "It requires real body-to-body teaching."

"OK, let's get back to it. Once we have closed the perineum point and tightened the pulley," she said, picking up the spiderman toy again, "relax and let the Dan Tien become the center of the web.

"The next step I'm going to show you will be by teaching you body-to-body. If you see/feel me doing it while touching my body, this will stimulate your body memory, and later something in you can remember how to embody it. When body knowledge is activated in this way then your body can remember well. I really don't know how it works but it does. Body memory is amazing.

"OK, come over here and put your hand on my belly," she said putting down her spiderman toy.

I moved over next to her. Standing at her side I placed one hand on her abdomen and the other on her lower back as she instructed.

"First, can you feel the ball?"

"Ummh," I replied.

"Now I'm going to move it."

I could feel the ball inside of her body move. She directed it to different areas. She moved it side to side, then up and down, and then diagonally across. Then it felt like it was going around and around, rotating one way and then the other.

"Notice that my hips stay stationary," Veronica said. "I could even do this sitting down and you would feel the same thing. You can feel it, right? At this stage we are just 'waking up the beast'," she laughed.

"Wow, this is really amazing," I said. "I have never felt anything like this before. I can't quite describe what I'm feeling. It's a whole new thing."

She looked at me and smiled, "I could try to tell you about this in words and point out a direction, and you might be able to put it together conceptually. But realistically, unless you're taught body-to-body it would be difficult to sense and then remember how to embody it. You felt the movement in my body with your own body. I am planting memories in your body which later can bear fruit," she giggled.

Veronica then went inside Angelique's house and returned wearing a stunning, colorful tight-fitting body suit.

"Now I'm going to show you some more things and explain them to you. So, just follow along as best as you can," she repeated.

Veronica went over to the cabinet and picked up another of Silvio's toys—this one was also a human-shaped doll, which I noticed was filled with something like putty or liquid rubber. She also took out another toy car, which made me wonder how big a toy car collection Silvio had left here in Phuket.

Revving the toy car up over her palm and walking towards me, laughing, she said, "We will now learn to generate electricity. I just want you to remember that every time you take a step you are generating electricity. Don't forget—where the rubber meets the road," she said again, laughing.

She put the car down and took the doll, going over to one of the posts of the sala and held it up against it. She stuck her thumb into the liquid rubber doll's left abdominal area, and I watched the putty-like substance inside the doll flow out from there into the arms, legs, and head. When she took her thumb away there still was an impression left there in the doll's abdomen.

*Dough boy*

"You see that?" she inquired.

I nodded.

She then pushed her thumb into the right side of the doll's abdomen, and I watched as the area which had been depressed previously fill, and then another ripple of putty go off into the arms, legs and head.

She then really got into it, delightfully repeating the sequence three or four times, pressing the abdomen of the doll first on one side, then the other, and watching the putty move through it.

"You see that," she said. "We do this by emptying and filling. After we have created the ball and filled our body with pressure, we then empty one side of our abdomen, and it sends a ripple of fluid out to the rest of the body. That is what you just felt me doing."

She put the doll down, then got into a stance in front of me and started moving. She said, "OK, I'm going to empty my left side in the same way I pushed with my thumb on the doll, but from the inside. And this creates a pressure that will push the ball I've created in my relaxed belly, pushing the fluids over to my right lower abdomen and out into my arms, legs and head. Can you see that?"

"Not totally," I said.

She then waved me over, "Come over here and feel my body again, body-to-body, so you can experience it and not forget it."

When I go into position, one hand on her back and the other on her belly, Veronica said, "Now feel it. This time I will empty my left lower abdomen and it's going to flow over to the right side. One side empties and the other side fills. OK, got that?"

"Umm," I acknowledged.

"Now put one hand on my leg and another on my arm," Veronica said as she moved the ball of fluid pressure in her abdomen. "And sense how they fill as the fluids move there. Feel that?"

I could clearly detect a wave of movement in her leg and her arm.

"Now move away from me and try to see if you can see/feel from a distance what you just experienced, body-to-body. I'm going to empty one side of my abdomen and fill the other side. Then, as I empty the other side the ball moves back over. Back and forth. See/feel that?

"But also notice that as I empty one side of my abdomen, a pressure wave moves down both legs. Just like what you saw when I pushed the abdomen on the doll. And when I start moving the ball from one side to the other, emptying and filling, I can feel the water wave go up from one foot up through the lower abdomen and down through the other side. It's like a ball bouncing in slow motion, from one foot up and across the abdomen to the other. This is something I can feel as I do it—can you see it?" she asked.

"Yeah, now that I have felt it in your body I can see it better," I replied.

"That's how it works," Veronica went on. "Since I can do it, I have embodied it, and I can see it in other people clearly. But since you can't do it yet, it's not so easy for you to see. You don't even know what to look for. Once you can move the pressure in your body as I do, you will be able to see/feel it better. This is the principle: to the extent that you have done and experienced it, you will know what you are looking for and can see/feel it in others. This is one of the important aspects of body-to-body teaching."

"Now we're going to move the ball around. We're going to combine some of the sequences Angelique taught you, but we will do it by moving water pressure through the body—not just moving Chi through the torso by activating the joints. Instead, we will squeeze the water pressure through the fascia and thus move our body in such a way that we will be able to bypass learned behavior's habitual muscle/movement patterns," Veronica beamed.

"Watch me do this. Remember that it is by emptying and filling in the way I just showed you that I will move the fluid pressure in my body."

When she began moving, I watched ripples or waves move through her body. She moved the three trunk segments Angelique had introduced me to, but I noticed her movements were smoother and more fluid and seemed to happen as a result of a 'wave' action.

She stopped, then paused to pick up the rubbery doll again, alternatingly pushing on different parts of the doll's torso. Briefly my attention drifted over to the top of the cabinet, and I noticed the tortoise shell that Angelique had shown me before, the last time I was with her. It brought to my mind a memory of the Ba Gua inscribed onto the underside of the shell. And then I realized that these were the same areas that Veronica was pressing with her finger on the doll. So, I asked, "Is what you are doing like emptying and filling the areas of the Ba Gua of the torso that Angelique showed me?"

"Yeah, you got it! Very good. We can initiate the movement of pressure from any of these areas,"

Veronica said. "And now look at this," she said excitedly.

Then I watched as she was able to swirl "the ball" up from her feet through her torso and out her arms, then back again to her lower abdomen, around and around in random snake-like fluid patterns that were like ripples running through her body, engaging all the Ba Gua of her torso in various patterns.

"Wow!" I said. "Now I can clearly see the waves of pressure that you were talking about. Fluid pressure initiating movement. That is way different than what Angelique had showed me—this is amazing!"

She stopped, and raising one finger, said, "That's why we call it 'waking up the beast'!"

I was starting to get a sense of what she was showing me and I asked, "What does this feel like from the inside?"

"Dough," she said. She once again picked up the rubberized putty doll and started squeezing it. "This is what we call a '*dough boy*'," she said, giggling.

"A *dough* boy?" I inquired, scrunching up my face.

"Yeah, a dough boy. Because what you feel inside is like what you see/feel when you watch one of those bread mixers slowly stretching and kneading dough. Once you have connected and compacted your body, created more pressure, and begun moving the fluids in your body, your movements become like stretching, squeezing, and pushing around this thick, pressurized substance.

"Just like our friend here," she said, picking up and squeezing the doll a couple more times with glee.

"You have to build up your internal strength to do that, though," she added.

"Well, this is simply amazing. I like it," I said. "Does it have any martial arts applications?" I asked, wondering.

"Interestingly enough it does, and it's very effective for those who want to use it this way," Veronica said. "I'm convinced that one of the reasons that it is so effective when used in a martial way is that you move at a different speed. It's not so much that you are moving 'faster', but that it is surprisingly unfamiliar, because it comes from a different system or moving dimension that we are not used to being in or seeing. A dimensional dislocation," she chuckled.

"People in their learned behavior are linked into muscular movement patterns, even martial artists. When you move in the way that I was just demonstrating, you're not moving your muscles in the patterns of learned behavior. You are moving outside of that realm and learned behavior cannot grasp how to respond when presented with it. The result is that it is like touching someone coming from a different dimension. Learned behavior's reaction patterns simply don't recognize what's happening. It comes as a big surprise and packs a pressurized, dough-boy punch," she said with a laugh, once again squeezing the dough boy.

Her face then lit up and she said, "I can remember once playing with this dog, who was very fast. He would run back and forth in front of me, and I would try to grab his legs, but I just couldn't get a hold of him. I thought he must have played this game many times before. Then it occurred to me, 'maybe I'll try moving the ball to catch him and see what happens?' The next time he moved by, I emptied one side of my lower abdomen and shot the pressurized energy out of my arm, and grabbed him by a front leg, and was met with the most startled expression I've ever seen on a dog's face. He just couldn't compute what I had just done within his movement world.

"If you were to see the world in terms of trained action/reaction muscle patterns and someone acts with movement outside that range, it's startling," she continued. "It has an invisible quality to it because it's rarely seen or experienced."

"So, it's like you can become invisible," I said, jokingly.

She laughed, grabbed a nearby cloth and wrapped it around me, saying, "Yeah, it's like a cloak of invisibility—moving into another dimension."

We both laughed.

Then after a bit she went on, "I remember one of Li Tse's stories about when he was learning to move the ball. One of his teachers was showing him how to apply these principles. The teacher would push him with this pressurized fluid energy and would send him reeling. Li Tse described to me the feeling he had at the time. He said he experienced a wave of pressure moving through his body as he flew across the room. He told me it was like being altered into a sense of slow motion, as if he were in car accident, and it was much different than being pushed physically or even being shocked and jolted by a burst of Chi. He asked his teacher to do it to him again and again, because he was mystified and really enjoyed the feeling of it. It really knocked him out of his usual way of moving and thinking. His teacher went on to tell him that unless an opponent knew how to move the ball and move this pressurized fluid energy in their own body, they were susceptible to this surprise, over and over again.

"It was Li Tse who put it together that the reason this happened is that it was really like the push was coming from another dimension—a dimension of movement from another realm, and now I agree with him."

"We use this technique and its ability to override the patterns of learned behavior stored in the body for healing. It disrupts learned behavior and frees up energy. In the same way that it shocked the dog and shocked Li Tse the first time he experienced it, it befuddles and confounds our learned behavior. So, we can use it to energize our healing-body template."

She squeezed the dough boy a few more times, smiling and said, "OK, now watch this. This is really going to be a little bit more subtle to observe because much of the experience is internal—whether it be tactile, visual or multisensual—but as you've been able to see/feel me moving the ball and your body has experienced that feeling, I think you'll be able to perceive some of it."

Then she raised her finger again and her face brightened up as if a light bulb went on. She laughed and said, "I'll draw you a picture."

Veronica went over to the cabinet and pulled out a sheet of paper and began to draw a side view of a human torso, neck and head.

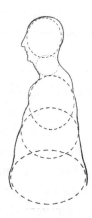

She then referred to the picture, pointing to the lower abdomen where the bowels and sexual energy reside. Then to the area of the upper abdomen, the chest area, the neck area and then the head—all of which she had delineated into separate zones.

"You have already seen and felt how the pressurized movement of fluids can be moved in many different ways. But now we'll use it to go to specific areas."

Again, as with Angelique, I was thankful that Veronica had put on her tight-fitting outfit, which helped me see/feel clearly what she was doing. I could understand what she meant by referring to the feeling of kneading and squeezing dough while I watched her massage her lower abdomen from within. Not only was it instructive, but it was also dazzling to see the energy move around through her tight body suit, especially since now I could see/feel her movements somewhat.

Veronica continued moving the pressure in her lower abdomen, saying, "This is a way to internally massage the lower organs, those in charge of defecation and urination and our sexual energy."

She stopped and smiled mischievously, remembering something, then raised her finger and said, "Do you recall how I mentioned that your penis and scrotum are really part of your pressurized sac?" She laughed, "Ever heard about 'genital weightlifting'?"

Before I had time to respond she excitedly went on, "This is how you can understand the principles behind it. Genital weightlifting can be done by a man by tying a soft cloth around his penis and scrotum and supporting weights with it. For a woman, this practice is done by inserting a jade egg inside her vagina with a string hanging down from it that weights can be suspended from.

"If it's done properly, it can be a method of increasing the pressure and compactness of the body within the body. This can be done by learning to hold up those weights by using the integrated pressure one can create in the body, rather than by contracting muscles. The 'grabbing' of these weights, using the dynamic pressure thus created, can be used to further compact and strengthen our body sac. You can even learn to do this by and while moving the ball as I just showed you.

"Normally we don't do this practice because it is dangerous, and it can result in injury if just done with muscles. But I thought you'd be interested to know how it works in the light of the principals we are discussing," she grinned.

"But let's move on."

She got back into her stance and rolled her shoulders a few times, then said, "We can move this pressurized liquid wave created by moving the ball in our abdomen and directing it with our inner focus to different areas. Now look at the picture again that I just drew for you. I'll move a ball of pressure through each of these areas."

She then began moving the ball and radiated pressure waves through her body through the different zones she had delineated. She finished and relaxed.

"You can even learn to grab an organ and squeeze it and massage it with this pressure," she said as she lightly closed and opened her fist in front of her.

She then continued, "Remember, you can move this wave in any direction or number of directions as you wish. But because you're moving what feels like dough or putty, this can be a very strenuous exercise. If you want to do this, you have to work the dough!" she said giggling.

Veronica stopped and then slowly began pacing in front of me.

"Remember, we're talking about a fluid system. Felina may not have mentioned this to you, but as you compact and pressurize your body you also compact and pressurize your life. As we learn to connect and compact more and more and strengthen this system by exercising it, we also gain access to more choice and fluidity."

"No, I don't remember her telling me that. Thanks. But what exactly do you mean by compacting and pressurizing your life?" I asked.

Veronica replied, "The result of this inner work is that what you do in the outer world changes, and your learned behavior can then be switched onto an automatic pilot mode. You can keep going deeper into yourself, exploring and enjoying as your learned behavior takes care of your outer doings.

Once you've de-charged your learned behavior it can become very useful," she chuckled.

She stopped and raised her finger again as if having remembered something, and then got back into her stance saying, "One more technique!"

"We can also bring this pressurized wave out to our wrists and ankles," she said as she twisted her arms in opposing directions, rocking back and forth on her feet. I could see why they called it the "double dragon," as I watched the undulating motions of her body and the twisting of her arms and legs. It was as if two separate undulating forces were running up her body from her feet out to her hands, connected by the Tai Chi Pole, animating the movements of her body. It reminded me of the ancient symbol of medicine, the *Caduceus:* two snakes intertwining a central pole.

She broke into my reverie, saying, "What you're seeing is actually another technique for pressurizing the body sac and moving the water wave. As I am sending the pressurized liquid wave out into my arms, I am twisting them, tightening them up. It is like kinking a hose, which creates even more pressure," she said as she torqued up the movements in her arms.

She stopped and went over to the cabinet and picked out a towel and began twisting and untwisting it,

"This is the principle. It's as if you are wringing out a wet towel. In this way you can create even more pressure as you move the pressure waves out to your arms. You wring them out," she laughed.

Veronica seemed finished with her teaching for a while as we took a break, drank some water, then walked over to sit in Angelique's gazebo, dough boy in tow. As we settled down, I reflected on what Veronica had just explained and shown me and I reflected,

"So, Veronica, I've learned about Chi moving through the body. Now we're talking about waves of water pressure generating more Chi and further energizing the body—how does all this fit together? Are we talking about two different systems here?"

She paused, pondering, then replied, "Well, think about it this way: using right structure and simply moving the joints, we are working much more with something like creating electrical power from air turbines. But when we move the water pressure wave, we're making pressure through 'hydroelectricity'! We are compressing the body sac, increasing the water pressure until it turns into heavy water or dough, then pooling it, passing it, and stretching it around the joints, along the bones and moving it through and around the body."

I could see Veronica's engineer coming out in the way she described these body processes.

She continued, "Chi is also created by water pressure as it moves throughout the whole webbing of fascia in the body. Do you remember our spiderman?" She said as she pointed with her chin back at the sala. "Chi is stimulated through a type of friction as it passes through the fascial webbing. Chi is generated as the fluid moves through the tissues and through the muscles and organs.

"And I haven't even told you this yet, but even more Chi is generated through friction as the fluid pressure moves over the bones, through and around the joints, and even along the spine. The vertebrae of the spine are movable parts too, like joints, and you can create more Chi-flow there, moving the water pressure up and down the spine."

She went on in a very technical tone again, donning the aura of a self-satisfied engineer, "Do you remember, previously I told you about how the joints are like electric transfer stations of an electric grid where the energy can be amped up? Well, the joints can also act like pumps and turbines that generate electricity and help move the water pressure through the body, creating even more energy," she smiled.

She stopped for a moment and then went on with her technical descriptions, "The water wave is more substantial than the air wave created through breathing. It provides a more sustainable pressure. And don't forget: Chi is created and stored in quality and quantity of pressure. Much in the same way as a car battery stores electricity, the body stores energy in its specialized reservoirs—in the specialized body fluids of lymph, blood, and the fluids in the organs. So, in the same way we need to keep the cells in a car battery filled with water to keep it charged, we must sustain the levels of essential vital fluids in the body to help it maintain its charge."

She looked around, noticing the light and gentle rain once again. I noted that it had almost stopped. She then turned to me and said, "The potential for using the waves of fluid pressure is enormous. Working at this level you can create a deep profound movement of Chi which is optimal for your health and well-being.

"Water and wind move over the Earth. These are the forces that create movement and weather on the Earth and inside the body.

"Chi and the essential fluids in balance. It is like what is out there," Veronica said, gently.

Chapter 15:

# Awakening

*It began with a flash of color, exploded, kaleidoscoping into a workshop. I looked right—puppets. One suspended by strings, dressed in blue-yellow embroidery. Hanging next to it, a face of a tortured demigod, white fangs flashing, clothed in deep greens strobing into reds. Next, a brilliant blue one with a human body and an elephant head.*

*To the left, an incomprehensible display of live musical instruments, a cornucopia of sound—drums of all description, bagpipes, flutes, guitars, xylophones, marimbas.*

*A huge cello sent a subsonic vibration into my solar plexus. I was overwhelmed.*

*I turned, out the window, a rice field pulsating in phosphorescent green. A water buffalo. A white crane landed on its back—colors exploding.*

*Droning back in the room—bagpipe playing on its own. A glowing gold-lit room, the light of oil lamps.*

*Tibetan thanka paintings, cloth talismans—gold on maroon, ancient Buddhist scripts in magical geometric patterns, old astrological charts, pictures of exotic deities and demons, bundles of bamboo tablets inscribed in ancient Pali.*

*A shining emerald and gold Buddha intruded, glowing with a light of its own. Below, an assortment of Chinese-looking tools on a worktable amidst the chaos of detached wooden body parts. In the corner, a hanging human skeleton—adjacent a case with three human skulls, emanating translucent bluish light.*

*Baskets, pots, and containers hummed and vibrated knowingly with an exquisite sound of their own. On a table, rubber dolls shape shifting one color to another—gooey toys throwing themselves against the wall, sticking then falling.*

*The workshop and attendant rooms were like a body operating in coordination and balance, breathing together.*

*Far away rain sounded on the roof. The bagpipe droning on with its own vital breath, wailing. Blue light entering and merging with the golden hue of the workshop, turquoise green and violet geometric patterns on a field of vibrating blue.*

*Suddenly an enormous slow motion wave came towards me through a tunnel of intense colored beams—portentous clouds of brilliant light, streaks of chartreuse phosphorescence. Finally, amidst a luminous golden amber glow, the shape of an immense green-gold iridescent beetle emerged. The illuminated beetle was on its back, trying to turn over, moving from side to side. Back and forth it rolled, again and again, struggling to regain its footing. Then at last with a mighty effort it righted itself, radiating light from its gold-green form.*

The melody of the gongs transformed and became the tone of a Buddhist temple bell. I came to, slowly—enjoying the feeling of the splendid colors and sounds of my dream. Enjoying just lying there, basking in it as it slowly receded into my body. So rare to be bathed in such sublime sounds.

A long way off I heard the temple bell again. I heard the sound of chickens, and then felt my head on the pillow.

"Where am I?" I thought.

Then the great, nourishing feeling from the dream enveloped me once again like welcome warm sunlight on a cold winter's day. I smelled the dampness in the fresh air from last night's rain and heard the waves lapping the sand in the distance—imagining their blueness as I laid there.

I heard the ladies talking in the distance, in counterpoint to the wailing of the Muslim "call-to-prayer" from the loudspeakers above the village. As down the road from the Buddhist temple the bell rang again, mixed with the sounds of chickens, waves, and the smell of newly fallen rain and salty sea.

I slowly became aware of my body feeling suspended, laying there in bed.

Out of nowhere...again, the feeling of the dream embraced me.

The vital pulsating greenness of the rice field—water buffalo—the phosphorescent green—living rice—the crane landing—an iridescent beetle.

Drifting gently out of this I slowly got up from my bed and looked out the window to see the morning light on the Andaman Sea, hearing the gecko family that shared this house with me scurry off.

I went over to the table to make some tea—some of my favorite *oolong* tea, grown by my eighty-year-old tea brother. For me he had always embodied and exuded the essence of tea. He had grown tea for almost fifty years in the stunning mountain environments of northern Thailand. I closed my eyes and I could see him, amidst seemingly endless terraced tea gardens—mountainsides shrouded in clouds, receding into the distance.

I raised my small ceramic cup with fresh *oolong* to my nose to enjoy the aroma. It was comforting and familiar. I then took my first sip. Ahhh, it felt good to be in Thailand.


My recent experiences with my newly-found friends were settling inside of me. They had taken root and their teachings were becoming clearer to me. I now had an understanding for that longing that had begun to stir within me when I had first felt my dissatisfaction with the world that I had been taught to perceive. I now sensed how this urge as it ripened had drawn me towards my own personal unfolding.

As I relished another sip of tea more realizations tumbled in. I could now understand how following that urge had propelled me. How I was being pulled and directed to absorb more energy to unite with my natural evolutionary path which had increased my feeling of health and vitality.

I could understand how I was being released from the iron grip that my past habits through my breathing and movement patterns had layered over my senses.

And I could sense the manner in which my path was correcting the imbalances in the relationship between my perceptions and my physical energy—opening me up to a new energetic world.

I became aware of the chirping of the birds in the trees, the sounds of the crickets and frogs, hearing the water dripping from the leaves of the trees from last night's rain. It all had a unique and direct freshness that permeated all my senses.

This helped me to relax further into myself and realize with great clarity how my sense of self is directly related to the rhythms of my daily breathing and movement patterns, which I was using to store my habits of "how to grab" onto the world around me. And that my habits—from the way I hold myself and move, to the way that I lounge around—form the basis for how I see myself and view the world.

And furthermore, that when I properly align the energy currents in my body, I initiate an alchemical transformation that allows me to manifest my primordial impulse towards wholeness and freedom.

And ultimately, that by changing the energy flows in my body, I change my life in every area that I can conceive of.

## SECTION 4—Up-country

Chapter 16

# Li Tse—House of the Four Thieves

"What is your body, where is your body?"

I grabbed my wrist and replied, "It's right here. This is my body."

"That's right! You see what you just did?" Li Tse said. "You froze the frame. Whenever we think about something we turn it into an object. Do you think your body is what you see when you look in the mirror? Stand in front of a mirror and close your eyes. Is your body still there?

"When we think about the body, that's exactly what we're doing—thinking. When you think, you freeze the frame, so the body becomes a static thing. When you think about it, in words, even though movement is happening all the time, movement gets frozen. So, you can see that it is very difficult to be aware that the body is constantly moving and to see it that way while thinking at the same time."

I was sitting in Li Tse's yard, talking to him at his home, which was on the outskirts of a small village outside of Chiang Mai. I had recently returned to Chiang Mai from the island of Phuket and only had a few days before I needed to leave the Kingdom. This time of year, it was intoxicating being here. The vitality and life in the radiant thick green carpet of rice stunned the eyes. The chlorophyll and sweet smell of the young rice shoots perfumed the air as well as the intermittent chirping of birds and insects.

Li Tse had been talking to me about body movement before he got into "freezing the frame."

He told me that when we walk in our normal way—walking forward, repeating our learned behavior over and over again—we are just reinforcing the way we're taught to walk or move in the world. We just go on and on repeating and reinforcing our habits through our movements. He explained to me that this is the main way which our learned behavior uses to transform and sustain the pulse of life in us into our socialized selves.

He went on to say that some folks in the "old" cultures, where the body and its relation to what was around it had been studied in depth, observed this fact, and used it in their transformative process: some shamanistic training entailed even walking or running backwards. He mentioned a place in China where some friends of his witnessed groups of apprentice shamans running backwards around a dirt track.

"In China? Where everyone is supposed to do the same thing all the time?" I asked surprised. This was based on the times I visited China in the 1980's when I had seen first hand how their behavior was even more consensualized than in the West. To me, at that time, it had seemed that they were being held to an extremely high level of conformity which was strictly enforced and difficult to escape, because everyone really knew what everyone else was doing.

"Out in the boonies there are a lot of interesting things taking place," Li Tse chuckled. "It's hard to obliterate the human spirit and China is a big country. And don't forget," he raised his index finger, "The Earth stores memories."

Li Tse then went on, smiling, "And as if that wasn't enough, the story goes, that these dudes were also making Chinese characters in the dirt with their feet as they ran backwards."

He laughed and said that walking forwards is in some ways like walking into the past—since you're repeating and strengthening the motions you've done innumerable times before. Whereas walking backwards could be a form of releasing your learned behavior. And that walking backwards, viewed in this way, could be seen as a form of walking into the future because you would be undoing your habitual way of walking. And in this way, you wouldn't be moving forward towards uniting with your evolutionary path.

"You see," he said, "In this context, walking backwards can be seen as disrupting the continuity of your learned behavior through time and space which then can help you to remember who you really are."

He finished by saying, "You know a good way to define Chi is to say that it is the energy which gets movement moving." He cackled, "And what a way to study it—by going backwards."

Now, as I sat here with him, Li Tse wobbled his head back and forth as close by a *Tohke*, a large multicolored gecko, called out "Toh-ke, Toh-ke."

Li Tse stroked his chin and began speaking, "Well, I heard you studied with those people in Phuket. They told me all about it, and Veronica told me that the last thing she introduced you to was this sac of pressure that we live in," he said reaching over to pull and pinch the skin of his arm.

"Now, before you leave, let's try and pack a bit more in there," he went on, tapping his temple as he peered at me, smiling. "I want to talk to you about the outer sac. It's part of and an extension of the physical body sac that Veronica showed you.

"The physical body is like the yolk of an egg," he said. Then there's another sac that encompasses it, which is like the egg white surrounded by the shell. It's the bubble we walk around in. It's a *movement* sac."

His description elicited an image in my mind of a Mexican healer Josefina, with whom I had studied in the city of Oaxaca in southern Mexico. She used to put eggs on her altar overnight and the next day she would use those eggs to diagnose patients. She would have a patient sit in a chair. Then, taking an egg, she would rub it all over their body. After it had absorbed the energy of the patient, she then would crack the egg open into a half glass of water. From this she would diagnose the person's health or spiritual problem by what she saw and sensed. Josefina could tell from the look and shape of the yolk and the filaments of white fibers made by the egg white in the water where the patient's problem lies and often who was at fault.

When my attention came back to noticing the surroundings, Li Tse was looking at me. He smiled, shrugged his shoulders, and then continued talking, "Let me put it like this: the extended range of our possible movements defines the circumference or perimeter of this secondary or outer sac.

"And it is the movements of the body in space, or the movement-body, that nurture the physical body, much as the egg white nurtures the yolk. It is as if we're living inside of a bubble in our routine day-to-day life and this bubble actually is what is moving through the world. It is the movements inside of that bubble that are nurturing us. And if we can learn to maximize the potential range of these movements, we can nurture ourselves more completely."

I burst out laughing, "Whoa! You bit a little off more than I can chew!"

"So, you're with me?" he went on, laughing himself. "We live within this double-pressurized sac with the physical body inside, similar to the yolk, and what I like to call functionally 'the movement-body', like the egg white, defined by our full range of potential motion, surrounding it. This movement-body is a secondary sac. And it is a sac of pressure as well."

"I think I'm with you," I said. "And I am beginning to get a feeling for how this pressure works in the inner, physical body sac, after we talked the last time I was here in Chiang Mai, and the training I received from Veronica. But how does pressure function in this secondary, movement-body sac?"

"Oh, excellent question! And an exciting one at that," he said amused, wringing his hands, giving me the impression of a cat about ready to pounce. "It's the pressure of movement. Movement has a pressure, and it leaves a wake. Just think about how water gets displaced and moved by the undulating body of a fish by its tail and fins, or the wake of a boat. The movements we make every day inside this sac also create a wake. And the rhythms and patterns of pressure that are created by our movements through time blend and mix, creating long lasting currents."

"Oh, I get it. So repeated movements leave wakes which make currents around our physical body?" I asked.

"Good!" Li Tse went on. "But I want you to remember when we talked about how thinking freezes the frame. I want you to take your mind off the body as a static object or something that moves from one fixed frame to another, and begin to think of it in terms of rhythms, patterns and movements in time, through space.

"This means, thinking about the fact that every movement you make predetermines the next movement, which in turn predetermines the following movement. The patterns of these movements leave a residue, like a wake. A residue that is alive. Once you become sensitive to this it can be felt like a gauzy substance left in space. Repeated movements create patterns of Chi-residue which, if they become static, turn to cobwebs."

"I can get a feeling for all this but I still can't quite grasp it," I said.

Li Tse brightened up, "That's just it. I don't want you to grasp it. I want you to see/feel what I'm talking about. You need to leave your old linear 'subject/object' way of thinking behind or at least give it some flow. We're moving into the realm of 'body language' where 'feeling concepts' are alive and moving. They cannot be grasped by the flat mummified world of linear thought.

"We're talking about life here!" he exclaimed, chuckling, leaning forward, pushing his chest out and spreading his arms. "This is the vibrating world of Chi."

He then settled back in his seat, considering just how to continue, how to talk about currents of movement and the residues that are left by them.

"Years ago, when Silvio and I lived and roamed around Mexico we visited the pyramids outside Mexico City. We went there often," he said. "While we were there, we could feel how the people, so long ago, had moved between the buildings. We could really feel the residue of their movements amongst the massive structures. The buildings helped to hold these old energetic patterns or residues in place.

"Thinking back about it, I now see that we really went there for a little cultural displacement and the little bursts of freedom that come with it. While there, we were surrounded by the different currents of movements that these ancient ones had lived in. The juxtaposition between them and the residues created by the pressure from our own learned behavior caused a disruption in our 'normal' way of perceiving the world. This then allowed us to feel and see things that we normally would not.

"Just because we could not see the living fibers around us in our normal learned way of seeing did not mean that they were not there. These residues were held in place in the way the buildings were constructed and their relative placement. And they were locked there by the Earth's memory.

"Remember," he emphasized, "The Earth holds body memory. These sacred buildings and their placement served to accentuate the memories held within the Earth itself of these people's body concepts that once thrived and moved there. When you begin to feel with your whole body you can notice things like this."

I drifted off into a reverie that rose within me—the memory of many American Indian legends which thought of beauty as something given to humans by spiders through their weaving of webs. Or caterpillars spinning cocoons from their saliva and then transforming into butterflies. These images that kept popping up contributed to a feeling that was making some kind of strange sense—the living saliva of the spiders, the living strands of the cocoons these folks kept talking about, the gelatinous white streaks of the egg whites in the healer's glass, the patterned residues of motion left through time in our movement bodies and how Chi residues were being reflected by the structures of the ancient ones.

When I again refocused Li Tse was gazing at me. His smile lingered over my body for a bit. He seemed to sense my mood and even read my mind as he continued on with another story.

"I also can remember a time when Silvio and I were in Mexico and we took a trip to Silvio's home, Zitacuaro, Michoacan, to see the monarch butterflies. In the mountains behind Zitacuaro they come to winter—hundreds, thousands, millions of them. They are some of the greatest travelers on the Earth. They have this most incredible connection to the living matrix of the Earth's cocoon.

"You know that every year they travel up to Canada and then back again to Mexico to winter. And it takes them a few generations to do this. It is not just one butterfly remembering where to go from another one who had previously done the trip. They are literally born to travel, with their direction imprinted upon them genetically, remembered through their connection to the Earth's cocoon.

"One individual flies northward for a while then lays its eggs and dies. The eggs hatch, turn into caterpillars, who then weave their cocoons and turn into butterflies again, continuing on their journey northward. They repeat this same process of regeneration and connecting with the living matrix of the Earth until they reach Canada. And then they migrate southward in the same way—reproducing and moving on.

"Their connection to the magical being, this Earth we live on, is just amazing. I remember Silvio and I lying there under the pine trees, looking upwards at those millions of beings and feeling somehow displaced as we rubbed against and absorbed their dream and their essence. The guiding knowledge within them that travels through generations is unbelievable! Their bodies know what they are doing. Stunning!"

Li Tse paused for a second, clearly enjoying his memories. He then went on, "But you know, we humans are connected to the Earth too, and are also full of evolutionary guiding knowledge. If we can get through the veneers that learned behavior has placed on our cocoons. the innate knowledge in our body knows what to do," he said, looking at me and smiling as he leaned over and affectionately patted the ground. "It's a promise made to us by the Earth."

Li Tse continued, "An understanding of our true connection to the Earth can only be reached when the language of our 'linear thought habits' has been de-charged. We've been working on breaking up our patterns of learned movement, which we didn't even know were patterns until we began to feel there were other possibilities.

"Now we need to break up the perception that this body is a static solid object by breaking up the crusts that have settled in and on our bodies, and the energetic blockages that have grown in our movement cocoons as cobwebs. In short, we want to clean the crusts and cobwebs created by the residue of movement patterns, both inside and outside of us, that our bodies are habituated to. These residues, lingering on through time in our movement-body, and the crusts that have settled on our physical body are constantly being compounded by how often these movements are repeated.

"Interest compounded daily in your very own 'body bank'," he said laughing.

"What happens is that we are left with only narrow channels of movement circulation within our body cocoons."

"*Crusts?*" I asked, already starting to feel overwhelmed.

Li Tse replied, "Yes, crusts indeed. Those repeated currents leave a residue in their wake. Our habitual movement patterns end up creating something like an energetic crusty plaster cast that then confines us through habit to certain movements in the future. Not only do they show up as blockages in our physical body, but they correspondingly occupy our movement-body. Together they form a barrier that we need to de-charge in order to regain our connection to this being out there," he said, opening his arms in an expansive gesture trying to capture the Earth.

I smiled. Then I stopped to remind him of an experience that I had eating in a small restaurant with him the day before. While sitting at a table in this small restaurant I witnessed the choreography of movements of the workers there. It was as if they were moving in visible rhythms and patterns and were involved in a pressurized prearranged dance, each knowing their steps to perfection. Not only could I see/feel how their movements were choreographed but I could also see how they, each one of them, left energetic patterns in space. And as I perceived the individual patterns more closely, I could even get a sense of the composition of their individual stories.

I asked Li Tse, "Why is it that I can see things like that when I am with you but not by myself or with other people?"

He looked at me and responded, "When you are with me sometimes the Chi-flow in your body increases as you start to experience the added energy that can happen when our cocoons merge. You begin to feel and move in a bigger cocoon. The collective cocoon of both of us allows me to naturally transmit energy and knowledge to your cocoon and thus you are able to reach beyond your normal perceptual range.

He then looked at me pensively and said, "And this can even extend to the deepest of levels. I can remember a time when I was in an interview with a Buddhist monk who was very advanced along his path. Just being with him and answering the most basic of questions totally exposed my learned behavior. My mind became crystal clear. And in that clarity that arose from being in his presence, I could perceive the root motivation of every thought as they arose from the vastness of the Mind—thus exposing the underpinnings of my story."

"But, getting back to our conversation and what I am trying to convey to you," Li Tse smiled, pausing before continuing, "it is because when I am with you, my body is talking to yours and this helps you to maintain your recently learned structural integrity. When you can maintain this right structure you can move beyond the pressures of your learned behavior, and to the extent that you do this you can see/feel the workings of the learned behavior around you.

"So, being with me helps you to maintain right structure and the resultant good Chi-flow which makes you a bit more immune to the structural pressures of learned behavior. This in turn keeps you from slumping back into your old habitual story, and so you become open to seeing other people's moving energy patterns and their stories. Don't forget—it is only to the extent that you have moved beyond your own story that you can see the story of others."

*Movement-body?* Is that what I was observing?" I asked. "What was this guy up to now?" I wondered, smiling inwardly.

Li Tse replied, "You were witnessing their living dance. But also, you were noticing their shields, the crusts on their bodies and cobwebs in their movement bodies, both individually and collectively."

"Oh," I said, "I am getting a sense of what you are talking about. People choreographing movement patterns in time-space that have a definite individual rhythm to them when seen over time.

"Like I do whenever I enter my home. I open the door, put my things down, and then do countless little things to 'organize' myself inside my place, and usually getting the urge to go pee, which often makes me wonder if I am subconsciously marking my territory," I laughed. "Then I feel settled in, and I am ready to relax."

I looked at Li Tse, who seemed to be encouraging me so I went on, "You leave a wake of energetic patterns of habitual movement behind. Not only because of the way you placed your things but even more importantly due to the patterns and rhythms of your living dance there amongst them," I said, my thoughts clearing. I can take it a step further and see how two people living together have their agreed upon movement arrangements. Or even, in a 'movement-pattern sense', how a guest would impact the choreography of a household.

"In this light I can even start to appreciate the Chinese 'Art of Placement' or Feng Shui," I added, as thoughts continued to tumble through me. "And how the practitioners of that art would want to emulate the natural flow of things while designing a house to create a more harmonious living environment. Or why the Native American Indians would want to 'smoke out' a place with sage to clear the energetic cobwebs of former residents before they themselves move in and start out afresh."

Li Tse nodded approvingly, pausing for a moment to playfully wipe his brow on my behalf, "Now, that was a mouth full."

He paused, smiled, then began speaking, "What we'll be doing with these next exercises that I will show you is learning to clean the movement-body of the lingering cobwebs that have arisen from the repeated movements of learned behavior. And instead, in our cocoon create a new web of living, pulsing fibers. This will put both your movement-body and physical body back into shape again, strengthening their alignment with each other. This then can serve as a foundation for reclaiming your perceptual options."

Li Tse looked at me, then said, "Do you remember when I told you before about the sequence? The sequence of perceptual awareness? Of how our perception moves from Chi, to touch, to seeing and hearing, then smelling and tasting? And how not only does the sequence begin and end with Chi but is permeated with it?"

I nodded.

He continued, "As we move through this progression our learned behavior grabs onto certain combinations of sensory inputs to create our story, sense of self, and concept of the body. And this pushes a feeling of 'solidness' out into the world. But however useful these selections may seem to be, they limit us. They keep us from realizing there are other perceptual combinations available and that there is a true self that knows. It's like having your face pushed against a window to see only one view and not having the strength to pull away to see things from any other perspective.

"Now listen closely," he said, raising his index finger. "These habitual selections of perceptual choices made by learned behavior are stored in our bodies and in the bodies around us. They are reflected in and activated by our movements and eventually become shields—crusts on our physical bodies and cobwebs in our movement-bodies.

"What learned behavior does is solidify perceptual choices. We become inhibited by the limited sensorial matrix of our learned behavior. And it binds us to uphold the image of the body as an object."

Li Tse paused before continuing, "So what we want to do is to clear up the perceptual incongruities given to us by learned behavior. We want to make both the physical body and the movement-body flexible, supple and pliable to allow more access to the energy of life.

"Through our Chi Gung we want to expand and extend the rejuvenated Chi-flow we've been able to create in our bodies out into the movement-body, so that the realization of who we really are can be grounded not only in our physical body but at the same time also grounded in the rhythms and patterns of our movement-body.

"We have to remember—we're not what we perceive but we're more than that. The perceiver is more than its perceptions. We want to allow the real essence that is beyond perception, beyond the five senses, to flow freely through us, to interconnect all parts of our being. And this in turn will bring happiness, health and well-being in its wake.

"And one more thing," he said, grinning, "Don't forget that Chi is what gets movement moving."

We sat there for a while enjoying the sights sounds, smells, and feelings of the pulsing rice fields around us. As I was mulling over what he and his friends had taught me, I realized that I was fascinated but still not quite sure about these fibers that they were talking about. So, I asked, "Li Tse, tell me more about these fibers? I want you to give me a better feeling for them."

He replied with a light in his eye that seemed to touch everything around him, "Look at them in terms of the movement-body. We have living Chi fibers running through our bodies along meridian lines that we've been cleaning and charging through the practices you've learned so far. We want to extend those lines of energy out into our movement-body so that new possibilities of being alive can be stored there too."

"I can get a sense of movement creating currents through time in space," I said, waving a hand in front of my face. "And how these currents could leave a wake, creating a structure like a sparkling, new spiderweb or a cocoon. I can also understand how repetitive movements can cause cobwebs if they're not re-spun." I paused, "I can just about see/feel it now. I like this idea of living in a cocoon."

Li Tse looked at me approvingly and went on, "I think you are beginning to understand that the sensations that you get from moving the Chi in your body are more vital, continuous, and integrated than the sense of body that you've been taught by learned behavior. The patterns and rhythms of learned behavior that makes up the 'body' are fractured—a finger here, a leg there, a look in the mirror here, a movement of the hand there—like I was trying to demonstrate to you before.

"Also, there is a sequence and rhythm to it that is familiar and comfortable. In addition, this sequence is reflected back to you by those around you which enhances that limited perception of your body that was taught to you by learned behavior."

"Enough said," Li Tse instructed. "Let's start. Stand up and close your eyes for a moment." I did as he directed, then he said, "Now, if you break the spell of your learned behavior's trained perception of your body and let the Chi flow through your body for a minute, I think you will be able to sense a body that has a continuity different from the body view with its 'scattered sequences' that learned behavior has taught you.

"Start to move your body, staying with the sensation and continuity of Chi-flow, and you will get an idea of what I am talking about."

With my eyes closed I began moving, while Li Tse continued, "Feel the energy moving. Feel the awareness in the flow of Chi that is your body. Like long extended fibers that have life in them. Move your hands and feel the trailers left behind.

"As you stay with these sensations and move them through your movement-body, realize that there is an interconnectedness that you are feeling that probably will go away when you open your eyes. See if you can envisage how you will think about your body when you open your eyes again—seeing a hand here, looking at a tree there, constricting then freezing your flow into a thought, or bringing up a part of your story, a drama you are involved in. If you watch closely, you can get a feeling for that sequence of who you have been trained to be.

"All you need is enough energy or attention to loosen the grasp of the perceptual linkage of learned behavior to get this perspective.

"Can you begin to see/feel how the fibers and the awareness in them has been taken over by learned behaviors' sequencing? And can you get a sense of the patterns and rhythms that it tells you make up your body?

"The Chi-body is a much more continuous multi-sensual feeling than the body taught to you by learned behavior. It comes with very different sensations than the sensual snapshots tied together by learned behavior.

"Can you get the sense of this?" he said with a silvery laugh.

I opened my eyes and looked around, but Li Tse indicated with his hands that I should close them again and keep moving so he could continue, "Keep your eyes closed and examine those sensations of Chi once again. If you deeply relax you will notice that there is a central column of Chi that runs from your perineum up to the crown of your head and from this column out to your extremities. Now as you move, and staying with feeling this column of energy, extend the sense of Chi all the way to your ankles and wrists, feet and hands. Then, as you see/feel the trailers left behind in the wake of your movements, try to focus your attention on feeling the movement-body, the fibers and their tendrils.

"Can you do that?" he asked, before going on, "These fibers extend through the limbs of your physical body to your movement-body to the whole cocoon you live in. Stay with that awareness."

Li Tse was silent. I kept my focus as directed. Then I heard his voice again, "Keep your eyes closed and I will read you something from Chuang Tsu who purportedly lived in China from 369 BC to 286 BC."

He paused, then began reading:

*Once upon a time, I Chuang Tsu, dreamt*
*I was a butterfly, fluttering hither and thither,*
*to all intents and purposes a butterfly.*

*Now, I do not know whether*
*I was a man dreaming I was a butterfly,*
*or whether I am now a butterfly dreaming*
*I am a man.*

*This transition is called*
*the transformation of material things.*[2]

"Some of these old Chinese guys knew a thing or two," I heard Li Tse say with a slow chuckle.

"You get free from your idea of your body and then you can begin the ultimate 'evolution of life'—the evolution back to your source and then to your true movement in creation.

"Hold those eyes closed for one more second and concentrate on that central column," I heard Li Tse saying. "This central channel in your body is what we are calling the life-giving part of the Tai Chi Pole. Moving the

Chi unimpededly out from there to your extremities and then through your entire movement-body and back to the Tai Chi Pole is what creates vibrant health and vitality."

"That's pretty cool," I said as I blinked and slowly opened my eyes. "I can begin to see where you are coming from with this cocoon idea. Can you tell me more about the process of weaving this cocoon?"

He smiled and replied, slyly, "It is a process on a grand scale that has physical and psychic components. Or it could be defined as the weaving together of your physical and psychic bodies. There is a certain rolling around in oneself that produces a result. Rolling around in your emotions, feelings, and sensations of your body while becoming aware of the focusing by that part within you that knows.

"This produces a result. You begin to weave a cocoon with fibers of truth as you remember yourself by putting back together the flows of Chi throughout your physical body and movement-body to coalesce into a grander Chi body—an evolving cocoon."

"So, are we creating a cocoon to hatch out of and turn into something else?" I asked.

"We believe it's something like that but of course we won't know until we get there. And to be sure—the part of us that thinks it knows won't get there anyway.

"Or an even better way to put it is," Li Tse said, beaming and rolling his eyes, then smiling, taking in the world around him, "We will just be here."

"Let's get back to the Tai Chi Pole," Li Tse said, "The mother of all meridians."

"OK, slow down a bit." I said. "For starters, why do you call it 'the Tai Chi Pole'?" I asked.

"We call it the Tai Chi Pole because we have studied Chinese traditions a lot, and we like the sound of it: 'Tai Chi—The Supreme Ultimate.'

"The Tai Chi Pole is a term out of Chinese Philosophy. I would say it mostly relates to the Taoist tradition, but it has other names in other traditions, even amongst the Chinese. Terms ultimately are a bit arbitrary and in this case the name is not so important.

"What is important is the feeling of this stream of energy. What we are trying to do is to describe an awareness, a full feeling that is a mixture of all the senses and more. We could just as easily call it the 'Bamboo Pole,'" he said, grabbing a bamboo staff nearby.

"As you know, the Tai Chi Pole, or the Bamboo Chi Pole," he said, looking at the staff in his hand, laughing, "is a column of energy that runs from the perineum to the crown of the head, a little in front of the spine. Now on the back side of this pole, closer to the spine, runs its active aspect, the 'life' or 'movement channel'. The way we perceive this life channel is a feeling, a pressure, composed of all the senses and more—Chi. It is packed with life-force. It is from here, this primary Chi channel, that the eight extra meridians that Angelique introduced you to, emanates from. From there the energy flows to fill the other energetic pathways of the body, to support the functioning of the organs and bowels. So it is from here that movement is engendered in the body and out into our lives.

"This channel is filled with what can be perceived as a full feeling of luminous light, with a consistency like the most subtle saliva, vaginal fluid or semen. Also, it is associated with the gauze-like feeling you have been able to sense in your hands, the middle of your nostrils and other parts of your body. These sensations are really out of the range of learned behavior, so they are very hard to talk about in language and sometimes very difficult to sense at first. But in essence, it feels like the most delicate of liquids filled with air, or like air with refined dampness, almost not there. But although subtle, it can be felt indeed, as a light pressure and it is very much alive."

Thinking about saliva and vital fluids brought to my mind another creation myth of certain Native Americans. According to this legend, Spider Woman created the world by molding two lumps of clay, then putting her spittle on them and thus they then came to life, becoming the first man and woman.

Li Tse had stopped talking and was once again looking at me, waiting for me to come back from my reverie before he continued, "You could feel the energy in this central column, right?"

"Umh," I mumbled.

He went on, "Now, if you study this column of energy you will come to realize that there is one primary place where energy flows out and is being captured and conditioned by learned behavior. This is right here," he said, pointing to his bamboo pole, at about eye level. Then, placing his index finger above his nose and between his eyes, he continued, "It is here where the senses of sight and sound blend with those of smell and taste—where they all come together and unite inside the head. And it is here that learned behavior does its 'magic', with the eye-sense usually being the number one magician," he said, chuckling, almost cackling.

"We have a name for this area in the middle of the head where learned behavior does its work. We call it the 'Outer Rooms' or 'The House of the Four Thieves.' Because it is from here that the energy is stolen by learned behavior, by the way it teaches us to see, hear, taste and smell the world around us.

"The great passageway on the inside along the Tai Chi Pole we call 'The Doorway to the Ancestors.' Because if the energy is not diverted by learned behavior at 'The House of the Four Thieves,' it continues to flow on to the crown of the head, completing our energetic circuits.

"The challenge here is to clear this ancient passageway, take it back from the control of the 'Four Thieves' and allow the energy to flow unimpededly up from the perineum to the crown and then connect out to our entire energetic body."

"This whole area up here," he said, touching the side of his head with his fingers, "is called the 'upper Dan Tien,' or place where energy gathers in the head region."

"How do you find it?" I asked interested.

Li Tse replied, "Actually, it is not that difficult to contact this energy center in the middle of the brain once you know what to do. You just follow any of the senses—the sense of seeing, hearing, smelling, or tasting—back to where they meet. And there you have it," he said, letting his staff lean against his body, then clapping and rubbing his hands together.

He looked at me before continuing to see if he had my attention, "The practice then is to build up energy, concentrating on this point. This nullifies the stranglehold of learned behavior and naturally allows the energy in the Tai Chi Pole to flow freely.

"If you disable learned behavior from utilizing the 'Four Thieves'—the four senses of seeing, smelling, tasting, and hearing—by focusing your awareness on this place where they meet, the energy then can gather and coalesce in the Tai Chi Pole to flow upwards and downwards then spread throughout the body in a more total way.

"Don't forget that there is a force within us that wants to be free," Li Tse said, smiling.

He tapped the bottom of his bamboo staff on the ground and lowered his voice to grating tone as he continued, "It is down at the bottom of the Tai Chi Pole where energy can be released through the genitals." He could not help chuckling at his own antics as he went on, "So we have two major places where the energy can flow out from this life-giving column of Chi—the genitals and the middle of the head."

Li Tse said peering at me, "This is one of the major reasons to seal off the perineum by bringing the sensation of Chi there. We can regulate the energy that may leak from the bottom of the Tai Chi Pole, the genitals, by learning how to open or close the perineum door. And direct it upwards to the lower Dan Tien."

He really had me interested now. It seemed like he was talking about the real stuff. "What do you exactly mean by energy leaking out the genitals?" I asked.

"What you really want to ask is: what do you do with an excited

Tai Chi Pole? Right?" he said, beaming, as he tossed the bamboo pole from one hand to another as if it were a hot iron.

"Well, I am glad you brought this up," he said with a grin, continuing to juggle his hot pole. "It is very important that you understand this.

"When there is a sexual attraction or interaction, it revs up and excites this central, life-giving Tai Chi Pole. But as the energy from within this column has been trained to move out of the body in only the prescribed ways that learned behavior has taught us, we're not presented with many options. Either do it the learned behavior way, or go crazy, or get sick because the learned behavior cannot handle it. So, often we seek release through orgasm," he said, cackling.

"Now, climaxing is fine from the learned behavior's point of view because the increased energy flow gets released quickly and it can remain in control. But in terms of our evolution and what we know to be the truth about ourselves, it is a great loss. We lose the opportunity of gathering enough energy to be able to perceive in other ways beyond those prescribed by learned behavior."

"I never thought of it that way," I said. "So, what shall we do? Not have sexual interactions at all?"

He began tossing his bamboo pole back and forth from one hand to the other again, then smiled, "No, no, no. It is never that simple. What you need to do is to see sexual energy from the point of view of gathering and storing energy, in order to better understand what it is that you are, and to further your evolutionary goals."

"But what actually happens when sexuality activates the Tai Chi Pole?" I asked.

This made Li Tse examine his staff carefully before he grinned, then said, "I can give you a simple example of how sexual energy activates the Tai Chi Pole and overwhelms learned behavior: Give me a depressed heterosexual man and have a beautiful young woman come up and flirt with him and see how long he stays depressed. The learned behavior can only deal with so much energy...then it loses control," he said, laughing.

"Sexual excitation stimulates the Tai Chi Pole. This is a great movement of energy. It fills the life channel portion of the Tai Chi Pole with energy. Now if that energy is maintained and neither leaked out via climax nor escapes via the conditioned senses in the head center, it then can be used for deep internal exploration or to invigorate the whole energetic system.

"In essence, what practitioners of many sexual yogas do is to excite the Tai Chi Pole using sexual stimulus. They then direct that energy up through the ancestral passageway, or 'Doorway to the Ancestors,' to overwhelm the traps created by the 'Four Thieves' trained in their craft by learned behavior. In this way a rush of energy can proceed up to the crown of the head, completing our natural energy circuitry.

"There are so many other things that go into sexual interactions. But these are the energetic mechanisms involved in terms of using sex as a path to help your evolution. What I recommend is that you understand what is going on and if you do have sexual interactions, you act with these things in mind. Understanding the principles involved is the key.

"You may even be able to find someone to teach you, body-to-body—good luck," he said, smiling knowingly from ear to ear.

He went on, "There are other ways to stimulate the Chi in the Tai Chi Pole, but the sexual example is very dramatic and helps to illustrate the underlying basics. Also, learning to stimulate and then to regulate the sexual energy is of utmost importance. Because, once you can do this then you are on the road to better health, longevity—and of course to greater sexual prowess," he added with a smile and a glint in his eye.

"It is very important that you practice to regulate this energy," he reiterated. "It may be just for mere survival, as Felina indicated to you when she told you her story. You can see how in her case the sexual energies of puberty overwhelmed her learned behavior and how she had to fight to stabilize a new flow in her life. And you can also understand how too much intense meditation could cause too rapid an opening of the energies in the Tai Chi Pole causing 'Zen sickness.' Then there are the 'twists of fate,' like someone getting ill, totally depressed, emotionally distraught, or frightened—which certainly can make one realize that there is more to life than the view provided by learned behavior. All of these could overwhelm the 'Four Thieves,' clearing up the 'Doorway to the Ancestors' a bit.

"But you have to be careful because the accumulation of energy in the

Tai Chi Pole without appropriate expression could so dramatically override learned behavior that it could be severely damaged—and we don't want that."

"You mean learned behavior is *not* something we want to get rid of?" I asked, trying to adjust my thinking.

Li Tse paused, looked at me then gazed at the pulsing green rice fields for a moment before continuing, "You see, on the one hand, learned behavior indeed is an impediment to our evolution. But on the other it is a friend, for it helps us deal with the world out there," he said pointing to some farmers working out in the neighboring rice paddies.

"To make it simple, learned behavior wants to use the energy of the Tai Chi Pole exclusively for its own self-perpetuation and its own preferred perceptual cocktail instead of allowing the energy to be used for the purposes of personal transformation.

"By closing off the genital area and allowing the Chi to rise from the perineum to the lower Dan Tien and then closing down the 'House of the Four Thieves' in the head, we can begin to reclaim the energy and means needed for exploration and evolution. When you close off the lower openings and focus on the place where the senses unite in the head you give your being a rest from learned behavior. You take a break. And then the energy can coalesce and find its true way."

He let his staff lean up against his body as he rubbed his hands together again, then continued, "Or even more simply put: by regulating how we think and perceive the world we can allow the true power of our sexuality to transform us.

"Basically, our challenge is to open up the Tai Chi Pole without destroying our learned behavior," Li Tse explained. "You want to keep your learned behavior somewhat intact so that it can deal with the world, but you want to be able to regulate it instead of being regulated by it, and not have it get in the way of your natural evolution.

"We must learn to reopen the 'Doorway to the Ancestors' without losing our marbles," he laughed. "When you understand this, then the same principles that we talked about in terms of sexual yogas can be applied to other practices such as Chi Gung for the purpose of our evolution."

He picked up his staff once again, looked at it, nodded his head a couple of times and then put it back against the pillar. "Let's look at this a bit more practically," he said.

"It is important to keep evolving your focus and goals. When they have developed to a certain point, the idea of loading up the Tai Chi Pole with energy and bypassing the 'Four Thieves' in the head area becomes very appealing. By concentrating on the upper Dan Tien, that point where the senses gather in the head, we can enable the Chi to pass through the 'Doorway of the Ancestors' unimpededly. Then, if we tighten up the pulley that Veronica told you about, between the perineum and lower Dan Tien, and adopt right structure, we can get the energy to stream upward and fill the Tai Chi Pole from the lower Dan Tien all the way up to crown of the head. And with further practice you can accustom your being to this new flow and use it to explore what you truly are and move along more freely in the evolutionary stream."

He leaned over, put his hand under his chin and smiled, "Once you know about this power you can then learn to regulate it. You don't want to overwhelm learned behavior too much, to the point that it becomes damaged. So, now and then, you can simply release some excess energy for example through orgasm," he chuckled.

"But you should also learn to activate and excite this energy to feed your body and further your explorations. When done over time this builds a fluid inertia, an ability to replicate itself according to new and different situations."

Li Tse paused to gather his thoughts once again, "To explore inner worlds and move along our path of evolution we need to allow Chi to flow freely in the Tai Chi Pole, then distribute it throughout our body. And as you gather your energy back you eventually start to notice the circulation of a very subtle crystalline liquid light in your body and around you."

As I stopped to absorb this last statement, I looked around at the lush green rice fields and listened to the chirping of insects, appreciating the rhythms of nature, and also wondering at the forces that had brought me here to be with this most enigmatic of characters. After taking a good drink of these feelings, I finally brought my attention back to our interaction.

"I am very curious about what this has to do with the de-charging of one's story that Felina talked to me about?" I asked.

"Excellent," he said with a satisfied grin. "The perfect question. Essentially, learned behavior creates your social self and your story by its special mixture of your senses. 'Special,' because it is made especially for you," he said, silently chuckling to himself. "And because it is made especially to make you feel special.

"The seat of your story and your sense of self that learned behavior has created for you is located in the 'House of the Four Thieves' in the head, in the upper Dan Tien," he went on. "This is also where language is created and where energy gets changed into thoughts."

"And what does this mean?" I curiously asked.

"Aaahhh," he replied. "It means that if you can override the particular sensual spattering of learned behavior that arises here," he said, putting his index finger to his head with his thumb up as if holding a gun, "You can move beyond or de-charge your story. And if you can do this well, then the body can relax into being within its rightful flow of energy while you can still retain the ability to function in the world."

He paused and scratched his chin, then continued, "These internal Chi Gung practices you are learning and the spirit you are learning them in, are out of the range of learned behavior. They cannot be co-opted by learned behavior's drive for self-perpetuation, protecting its 'culture' or the accumulation of material things.

"Instead, with the right focus these techniques deal with our transformation and evolution. Through these practices we can immerse ourselves within our guiding evolutionary force and become involved in a process much like a caterpillar weaving its cocoon. Knowing in an inexplicable way that we will emerge later into something which we can at this point only intuit."

"OK, so tell me more about this cocoon and these fibers of energy you keep talking about," I said, interrupting his flow.

He stopped for a moment, looking at me with a piercing gaze, then dropped his shoulders and hung his head in mock resignation, then asked rhetorically, "Aren't you getting tired of all this talking?"

He then seemed to have a change of mind, perked up, and then chuckling said, "OK, just a bit more, then we have to get to work.

"The webbing of our cocoon is made of fibers, a vital essence, a fine clear fluid, similar to subtle vaginal juices, semen or saliva but full of Chi. It is so fine that it can appear to be made of a gauzy substance, forming a lattice work like a spiderweb throughout our physical and movement-bodies. It can be felt as a gauzy sensation or like infinitesimal moving pinpoints of pressure."

"Why do you call them fibers?" I interjected.

He replied, "Because they feel like fibers on and in the body when you breathe them or touch them. And they sound like fibers to our internal hearing and look like fibers to our internal sight. These fibers are alive and have awareness in them. Silvio tells me that some healers in Mexico call them 'La Cabaerra de Nacar,' translated loosely as hairs of mother of pearl.

By realigning or untangling the fibers that have been redirected away from their natural flowing patterns, we can become more aware and feel more connectedness."

He peered at me, his eyes bulging, then exclaimed, "*So, untangle the fibers!!!*"

"Think about a kinked cocoon," he went on, laughing, yet continuing to peer at me.

"A *what*?" I asked.

"Yes, think of a caterpillar weaving a kinked cocoon. What do you think would hatch out of that? A kinked butterfly, eh?" he laughed. "And speaking of a kinked cocoon—what kind of cocoon do you think you've been living in?" he said, grinning, the twinkle in his eyes getting brighter if that were possible.

I didn't know what to say and I could see that Li Tse's inner trickster was beginning to come out and I did not want to be duped. So, wanting to get the focus off me, I asked, "How do you do this? Fix a kinked cocoon? How do you do it, not just talk about it?"

"I've been waiting for you to ask me that," he said, amused.

"First, you raise the energy level in the Tai Chi Pole, then send it out through the meridians and finally, back to the Tai Chi Pole," he explained, grabbing his staff again, playing with it, poking it at me, then moving it in a quick striking motion first to the right and then to the left.

He put his staff down and went on, "It is as if learned behavior creates a thin elastic coating or webbing that is very hard to disentangle from. This web winds its way through the body like a net, sticking energetic fibers together for its own purposes. As you know it is very much like a parasitic growth.

"We need to clean things up. We need to create a new flow of energy, one that is free from these old cobwebs. We want to get closer to our wholeness and create more healthy relationships inside and outside of 'ourselves' so we can generate more internal integrity."

Li Tse then went on, "This is how working with the movement-body is helpful. Cleaning up your movement-body can make you feel more complete. You will need less pressure coming from the people around you to fill up the holes left by learned behavior's attempts to control your energy flow. You can learn to get sustenance from your own completeness.

"You will also notice how this then improves your interactions with people. Change your movement-body and you change the way you inter-relate. And you will be able to maintain this transformation because the new Chi-flow structure you have created in your body has staying power. That is why you have been learning right structure—to help this flow and to become more aware of it."

"OK, time for another chapter in the book of the body," he laughed, then exclaimed, "We're born to move! Life is movement! Chi is the mother of movement! The study of movement is the study of life!"

Chapter 17

# LI TSE—MOVEMENT BODY

"Let's get moving before our cocoons ossify!" Li Tse said enthusiastically.

He stood up and motioned for me to do the same, then said, "When the fibers in the movement-body are not kept clean or preened through usage, crusts are formed in the physical body that can eventually cause disease. The Eight Point Chi Gung we teach is all about moving within this web of energy that I have been explaining to you—our cocoon. We work on cleaning this web of undesirable wakes of Chi-flow that have built up as cobwebs in our movement-body, and which correspondingly cause the calcifications that have created crusts on our physical body.

"We want to activate the Tai Chi Pole and move Chi to the wrists and ankles and back, straightening out the energy lines to all essential parts of the physical and movement bodies. Then the subtle-body can take it from there."

He told me this as we walked to his sala, a rustic but beautiful structure, overlooking the surrounding rice fields. A perfect place to practice Chi Gung and also to absorb the rhythms of nature.

"Just stand there for a bit and listen," he said after we had arrived. With his staff in his hand, he started walking back and forth in front of me, then began speaking, "Let's recap briefly what you've learned so far. We're going to put together everything into a form with a focus.

"First, you learned to focus on Chi by bringing your attention to the fuzzy feeling or slight pressure that occurs when the air enters and leaves the nostrils. Then you trained to detect that same sensation of Chi in the belly, hands and feet, right?

"By now you should be able to understand that by directing your attention on your breathing in this way, this can be a method to concentrate awareness in the upper Dan Tien, where the senses of the head meet. A technique that disables the 'Four Thieves.' This seemingly simple exercise, along with sealing off the perineum, leads to stimulating the energy flow in the Tai Chi Pole," he said. "Can you see that now?

"We also taught you about reconnecting, compacting and segmenting the body. Doing this initiates the breakup of the crusts and tissues stuck together in your trunk and limbs, further opening the Chi channels in the body. Still following?"

"Mmm, I am beginning to get the picture," I replied.

Li Tse continued, "Then Veronica introduced you to right structure—a natural energetic framework in which these exercises function. Right structure creates a proper container for maximizing Chi-flow by balancing your energy with the gravitational pull of the Earth.

"Finally, you learned about the dough boy; and how by creating an energy ball in your abdomen you can utilize directed pressure to move the water waves in your body. I am not sure if she told you or not, but it is like 'heavy' water, and that moving the dough boy gives you the sensation of being a bread-making machine, moving the 'heavy' dough around."

As he said this with a delightful grin on his face he began twisting and flexing his body—staff and all—moving the ball in his abdomen, pushing waves of 'heavy' pressure through his body and seemingly out through his staff.

Li Tse continued, "All of these instructions created a foundation for you to understand the form I am going to show you now. We will combine all these principles of body mechanics with the knowledge of the eight primary meridians that accompany our embryological growth as Angelique taught you. We will focus on cleaning out the cobweb-infested movement-body, and thus breakup the resultant crusts on our physical body."

He stopped moving, looked at me and said, "With Veronica you learned about the mixing of Chi and fluids. Now I will teach you about a bigger mixing—mixing the physical body with the movement-body.

"Let's get to it!" he continued, beaming.

"First, we will open and energize the Tai Chi Pole. With the Tai Chi Pole activated, and our right structure intact, we will then move Chi out from it through our physical body. Then we will direct it to flow further outwards throughout our movement-body and then back to the Tai Chi Pole to complete the circuit."

He started walking back and forth in front of me again, then said, "We have developed a systematic approach for loosening up the Chi stuck in the physical body. Now we can work on extending it out to and cleaning the movement-body.

"At this point you haven't yet consolidated the exercises we have shown you, so your habitual perceptual patterns are still quite strong. But later on, you will grow to understand that it's all about changing the way we walk on the Earth. This then will create a basis for altering the way you perceive yourself and hence the way you see the world around you.

"Hard to keep carrying around a kinked cocoon," he said, chuckling. "Hopefully we will be able to fix that by freeing your habitual perceptual patterns and revitalize your health.

"But for starters, let's talk a little bit about the form we're going to learn."

I was feeling a bit overwhelmed again and must have looked like it. Seeing this, Li Tse stopped to consider for a moment and then said to remind me, "With Angelique you must have learned about the embryological growth of the fetus, the twisting and flexing of the body, and the eight points that control these motions. These eight points are the eight points of the moving body compass. We will combine all the techniques you've learned so far and use this embryological knowledge to give you a set of internal coordinates."

A question came to my mind, and I opened my mouth to speak, but he raised his hand to cut me off, smiling, then saying, "Wait a minute, let me finish first.

"You remember that the eight primary meridians formed the major energetic pathways during the growth of the fetus, and that from them the entire physical structure of the body evolved, right? They also form the major energetic pathways that define the range of movement that can be made by the body. Do you remember?

"'Flexing' and 'twisting'? So now we're going to concentrate on stimulating these meridians by using movements that incorporate our Eight Point Chi Gung."

"HNNNGGH!!! Did he really say all that in one sequence?" I thought, as the vision of an egg turning into a fetus and then into a human adult flashed before my eyes.

I noticed that as he spoke about this Chi Gung, he became quite animated, and then I remembered that Angelique had said that he was the one that had put together the concepts of the Eight Point Chi Gung, with a little help from his friends.

Li Tse picked up his staff, looked at it for a moment, then placed it back against the pillar. He then said, "Veronica began to teach you about the mixing of Chi and fluid and how to move this fluid throughout the body to create more Chi. Now we will learn about moving energy to and through the eight points on the movement-body grid.

"Each of the primary meridians is activated by stimulating a point on your wrists/hands or ankles/feet, using a twisting or a flexing motion," he said, twisting his arms and flexing his ankles in undulating motions.

"In acupuncture theory we couple these eight meridians into four pairs. The two points stimulated by the twisting actions of the ankles are paired with two points of flexing action of the wrists. Conversely, the twisting actions of the wrists are paired with the flexing action of the ankles," he said, demonstrating these movements for me as he spoke. "These make four pairs that correspond to the four postures I am about to show you."

"So," he said, grinning and brushing his brow as if to clean off the perspiration gathered there. "That's a quick outline of the major things you've learned so far and what we are about to learn."

"This guy could go on and on without losing focus for a single breath," I realized. I felt like I needed to slow him down so I could ingest it all, so I blurted out, "I remember now that Angelique told me you compiled this Chi Gung with the help of some sky beings. How did you really come up with this?"

He smiled sheepishly and replied, "Yes, I first met my other world friends in the mountains of Mexico where they pointed out the overall direction. Then later in the Peruvian Amazon they helped me to see it even clearer, helping me to flesh out the concepts. After that, my body showed me the rest."

He paused, then continued, "You must realize that movements come to you naturally when you're reading the 'book of the body' every day. If you listen to your body's teachings, you will gently be taught how to remember yourself. And in this way, once I had been pointed in the right direction, knowledge about which movements to do arose from within me. The evolutionary path is there for all of us. It is slowly pulling us towards itself and reveals its presence in the most surprising ways."

"Were these friends real?" I asked, wanting to understand more clearly what his experience had been.

"Very interesting question, Mr. Watson," Li Tse said, stroking his chin and beaming me a smile.

"It is learned behavior which defines for us what is real and what is not. Anything outside of its limited definitions, or outside of its special perceptual cocktail, is brushed aside and discounted. This not only affects the way we look at the world but also the way we interact with others. I can assure you that there are things roaming around out there," he said with an eye roll and warily wobbling his head from side to side, "that do exist and can have an effect on us."

"Are these beings inside of us or outside of us? Are they just apparitions that we see?" I asked intrigued, trying to comprehend his experience so that it might shed some light on some of my own.

"This opens another can of worms," he said with a rolling chuckle. "What is 'internal' and what is 'external'? When we speak of internal energetic movements and feelings, what we are talking about are energetic phenomena that are just on the edge of the purview of learned behavior and beyond. Learned behavior cannot really grasp or qualify these feelings, so they are usually referred to as internal or 'subjective.'

"Along these lines, here is something for you to ponder," Li Tse continued. "When you are dreaming or in a dream—is that internal or external?"

I then watched a smile dawn on Li Tse's face, "What is more 'real'? Twenty-two people you pass in the streets? Or a person that you meet periodically in your dreams? Or someone who occasionally speaks to you through a 'vision'? Ask yourself what has more impact? What is more real?"

Then after a slight pause he went on, "But to get back to your original question—yes, my helpers were very real and affected me profoundly. Helping me as best as they could with my personal evolution.

"Our path talks to us in many ways. Though at first, because of the rigid structure of my learned behavior, I could only accept my friends as mythical beings."

"Do you still talk to them?" I asked fascinated.

He looked at me and replied, "Not really in the same way. They have become more 'internal'", he said, bursting out laughing.

After he had finished reminiscing about his "friends," Li Tse then walked over to a post where there was a chart, a replica of one Angelique had shown me: a diagram of the human body showing the points that activate the primary meridians, the points of Eight Point Chi Gung, the master points for the twisting and flexing of the body. And I was also able to remember from my time with Angelique how each of these meridians and their related master points had an associated Ba Gua. And how each of these Ba Gua were related to a primary force of nature, and that the relationships between the Ba Gua illustrated the way these forces flowed in the world.

Li Tse also had the smaller pictures inserted into the illustration, with the locations of the points on the hands and feet specifically marked.

*Eight Point Chi Gung*

"Bear these points in mind while I show you the next movements. These are the eight points of the body compass through which you can get your internal bearings," he said enigmatically.

He then walked me over to another post where there were a series of four different pictures depicting body postures. He pointed to the first picture:

*Lilies on the Water*

"Start by activating right structure in your body and move into this first posture. Then put your feet/ankles into a pigeon-toed position and let yourself sink into it. Can you feel how this activates the point on your

277

foot as you twist the ankle inwards?" he said, pointing to the diagram of the first posture and the "X" marks on the outsides of the feet.

"The corresponding point of this pairing, the flexing position, is just above the wrists. You can see it marked with an 'O' in the picture. Push down with your palms facing the floor until you feel this point being activated. This particular position of the hands and wrists is sometimes called 'Lilies on the Water' because it looks and can feel like your hands are floating on a pond like lily pads.

"As you do all these postures, you will want to maintain right structure in your body as best you can. Direct your focus to prevent the escape of energy from both the upper or lower openings: by bypassing the 'Four Thieves' of the upper Dan Tien, as we have shown you before, and by bringing the sensation of Chi to the 'Meeting of Yin' point on your perineum. You will find that you can do both actions at the same time."

Li Tse continued, "This will allow the energy to build in your Tai Chi Pole. You can then direct it from there out along the meridian lines. In this way you can hook into the underlying natural rhythms and patterns of flow that your body intuitively knows and begin to move them throughout your body.

"Veronica must have at least introduced you how to create right structure before she showed you how to create and move the energy ball and waves of liquid water pressure throughout the body. So, make sure your body's structure is as compacted as possible. We want to transfer all this connectedness and power from your physical body into your movement-body."

He stopped for a moment to peer at me, making sure I was following, then said, "From the posture I'm showing you right now we want to move our bodies—but keep holding our wrists in this 'Lilies on the Water' position. We want to stimulate these points on our wrists as we move those through as many areas of the movement-body as possible. This will bring the Chi in these two connected meridians out into the movement-body where it will begin to sweep out old cobwebs, combing out the fibers which will enliven the cocoon. At the same time this will further break up the crusts held in your torso."

"I'll take you on a tour of the movement-body in this posture," he said, then began moving.

*Chi residues*

I kept my eyes slightly open while still maintaining the static posture he had left me in. I watched his body undulate, his arms moving from side to side. He then raised his wrists to the level of his diaphragm, then up to shoulder level, while continuing to send waves of energy rippling out through his arms.

After attempting to practice what Veronica had introduced me to, I knew enough body-to-body training to be able to see what Li Tse was trying to show me. I could even see/feel that he was moving the "dough" in his body, even though he was wearing looseflowing clothes. I could make out the water wave moving alternately up from his feet and legs, then through his torso, then out the wrists, and back again, while he consistently kept activating the flexing points on his wrists.

"This reminds me of a Silvio toy that I have not seen yet," I chuckled to myself as I stood there watching him.

Li Tse said, "This can get to be really fun. Can you see the water waves in my body? On the inside it feels like I'm a fish in water, undulating back and forth."

He then stopped his movements and said, "I just completed a circuit of my movement-body in this first posture. The important point in this posture, and in all the others I am going to show you, is to keep the specific points in your wrists/hands activated while you move. Remember, the points in the feet are automatically stimulated because of the initial position you put them in, in this case the pigeon-toed posture in your stance.

"Now I am just trying to show you some more possibilities. You would normally do this for a longer time than I just did, covering as many areas of the movement-body as you can conceive of with this wrist posture, using all the techniques you've learned to send the Chi out into your movement-body."

As we both relaxed, he from his moving and me from my static posture. I asked him, "Why do you do this movement first?"

He replied, "Remember when you studied the Dai or 'belt' meridian with Angelique? This is the only meridian that encircles the body horizontally. We do this posture first to loosen and regulate the movement of energy from top to bottom, adjusting the belt vessel so that Chi can flow properly throughout."

"What do you think of all this?" he then asked, grinning, trying to illicit a question or two from me.

I obliged him by asking something that had been on my mind ever since we started talking about the movement-body, "Can you explain a bit more about what you mean by 'meridians moving' outside the body?"

He smiled in acknowledgement and said, "Something in me always knew that the meridians extend outside of the physical body. It seems so obvious to me now, but it took me a long time to figure it out. It wasn't until I had enough energy to move beyond my learned behavior concepts of the body as an object that I could really understand this. The answer was always right there in front of my nose. I just had to sink down inside myself deep enough to see it."

He then looked at me, and continued, "You understand by now that when your body is connected, and you move your wrists and arms in certain ways this directs the energy flow through your shoulders and hips through the torso along specific channels. When this directed energy moves through the trunk of the body the individual energy lines stimulated affect the inner workings of the organs and bowels along their pathways."

I looked a little perplexed, which made him smile.

Li Tse explained further, "You remember how you learned that by putting your body in certain postures you could stimulate different meridians? Well, then it is easy to understand how each different motion we do within our movement-body triggers a corresponding movement in our torso or physical body, especially if the body is correctly compacted and connected.

"When you extend your limbs, especially your arms, out into the movement-body, then with every turn, twist and flex you are also stimulating points on the meridians within your torso. Each different nuance has a resonating effect in the trunk of the physical body. Essentially because we have a whole energetic replica of our body around us in our movement-body."

I scratched my head, concentrating, before asking, "Is what you're trying to say is that energizing the movement-body can help one to become more whole and experience greater well-being?"

Li Tse nodded in agreement, "That is exactly what I am trying to say! The so-called physical body and the movement-body have a reciprocal relationship."

Before he could say more, another question popped up in my mind related to the exercises he just showed me. I remembered his hands and wrists had been moving, but his feet and ankles didn't move at all. I wondered how the corresponding points in the lower extremities were being activated.

So, I asked, "OK. But what about the legs and ankles? You mentioned that the points there were automatically activated by simply maintaining the posture. You were not moving them at all, so how were they being stimulated?"

"Didn't you see the waves of energy moving through my body?" he replied. "So, didn't Veronica show you her 'dough boy'?" he chuckled, a picture obviously coming to mind.

"By holding your feet and ankles in the correct posture you stimulate the appropriate points and then further energize them by connecting and compacting your body. Then you accentuate that even more by moving the 'dough' from your torso to your ankles and feet and back.

"Later on, you can move your feet and ankles while doing a more complete moving form and even mixing the wrist positions, but first I want to show you this more basic static form so that you can develop a better understanding for some of the applications of our Eight Point Chi Gung."

He briefly checked my level of attention, then continued, "What we essentially have is a whole body in front of us—an energetically connected extension of the meridians of the physical body within the sphere of movement.

"By now you understand how meridians have a flowing aliveness in them that can be felt. Every time we move our bodies, we are stimulating meridians. In addition, you have come to see that each different motion in the movement-body triggers a corresponding motion in our physical body. The movement-body moves in consort with the physical body. They are aligned. They move together. They dance. In the movement-body are all the possibilities of energetic motion that lie latent inside the physical body. It truly is a replica, an alive, human body."

He stopped for a minute, lost in his own reverie, then slowly with tenderness said, "In essence you have another body out there in the energetic fabric of your movement-body which you stimulate as you move your limbs. Becoming aware of this can be similar to the experience of caressing and even merging with another entity.

"Sometimes I even think of it as a lover," he said slowly, "I know I like my moving conversations with it and the way it makes me feel."

Li Tse went on smiling and reflecting for a moment, before continuing, "We are talking about the coalescing of these two bodies, the movement-body and the physical body, by first aligning the Tai Chi Pole correctly, then allowing the energy to flow rhythmically out to the extremities and back again using our Eight Point Chi Gung to give it direction.

"This process helps to unite the 'subtle energy-body' with the physical body and stops the escape of essence. And as you restore your natural energy flow this essence starts to circulate light in your body. This circulation of liquid light helps to engender better health, longevity, and a better understanding of your sexual energy."

He was quiet for a moment, looking wistfully at the trees around him. I stood there considering what he had said before asking, "The physical body and the movement-body are not actually separate at all? Is that what you are getting at?"

"Yeah, fascinating, isn't it?" he said with a twinkle in his eye. "I think it is sinking in a bit more. Let's go on!"

He pointed to the second picture in the series.

*Man holding Trays*

He assumed the posture in the picture and motioned for me to do the same. "Move into this posture with your arms pushing upwards as if they're holding two trays, one out to either side. Your feet should be placed in position as if you're shuffling about like Charlie Chaplin," he chuckled. "Hold this posture while I go through the second part of this form."

He once again began by moving the energy ball in his abdomen from one side to the other, with his hips not moving at all, fixed as if in a sitting position. Next, he brought his hands down to waist level in front of him, palms up, and began to move them, alternating pushing one forward while retracting the other. He initiated these movements from his abdomen, moving the "dough." I could see/feel the energy wave go down to his feet, then bounce back up through his lower abdomen, then out his wrists and then back down again.

I was beginning to understand Silvio's fascination with toys and the body. I was looking at a living moving human body, but the underlying mechanical principles could be seen and understood by using those simple child-like gadgets that these people had introduced me to. This also helped me understand the natural fascination a child would have with these toys. They really depicted actual movements in the body.

I heard Li Tse say, "Remember, it's important to sweep the movement-body by moving the activated points in the wrists through as many positions as possible. Right now, I'm into the 'teacup' routines where we aren't allowed to spill a drop," he said, laughing.

He twisted his right hand beneath his right armpit as if holding a small cup of tea in his palm, then rotated his hand out to the side. He continued the motion upwards over the head reversing the twist, then bringing it back to its original position. He then repeated this motion with the other hand.

*Teacups*

"This is where it starts to get fun," Li Tse said as he started alternatively twisting his "two teacups" at the same time. One hand descended intermittently as the other ascended. Back and forth they went as I watched his body undulate from one side to the other. I was able to see wave after wave of energy moving up and down each side of his body.

"That's really beautiful," I said.

After a few minutes he stopped, then gathered himself. He opened his half-closed eyes fully again and said beaming, "You should feel what it's like on the inside."

I then asked him why this was the second posture of the series. He told me that after opening the body in the first position this was the posture that really activated the energy and moved it around. The next two postures, he went on to say, would be more meditative and could utilize the energy that these first two forms had freed up. He also mentioned that the postures could be done in reverse order when wanting to bring internal energy back out to the physical body.

I registered this information, then told him I had a question. I asked him why he was twisting his arms in this posture when he had previously described the movement of the wrists here as one of flexing and not twisting.

He smiled knowingly and said that even though he was twisting his shoulders and elbows, his wrists were actually being held in a fixed position. "In this way I won't spill even a drop of tea," he chuckled.

He went on, "Veronica must have shown you how you can kink and twist the arms like wringing out a wet towel to create even more pressure in the system. In this case not only do we twist the dough around and push it out to the wrists and hands, but by doing so, and keeping the wrist points in their flexed position, we can stimulate these points even more.

"Incidentally," he went on, "don't forget that the primary flow of energy in the body is from the feet to the trunk and then out the wrists and hands, with which we manipulate the world. The wrists and hands are the places from where the most energy goes out from your body into the physical world, where you grab things from the outside world to bring them into the body sphere, like the people we touch and the food and liquid we imbibe."

He then added, "But even though we keep the wrists flexed, so we can maintain an unimpeded energy flow from the trunk to the wrists, we allow the fingers to stay loose and full of Chi which allows us maximum flexibility in manipulating the world."

I nodded and thought, as I looked down at my hands, "Oh my god, he's right."

When I looked up again, I noticed, not for the first time, the calm and radiance of Li Tse's bearing in the midst of his joking around. It was beginning to dawn on me the major effect of being in his presence, or of learning from him body-to-body as he would say, had on me. I could see how being exposed to his energy had definitely opened me up to new ways of experiencing and being in the world.

I wanted to learn more, so I probed, "In essence, we are cleaning out the fibers in the movement-body and bringing that released energy back to strengthen the physical body?"

He leaned over and picked up a short Thai grass broom and whisked away a few leaves from the floor of his sala as if to refocus.

As he continued sweeping, he then cackled, saying, "Fibers are an energy substance. By breaking the crusts, cleaning the fibers and bringing the released energy back into the body, the being becomes light and pliable. Problems in our physical body are always going to have corresponding entanglements in the movement-body cocoon. By combing out the knots in the fibrous web of energy channels in the movement-body, we help to heal the ailments we may have in the physical body. These movements stimulate the meridians to their natural extension, and that pumps energy through these channels and keeps the Chi in the body flowing. Once the meridians are made fully functional through movement then it is difficult for diseases to take hold in the body.

"So, we need to keep sweeping out those cobwebs in our movement-body," he energetically stated, punctuating that with a couple of sweeps with the broom before putting it back in its place with a flourish.

Suddenly the house cat appeared, gracefully grabbing our attention. Slowly it assessed the situation, moving its head from side to side, acknowledging our presence in its domain. It rubbed against the broom, then looked up appreciatively as Li Tse bent down and stroked it between the ears. It reminded me of being with Li Tse and Hollow Bamboo at the temple when Mr. Hollow had scratched the cat there in a similar way and had said, "For sure, purring is the life-force moving through the body."

"OK, let's get back to the book of the body," Li Tse said as he energetically rubbed his hands together. He then motioned for me to walk over with him to get a closer look at the picture of the third posture.

*Phoenix Feather Fingers*

He reminded me that the first posture was to loosen and free up the energy, and the second was to mobilize it, and that the next two positions were much more meditative.

"Place one foot in front of the other, as illustrated in the picture, the palm twisted in, stimulating the outer part of the hand in such a way that it would open up the back of your body."

I remembered that putting my hands/wrists in this position was how Angelique had taught me to open the 'Governor Vessel' meridian that moves up the outer part of the spine.

"We will also be activating the 'Yang heel meridians' with our foot postures," he said. "These points below the little fingers on the outside of the hands and below the ankles on the outside of the feet will do the trick," he went on, referring to the points in the picture. "The twisting point on the hand is marked by an 'X,' and the flexing point on the heel is marked by an 'O.' See that?"

He then began rocking back and forth, shifting his weight from his front foot to his back foot. When his weight was back, he would raise the ball of his front foot. While when his weight shifted to the front foot, he would raise the heel of his back foot. Li Tse then gestured for me to follow. He assured me that this movement provided a wonderful way for stimulating the heel vessels.

After getting used to this slow rocking motion, he had me focus on twisting my wrists to stimulate the points on the outside of my hands so that I could feel my Governor vessel along the length of my spine.

"Let's keep this simple so you can get a feeling for this posture," he said.

Li Tse began making huge circles, rotating his arms in unison, holding his wrists twisted outwards, keeping the points there stimulated as he slowly shifted his weight from his front foot to his back foot.

He explained that through these motions we would be able to scrape the cobwebs off the outermost edges of the movement-body. This particular posture, because of its meditative nature, was a good one for opening the "The Doorway to the Ancestors" in the upper Dan Tien—by focusing on the sensation of Chi at the nostrils, directing the eye sense and ear sense inwards and putting the tongue gently on the upper palate.

Li Tse continued, saying, "This and the next movement sequence bring the energy up from the 'Bubbling Spring' point at the sole of the foot to the ankles where both the 'Yin and Yang heel meridians' connect internally to the upper Dan Tien, connecting the essence of Earth and Water with the center of the brain. As I said earlier, stimulating these meridians can help to neutralize the 'Four Thieves' and open the Tai Chi Pole, thus establishing a good connection with your movement-body.

"Using this posture we can clean the outer edges of the cocoon," he reiterated as he continued moving slowly back and forth, making huge circles with his arms. "Make sure as you do this you maintain the wrists twisted outward and keep the two points you see on the chart activated."

He then pointed at the picture of the fourth posture.

*White Ape Offers Fruit*

"One minute," I said, raising my hand with a smile, "How does right structure fit in with Eight Point Chi Gung?"

"Hmmm," he mused. "As you know by now, one way to move outside of learned behavior is to move outside of its habitual movement patterns and the muscle configurations that support it. There is a difference between maintaining a posture in the movement-body by moving the muscles and moving into and through that position with right structure. The latter allows the feeling of Chi and fluidity to permeate the movement.

"So, in essence, right structure overlays the Eight Point Chi Gung. That is why we taught you right structure first. All of our postures are done while maintaining right structure. The Eight Point Chi Gung is an efficient way of spreading out the energy after you have embodied it, thus establishing an efficient gravitational structure that supports maximum Chi-flow.

"We shift from the continued overuse of the muscle patterns instilled in us by learned behavior to a way of moving and being in the world that helps to recuperate our wholeness. This is good for an old man like me for it gives me a whole new way to be. We have to become more efficient with energy as we grow older, you know," he said with a twinkle in his eye.

"OK, let's get on with the last posture. It has the same leg position as the previous one, but for a change put your other foot forward," he instructed.

He then directed me into the same rocking motion as before, first raising the ball of my front foot when my weight was on my back foot, and then raising my back heel when my weight was on my front foot.

Pointing with his chin to the picture, he then said, "Now, as you continue shifting your weight back and forth, twist your wrists outwards in front of you with your thumbs out. This posture comes from a healing/martial arts tradition and is called 'White Ape offers Fruit' or sometimes 'White Ape offers Tea.' These types of metaphors can be helpful reminders and stimulate associations as you go through the various movements."

After we had been moving repetitively for a while he began to speak, his voice becoming soft and hypnotic:

> *The primary pulsing of life,*
> *moving fluid in the heart.*
> *Feeling of clear water*
> *sliding over smooth rocks,*
> *Air caressing a flame,*
> *the curve in a river,*
> *A gentle breeze flowing off the lake.*
>
> *The friction between the elements,*
> *Here is where life begins.*

After a bit we stopped to drink some water and relax and to take in the world around us.

I then asked Li Tse about the benefits of combing out and enlivening the fibers of the movement-body that we were doing with this sequence Eight Point Chi Gung.

He responded in a very interesting way, "Living life is an art, a moving art. The way this art is breaking down the crusts of objectivity—the way we freeze life by freezing the image of our bodies. And de-charging the story of who we are taught to be. We need to loosen the moorings of learned behavior and allow it to flow freely in the currents of life."

Li Tse said that the Chinese had associated each of the eight extra meridians and their associated cardinal points of our moving body compass to the eight Ba Gua symbols. He then explained, "These are the points we activate in our Eight Point Chi Gung." And then asked, "Have you noticed in some of our drawings that each hand/wrist and foot/ankle position and its associated meridian always has a corresponding Ba Gua symbol attached to it?"

He went on to say that in the Chinese system these same eight trigrams of Ba Gua were also used in Feng Shui, the Chinese art of placement. In Feng Shui they are used to represent the eight cardinal points of our personal compass, like career, health, wealth, and intimate relationships—or the basic eight coordinates of our being.

"If we put these two systems of correspondence together, it gives us a way to see how bringing the sensation of Chi to the eight primary meridians will be reflected out into the related areas of our lives. This is one way we can see and experience how doing Eight Point Chi Gung would begin to affect our story and begin to liberate us from the pressures of the learned behavior around us. We can better understand how there begins to be less friction, which allows for more contact with the outside world, as we enliven the eight points of our internal movement compass with the sensation of Chi. Even to the point that we, or at least our learned behavior, can become invisible," he said with a chuckle.

Li Tse went on, "Looking at it in this way we can see that cleaning the movement-body with the Eight Point Chi Gung is a form of psychic self-defense, protecting us from, and moving us through the onslaughts of learned behavior embodied around us.

"For example, when we are not interested in participating in the same dramas as others there is less for the learned behavior coming from them to grab onto. We don't give out the same energy that we once did to be reflected back. Spreading the Chi throughout the meridians recharges the body with internal pressure and makes rough patches in our life, and accidents less likely to happen. We become less tempting morsels for our own and other people's learned behavior and in general much less susceptible to the overall imbalanced forces that we are exposed to in our world."

Li Tse paused, slowly sweeping his eyes from side to side, taking in the scene around him. While he did this, an image of a many-armed Hindu deity came to my mind, dancing the dance of life.

"You know," I said, "seeing you move through these postures, seeing them in motion, and taking my mind out of its fixed frame way of seeing the body, the many armed figures I see in Buddhist and Hindu iconography pop into my mind."

He peered at me for a few seconds then smiled, saying, "Very good, my friend. One of the major concepts that is being transmitted through those images is the power of the movement-body. I think that in fact those ancient peoples were depicting the movement-body. And that the postures and symbolic objects that they hold represent the powers that those particular positions have on and in the body and the reflected world around us.

"But of course, you have to consider that over time some of the direct transmissions of these images may have been changed due to artistic license and a little learned behavior co-opting," Li Tse chuckled.

He then stretched his hands high above his head, then spreading them as far out as they would go to his sides in an expansive gesture said, "We live in a world of Chi. When it swirls together it creates a feeling composed of all the senses in just the right order, in perfect proportion.

"As it begins to coalesce from the bliss of the clear light of awareness you want to fill your body with it. As your life becomes more and more united with the Chi-flow and life itself, the spiral of your path grows ever tighter and tighter.

"And what is this life-force?" Li Tse stopped for a moment, looking at me once again, taking in all that was around him. "It is a feeling that encompasses everything. Life is a feeling. It is the root of all our feelings. It is the song of the Earth."

He went on, "How can we be with this feeling while walking around in this world? How can we feel it sparkle out of our eyes? Hear it in the wind? Smell it in the air? Taste it when we eat? And feel it ooze out of our pores?

"What we are really trying to do is to merge with the stream or feeling of life all around us. We want to keep de-charging learned behavior so we can accumulate enough energy to ride the currents of life. To bring what we know to be ourselves out into the world. To merge with the ever-undulating motion of the universe. We literally want to embody it. It is what we really are. Everything is in motion and alive with motion. Riding on currents of life is like riding on the back of a beast."

As if on cue, I heard the roar of a motorcycle and turned to see Silvio showing up on a 650 Kawasaki. He stopped, smiled and pointed to a powerful beast lurking inside Li Tse's garage, motioning for me to get on.

After I walked over to it and mounted the beast, Li Tse's silver cycle, another Kawasaki, Silvio looked at me, grinning and said, "Get on it and ride! Ride on the currents of life!"

Li Tse grabbed his staff, beaming and waving as we were pulling away, "Rip through the veneers of learned behavior that cover you. Experience total body awareness, allow yourself to embody it. Then take it for a ride. Take a ride with the rain on your face and the wind in your hair. Enjoy being alive and the awareness of being aware."

Chapter 18

# SILVIO—PATH OF THE HEALER

I found myself walking on a dirt track headed to Silvio's house. I had never been there, and I was touched with anticipation. I really wanted to see where this guy lived. It felt good walking as I drank in the sweet, scented smell of the young green rice all around me. I heard the birds chirping, their songs sounded through the still air, and I noticed the whorls and patterns of their slipstreams as they flew by.

As I thought about what a gift living in Thailand had been for me, a sense of well-being filled me with gratitude. Life: the place is pulsing with it, on the streets wherever I go—so many young people—the food—and the smiles, "that secret Thai anti-depressant," I chuckled to myself. "Just try to stay depressed in Thailand when you get smitten by those smiles."

Being here with the Thais had transformed my life. For starters, the way they think and how they move differently had given me a small break from my Western learned behavior. This was especially true since my Thai language skills were limited and most of the time, I did not understand what they were talking about or at least I could turn it off easily. My spirit had basked in this little slice of freedom.

As I continued walking, a scene arose in my mind's eye of monks in their saffron robes, barefooted. A line of them with their huge bowls, receiving alms from the people. This ritual was enacted each day in the early morning hours, long before the common tourist woke for breakfast. It is a strong thread that underlies all Thai culture.

I watched as the villagers *wai*-ed and bowed to the monks and then placed food and other offerings in their bowls. They were expressing their respect and awe to the monks' practice—as an embodiment of the stream of realization.

Thailand was one of the few Buddhist countries in the world, and within its culture the life of the renunciate had value. This was a culture within which the practice of withdrawing from the pressures of day-to-day life to explore one's inner nature is alive and revered. I was glad that this tradition of self-cultivation was still alive enough to be felt as this palpable tradition had offered me a welcome opportunity for the type of internal exploration I liked to do.

Here I experienced a special freedom of not being confronted daily by the cultural collusion that I had grown up in. The judgments that underlie my early training and that would normally be reflected back to me by the learned behavior around me were significantly juxtaposed and short-circuited just by being here.

"Ahh, Thailand!"—it was special.

The fabric of Thai culture contains a certain kind of reverence that permeates every single moment. Partially molded by its warm subtropical climate, time slows down. Thai everyday life provides a profusion of life in the streets of ever-changing overflowing abundance; a vibrant, subtly-surreal collage of colors, smiles, and sounds.

Coming back from my reveries, and feeling the muscles in my legs, and my feet touching the Earth, I neared the gate to Silvio's abode. I could make out a couple of different separated buildings partially concealed beneath huge trees. His place seemed to radiate a special energy like a hidden treasure appearing out of the surrounding lush green rice fields. I also noticed the clouds and mist feathering the green-blue mountains in the distance. It was all so alive. There was even a large pond to swim in, with a floating bamboo platform.

As I opened the gate, I moved into the presence of old *lamyai* trees and basked in the energy provided by their moving shade. It brought to mind something that a teacher of mine had once told me, that "the trees are the soldiers of the world. Where there are trees there is life."

Off to my left I noticed a single water buffalo in one of the neighboring rice paddies. It was knee deep in water. It had a white egret on its back. A little dazed from the sight, but not quite sure why, I was drawn to a structure on my right-hand side. I knocked on the open door that I saw in front of me. Not receiving an answer but knowing I was expected, I walked in.

Walking in, and already feeling a little overwhelmed, my memory began doing a kaleidoscopic shuffle—déjà vu. The past. The future. I was there and not there. Meandering memories put time and place together in a different way. Out of this vortex of experiences a reassembling and reshuffling of forgotten feelings arose and faded repeatedly. Objects appeared with renewed undulating focus, as I remembered I had been here before.

Within this sense of disorientation and dislocation, I remembered my dream in Phuket with its colors, sounds, and feelings.

It seemed so long ago.

I slowly began to take in what was around me. It appeared to be Silvio's workshop. In a corner of the room, I made out an incomprehensible cornucopia of musical instruments—bagpipes, marimbas, gongs, cymbals, flutes, a gamelan, singing bowls and drums of all description.

Still partially in my déjà vu, I felt like I could still hear the haunting sound of bagpipes in the distance from my dream.

I saw acupuncture paraphernalia, needles, and an herbal cabinet with Chinese characters next to Tibetan thangka paintings, cloth talismans—gold on maroon, ancient Buddhist scripts with magical geometric patterns, old tattered and frayed astrological charts with pictures of demigods, bundles of bamboo tablets inscribed in Pali—the language of the Buddha.

On a worktable, amidst the chaos of detached wooden limbs and body parts accompanied by some strange looking tools, I saw a variety of mechanical toys and puppets in various stages of disrepair.

Alongside these there was a human skeleton next to a stacked array of gears, winches and pulleys.

I felt as if I were in a toy maker's workshop and smiled as I began to get a sense why Li Tse affectionately referred to Silvio as "the toy maker". It then became clear to me how the way the human body moved would inspire toys.

After once again getting my bearings and settling back into myself, I happened to look out one of the windows to see Silvio under the trees. He was flowing through sequences of movements that were nothing like what I had been introduced to before, although I could identify some elements and principles of body mechanics underlying his postures.

He went on for a little while then stopped, smiling shyly, acknowledging my presence in his workshop. Then he looked at me with his eyes on high beam and his signature smile. He then walked towards the workshop with a bouncing exaggerated stride.

I had hardly time to notice the acupuncture needles in his face as he appeared in the doorway, opened his arms and bowed slightly, and said, "Welcome to my world!"

I was very glad to see him, but before I could tell him that I blurted out in surprise, "You have needles in your face? You leave those needles in when you do your Chi Gung?"

He laughed and said, "You should see what else I do."

And then mysteriously continued, "Using needles while standing and moving is a way to direct the Chi-flow created from gravitational alignment. We use everything at our disposal, anything available to help us evolve."

He smiled and said, "We are hunters, looking for energy wherever we can find it."

"Tell me more about this," I said.

Silvio went over to a counter and took the needles out of his face before responding, "This is just part of my latest exploration. I simply cannot stop reading this book of body navigation. It has so many different chapters and pages, intertwined plots and subplots," he grinned.

"When we begin to break the bonds of learned behavior, we contact more energy, and then we have to train ourselves how to store it and use it."

He motioned for me to come and sit with him in some soft-cushioned chairs in the middle of the room. I went over and as I was sitting down, I noticed that this part of the workshop seemed to have a feminine touch. It had never occurred to me that Silvio might have a lover. Being around him had always been so overwhelming that I somehow had only been able see him as a teacher and friend, but not as man filled with a living passion for life. So, I asked him about that.

"That is another story in the Naked City we are not going to get into just yet," Silvio responded with a wink and a smile.

"OK then, can you give me an example of what you were just talking about—the many chapters of the book of the body?" I inquired.

He winked again at me and said, "What I am getting at is that we use anything that works, anything that we can get energy from, and any system that enables us to understand and enhance the use of our energy. This includes for example things like movement practices, breathing, sexual yoga, Chi Gung, and acupuncture. And also, more internal practices like meditation, inner alchemy, even psychology with the right focus. Any way or discipline that can make us become more efficient with our body energy and enhance our evolutionary path."

"OK", I said, "but what's all this?" I asked, smiling, pointing at the pile of dolls and toys in different states of disrepair. At last, I had a chance to learn more from "the toy maker" about his toys.

"I see you noticed my friends," he replied. "The body is so difficult to talk about, so I have my toy cohorts to help me," he said, beaming.

"There are so many ways to make a toy and so many ways to talk about the body. I have found that it is helpful to see or imagine our bodies as a strange combination of mechanical principles that I can show and explain with my toys and props."

He got up and went over to one of the workbenches and picked up a couple of gears with one hand and a pulley with the other. Grabbing them and dangling them in front of me, he laughingly, said, "This is how the body works."

Some blue-yellow embroidery caught my eye. I saw a puppet hanging above me next to the face of a tortured demon, white fangs flashing. And

I chuckled, thinking about Silvio's universe. As I continued turning my head my eyes made out a colorful painting on the wall. It featured a group of people with two people prominently in the foreground—figures confined in structures, people appearing to be frozen inside colorful cubes.

"This is an interesting picture, Silvio. What's this all about?" I asked.

He replied, "Cubes, frozen cubes—I use this to remind myself of the ways learned behavior has set people up to relate to each other through interlocking cubes of pressure and how our movements and rhythmic patterns are locked into place through the force fields that it creates around us.

"I sometimes like to look at it before I teach my students because it reminds me of how pressure from the outside, like social pressures, will flow along the usual lines given to us by learned behavior. And it reminds me that the real teaching is about dissolving these cubes of pressure with our practices, so that we can feel more complete and have less need of the collusion to feel the way that was taught to us by learned behavior."

I then noticed some deer horn knives, swords, ninja stars, some short staffs, and other martial arts equipment over in an alcove. It brought to mind a question I wanted to ask Silvio when I had seen him practicing his form outside, "What kind of movement were you doing out there under the trees?"

"Right now, I was doing a moving Eight Point Chi Gung sequence. It is more or less a free form incorporating the principles of body mechanics that I know. At the same time, it is loose enough to give my body the opportunity to teach me something—if it chooses to. A form after all is just a vehicle for moving realizations into the body and storing them there. And our Chi Gung can create a stable base for that."

He came back and sat once again in his chair.

Looking at him I asked, "Silvio, your universe is fascinating. How did you get into all these different things?"

He relaxed into the cushions of his chair and said, "So you want to know my story?"

He grinned from ear to ear. "Well, I will tell you one version.

He closed his eyes for a bit, before slowly opening them, "I grew up in the dynamic, surrealistic landscape of Mexico, a land of volcanoes, lakes, oceans and jungles. A vibrant and violent land where Christianity has overlaid the native Indian beliefs and traditions with its own ways."

He paused, then continued, "Once, when I was a small child, my mother was sick and since the Western medicine she had been prescribed wasn't working she sought out a local healer for advice and treatment. While there the *curandera* took me aside and looked me over, then came close and poked my little body a few times. She then turned to my mother and said, 'Uh, this little guy is not well. But don't panic. I can see that he has *something*.' Her lined face moved into a smile and with a twinkle in her eyes, she added, 'I'd like to give him my blessing.'

"My mother returned her smile and nodded in ascent. The healer then put her hand on my head in concentration for a few minutes murmuring incantations. I thought nothing of it. But a few months later I started noticing little things that I never had experienced before—like spirits in the forests who wanted to talk to me. I also noticed a newfound fascination for the plants around me.

"I now understand that she had 'touched' my body with her body and in this way had opened me in a special way. This 'touching' had transferred to me, in a strange way, the ability to experience and perceive the world in the exceptional way that she did."

Silvio again paused in reflection, before going on, "Throughout the next few years intermittently I had more of these kinds of experiences. Something was growing inside me.

Then my life took a tumultuous turn when the sexual energies started to be activated in my body. I really wasn't sure what to do or where to go. Luckily, I found a cohort, bonding with a childhood friend of mine who was going through similar experiences. Fortuitously we were drawn to a physical practice, a local karate school. I know now that what I was being taught there was very rudimentary in terms of martial arts. But it definitely served its purpose at that time—to ground our energies down some and to give us a sense of purpose," he chuckled softly.

"During that time, I was also 'accidentally' led to visit some of the mushroom shamans in the mountains.

I soon found myself apprenticed to one of them and immersed in their world. It was an animistic world of spirits, evil eyes, and personal vendettas overlaid with Jesus, Mary, and The Holy Spirit.

"Looking back, I can understand the role of these shamans and the way they used their sacred mushrooms—'footprints of the gods', as they called them. They were providing a service to their community, by administering individual healing and treatments that somehow helped to give a cohesiveness to the internal fabric of their society. High in the mountains people would come from miles around throughout the night. Sometimes it seemed as if the trails to my shaman's house were swarming with them.

"During our inspired exalted states that we were able to attain while under the influence of 'the footprints of the gods,' it felt as if we were actually involved in a type of divine intervention. In one of our healing sessions, I had a vision where I became aware of a power that somehow had been guiding me, had been leading me along a path—from meeting the healer, to martial arts, and to the shaman I was studying with. It awakened wisps of deep memories of the evolving forces working through and around me. What I can understand from the perspective that I have now was that I was sensing the spiral-like current that was my 'path' moving through my life."

Silvio continued, "It was after that experience that I made the decision, perhaps on an unconscious level, to allow this force to give my life meaning. As a result, I decided to go out into nature and live alone to figure out the confusion and pain I was feeling. I felt like I needed to know what I should do next and how to deal with the bursts of energy that were overwhelming me at that time to the point of sometimes making me physically weak.

"It was a difficult time. I had to begin to learn to nurture myself. But it gave me opportunity to become more aware of and evolve along my path. It was then that I began to study herbs and tried to talk to plants. I somehow understood that it was the next step along my path. I could see how my training with shamans and mushrooms had opened me to the world of plants. It was a quite illuminating experience as the plant and animal spirits of the forest began teaching me about themselves and the energy centers in the human body. When I finally left the forest, it was with a sense of purpose."

Silvio went on, "Then I began wandering for a bit. And at one point, on the outskirts of a small town under a big tree, I saw a middle-aged man looking at me. I had that eerie sensation as though I had met him before. When he caught my eye, he waved me over. We sat down and began to talk, and I found out that he was into acupuncture. He took me into his home where I stayed for some time. There I studied with him the Chinese medical model which opened a whole new world for me, where all my feelings and emotions and illnesses were at least accounted for.

"He also introduced me to Chinese herbology, which I studied enthusiastically, wanting to know more about my plant friends. But, after a while, these studies began to disappoint me. I was studying what had been written down for hundreds of years. I found these writings both extensive and informative, but on the other hand they had lost the spirit of the plants that I had tapped into naturally in the forest. I opened my heart to my teacher and shared my disappointment and doubts. I can remember his face, nodding at me knowingly and then recommending that I should go to the Amazon where a living plant science still existed."

He paused, then said, "And that's just what I did. I went to the Peruvian Amazon, and there synchronistically I found an *ayahuasca* master and healer. With him I learned about the ten master plants and the spirits of the others. I was literally plunged into a world of talking to plants, animal spirits and the overall cosmology of their 'science' when I watched my teacher work.

"He would take 'the medicine' before a client would come to him to be healed. When the client presented himself in front of him, he would begin to sing. He would call in all the healing plants that he knew might be appropriate for this client's condition, to communicate with them. He described it to me as a long hallway through which he walked where the spirits of the plants would line up. The ones that were appropriate for a cure would talk to him."

"*Singing?*" I asked. "*Talking to plants?*"

"I asked my teacher exactly that," Silvio replied.

"At first, he was amused, but when he understood that my question was serious, he told me that if I were to listen closely in the evening I would discover, as he had, that everything sings. The frogs sing, the insects sing, the birds sing, and even the snakes and crocodiles sing. He added that when we humans sing through our song, we can re-establish a vibrant connection with the universe and bring this back to the people.

"One night after taking 'the medicine' we were listening to the songs of the stars together. My teacher looked at me and said, 'Taking the medicine is wonderful, but taking the medicine with friends is truly magical. Sharing this magical universe that is so very much alive with others is one of the best feelings there is.'

"On another night I wandered off into the jungle alone. Because of my heightened sensitivity I could feel many energies moving around me. They enticed me into movements. As I slowly walked, then paused, then moved again, I began recalling my old martial arts movements and I could begin to understand how certain movements stimulated certain acupuncture meridian lines. There was a wonderful feeling of realization, a feeling of things coming together."

Silvio cleared his voice, then said, "After spending a few months immersed in that transformative world, I returned to Mexico, where I was drawn to study Buddhism. This brought me to Vipassana meditation, the path of *Theravada*, the path of the 'Elder Brothers'. And it was during this time that I met Li Tse, who was very much into Buddhist thought and meditation, having studied both the *Sutrayana* and *Tantrayana* paths. He had also spent some time in India and was well-versed in Taoist thought and practice. In addition, he had trained in some internal Chinese martial arts and practiced Chi Gung. And with that we're back to Chi Gung again, eh," he said, smiling.

He then looked over at me and said, "That's one description of the footprints of my path."

Silvio continued, "After I met Li Tse, my life really changed. I finally found someone with whom to deeply delve into the explorations of body-to-body communication. Maybe it was because of the synchronicity of our past training, but our paths were able to merge and evolve together. By spending time together there in Mexico, not only did we verbally share our knowledge, but our bodies talked—transferring the knowledge that each of our bodies carried to each other. It felt like a transmission of vital and natural body-knowledge, link by link, that connected us back to our sources in the depth of time. This knowledge poured out from each of us and mixed into something greater."

Silvio, it seemed, was enjoying listening to the sound of the words flowing out of his body, and so delightfully went on talking, "If you are fortunate this special type of communication can sometimes last for long periods of time. This can happen with the closely-knit relationship of teacher and student and sometimes amongst friends like Li Tse and myself. You can form a communal cocoon that raises and sustains the vibrational level of both people and moves you collectively away from learned behavior for much longer periods of time than you could on your own."

After some moments of silence, Silvio began speaking again, "It's like the picture you noticed earlier. That one of the people held in the cubes of colors," he said, pointing back at the picture. "Those interdependent squares that both mold people and hold them back from their true nature. When we can creatively loosen up our learned behavior it allows for a freer flow of energy.

"We are like this caterpillar, inside," he went on, slightly closing his eyes and allowing his hands to undulate forwards and back, his fingers moving as if he were playing a harp in front of him. "You're weaving this cocoon. But when you share these states with others it can increase the personal weavings in each of you. These shared states are part of the path of evolution. This is a special way that we can continue to weave our cocoons with strands and knowledge and realization while with others."

As I heard Silvio's words, I reflected on my own past.

"Oh yes," I thought, "This has happened to me many times. Walking with a friend and feeling energies merging for short periods of time."

And I realized that it even used to happen in my clinic back in the US.

I understood now how the placement of needles in my patients had been a way that I had unconsciously used to establish a field within which to merge our energetic bodies. This had created a framework for a kind of communication which not only allowed me to establish greater body-to-body contact with them, but also allowed the needle patterns that I had inserted in them to work at a deeper level.

Silvio's voice brought me back into his workshop, "Remember that picture with those people in their cubes," he said. "This is the state we will revert to if realizations are not grounded down and stored in the body, or if another special person is missing to sustain and stabilize that higher vibrational state."

I quickly now realized part of the frustration that I had felt when I had taken the needles out of my patients and then when they left my clinic. I could now see what had happened to them the moment they got off the treatment table and placed their feet on the ground. They began once again calling in the walking and moving patterns of their old, learned behavior in anticipation of meeting the learned behavior patterns of their world that was about to come at them from all sides when they left my clinic.

I liked this feeling of being with Silvio. I felt somehow light, liberated and somewhat expanded. As I looked around his workshop with renewed focus, I noticed the acupuncture paraphernalia, the skeleton, some anatomy books, and a medical dictionary on his bookshelves.

And I finally asked him, "When were you drawn into this healing path, Silvio? What did it feel like from the inside?"

He once again moved his eyebrows up and down, smiling, and then punctuating his first few words by waving his index finger, "First, let me make it clear that there is my personal 'path' upon which I tread, or better yet: an impersonal force that is pushing and guiding me through life. And that then there is the generalized path of the healer with which this personal path of mine merged."

He paused, reflecting, before continuing, "As I look back now and detect that spiral-like path that has been moving through my life, I understand that it has been directing and pushing me towards healing.

"This is what I was trying to describe to you when I told you that version of my life story, the series of events unfolding along my specific path: my early years of ill health as a child and the empowerment by the curandera. The initial introduction to mushrooms and sacred rituals by the local shamans. Then being alone in the forest and discovering the richness and aliveness of nature. And the attraction to acupuncture and Chinese herbology. Being in the Amazon and conversing with the plant and animal spirits. The way in which I was called to and studied Buddhism and meditation. And finally meeting Li Tse.

"This was my tale of synchronicity that linked my personal path to the broad framework of the path of the healer."

"Silvio, can you tell me more about this path of the healer?" I asked fascinated.

He smiled and looked up to the rafters of his workshop, focusing on his collection of dangling Burmese puppets, then looked at me for a bit before he proceeded, "The path of the healer comes with a different frame of reference than other paths. It is dedicated to studying and exploring how the life-force moves and functions in the body and how to maximize the efficiency of that movement. And if it is followed to its logical end, it leads one to not only the study of how energy manifests and moves, but ultimately to the study of where energy comes from.

"A big advantage of being on the healing path is that you become more versed in reading the book of the body than you would on some other paths. When healing becomes part of your path of evolution, you begin to look at the incorporation of all the forces in the body and their relation to the healing-body template.

"Healing is about understanding how the body processes work and helping them work more efficiently and then getting out of the way.

"In other words, the path of the healer enables you to see the workings of the body from an energetic perspective. You learn to see the subtle-body sheaths as different energetic layers on which the body operates. And you study how to unify these layers with the essential energy emanating from the Tai Chi Pole.

"The advantage of the path of healing for me personally was that it gave me a certain kind of awareness—an overview and a sense of direction and an understanding that allowed me to look at and streamline the path of re-integration. Through the path of healing, you can begin to see and understand what's right and what's wrong with the internal relationships within your body, as well as in the bodies of others," he said.

"And getting healthier and more vital is an important ingredient in weaving our cocoon," he exclaimed.

"So, overall," I said, "What you are saying is that from the point of view of the path of the healer, you will be led to follow the life-force back to its origin?"

"Yep," Silvio responded with a grin, "And in addition to that, the perspective that you gain along this path about the workings of energy in the body can come in handy when you move into the deeper levels of integration and seek to create a system of grounding and storing the energy of realization in the body."

In a more pensive mood he continued, "I want to remind you that the root source for most of our illnesses is learned behavior and the constraints and deformations it imposes on our natural evolution. The path of healing can help you begin to break away from these debilitating patterns of learned behavior and instead develop a healthy and natural method to ground the flow of energy in your body.

"And if you follow this path to its natural end, you will incrementally merge with the stream of realization. You will be involved in evolution through healing. The urge to heal and the urge to realize will become one.

"Also, a wonderful side effect of this path is that it can provide you with a helpful way of relating to others. This not only helps one by giving one a way to relate, but since we are in this world only for a very brief period of time, it allows us to also help and enable other people to live their lives in a healthier and longer fashion so that they have more and better chances of evolving."

Silvio stopped talking and went over to his bookshelf, scratching his chin and letting his fingers dance over some of the spines of his books.

"There it is," he finally exclaimed and pulled out a worn brownish-looking tome and slapped it down in front of me. He pointed at it and said, "I kept this book because I really liked the title: Where Energy and Health Come From."

With a smile I uttered, "Um, I like that title too, Silvio. So where is it coming from?"

"Ahh", he said, smiling, "Healing is the study of energy. A healer studies the nature and functioning of movement—Chi. What is it? Where does it come from? To really follow the path of the healer is to follow the life-force to its source and that ultimately leads you to studying the nature of reality itself."

Silvio peered at me, then after taking a dramatic pause raised his index finger and said, "Following energy back to its source is the natural predilection of a healer. But not only that, the path of the healer can also help you to understand how to bring that energy from its source back out into the world and beyond," Silvio said as he affectionately picked up one of his mechanical toys to play with it.

"OK, Silvio, you sold me: I'll take three. Is there any downside to this path of the healer as you call it?" I intervened.

He turned with a solemn and grim face, just hiding a smile, "The downside that most healers get caught in is using healing methods only to prop people up, returning them back to their lives, even more attached to their old, learned behavior patterns than before. And an even bigger downside, with respect to the healer, is that it is very easy to slip into superior/inferior patterns that strengthen their own patterns of learned behavior."

He reiterated, "The important thing is correctly directed focus. Instead of focusing on how to get rid of symptoms to better function in society, you change your focus to understanding how to use symptoms of ill health as steppingstones on the path of personal evolution."

I stood up and walked over to a counter that was filled with acupuncture paraphernalia—needles in different lengths and sizes, small needle hammers, three-edged needles for bleeding, one or two gold needles, glass cups, and moxa used for cauterization. This cornucopia brought to mind the whole intricate, ancient universe of understanding within Chinese body-knowledge.

"I see you have all these acupuncture paraphernalia around, and that you had needles in your face when I saw you doing your Chi Gung form. Do you still have a regular acupuncture practice?" I asked.

Silvio replied, "In days gone by I did. But as my focus evolved it became harder and harder. I felt my interest evaporate. Putting people back together only to function better within their old patterns of learned behavior did not feel good enough anymore. I was very disappointed by my experience with patients who would get better lying on the healing table, but then would get up on their feet and go right back to their same old lives and movement patterns.

"I realized that acupuncture used only in this limited way did not really help people all that much. And of course, as I mentioned, I was very suspicious of how my own learned behavior might be using the role of being a healer to sustain itself."

"So then how do you acupuncture nowadays?" I asked.

He replied, "I use it to give the being a jump start into what it already knows. For example, even before your body can embrace and understand right structure you can enliven those points along that framework, and that begins to accentuate that knowledge in your body. This is one way acupuncture can be used to stimulate your attraction to your path. And if you include acupuncture with Chi Gung, you can also get added benefit," he said, tapping his face to remind me of the needles he had in place when I first arrived.

"Remember, we need to use everything at our disposal to understand and use energy—Chi. Personally, if I did not have acupuncture as one of my foundations, I think I would be wandering around lost and in disarray. When I first was introduced to acupuncture, I could not conceive of the fact that it would later prove to be such a strong cornerstone of my own personal path."

He then reflected a bit before saying, "Doing Chi Gung every day has also provided me with a very valuable tool. It can provide an evolving stable platform for your health and well-being."

As I sat there with him surrounded by the many facets of his life, I once again appreciated the fact that I had been lucky enough to meet this unique and wonderful human being.

Silvio went on, "Life is an ever-unfolding experience and so should your practice be. As you become more aware of the unfolding of your personal path and its spiral-like nature through time you'll need to create your own system which best reflects it. You need to develop a personal system whereby you give your body the best chance to unwind itself and talk to you. What we each do will have to do with our own predispositions, past exposures and past experiences. You can go to other people to get information, but ultimately it is you who has to figure out who or what you really are."

With a wide grin he added, "For me it was a long process but I slowly understood that there was no hope of anybody else doing my work for me and so I had to give that up. When I finally came to terms with that it changed my life.

"The process is an internal one. I realized that all I have is my path— one foot after the other.

Sometimes not even knowing where the next foot will land, where the next sparks of truth will come from. Sparks of truth come to us from different sources, places, people—even dimensions. We each have our own path that we can feel spiraling through our individual lives."

I looked around the workshop and I saw reflections of his shifting focus and passions through time, the many ways that his path had reached out and hooked him. With all that knowledge that he acquired at his disposal—how had he put it all together, weave it into some kind of path? Looking at all this disparate stuff I felt overwhelmed. And I asked, as I gestured at all the stuff around us, "Silvio, how did you weave all these strands together?"

"Trust yourself and things will hit you, things will come to you," he said, as he gently slapped the side of his face. "And you will make sense of it. You never know where the next steppingstone will come from.

"What you're looking at around me," he said, turning his head from one side to the other and then rolling his eyes to encompass everything in his workshop with a grin, "is an assortment of 'my little caches,' my secret tools given to me by my path. They are here to help me, to reach out to me the very moment I find myself falling off the edge.

"Consciousness is always re-patterning itself and the next answer may come from any of these," he said, beaming, while slowly looking around again, pointing with his chin at the collage that was his workshop.

"Sometimes an answer will come from Chi Gung movements, sometimes the answer will be supplied by herbs, sometimes it'll arise from acupuncture, sometimes from my books. You never know from where the next step of your path will arise; or from whom the next realization for the weaving of your cocoon will come from. But you develop a sense of it and the ability to intuit it gets stronger over time."

"Everybody is on their own path and has their own resources. Truth comes to each of us in different ways and in different patterns, especially in this day and age. These days we find ourselves in the strange situation where 'traditional paths' no longer exist the way they once did. Instead, we are trying to find our own path in the midst of all those things we are exposed to."

Silvio paused, before continuing, "You can get inspiration from others, but you have to make it your own and keep evolving it. This is really the only way to stay inspired and kindle your interest. Otherwise, your experience of life will become dull and boring. You will be living other people's lives.

"I know this from experience. I can show people how to move their bodies in new ways, but they won't keep up the practice if inspiration is not ignited inside. The most important thing is to keep on honing and evolving your individual path—this is what will take you through thick and thin."

"Silvio, I did not know you were such a serious dude," I said kiddingly.

He smiled at me, peered at me intently, then vibrated his lips to utter a "Phuuuuuuh" sound before breaking into a grin.

"Is this why I am so rebellious? Because I already know who I am? Because I'm already enlightened?" I then asked, laughing.

"That's it," he stated, directly taking the lightness out of my questions. "You know already. Deep down you know. Deep down you're connected to everything, and you know from where true knowledge arises. You're just waiting to bring out your own inner knowledge.

"You can be rebellious. But what's not so good is to be rebellious and stubborn," he said, raising his eyebrows a couple of times, before chuckling.

"You are doing to me what people often do. You're just trying to set me up. You're trying to find someone to tell you what to do so that you can rebel against what they tell you."

Silvio chuckled as he raised his index finger, pointing at me and said, "Watch out, hombre!"

I laughed with him for a bit. Then I stood up and walked over to the cooler and got us some glasses of water and brought them back to the table.

I then said, "When I first arrived earlier today I was watching you moving under the trees. To my surprise, I could feel my body understanding some of what you were doing. I understood a little of the underlying principles involved. But what I saw was very different from what I learned up here in Chiang Mai and in Phuket."

Silvio got up and picked up a Spiderman and a dough boy, replicas of the dolls that Veronica had shown me. He squeezed them repeatedly as he brought them back. And I laughed inwardly, thinking, "The spirit of 'the toy maker' has left footprints everywhere in Thailand."

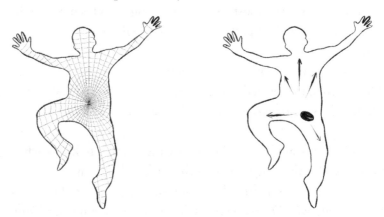

After he sat down, he continued, saying, "There is no one way. Everyone has their own way, but the mechanics of body movement underlay them all. Everyone learns within their own frame of reference. Forms of movements are like learning scales to be able to play music. First you learn your scales, then you're ready to play music and then by practice you can become a master. You need to work on your body mechanics and at the same time know that you are moving towards an ever-evolving form."

"Why call it ever-evolving?" I inquired.

Silvio responded, "Because in my life I have seen the forms I do change so many times, even if I am attached to them. Everything changes. You sometimes need to change your forms continually to explore your nature. And your forms should reflect your ever-changing focus and expression."

"What about all the forms and movements I have learned before?" I asked.

"Once you understand and embody the principles underlying our Chi Gung you can put those into any outer form or movement you choose. But some forms lend themselves better to understanding and cultivating those principles. However, you also need to be careful of Chi residues passed on to you through the forms that you study from others. Often their focus is not about one's evolution. So, take what you can from them and keep evolving, allowing your form to reflect your path," Silvio explained.

"OK, then what makes a good form?" I wanted to know.

He said, "Talking and working with the body gives one a practical and pragmatic way to explore one's inner dimensions and to induce realizations and a practical way of stabilizing them. A good form is one that supports this way of energy stabilization while continuing to advance your internal inquiry.

"When I teach, I like to accentuate principles that can be applied to various forms, something flexible that you can combine into an exercise regime that can be personally modified. Or that the principles can be incorporated into your already existing exercise system, according to your predisposition and previous learnings.

"If you know your principles well you can detect them in many forms. Similar to your earlier experience when you were watching me move in the garden: your body already relates to the underlying principles it has embodied though the outer form appears unfamiliar. You can even use these principles of body mechanics while you are taking a walk down the street."

Silvio got up and stretched his arms, rolled his shoulders and then kneaded his lower back. After that he sat down, looked at me and said, "You know that truth is a mystery because we really don't know. We are engaged in a balancing act of walking on the edge. Allow your connection to your path to become an ever-changing web to catch truth as it comes."

As happens often here in the countryside, the signature melody of a moving ice cream cart trolling along a nearby dirt road hit our ears. Immediately after that we could hear that joyful screaming and laughter of village children running for it. It brought a smile to Silvio's face and reminded us that we were still in Thailand. Being here in Thailand with Silvio definitely supplied ample opportunity for shifting moods in the blink of an eye.

Silvio winked at me and said, "Keep evolving and rewriting your story and rewiring your body."

"What about me?" I asked. "What about my story? Silvio, with all your experiences and understanding, looking back at your path unfolding, can you feel the spiral of my path weaving its way through my life and where it might lead?"

Silvio scratched his chin for a moment. He then said, "The path is such an internal experience. It is for you alone. The story of your own evolution and personal dissolution."

Suddenly a question surfaced, and I blurted it out, "Can I put what I am learning here with you into words?"

Silvio quickly stared at me with a penetrating yet questioning gaze.

Then I continued, "What if I write a book?"

Immediately doubts arose. And I began voicing them, "But all this is such an internal experience. How can I even conceive of words to match my experiences? How can I convey these shared body-to-body experiences with you and Li Tse within the limitations of language?"

Silvio looked at me approvingly, then said, "We're not talking here only about conveying this information to others. But more essentially is the process of writing itself that will help you to integrate and develop the feeling of where your path will lead to. Take one step after the other. You don't have to be sure what it'll all lead to. If it turns out to become a book, then that's fine. And if not, you have the experience of consolidating what you know into some kind of material form.

"Another way you can look at it is that it might be a perfect way to beat things out of yourself," Silvio said, laughing.

The combination of Silvio's words and the peripheral flash of iridescent lights reflected off the rich texture of the puppets' costumes intensified my awareness of being present in this vibrating scene again.

"Déjà vu number two," I chuckled to myself.

Once again, I heard the melody from the ice cream lady's cart. She must have finished with the children as the sound slowly receded while she went on down the road.

Silvio cleared his throat. I looked over at him and saw him wriggling his index finger in circles in the air in front of him.

"One time Li Tse shared with me what a Taoist had once told him. He had said that it is sometimes a good practice to learn to write without ink or paper. Writing with your fingers on the firmament around you," he said, chuckling, bringing a picture of Li Tse to mind.

"Or even writing with your whole body," he said as a wave of energy rolled out from his lower *Dan Tien* out through his wrist.

"Writing—without leaving a mark!" he continued. "Just writing, any kind, can make you clearer and teach you many things."

Silvio seemed to like the idea so much that he went on, "You have to really absorb from someone body-to-body to learn many of the things we are teaching you, but you can share some principles about how moving one's body in new ways can lead one to greater freedom, health and happiness.

"And perhaps some of your readers already will have some experience in martial arts, meditation, Yoga, Chi Gung, and Chinese Medicine, so that this could help to inspire them and to fill in some of the blanks.

316

"Hopefully those that read it will have a good and intimate conversation with what you write. And then there is their own ever-evolving living exploration."

He rubbed his palms together and said, "By giving them a glimpse of the Spirit, it could help them in the evolution of their own systems. Knowledge of oneself is acquired slowly, it builds over time. Like grinding something down, like water dissolving rock. Slowly accumulated.

"So, if your book were written in just the right way it might contribute to their own personal practice and their commitment to it. Maybe you can help them jumpstart their connection to the feeling of life. Just throw around some sparks. I mean, how do you tell a caterpillar how to weave a cocoon? It knows already!"

He paused, scratched his chin, then continued, "Different people start from different places. We all are like caterpillars in the midst of weaving our own cocoons. We have to let our bodies unravel. We only need space and sparks for transformation."

The sound of my smart phone intruded. I leaned over and opened its protective case. I looked at the screen and turned it off. It reminded me of a question I had been looking for the right time to ask, "Silvio, we are talking about this body-to-body space, the learning of movements. What does it all mean with regards to computers and globalization?"

Silvio smiled, then got up and walked over to one of his piles of toys and pulled out two small rubber plastic statues of white baby Buddhas in saffron robes talking on their black cell phones.

"Have you ever seen one of these?" he asked, grinning. "They're everywhere. It's an unstoppable invasion," he said, squeezing first one then other as they squeaked out the ringing tones of now antique cell phones.

I had seen those statues around. But seeing him pulling these toys out in this context made me laugh. He came over and sat in a chair next to me, placing the little statues on the table between us. He then leaned over, turning them to face each other giving each of them a final squeeze.

Silvio then looked at me and said, "Authentic body-to-body communication is actually somewhat imperiled by the ever-increasing speed of this global fusion of learned behavior. We are becoming ever more riveted to one dominating perceptual system. Because of this galvanization of our perceptual options, we lose the gaps that can be created by living in a different culture or speaking a different language. As we lose more cultures and languages and their systems of motion and ways of being we lose options. Much less can slip between the cultural cracks. These are disappearing. And without breaks in our habitual behavior it becomes much easier to forget our true selves."

He continued, "You need to realize that the Spirit quickens around the edges of our learned behavior. The more edges, the more Spirit you will be exposed to. This is where the true teachings hover. You always find the right people on the edges. But those edges are changing. The 'edge' is no longer between different cultures, languages, and body systems. But it seems as though more and more the only edge we have available is located on the periphery of the unified pressure field of globalization."

Silvio squeezed each one of the baby Buddhas a couple of times again, then paused to point with his chin at the painting with the people frozen in cubes. "Consensualized pressure. See it? This pressure increases with mass. The bigger the population with a uniform perception and synchronized body movements the stronger the urge to conform. And thus, it's harder to keep body-to-body communications that are not part of that consensus alive and intact.

"Another aspect in this age of globalization is the speed with which things are co-opted." He picked up one of the baby Buddhas again, squeezed it, then moved it back and forth in front of my face a few times as if he were a magician trying to distract my attention, which brought a smile to my face.

I wanted more clarification about the ways that globalization impacts us, and so I asked, "Don't computers allow people to communicate beyond the ingrained patterns of learned behavior stored in their bodies?"

He replied, "Yes, in a certain way computer and information technology can momentarily free you from the movement patterns of learned behavior held in your body. And indeed, a respite is given that allows the body time to rest and reset, and a transitory feeling of freedom. But because it is so fleeting there simply is not enough time to engender new movements coming from within your body's own innate knowledge or to ground down that sense of freedom back into the body.

"In this way 'speed is not magic at all.' It's just an ephemeral appearance that keep your body movements fixed, promising freedom but not delivering it," he grinned, while rubbing the baby Buddha's belly.

"So, in the end, learned behavior actually perpetuates itself through this wonderful subterfuge. People feel free but then get caught up in the content of their very escape. Easy pickings for learned behavior. It can continue to get the energy from the bodies' habitual movements or lack thereof, but even more so in this milieu because this 'freedom' is not grounded into any body movement—very difficult to stay body oriented when on a computer or device."

A scene appeared in my mind's eye that I had witnessed earlier, people in a coffee shop. None of them were talking to each other. There was one group of three people, two men sitting opposite to each other and a woman next to them. A tablet computer was set up on the table, showing a live news feed. Everybody was glued to the screen, their bodies inert. Next to them was a young teenage couple who were both intensely interacting with their devices.

They all seemed to be disconnected from each other, but at the same time connected to something else. I could see what Silvio was talking about: today's smart devices operate like a learned behavior box that people use to connect to the world.

And another scene arose in my mind: of the time I had been in a restaurant with Li Tse recently. In this case, because he had shared his energetic presence with me, I had been able to recognize the flow of pressure between people—a body-to-body dance.

I juxtaposed these two scenes and saw that in the coffee shop I was watching a dance between people and their devices and not with each other. They seemed disembodied. Their bodies seemed locked as if in a freeze-framed moment of limbo.

I was seeing that the moment of disembodiment frozen into this frame appeared to hold a promise of freedom for these people—a momentary respite from their learned behavior, a break from the ways of their learned behavior body patterns that they grew up with and were accustomed to. In some ways similar to the joy of rebellion that Angelique had explained to me when she told me about the co-option of Rock'n'Roll—but with an ephemeral ecstasy created by connecting with devices that lacked the body component to give it more stability.

And suddenly I could see what Silvio was alluding to. The speed at which this co-option was happening was both astounding and overwhelming. The speed's magic arose from creating a disconnection between the individual's body, and its power to induce a trance-like state. I could also intuit that in this disembodied state learned behavior would have no problem in holding the upper hand.

Suddenly I noticed three butterflies outside of the window. They had their own movements, a circular dance, their particular weaving within the matrix of the Earth's cocoon without relation to our human world and patterns of interaction.

Silvio looked over and saw them too.

He laughed and said, "There is less and less room for magic in the world these days. But who knows—the pressure of conformity may become so great that the human spirit might just rebel and find a whole new way to express itself."

Chapter 19

# SILVIO—DISCIPLINES

The next thing I remembered was that I was looking at Silvio's chaotic heap of mechanical toys and dolls again. It brought to mind an underlying confusion that I still could not resolve. A while back Silvio and Li Tse had talked to me about the energy-body, the healing-body template, and the truth-body. And then, Angelique had explained to me her ideas about the subtle body. And recently it had been Li Tse again who then had talked about the movement-body.

All these systems!

"Body, body, body—again! How am I supposed to make sense out of it?" A cartoon character arose in my mind, lightning striking around him, shrieking in panic. I smiled at that.

Silvio caught me smiling and I unburdened my confusion onto him.

He chortled, "Bodies, bodies, bodies, yeah. But I hope you get the overall idea: that we have some misplaced energy that needs to be woven back together. We have been using different metaphors to introduce you to the underlying feeling of what is going on. We were utilizing different body models according to the level of understanding you were capable of.

"You might say, 'we were working from the outside in,'" he grinned. "I'm sure you can remember when Angelique was teaching you how to integrate your body by showing you how to move by focusing first on the movement of the wrists, then elbows, shoulders, and finally leading you back inside to your lower Dan Tien. Here we are using that same principle—we are peeling away useful but overlapping concepts to help you identify your essence."

Silvio stood up and he took me by the arm and excitedly said, "Come over here, I want to show you something."

And he turned me around and took me to the opposing wall.

"See this, I think this will help!" And he pointed at a picture, an illustration of a body in sitting pose.

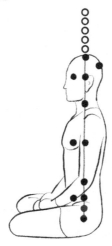

*The Three Dan Tiens*

As we stood on either side of the picture, he began explaining to me about the three Dan Tiens. "At this time, for me the most comprehensive way of looking at our body/energy is to look at the three energy centers that reside in the head, in the heart and in the lower abdomen: the upper, middle and lower Dan Tiens," he said, while pointing to the corresponding three areas.

"The lower Dan Tien is the center of life-force, the upper Dan Tien the center of light and bliss, and the middle Dan Tien 'the great mixer.' The upper Dan Tien is the source of light, it gives you internal seeing. It also includes this," he pointed to the area of the head and above and explaining, "This is where focus comes from.

"The lower Dan Tien is the source of vibrant energy that powers the body and gives you heat and internal feeling," he continued as he pointed to the area of the lower abdomen. Finally indicating the heart area, he said, "And here in the middle Dan Tien is where all the energies are mixed and merged, and essentially where they all came from."

Clearing his throat, he went on, "I feel it's best to describe the body's energy with broad strokes so that it is more inclusive and easier to incorporate many of the systems we get exposed to. Indeed, many cultures and traditions have put a great deal of study into the relationship between the psychic and physical components of our 'body'—the movement of energy, vortexes, and centers where energies gather and where the psychic body most strongly interacts with the physical.

"In this day and age, we have access to a wide variety of traditions, lineages, and schools. The broad stroke model of the three Dan Tiens simplifies our task and enables us to use the understandings that can be gained from many traditions. And by using this model we put ourselves into a position where we can synthesize and incorporate those aspects that seem most appropriate."

He took a deep breath and then began pointing at different centers or focal points in the diagram, "For example you can see how the seven energy centers of the Hindu system, and the major four energy centers that are used in Vajrahana Buddhism, can all be reduced to the three Dan Tien system, at least for our purposes.

"The so-called 'subtle-body' fits in here too. In our system we utilize the idea of the subtle-body to describe the various energy sheaths that encapsulate the physical body. We use it usually in the context of trying to unify and integrate these. There is also the Vajra body or Bliss body that the Tibetan folks use, which is perhaps the most subtle."

"OK, Silvio, but what about the movement-body Li Tse taught me about?" I inquired.

"Good question," he replied, "That's where the energy-body comes in. Our energy is floating around, 'disembodied,' in the movement-body because of the distortions created by learned behavior. Clearing the movement-body of unwanted Chi residues and the reflected crusts that attach to the physical body can re-establish the connection of the energy-body within the physical body, and thus truly integrate us with the earth's gravity. You see the energy-body includes both: the physical body sac and the larger movement-body sac and their relationship to each other."

Silvio stopped for a moment, then directed my attention once again to the drawing and said, "The link between the upper and the lower Dan

Tiens is very important in creating and sustaining life. Their right connection is key to our health and well-being. The biggest impediments to their correct energetic functioning are the residues of learned behavior stored in our movement and breathing patterns."

"In terms of healing, what would be your best suggestion?" I wanted to know.

Silvio replied, "Lower Dan Tien practices that work with movement and breathing patterns joined with right focus from the upper Dan Tien can help by giving your body enhanced Chi circulation, maximizing the energy flow within the life-giving channel of the Tai Chi Pole and then distributing it throughout the healing-body template. This then can point you in the right direction."

"Now let's go back to our drawing and look at the middle Dan Tien. By going back into the depths of the heart center we can allow energy to reform and re-connect the upper and lower Dan Tiens so that we can evolve freely.

"The first step is allowing the upper Dan Tien to connect naturally with the lower Dan Tien. Then, when these forces meet in the middle Dan Tien, this opens the door for a type of healing that will lead you along your path of evolution. This can help the body attain a malleable, soft child-like state," Silvio said.

After gathering his thoughts for a moment, he said, "Li Tse at one time related to me what an enlightened Chinese sage once wrote: that the bodies of all the eminent monks of great virtue were as soft and supple as a baby's."

"And very importantly, as you well know—this is where sexuality resides," he said, tapping the area of the lower Dan Tien in the illustration.

"And the dysfunction in the energy flows between the upper and lower Dan Tien areas can readily be seen in learned behavior's ideas of sexuality, and more specifically in the male/female agreement that you heard about earlier. And it radiates out into many disease patterns that occur because of the lack of right connection between the two," Silvio said,as he moved his fingers back and forth between the two Dan Tiens along the Tai Chi Pole depicted in his diagram. "It is important to note once again that the male/female agreement, or the way that a person is taught to relate gender-wise," he chuckled, "is the lynchpin that holds learned behavior together."

Then moving his finger upwards from the lower Dan Tien area to the center in the head and tapping that area in the diagram repeatedly, he said, "Li Tse must have told you when he was instructing you in move-ment-body practices about how learned behavior was implanted in the lower Dan Tien and how this can inhibit our life energy from rising up the Tai Chi Pole to the crown of the head and then to the rest of the body. And I am sure you have intuited how the 'House of the Four Thieves' influences that.

And how this enables learned behavior to store its preferred version of reality, of how we touch ourselves and the world around us, in our move-ment and breathing patterns.

"I know that by now you've got that. Right? But that's not all," he turned to face me, grinning. "As well as inhibiting the energy from the lower Dan Tien rising up the Tai Chi Pole, the 'Four Thieves' also holds ransom the power of focus that comes down from the top of the head and beyond," he said, this time moving his fingers downwards along the line starting above the head then down through the body.

"These thieves weave a cobweb of stuck fibers, so to speak, that per-meate our breathing and moving patterns to make the upper Dan Tien replace the middle Dan Tien as the 'great mixer.' So, you can see that not only have they absconded with the life-giving power that resides in the lower Dan Tien, but they also have diverted the light-giving focus from the above-the-head aspect of the upper Dan Tien. This is how learned behavior manipulates perception so that it can perpetuate itself."

Silvio paused, considering his next statement before going on, "Learned behavior residing in the upper Dan Tien spreads its influence throughout the body. And this is also where focus and feeling are mixed and turned into language by learned behavior, and this is where it is charged. Here is where our charged discursive/linear 'thought patterns' are shaped.

"But if the learned behavior can become de-charged, then language becomes liberated and can be used without the debilitating effects of learned behavior. Not only that, but we are opened to the voice of realization whose presence becomes stronger and clearer as we de-charge language."

He cupped his right ear with his hand and said, "Charged language can actually be de-charged! And then through it you can hear the voice of the Spirit. But the Spirit talks in a different language." He laughed.

Silvio got up and walked over to a nearby table and picked up a small mechanical music box in the shape of a carousel. He wound it up and set it down between us.

The carousel started to rotate. It played "The Blue Daube." He started speaking as we heard the tune,

"Learned behavior works through the power of rhythm and repetition. But we can also utilize these same principles in disrupting its continuity. When you disrupt the rhythm of learned behavior with another pattern, you can generate a creative dissonance, breaking up the inertia of learned behavior so other energies can enter and begin to circulate again in the body. This is one of the main focuses we have in our Chi Gung.

"But only when something is taught body-to-body with the right focus does it stand a chance. This is how you can keep co-option at bay. It is exceedingly difficult for learned behavior to co-opt body-to-body teachings that are inherently of a greater scope than itself."

"Goals and purpose beyond the reach of learned behavior? What is this all about, Silvio?" I asked.

He grinned wickedly, "Here is a secret of our other-worldly martial arts: with this one-two-punch learned behavior doesn't stand a chance. On the one hand our goals and purposes are too fluid for learned behavior to grasp," he said, punching the air in front of him with his left hand. "And on the other hand, through body-to-body teachings with the right focus, we increase the energy in the body, which overwhelms learned behavior's ability to engage," he said, punching the air with his right hand.

Silvio continued punching the air in front of him, laughing. He then opened his arms and placed them on his thighs, grinned and said, "When there is a strong body component, we stand a good chance. When you can get the energy freely moving in the body creating a strong energy current with the Earth it clears the mind. By learning to listen to and to trust the body one can learn to walk a tight rope on the edge of one's learned behavior, creating a new life full of magic and mystery."

A slight breeze caressed my face, carrying the scents of young rice, wildflowers, and fresh running water.

Silvio got up and started pacing back and forth. My eyes moved across his bookshelves and I noticed the titles of some old-looking tomes of the Upanishads, the Vedas, and the three seminal works of Chinese culture: *The I Ching, The Book of Changes*; *The Nei Ching, The Canon of Internal Medicine*; and *The Su Nu Ching, The Counsel of the Plain Girl* or *The Plain Girl Classic*, in which the "plain girl" descends from the spirit world to answer the Yellow Emperors' questions about sexuality and long life.

"Now his was ancient written body knowledge!" I thought.

It reminded me how in India, China, and Tibet the shamanistic cultures had reached their apex and were turned into a written tradition. This then brought to mind what Angelique had told me about the downside of written tradition and the way in which it can erode authentic oral and body-to-body transmissions.

But she had also mentioned the upside to these old writings: that they preserve, amass, and collate that original knowledge. And that indeed still amongst these writings were remnants of the original truths that the old sages once discovered that still show through.

"I see that you've noticed some of my old books," Silvio said, stopping by a bookshelf. "I remember how I once was drawn to study many of them, and how at that in time I had made the following observations: that there were those disciplines which had strong elements of knowledge, but they lacked its application.

Then there were others which were strong on practice, like the martial arts, but they were weak on knowledge and lacked the right focus. And I also came across some shamanistic practices which were strong on focus but lacked the detailed heights of the knowledge discipline, and although they had developed some physical exercises, these could really not be compared to the movements evolved by the practitioners of the internal martial arts or by some Chi Gung masters.

"You may need to combine elements from a wide variety of disciplines as you are guided along your path," he raised his right index finger, slightly for emphasis, as he continued walking back and forth in front of me.

"It is important to understand them so that you know the benefits as well as the shortcomings of the systems you come across. Their pull can be very strong. Remember, use what seems true for you, but at the same time be careful that these teaching or trainings do not co-opt your personal path."

He paused, before continuing, "Our Spirit seeks Union. There are many ways and schools of thought that have sought to meet this need. You can pick your way through these and find what's most appropriate for your personal evolution."

With his penchant for drama Silvio then stopped, peered at me and said, "Everyone has their own path—even if you don't realize it in the beginning. A good so-called spiritual path is one that allows you to go 'crazy' while still maintaining a foot in this world. It enables you to deftly loosen the grasp of learned behavior and allow your True Self to surface."

Silvio grinned and intensified his gaze, in order to punctuate his next statement, "You have to know that your own personal path is your protection! And so, you must guard your connection to it—it is your most precious treasure. It is the unrelenting focus on, or better yet your surrender to your integrity of being, that allows you to keep learning and adapting to the next appropriate form as you go along. It takes unbending internal focus on the connection to your path to change whatever you find into something powerful and potentially transcendent."

I looked around the workshop again with a new perspective, then asked, "Are all of these things, stuff, artifacts you have collected about 'enlightenment'?"

A smile slowly lit up Silvio's face and he said, "Ah, so you are noticing my personal laboratory," he said with a laugh then continued. "We don't call it 'enlightenment'—we call it 'evolution.' There is a force within us, flowing through us. What we are really doing is looking for the secrets that the body has within it. We have to mine them. The body knows! It is the process of remembering and embodying the possibilities of the power both recuperative and creative that you have within you. And finally, when your personal body cocoon lines up with the body of the cocoon of the Earth, a union happens that enables you to move beyond."

He then paused again before deliberately continuing, "You know, my personal path turned out to be tightly joined with what we call 'the path of healing' or 'the path of the body.' Being a healer and studying the moving energetic path appeals to me more than the philosophical one. And while this path can enhance the healing-body template, you have to understand that its main purpose, as with all other paths, is to realize who or what you really are."

He paused for emphasis before he said, "And it is important to keep this in mind as you move in and out of different perceptual alternatives."

Silvio turned to look at his books, and as he brushed his fingers along their spines he explained, "In general, most of these disciplines fall into two classifications: the emphasis will be either on the upper Dan Tien or the lower Dan Tien. And each has inherent limitations. What we prefer is both, integrating the energy along the Tai Chi Pole at the heart center from both ends. We are interested in learning how through concentration we can circumvent the 'Four Thieves' in the upper Dan Tien by applying knowledge practice. And we want to know how to utilize the life energy of the lower Dan Tien through physical practice to overwhelm them from down below and to create a stable platform from which to operate."

Silvio looked above his bookshelf and pointed to a framed quote in beautiful calligraphy that had been placed above his books and smiled.

*They are doomed to darkness those who worship only the body,*
*and to greater darkness those who worship only the mind.*
—Isa Upanishad

"These guys really knew a lot," he said as he leaned over and patted a volume of The Upanishads as if it were an old friend. "It is too bad that now it's all just written words and these guys are no longer alive to be with," he said with a sense of regret. "But we still can learn a lot from reading these texts.

"Listen carefully," he said looking at me and shaking his index finger. "*I am not the mind. I am not the body. There is no personal I.* This is the foundation of the realization of our True Self."

Silvio paused smiled and continued, "What I want you to see is that in this Upanishad they are backhandedly showing a progression as to how to proceed with the dissolution of the little self, which then allows the True Self to surface. The ultimate aim is not to be the best Chi Gung practitioner in the world but the realization of the True Self. But for many of us there are steps. There are steps to breaking down what we call our learned behavior and doing it in a systematic way. And being able to digest the huge burst of energy released while doing this. This involves needing to take care of and stabilize the so-called body so that we can have the strength to pursue our path.

"The old rishis who lived in India millennia ago created Sanskrit to reflect their probings into our inner workings and the nature of perception and reality. In these works, they describe the path of Advaita or 'Non-Duality.' This philosophy uses the innate binary nature of language itself to short-circuit and de-charge linear thinking and paralyze the 'Four Thieves.'

"You see this is a very tricky path," he scratched his chin, then continued, "The techniques used in this kind of mind discipline, whether it comes to us from the Upanishads or in the form of Buddhist koans, come from the realization that thought or linear language 'fixes the frame.'

"For example, the koans of the Japanese Zen tradition tie the mind up in knots. This shattering of the frame temporarily frees up the energy that the 'Four Thieves' in the upper Dan Tien have stolen so that one can momentarily experience the rapture of the True self. And the old teachings of the rishi's are either constantly juxtaposing opposites or providing images that stretch the mind and allow essence to enter.

"So, in a real way their applied techniques cancel out linear mental processes, cracking open and paralyzing the thought patterns of learned behavior for a bit—thus allowing a glimpse of another world.

Also, in addition to breaking up the thought patterns and their underlying psycho-emotional structure in this way, these techniques briefly, shockingly disrupt the body's movement and breathing patterns. This can give not only the mind but also the body a chance to perceive differently.

"The fault of this mental path by itself is its lack of lasting embodiment, sustained engagement with the body, and enhancement of the body's storage capacity—its innate ability to house living energy.

"The rishis knew about this and gave fair warning even as they wrote down their findings, well knowing the shortcomings of writing," he said as he pointed to the framed calligraphy above his bookshelf once again. He then picked up a volume of The Upanishads, flipping through the pages until he found what he was looking for:

*"Clarification of* Advaita *and* Vidhya: *non-knowledge and knowledge are both in confusion. Because spiritual knowledge which does not lead to the transformation of oneself is not true. It is complacency. Just as understanding the rules of the game is not playing it."*

"These knowledge paths are very good to use to disable learned behavior in the upper Dan Tien, using the rational mind to cancel itself out, but they usually tend to not go far enough and to neglect the energies of the lower Dan Tien, and of allowing the energy of the upper Dan Tien to settle down into the Heart.

This makes them somewhat impotent for dealing with the patterns of learned behavior stored in the body.

"The underlying message is that it is brains that matter and our body does not. And what this does is essentially direct our attention away from the life-force and sexuality. You can see why learned behavior would be very happy with these knowledge traditions because they allow the Tai Chi Pole and the physical energy of the body to continue to be drained.

"The basic ploy of learned behavior is to have the upper Dan Tien control the lower Dan Tien. If you stay in the realm of the upper Dan Tien, this puts learned behavior at ease. So, you can understand why learned behavior is not threatened when religions, its proxies, extol the benefits of the upper Dan Tien and ignore the lower Dan Tien. This is how learned behavior maintains its control—sometimes crudely and sometimes very craftily in the most beautiful ways—but the mechanics are the same. You can see reflections of this in 'acceptable' religions of today which use the same ploy."

He then looked down at his crotch, chuckling, and said, "To try to embody realization without a body is like trying to masturbate without a dick. It's like staying away from it and poking at it with a stick," he said, laughing, wagging his finger at me. "They believe realization and sexuality are separate—this is often their downfall."

Silvio laughed at his own joke before once again running his fingers lovingly across the spines of his books, "As you will see, each of these disciplines have their upsides and downsides. There are many belief systems. Their leaders are confident in their own beliefs and practices. We have to meander through this maze. But you must be careful, as most important traditions keep some of the original source energies intact, but almost always, they have been, to a great extent, co-opted through time. And because of this their meaning only become clear when you already know."

Silvio stretched, looked up at the puppets above our heads once again and a mischievous smile appeared once again on his face. He then pulled out another volume and showed it to me, "Here is another brick to build and maintain the walls of ignorance—it is called 'The Encyclopedia of

Psychology,'" he said, chuckling.

He turned and looked at me, saying, "Initially these days, a lot of people are drawn to study psychology because they have touched some deep currents within themselves, and this has made them look for healing in a profound way. They look for answers in what society has to offer. They have been exposed to the stirrings of realization and evolution inside, but sadly this natural impulse gets co-opted by wrong focus and the resultant theories of psychology. You know that psychology is taught and nurtured in universities, and universities by their very nature and funding are institutions and thus among the strongest agents of learned behavior."

He grinned, "If you go to a psychologist s/he'll make you feel 'special.' And or s/he will assign you a condition that can make you feel even more 'special' than before. It's like another turning of the screw—learned behavior feeds you an illusion of liberation while tightening its grip on your energy.

Learned behavior makes you 'feel special'—that's certainly one of its best tricks." He chuckled.

"But Silvio, people who go to psychologists sometimes have realizations and release a lot of energy, don't they?" I asked.

He replied, "Yes, that can happen. But it's the focus of psychology that is the main problem. It sets the agenda. Instead of studying the nature of the psychic and its relationship to the physical and to the path of liberation, psychology negates the physical, obscures the psychic, and does not treat psychological imbalances as opportunities to move beyond learned behavior.

"Psychologists should grasp that so-called 'dysfunctions can serve as an opening, as a way to move deeper and deeper, and as a way to follow one's personal path.' They may find that underneath these 'pathological conditions' there is a pattern of personal evolution. And that these 'pathological conditions' relate to emotional charges stuck in one's body, because released energy is not being grounded in the body.

"As they don't use physical techniques to help their clients re-channel and store energy, psychologists just re-shuffle these charges, they keep their clients at the same energetic level. And also, they don't use this released energy to help their clients redirect or redefine their focus. Instead, energy is usually directed into how to cope better and reinforce one's story."

Silvio went on, "A psychologist should be one who teaches us how to stabilize ourselves by incorporating body movement practices, and an emphasis should be placed on puberty and the few years following that. It is during these years of transition that a psychologist could be a wonderful teacher to lead one back through the doorways of perception to one's source and to one's evolutionary path," he said, smiling.

I leaned back into my chair and looked around the room, and once again I felt the stirring within myself that had been initiated by the dream I had in Phuket. I noticed the fleeting sensations of déjà vu still coming and going: *the flickering of iridescent light, streaks of chartreuse phosphoresce that finally took shape as an immense gold beetle, and the haunting sounds of the huge bagpipe.*

Coming back from my reveries and seeing Silvio with his Cheshire grin standing there by his books I noticed some books on martial arts, yoga, and Chi Gung.

"What about these, Silvio?" I asked, pointing to that section of the bookshelf.

"Well, I've introduced you to some disciplines that focus on trying to de-charge learned behavior's control of the upper Dan Tien. The books you are looking at now refer to techniques for strengthening and utilizing the energy flow of the lower Dan Tien.

"And this is both their strength and their drawback. With these more physical practices you can find good methods for grounding the energies one's realization. The biggest drawback of these physical systems is their lack of knowledge about focus. Their focus gets skewed. And to a large extend they're not interested in correcting it."

"So, then, Silvio, how can we use body movement correctly?" I wanted to know.

Silvio scratched his chin for a moment and then explained, "Exercise for union is activating the energy-body through 'physical' movements. Body movement is a language. And expanding the way in which we move our bodies in relation to gravity will expand the way in which we can be and interact with the energies of the Earth. This also can help to stabilize huge influxes of energy and thus can enable us to move through and alleviate the jolts and effects that arise from 'Zen sickness.' The more exposure to your energy-body the better. It helps offset the deleterious effects of the 'body concept' taught to us by learned behavior. Correct body movement with right focus can help us with that significantly."

"Yeah, I see what you mean," I said, making a connection. "It is about developing a healthy balance between the lower and upper Dan Tiens. Is this what brought you to study martial arts?"

"Not consciously," Silvio replied. "I studied them because my path led me there. And while studying them I discovered that these folks, especially at the higher levels, have a good practical understanding of the mechanics of how the physical body functions," he took up one of his toys and dangled it in front of me.

"And remember: when you are a hunter you go where the scent takes you." He considered for a moment then added, "Or where the path pulls you."

He grinned again before going on, "In the past, martial artists were the consummate investigators of physical movement—but alas, for our purposes, their focus was skewed. Traditionally their exploration by and large was not for self-cultivation, but for self-defense or fighting. The martial arts often originated and were taught in village and temple settings for the main purpose of self-protection. The result being that these people became stuck in a specialized view of how to use, and for what purpose to use the physical body."

He explained, "This is not an attempt to knock them down, but to put them in the context of the bigger picture. I want to acknowledge what they discovered and tempt you with the possibility of what could happen if these techniques were used with the right focus placed on the path of evolution. Because they cultivated within their internal martial arts systems many secrets of body movement, some of which we can't even imagine today.

"But here's a warning: be careful here! Their lineage or body-to-body teaching is very powerful, but their martial focus leaves its imprint on

335

their forms. Having done the same movements again and again over time and through space with this same focus as past martial arts masters have, these forms—being handed down for generations—have become imbued with their particular Chi residues. Trying to emulate them through their forms will transfer their intentions to you. Just be aware of the trade-off!

"But certainly, you can use these underlying principles of body-movement that they have unmasked. And if you are skillful, you can transform their discoveries into new and evolving forms for healing, psychic self-defense, and for storing released energy."

I reflected on what he had told me for a minute and then a thought came to mind, "What do you think about the healthy ways of Hatha yoga?"

He chuckled, "You mean the contemporary mass co-option of Hatha yoga—'beautiful people meeting in exotic locations, socializing and perpetuating learned behavior'?

"Don't forget that pimping learned behavior sells," he grinned mischievously.

"What do you mean?" I said, looking at him a bit offended and surprised.

Silvio looked at me, grinning. "OK, OK, I see we have tapped into a tender spot in you," he said as he continued smiling.

"So let's go slow and remember, first of all, we are looking at modern Hatha yoga and how it has been adopted in the West. And we're looking at it from the point of view of how exacting information from it can help us along our path, and how to stay cognizant of the pitfalls that may exist because of learned behavior's co-option," he said, continuing with an impish grin.

He then took a deep breath and said, "Let's look at the term 'yoga' and how its roots go back into prehistory, even before the ancient Vedas or Upanishads. Remember: writing always happens after the fact."

He cleared his throat, "When looking at its written history we see that the word 'yoga' comes from a Vedic Sanskrit term, meaning 'to join' or 'to unite.' This for example is the root of the English word 'yoke.' A yoke is used to bind together the dynamic forces of two strong animals to do focused hard work.

"In this same way, yogas are ways of binding together various techniques to enhance the union of a person with her/his essence. The ultimate focus or goal of Yoga is liberation or the realization and embodiment of our True Selves. Which, in other words, means uniting with our natural path of evolution."

"There were many paths or disciplines of yoga, such as Hatha yoga, developed in the ancient world for doing this and thus many types of yogas: Jnana yoga, Bhakti yoga, Karma yoga, Tantra yoga, and Kriya yoga, to name a few. Each usually has a psychic as well as physical component.

"Interestingly, due to the intense spiritual focus of the ancient peoples and body to body transmission, the yogas, including Hatha yoga, have been able to maintain a relatively vital connection to their roots. So, the roots and practices of yoga run very deep and come from very ancient sources reflecting the spirit of these people's deep inner searchings. Because of this relatively pure focus there are comparatively less Chi residues that have accumulated around them through time."

I nodded, agreeing, and at the same time a little taken aback by Silvio's extended knowledge about the ancient roots of these spiritual traditions. So, with great anticipation, I asked, "Can you tell me more?"

Silvio chuckled before continuing, "So you see, Hatha yoga is undoubtedly part of an ancient tradition for union with our path of evolution. But this to a great extent has now evolved to become another branch of the Western exercise movement. Although Western exercise systems go back to the ancient Greeks, it was just in the 19th century that the modern roots of the exercise traditions now seen in the West began to appear in militaristic and nationalistic contexts. If you look closely, you can experience how these martial origins to establish uniform and homogenized group activities still permeate and can be felt today in Western exercise systems.

"In contrast to this, Hatha yoga has a rich history of body-to-body transmissions. A teacher would pass on tremendous amounts of energy

337

and information to individual students for their specific needs within the context of helping them evolve along their path.

"Do you see the juxtaposition in focus here?" he asked rhetorically. "On the one hand, you have individualized trainings to help one on the path of liberation. And on the other hand, we have group activities based around physical exercises and socialized goals which very easily lead to co-option by learned behavior."

"Sometimes the most obvious is the hardest to see," Silvio continued, pausing before reiterating, "Hatha yoga was not created to be the center of social gatherings, but to be an aid or an adjunct technique to our personal path of evolution."

He waited for a bit to let that sink in. "It was in the 1980s that yoga became popular as a system of physical exercise across the Western world, melding with the established Western exercise tradition. And I am sure that Angelique talked to you extensively about the 'Westernization' process. Do you remember when she told to you about her experience with co-option and how it changed acupuncture and Chinese medicine when it was incorporated in the West?"

"I remember what Angelique told me, but not in this context, Silvio. Are you saying that Hatha yoga has been co-opted too?" I asked with a challenging tone.

Silvio's eyes lit up, "Similar to acupuncture and Chinese Medicine, Hatha yoga has been and is being co-opted at this very moment."

"But doesn't Hatha yoga serve a purpose in alleviating health problems, reducing stress, and making the spine supple?" I countered.

Silvio replied, "True, but using this type of yoga for this purpose should not obscure the bigger picture of its quintessential usefulness for the journey of self-remembrance. Don't forget: Real healing is helping people reconnect to their evolutionary path."

I wanted him to clarify this more for me, so I asked, "What do you mean? It's claimed that yoga can be excellent training for children and adolescents, both as a form of physical exercise, and for breathing and stress relief. Even primary and secondary schools have considered incorporating Hatha yoga into their physical education programs."

Silvio said, chuckling, "This is such a blatant act of co-option that sometimes it escapes scrutiny. But I am sure if you examine it, it will become apparent. And you might even notice the reflections of militaristic and nationalistic aspirations rooted in the very setup of schools.

"So here you can see the co-option of these beautiful ancient practices: co-opted by learned behavior and put under its purview as it were, just as we saw it happen to acupuncture and Chinese medicine."

He then peered at me, beaming, "Strangely, today Hatha yoga also resembles psychology, as these days it's mainly used as an exercise to enhance the ability to function better in the realm of learned behavior.

"Hatha yoga is a physical practice, but to be useful for our inner probings it needs to be used with techniques such as meditation or other methods that enhance realization. And as with martial arts, it quite often lacks the right mental focus."

Silvio then looked at me before continuing, "Hatha yoga supplies some health benefits as it disrupts normal gravitational alignment. It is especially good for stretching the spine and loosening up the sacrum.

"It can be used to get in touch with certain kinds of structural alignments 'beyond the force of gravity' that are reflected in how we are trained to walk on the Earth."

He then looked at me and said, "But you rarely hear a Hatha yoga teacher talking about how to place your feet correctly on the ground. You see, Hatha yoga does not directly deal with walking around in the world. I mean, literally 'walking around in the world.'"

He stopped and reflected for a moment, before saying, "I once had this friend who was quite accomplished in Hatha yoga. I actually learned some useful things from him. He got a lot of energy from his practice. But he would constantly complain to me how 'walking out into the world' would quickly drain him and destroy his sense of well-being and feeling of connectedness that he experienced right after his practice. He would then be forced to return to his yoga mat so he could regain his equilibrium.

"You see how this reveals one of the shortcomings of Hatha yoga if it is to be applied to our everyday lives? It really needs to be balanced with standing and moving. It is not enough to open up the energies of the sacrum and spine. We need to get the energy moving from the Earth through our feet and up to the sacrum as well."

"So, what about Chi Gung? Isn't that a kind of yoga too? How does that fit in?" I asked.

Silvio replied, "Indeed it is a kind of yoga, or 'union.' It emanates from the Chinese system of unifying man with the cosmos. But when you look at the difference between Indian and Chinese yogas, you will see that in the latter there is much more emphasis on the way that we place our feet on the ground and thus the connection between the sacrum and the energy received from walking the Earth."

"Compared to Hatha yoga, Chi Gung provides more opportunity for energy storage. Because you can more easily translate the energy you have gathered through the practice of standing and moving into everyday life. More specifically, Chi Gung moves the energy out: from the trunk to the wrists and ankles and back. Through our feet we connect to and gather energy from the Earth, and then we can move this energy up to the sacrum and trunk, and from there out through our arms and hands to interact with the world."

He paused, "Also, as opposed to Hatha yoga's emphasis on the spine, the approach of Chi Gung is to work with the meridians, including specifically those going to the wrists and ankles. Our Eight Point Chi Gung is a good example of that.

"Remember," he emphasized, "The way the foot is placed on the ground is really important. Think about the images of the Buddha's feet that you see in the temples here and in Buddhist literature and you can detect the reverence that is expressed for how we place our feet on the Earth, for the way we walk our path."

He went to his bookshelf again and pulled out an anthropological tome. He flipped through the pages until he found two pictures of Buddha's feet and showed them to me.

"Many of the older cultures throughout the world express this innate feeling that the way we walk upon the Earth is a reflection of how we are in the world, a reflection of our sacred immersion in the universe.

"So, watch your step!" he said, laughing.

And then he said laughing again, "The more our body concept gets gravitationally lined up with the Earth's gravity, the more the so-called body disappears."

I thought to myself that perhaps this was one of the reasons that I liked living in third-world cultures because these people seemed to still have "their toes in the Earth," so to speak, and in many ways are not quite so removed from the rhythms of nature in their everyday lives.

Silvio interrupted my musings, "The standing and moving postures are very good for dealing with the world because they stress the way we plant our feet on the Earth and thus provide us with a strong contact to its gravitational force field. You see, planting our feet correctly maximizes the stimulation of the 'Bubbling Spring' point on the soles of our feet from where the energy rises up to charge and nurture our bodies.

"All in all, our Chi Gung enhances our natural alignment with gravity, maximizing natural energy flow. Veronica once shared with me a vision of literally seeing sparks arising from people's feet when they were correctly aligned each time they put their feet on the ground." He laughed.

He paused for a moment, reflecting, "Do you remember when Angelique introduced you to the idea of evolution? How our legs and arms form to help us relate to the new air/earth environment we are born into? And what we may be evolving into, now? Remember how she posited the question of what may come next?"

He paused, to look at me, checking to see if I was following. "By now you should be able to understand that the emphasis of our Chi Gung really is on our evolutionary path. We are using Chi Gung to help us hook up to our healing-body template and into our own evolution."

"Also, you should be able to understand how moving is really the flowering and integration of all the postures. It is through moving that we reach our full potential.

"Now, think about this in terms of global technological society. Think about how much you move while being glued to a screen," he said with a big grin and then a laugh.

I laughed along with him, then reflected back, "OK, Silvio. I get your point that better contact with our feet on the ground sends a fuller charge of energy through our bodies.

"So, you think that Chi Gung is a better path to integrating the body." I asked

"Not necessarily," he said smiling. "But I am biased and know more about it. Chi Gung was the path I was given. And I have more experience with it and want to pass that on to you."

I paused to consider how to phrase my next question but nothing came to mind so I blurted out, "After all you have taught me before, this may sound like a stupid question to you—but I really want to know how can Chi Gung help me cure my ills?"

"Actually, that is a good question. Sometimes the most basic questions are the best ones," Silvio replied. "For starters, both Hatha yoga and Chi Gung are excellent methods for overall maintenance. Chi Gung helps to increase and stabilize your overall energy flow and chips away the illnesses you may experience. When you stay on your path it helps your well-being and body functions in general which eventually, in this way, can make specific illnesses go away. By harmonizing your so-called outer world and inner world you become healthier.

"Chi Gung can become a stable platform with which you can do your self-exploration and train your body so it has the strength and suppleness to sustain your realizations. It also helps to preserve those realizations while standing your ground when you are facing the onslaughts of learned behavior all around you that do indeed cause illness."

Silvio smiled at me, then went over and picked up a statue of Xochipilli, the pre-Columbian god of plant allies. The statue had patterns on its body representing the many transformative psychoactive plant substances used in Mesoamerica. The figure had its head tilted up, mouth half open, jaw tensed, and its arms opened to the heavens.

Silvio said, "He's absorbed in 'the flowery dream.'"

"This represents another way to deal with your learned behavior, something else that can help you to go 'crazy' for a while, but still maintaining a foot in this world. These plant medicines can help you to face the gruesome limitations put on you by learned behavior. The initial shock these substances produce can be very beneficial. And some of these substances have even been known to have curative effects on the physical body, by spreading realization throughout the healing-body template."

"Wait, wait, wait, Silvio," I interrupted. "Are you telling me that drugs can be compared to Chi Gung?

If so—how?"

"Again—good question!" Silvio chuckled, smiling. "Chi Gung is great for releasing energy slowly and creating and stabilizing an energetic platform with which we can store realizations, whereas these psychoactive substances are much more useful for dramatically disrupting the perceptual co- ordinates given to us by learned behavior. But these natural substances, as well as processed mind-altering drugs, can only give you a kick-start, give you a taste of experiencing what's out there beyond learned behavior," he said, opening his arms to the heavens, pantomiming the stature in front of him.

"They can rock the stabilized platform of your learned behavior and allow you to get a glimpse from beyond, to realize that there's something else. This in turn can begin to intensify the pull from your path."

He went on, "But you need to be very careful with these substances."

"Why do you need to be careful?" I inquired, very interested.

"There is a downside to them too," he said, pointing and waving his index finger at me. "Number one, you can begin to rely on them too much and develop an attachment. And number two, they can have deleterious effects on your physical body and on your learned behavior. Again, you have to look at the trade-offs!" Silvio said as he sized me up.

"You know by now that it is important to keep learned behavior somewhat functionally intact, so you can deal with the world of people. It needs to be skillfully disassembled and de-charged—not haphazardly ripped apart. Indeed, these substances have shock value, but they don't offer a sustainable way of maintaining the process of breaking down and re-assembling your learned behavior.

"So be careful here, watch the trade-offs. If you are not careful the price can be too dear, my friend."

He paused to reflect, looking over at some shoulder bags, weavings, and brightly colored headdresses from the Amazon.

"Ayahuasca was one such substance that I studied in the Amazon basin. It is truly remarkable and its discovery and use attests to the incredible plant knowledge that the native peoples of the Amazon possess," he went on.

He now had my rapt attention, for I had had a run in or two with this substance myself.

"It is made from a combination of at least two distinct plant species. When one thinks of the vast number of plants available in the jungle it seems to us—at least from a Western point of view—miraculous that these indigenous people were able to figure out how to combine them to achieve the 'ayahuasca' result. But when you live and study with these people you realize that they in fact have a 'science' of their own, and when we have the time I can tell you more about it," he said, grinning.

Silvio continued, "Ayahuasca is one of the better mind-altering substances. I consider it the queen of them all because its psychoactive component, DMT, is produced naturally in the human body, and this I believe, is one reason that its side effects are less harmful to the body itself.

"Purportedly, a large amount of DMT is secreted from our pineal gland both at the time of birth and death—so it can be inferred from this that it is truly an agent of 'transformation.' In addition, we find DMT in thousands of plant varieties all around us," Silvio said, looking around and moving his arms to take in the natural world around us. "Which gives us, you could say, a 'chemical' link to all that flora out there," pointing with his chin out the open door.

He continued, "Ayahuasca affects the whole digestive system and can cause both vomiting and diarrhea. Which is a safeguard when taking it. If your body gets too much it goes out fast," he said, laughing. "In fact, in the Amazon it is often referred to, in addition to its other more loftier names, as La Purga or 'the purge.'

"This is not your 'party substance.' You get what you pay for," he said, laughing, obviously recalling either his personal past experience or what he had seen others go through.

"It really affects the whole body," he stated as he rubbed his belly, "Because the source of DMT in the body is the pineal gland, which is located in the area of the upper Dan Tien, and the purging effect happens in the belly, which definitely affects peristalsis in the area of the lower Dan Tien," he said as he laughed, continuing to rub his belly while patting the top of his head.

"With ayahuasca we really can experience our awareness moving beyond our learned behavior to touch the body of the Earth, and thus the truth-body, the body that knows.

"But even with all its seemingly beneficial characteristics and minimal deleterious effects on the physical body, ayahuasca should only be used as an occasional kick-start. The plant alkaloids that surround and give its DMT a special character are not exactly the same as what the human body produces, and these have specific side effects. And certainly, even chemically produced DMT is not the 'pure' DMT that the body generates with its special cocktail of chemicals that Western medicine will probably never trace," he said with a Cheshire grin.

"If you take ayahuasca, things can start to happen and to fall into place in your life, but as everyone has their own particular path, the experience is different for each person. There are other natural substances available but ayahuasca is one of the best that I have found. In addition to the disruptive effects to your learned behavior, it seems to have a special 'protective spirit' about it that eases your re-entry back into the world of learned behavior."

He paused for a moment, before going on, "In general I would not recommend human-made mind-altering chemical substances even if they have great party value," he said, again grinning. "Because overall they tend to produce much more skewed effects. They don't have the 'wholeness' or 'intactness' to them that the plant medicines have. They do not exist as living entities between heaven and earth in the same way that plants and our bodies do.

"But nonetheless, all of the mind-altering substances do have an effect on learned behavior. And in this regard, they can provide an opening."

Silvio then said after reflecting for a moment, his eyes shining, he turned his eyes on me. "You can look at a drunk as a drunk or an addict as an addict, but from a deep perspective you can't deny the initial impulse that drove them to experiment with these substances. A yearning deep inside of them knew that there was something more out there. A searching for true freedom."

He then walked over to a counter and picked up an old-looking opium pipe. One of the kinds I had often seen for sale in the small local markets of hill tribes around Chiang Mai.

"This is how undisciplined people can run into problems," he said, holding the pipe in front of me.

"Quite often they can become attached to that special feeling of being liberated from learned behavior. But they're unable to, or do not even care to, ground that feeling back into their lives.

"What happens for addicts is that they have a lot more ground to cover to get a good connection going with the process of evolution. They've taken a step and repeated it enough times that to a lesser or greater degree they have created a damaging condition to their learned behavior so that it has become partially inoperable.

"Again," he said, waving his index finger at me, "Be aware of the trade-offs!

"In one way the life of an addict is very appealing. Once you're seriously addicted, life becomes very simple, very basic. Suddenly your whole life becomes reduced to one single focus—to serve your addiction. Everything else, your whole reality, simply falls apart. On an individual level they have gone so far out, so many times, that the functional underpinnings of learned behavior are being eroded."

He explained further, "The process of our evolution is about learning to dissolve our learned behavior and to put it back together smoothly, skillfully, and each time suffusing ourselves with sparks of realizations. The point is not to blow your mind," he said, looking at me with his eyes bulging out, grinning, "That's easy! The point is: once you've blown your mind, to put it back together skillfully.

"And addicts and drunks are not very skillful," he laughed, going to a table nearby picking up an empty Tequila bottle with a worm still in it and swirling it up in the air and humming an old Mexican tune.

"So, in the end, my friend, the real challenge is to tweak the initial impulse that leads you to addiction into becoming addicted to realization."

Finally, Silvio put the opium pipe and the Tequila bottle back into their places, then walked over to an area in his workshop filled with ancient scripts. As I looked at them, I could see magical looking geometric patterns with inscriptions and drawings of mythical beings which evoked in me an eerie recollection of entities that I had seen in my dream.

Silvio smiled and grabbed a small Tibetan hand drum whose membrane he said was made from human skin. Playfully he started twirling it back and forth until he had a steady beat going. He sped it up, then dramatically stopped it.

"Talking about addiction," he said, "You know that in Tibet these small drums are sometimes used by magicians. And magic can turn into some serious addiction," he cackled.

"How come, Silvio? You talked about drugs and now you say magic can become an addiction too?" I asked, wide-eyed and perplexed.

"The best magicians know how to manipulate perception, even going to other worlds and sometimes even taking people there with them. They definitely have learned to move beyond learned behavior. Some of them may even have been able to use this accomplishment as a steppingstone to merge with their evolutionary path.

"But on the other hand, these folks face a very specialized trap in their chosen discipline—as most magicians manipulate perception and can get overly attached to it, lured by their addiction to power. And they can get stuck in the other worlds of their own creation—just a very elaborate way of getting caught in your own story.

"For, as I've heard, out there," he bulged his eyes, opened his mouth, and spread out his arms, "Out there, there are particularly enticing places to remain stuck."

He then burst out with laughter.

"Another enticing arena where one can get stuck is...," Silvio said with a dramatic flourish as he pulled out an illustrated book that contained some twelve basic sexual positions, flashing its cover in front of my face, "SEX!!!"

"Want to get away from your story? Want to get out of your head? Nothing better to change your mood than to get those sexual juices flowing," he said, gyrating his hips, grinning.

"Sexuality is definitely an especially important part of the mix. Everybody has an opinion about it. And a definitive text is very difficult to find," Silvio said, pulling out a notebook that he said was once given to him by one of his teachers. He flipped through it, then put it down before starting, "You have to respect that sexual energy powers the body. And thus, you should also realize that to regulate and use it can be of vital importance.

"Sexuality is in many ways like a plant medicine. It can be used to move your awareness beyond the realm of the 'Four Thieves' of the upper Dan Tien by overwhelming learned behavior's capacity to deal with the huge influx of energy it can provide. But like plant medicines and human-made chemicals, the sexual path is intense and dangerous and can also lead to addiction. You enter it at your own risk," he said, laughing, before he added more seriously, "And you need to treat it with great trepidation.

"Learned behavior wants to bring sexual energy out through the five senses and play with it in its own prescribed way. Getting sexual fiercely activates the patterns of learned behavior because sexual patterns form the bedrock from which learned behavior springs. And as you know, it is of primary importance for learned behavior to protect its interests. Thus, it created the male/female agreement, and the resultant agreements of courtship and rhythms of touching proceeding the sexual act.

"In order to proceed along our evolutionary path, we need to free ourselves from the lattice work of emotional charges that form our karmic patterns that are rooted and housed in sexuality and the resultant male/female agreement."

Silvio patted his notebook and glanced at it once again for reference before he continued, "It is important to look at sex in terms of saving and re-channeling energy. So much of being successful along the sexual path has to do with putting sexual energy into the right perspective, free from the views and restraints imposed on us by learned behavior and its desire to perpetuate itself. That is why it is recommended that when dealing with sexuality, it is advantageous to have your state of awareness aligned with at least the Chi-level which is energetically beyond the accustomed range of learned behavior's moving and breathing patterns."

"Why do we have such a strong interest in sex?" I asked. "Why do we want to be sexual?"

Silvio replied, "It's the life-force. Inherently we know it is important. Through sexual practice we can connect with this force and use it to invigorate our bodies. The energy of the lower Dan Tien, where sexual energy resides, has been alienated by learned behavior and needs to be re-integrated. So, one of the things that sexual practice can do is to move life-force beyond the layers of learned behavior and the related maladies it creates in the body.

He began pointing at various Tibetan thangkas with depictions of a male Buddha in union with a female consort. "The primordial celebration of all our senses," he smiled. "The metaphor of sexuality is one of the most potent images of union that we have. So, it is often used to evoke the awe of the sacred, of uniting oneself with the life-force and beyond, or to show the breaking down of the barriers between what we 'think' we are with what we 'think' we perceive.

"Notice carefully what happens during the sexual act. All your perception, seeing, hearing, tasting, smelling, touching, and the intellect— everything gathers, before and all around you, like a consort. At orgasm, the inner and outer merge. You become one with the life-force with evolution and for a millisecond your 'being' merges with the True Self."

Silvio then went on to say, "And when you can stay on the edge of orgasm you will be on the edge of realization. Also, you can infuse your body, and what is your body but an amalgamation of all of your perception, with life-force which then can imbue your body with healing energy."

Silvio stopped for a moment and looked at me. He then picked up a magnifying glass and peered at me through it wide-eyed and said, "The key to the sexual disciplines is regulating and extending orgasm so that one can maintain and explore awareness. You see, right at the edge of orgasm we are free from learned behavior.

And this may well be the reason why the French call orgasm 'the little death,'" he said laughing.

"So, apply focused concentration to prolong orgasm. And let your awareness reside in the gap on the edge of orgasm!"

He put down the magnifying glass and continued in another vein, "We are talking about uniting with the pressure to transform and evolve that is pushing us to manifest along our path. Contrary to popular belief, you need to be able to somehow use your sexual and or life energy to move along the spiritual path of evolution and transformation. We need to learn to redistribute the life-force that permeates our sexual energies and that have been diverted by learned behavior and bring them out into the world with our practices."

He paused, then looked at me and said, "But you have to be careful.

There is a balance to maintain.

"On the one hand—if you get too much of that juicy life-force/sexual energy going you can become 'oversexed' and that scatters your concentration. You don't have to be a rocket scientist to see that 'oversexed' people are a little crazy," he laughed. "Way too much energy, and learned behavior freaks out and can become damaged.

"On the other hand—if you don't have enough juice flowing you won't have enough energy to build up your concentration to allow the pushes and pulls of the path to move through you."

He then reiterated this so that it would sink in, "We have to maintain that delicate balance. Orgasm releases energy and can lessen our ability to concentrate. But when we store more energy than we can handle we can go a little crazy and our concentration can become unfocused.

"You have to look closely at your own sexuality and its effect on your being, and then devise a strategy for how to use it. Get your priorities straightened out. Try to look at sexual energy from the perspective of your path or your personal evolution. Place your sexuality in the context of gaining energy to unite with your path."

Having said that, Silvio paused to glance once again into his notebook, then looked up at me and put his finger in the air, just saying, "Love and affection!"

He started speaking again, "As the evolutionary life-giving force spirals out from our sexual core into our 'humanness,' it generates the feelings of love and affection. This is a natural progression, but the latticework of parasitic learned behavior interrupts and distorts this flow for its own ends and creates the male/female agreement to abscond with this energy.

"You can begin to understand why the practitioners of sexual yogas would say that if you can get the energy straightened out on the sexual level the effect of this radiates outward to the rest of your life. It spirals out and purifies your feelings of love and affection.

"As you loosen control of the patterns of learned behavior, you get in touch with the evolutionary forces and allow these to flow out through the moving language of the body. This then can produce some very beneficial effects both in your physical body as well as in your personal psychology as you move along to the next step.

"But you must watch out for 'looking for love in all the wrong places,'" Silvio said, laughing mischievously.

"So, Silvio tell me more about love and affection?" I asked, trying to get a grip. "And how does falling in love fit in?"

Silvio smiled gleefully, "Magnificent question! I have been waiting for you to stir up this bee's nest.

"Yes, you could say that 'falling in love' leads to a massive activity in the Tai Chi Pole and overwhelms the 'Four Thieves' and their master: learned behavior. And in this way, it could catapult you into the power of the evolutionary stream. The new brightness in your eyes, ears, taste, smell you can experience are a testament to that."

With a sparkle in his eye he continued, "And then we attempt to merge our stories with these feelings, and they become 'personal,' then suddenly," he gleefully continued, "POOF—the feeling goes away, eaten up once again by learned behavior.

"Talking about where learned behavior lurks: watch out regarding putting too much of your money into the love and affection account at the bank of learned behavior," he continued laughing.

"Silvio, are you seriously making fun of human affection," I asked, feeling offended.

That made Silvio burst into some serious laughter. And slapping his thighs he pointed a finger at me and said, "Got you!"

After he calmed down, he continued in a more focused manner, "Whether it be sex, love, or affection—the key to this attraction is that deep inside underneath the patterns put there by our learned behavior is the power of evolution that we are seeking to become a part of, united with. In the midst of our sexuality is this power, and as it flowers outward through love and affection learned behavior attaches more and more of itself to it. So you can see that if these patterns can be dealt with at the edge of orgasm there can be far reaching effects.

"Affection—there is nothing wrong with affection," he added. "In fact, it is essential. Creating feelings of joy is a wonderful way to treat this human vehicle," he said, patting his thigh. "While we are human it is the core of everything that is good in us.

"But on the other hand, due to its co-option by learned behavior, it is also the core of everything that is rotten. Human affection—the most difficult to unravel. The reason is that this is so is because love is impersonal. It exists as a force all on its own. We can tap into it. But it is not ours. It exists outside of our story."

He continued, "When you get in touch with the life-force and bring it back out through the layers of your being it can free you from the tyrannical grip of your story. You have to understand that our charged stories overlay our natural human affection.

"We are basically taught: no story, no personal affection. We have a deep affection for all that we create through our perception. So, then really, the reverse is true: no personal affection, no story. Our charged story is a skewed interpretation of affection. We have been taught to run affection through our stories to the point that they become indistinguishable. Thus, we see de-charging or tampering in any way with our learned story as a threat to getting our needs for affection met.

"Now listen closely, friend," he said as he moved his head abruptly, to focus on me. "Can you now see how when we are young our story and our breathing and moving patterns are merged? Can you see how this story and its resultant patterns are placed in your body, seemingly innocuously, when you are young?

Can you see the resultant tension that occurs at puberty when learned behavior tries to control the outpouring of the evolutionary forces? And can you begin to understand our approach?

"How we are trying to align ourselves more directly with the evolutionary forces within us and spread them throughout our body? And ultimately—how de-charging your story can have a positive effect on your health?"

After this dramatic elucidation Silvio wiped his brows and said, "Affection is where you can judge the real proof of the pudding."

After a pause he went on, "Do you remember how I talked to you about 'creating your own system'? One has to know one's own body well, as for each person the physical particulars are a bit different. You must understand yourself, both physically and emotionally. You also need to become aware of your emotional proclivities or predilections—how one's sexual balance affects one's emotions and concentration. You have to understand your own dynamics amid the expectations and pressures created by learned behavior around you. If you don't change how you talk to your body and how your body talks to the bodies around you, nothing really changes.

"Remember—you are on your own path!"

Silvio looked around his studio and with a big smile faced me and said, "The downside of sex is that it is clouded with desire, passion, and so-o-o much pressure that you can rarely control and enjoy it at the same time—and it is very quick.

"Like dying in an accident—quick, quick, quick."

Silvio grinned, then said, "To use this path you need to build your concentration to deal with all that pressure.

"And if you are lucky enough you will find someone to explore it with."

# Chapter 20

# Li Tse/Silvio—Pull of the Path

Silvio suddenly cupped his right ear with his hand as if he was hearing something. His face lit up, he then scratched his chin and grinned, "It would be good if Li Tse was here to help me discuss meditation, as he is truly a master weaver of the path."

As if on cue, I saw Li Tse on his silver Kawasaki approaching, with three iced coffees and packages of food swinging from the handlebars. It was as if the party had finally started. Silvio waved me outside and I went to greet Li Tse. Silvio began bringing chairs out into the courtyard in front of his house, placing them next to a table with a blue and white tile checkerboard embedded in it.

Li Tse and I soon were sitting down sipping our coffees while Silvio went back and forth bringing out paraphernalia and setting the scene to his liking.

"Thanks, Li Tse," I said, pointing to the coffee. "This comes at the right moment. Silvio really had my head spinning."

Silvio finally approached the table, overjoyed, saying, "Li Tse, right on time as always. I was just about to talk to our young friend here about the discipline of meditation.

"And not only that—you came just in time for lunch. Coming right up," he said, laughing, as he went into his house carrying the assortment of food that Li Tse had brought. He returned with barbecued chicken, a big bowl of *som tam*, spicy papaya salad and sticky rice, a famous dish from northeastern Thailand.

"I made this som tam myself, so have at it," he exclaimed, laughing, while rubbing his hands together in anticipation. And the feast was on.

For a while the world receded and the only sound to be heard was the silence of munching.

There's a moment when your stomach is full and your mind settles. When this happened, I looked around and appreciated the scenery, starting with the hills and mountains around us. The nearest peaks were purple, the next one is mauve, then there were blue ones and light blue ones, going off into the horizon which blurred into a pink haze.

"What did they put into the food?" I mused, smiling.

Then I took in the mysterious allure of the close-by rice fields where I could still feel the spirit of the verdant jungle that they replaced.

I turned my attention to my two friends as we sat in peaceful digestive silence. Then I remembered, as I had many times before, something that my ayahuasca teacher once told me, that "it was best experiencing 'the medicine' with friends," and then I thought "eating must be the same" as I recalled the old Thai saying that "eating by oneself is not delicious."

As I was mulling over these thoughts Silvio rose and started cleaning the table. When he had finished, Li Tse began, "Aaah, yes, meditation," he said, turning his attention to me, smiling.

"Calms the mind as when you ride your motorcycle at just the right speed—when somehow the outside wind matches the speed of your inside winds and thoughts etc. are vaporized and you can just be there. I like it. It's a kind of meditation. It's a break, a feeling of flow and oneness," he chortled.

"We were just talking about how to take a break," Silvio said. "I was introducing our young friend to the various disciplines that attempt to do that. We were just waiting for you to come along to help us understand more about the art of focusing the mind."

He grinned, then made a gesture with his hand, giving the stage over to Li Tse.

"I knew there must have been some reason that I was coming over here," Li Tse said.

He cleared his throat and then with a ceremonious chuckle and a nod of his head he began,

"Eventually, you most likely will be led to sitting meditation because the sitting posture is perhaps the best way to examine your inner warrings. Most people think of meditation as a technique to calm the mind and experience peace, but actually meditation is about mining for realization.

"In sitting you can still your energy and sink back into yourself to explore your source."

Silvio fumbled through the paraphernalia he had brought out and laid a straw mat on the ground. He brushed it off with his hand then promptly sat down in a lotus posture and rolled his eyes up to the top of his head.

All of us started to laugh.

It was a joy to have Silvio around to lighten things up, and I could feel how these two enjoyed each other's company.

After a moment Li Tse continued his elucidation, "In the sitting posture the spine is erect, aligned with gravity. It is in effect the most basic of the erect postures. The energy flowing through our arms and legs is diminished, thus limiting our energetic connection with the outer world, and so this posture can enable us to go deep inside, providing a very concentrated way of probing the deeper strata of awareness."

He stroked his goatee for a moment, before continuing, "But sitting meditation has its limitations. I would recommend that sitting be coupled with some kind of moving or standing and even lying. Sitting is a great posture for going back into essence, but standing and moving are better for engaging the world around us. And lying provides us the access to the dream worlds and deep sleep."

Silvio stood up and moved through an Eight Point Chi Gung form, then stopped and looked at me, saying, "Do you remember how I told you that Chi Gung can become a stable platform for your self-exploration? And how it can help you to store realizations while you stand your ground, being battered by the learned behavior all around you?"

Silvio grinned then gestured towards Li Tse, giving him the stage once again.

Li Tse nodded in return, "You don't perceive and think the same way when you're standing, walking, lying, or sitting. Each posture gravitationally organizes the body in a different way and thus contains its own certain kind of knowledge. Movement for example affords us the possibility of a greater capacity to actively stimulate the healing-body template than sitting does. It can actively stretch your perception out to cover the inner and outer sacs of your energy-body.

"In the sitting position on the other hand there are only limited ways of grounding realizations into the body. However, a natural way of integrating realization into the body while sitting can occur through involuntary shaking. Shaking is a form of gravitational re-connecting which can lead to release of old energetic patterns. Shaking can be an expression of releasing the pent-up energy held by old karmic patterns and re-aligning oneself gravitationally. Realization creates energy, and shaking is one of the body's natural ways of allowing Chi to flow more freely so that it can clear and strengthen energetic pathways in the body."

At this moment Silvio once again got into the lotus posture and began exaggeratedly shaking. We all laughed again, but at the same time I was aware that Silvio was giving me a useful picture that I could take home with me.

Li Tse said, "You could just sit in meditation releasing the shackles of your learned behavior, but there will come a day when you will have to get up and interact with the world somehow.

"And learned behavior will be lurking there," he said, chuckling, "Waiting to pounce. Learned behavior does not care so much about the benefits of sitting meditation, going back in and exploring your source, but it is deathly afraid about this energy being integrated, directed, and manifested in engaging with the world," he explained, waving his index finger at me.

"It is deathly afraid of disruptions of its pre-established movement and breathing patterns that will occur when we re-connect our bodies naturally with the Earth's cocoon."

As the impact of what he just told me reverberated, inside of me images appeared in my mind of so many people I had known in the past who practiced sitting meditation. So, I blurted out, "What about all these Buddhist people who meditate?"

Li Tse got up and cupped his hands over his mouth like a megaphone and said, "Now listen to this! Now listen to this! Buddha was not a Buddhist."

He chuckled, then added, "You see, we are dealing with hand-me-downs."

I looked over at Silvio and saw a smile creep mischievously across his face.

"You guys are terribly irreverent," I said in frustration. "You seem to not believe in anything! What are you guys into anyway? Are you rebels without a cause?"

They burst out, laughing at my discomfort. And when they calmed down a little, Li Tse said, "He caught us red-handed, didn't he?" He smiled, rubbing his hands as if trying to remove red paint from them.

"Seems the conceptual underpinnings of our young friend are getting rumpled," Silvio added.

Which started another round of laughter at my expense.

Finally, after they settled down, and Li Tse had pulled himself back together, he scratched his chin, and said with a chuckle, "I guess we are rebels. We rebel against learned behavior and work towards something unexplainable. At the same time, you could say we know where we are going, but not really. And we can't even say who or what we are." Then beamed me a smile.

After having said that he gazed around the yard until his eyes became fixed upon a moss-covered Buddha statue, and he then said, "Even the Buddha had to change his terms several times during his life so that he could keep the essence of his teachings intact without the pervasive encroachment of learned behavior."

He went on, "One of my teachers used to say that written traditions are just the outer husks of long forgotten knowledge. This knowledge has been separated from us because it comes to us via the written word. And as you may have figured out by now, written language is the first lieutenant of learned behavior.

"Not only that, but many of these traditions come to us from a time long ago when the learned behavior in the world was very different, which makes these teachings difficult to understand in our present-day context, but on the other hand makes them truly more understandable," he said chuckling at this paradox.

"But as I have said to you before—amidst the husks of written traditions some nuggets of truth get through around the edges."

He pulled on his goatee, and continued, "But then, there aren't that many writings within those traditions that come from beyond."

Spreading out his arms he said, "Because they don't write letters back from the other side."

They both laughed.

"But there are hints here and there if you look for them. Like Chuang Tzu's poem I read to you earlier."

He then raised his index finger for emphasis and said, "But never forget—butterflies don't write letters back to caterpillars."

Silvio then suddenly pulled out another plastic baby Buddha statue that I had not seen, from his pile of paraphernalia. This one had a smart phone in its hand and was texting.

He interjected excitingly, "And the Buddha doesn't text us back from the other side either."

Which started another round of laughter that pulled me in.

When we finally calmed down, I raised my hand to grab their attention and asked, "What about the moral rules they talk about in these traditions?"

Li Tse, collecting himself, replied, "First of all, as I just told you, these traditions, to a large degree, are in the state of co-option. So, you need to be diligent. Your actions should be based on what helps your practice or evolution and not doing harm to others. But I don't mean harm in a moral sense, in the way that learned behavior creates morals to perpetuate itself. I mean, construct your life so it leads you along your path towards your evolution. And usually that means treating the learned behavior of the times as lightly as possible.

"Remember, we are disengaging from learned behavior, but we still need it. We have to keep our learned behavior and its concepts of reality somewhat intact, like putting it into automatic pilot, so that the world can be engaged gracefully. But even though you understand and realize that it is important to keep your learned behavior functional, you neither need to nor want to be ruled by it.

"It is by keeping these principles in mind that rules of right conduct should develop. When you are aware of these principles, then the so-called 'rules' or 'morals' that are espoused by tradition become transparent and you can decide for yourself."

I could follow what he was saying, but it was difficult for me to integrate this. I thought it would help to look at it in a more personal way. I asked, "How did you get all into this stuff? Why did you start looking at your patterns anyway? How did it all begin for you?"

Silvio got up, bent over, and started hobbling around with one hand in front of him as if holding a cane, shaking. Then he raised his left index finger and waved it at me and said with a creaky voice, "We were sick, son!"

Li Tse chuckled.

Silvio bolted upright, then dropped his imaginary cane and with a full voice said, "I thought we made this very clear to you already—we had to track down our basic patterns and de-charge them. Our path pulled us. We looked at healing ourselves. We had no choice."

I noticed a difference in Silvio's demeanor since Li Tse had arrived. I could see how he was appreciative of Li Tse being around so he could be more of his natural active self than he had been while with me alone in the morning. And this on the other hand allowed Li Tse to take on his more scholarly role.

Li Tse cleared his throat, "Sitting with the spine erect is an optimal posture to slow your breathing and moving patterns—to move beyond them and to explore the Chi level.

"In sitting meditation, it is possible to slow down your metabolism to the point that your external breathing becomes subtle and refined even to the point that is basically stops. You can then revert to a type of internal breathing, which then helps you slow down both the intensity and the rate of your heartbeat. At this point you can open more of your awareness to the Chi level where it is possible to strongly contact the psychic centers in the Tai Chi Pole."

"Stopping my breathing? Can I really do that, Li Tse? It sounds frightening," I burst out.

"Don't be simple-minded," Silvio said, grinning. "The whole point is not to stop breathing or to make your heart stop beating. What you want to do is to move your awareness first beyond your breath and then beyond your heartbeat to allow it to reside at the Chi level. You move your awareness beyond your idea of your physical body to the edge of perception."

He then looked at me, smiling, and continued emphatically, "Who cares about your breathing or your heartbeat? What is important is where your awareness resides! All we are trying to do here is put the breath and the heartbeat in the right perspective. What we are doing here is moving awareness—not killing ourselves," he said laughing.

Li Tse smiled and shook his head at Silvio's remarks, he then looked at me and said, "I have heard that stopping breathing is not that hard to learn, especially if you keep in mind what Silvio just said. For example, you could start by balancing the pressure of the in-breath and the out-breath and relax into that more and more. And I say 'relax into it' because all you'll be doing is following a natural progression to your source. A progression that increasingly becomes more and more subtle."

He stopped, looked at me, then added, "But it is really just about relaxing. Exploring relaxation."

"Let's take a closer look at breathing," Li Tse said. "The shallower and more even your breathing becomes, the stronger your concentration. And as your concentration builds, you begin to clear up focus in the upper Dan Tien.

"When your breathing gets shallow enough, increasing your concentration, you can then move your awareness from the level of the breath to your heartbeat. Having thus moved your awareness beyond your breath, you begin to naturally clean out your habitual breathing patterns.

"Then as your concentration increases even more and your heartbeat slows, you can then move your awareness from the heartbeat to the center of feeling in your belly.

"And finally, as the breath becomes even more and more subtle and the heartbeat slows more and more and the belly relaxes—then your awareness can open up to the Chi or psychic level deep inside."

Silvio chimed in, grinning, "And this will make your vision brighter, sounds sharper, tastes more delicious, and smells intoxicating and provocative."

Li Tse looked up at Silvio, then went on, "OK, you've learned about the three main energy centers, or Dan Tiens. While discussing learned behavior we also pointed out that it controls us primarily via the 'Four Thieves' which reside in the upper Dan Tien. This also is the place where language forms and concepts reside.

"It is here in the upper Dan Tien where the breathing patterns of our body become the battleground. Traditional meditation keeps awareness on the breath, the area of the nose, the upper Dan Tien. This kind of practice may go deeper and develop some awareness of the heart, 'The Great Mixer,' the middle Dan Tien. But here we are still dealing with a subject and object, something watching something else. We will get into that a little later.

"But quite often traditional meditation evades the lower Dan Tien, the realm of sexuality and life-force—because of learned behavior's inherent fear of awakening this dragon power. So, quite often you'll find meditators who intently fight their own sexuality and life-force—and thus they have a very hard time cultivating their own path as they have cut themselves off from their natural vitality.

"This reminds me of what the famous Mahasiddhi Tilopa once said, 'The problem is not enjoyment. The problem is attachment,'" he chuckled.

Li Tse stroked his goatee and went on, "There are profound experiences that we can explore during meditation. For example, the fears that arise as our breathing becomes shallower.

"As your breath gets shallower and more subtle, you will experience a friction at the edge of your breathing which is caused by physically confronting the patterns of learned behavior. This friction stems from learned behavior's fear of its own death. This idea is at the root of its functioning patterns. The more that you understand that this fear is merely an effect of learned behavior's grip and control, you'll be able to relax through this fear, relaxing towards your essence.

"In this way, relaxing through breathing can begin the pathway of finding out where you come from—finding your source. By moving awareness along your breath, as it's becoming shallower and shallower, you're moving closer and closer to the essence of breath. Subjectivity and objectivity begin to merge. Closer and closer to the subtle pulse of life that was sparked at conception.

"Also, while shifting your awareness in this way you are slowly de-charging patterns of learned behavior, if you have the right focus. And at the same time, quite naturally, you are transferring recovered energy to your energy-body. This simple practice can give you a glimpse of the power of your evolutionary path."

"As you do this you will understand more and more, at an experiential level, how your learned post-natal patterns are held in place by your breathing. The friction that occurs as your breath becomes shallower and shallower can create a pressure, even a heat, that increases your concentration, which then allows your awareness to burn and move beyond those patterns. Simple as going through the gears of your car," he smiled.

Li Tse continued, "I have always found it interesting that as you relax the overall pressure within your being increases as it is pulled, or to merge, with what is outside. And when you gain more pressure, it is as if the spiral of your path around you is getting tighter and tighter and is squeezing out learned behavior, and what is outside gets closer and closer.

"At the same time, you may notice that your senses become clearer, crisper and more precise. These practices begin to take out and transform the energetic charges left there by learned behavior. And as a result, you move beyond those patterns, and as you do so you become aware of them. Thus, if you stay with the practice they show up, lose their grip and fall off. They should be observed through the eye of awareness and let go."

Li Tse went on, "As you move towards the edge of breath, you're closer to death, particularly closer to learned behavior's idea of death. This same phenomenon happens on the edge of orgasm. The closer you get to that edge, the more your concentration builds, and you move further and further from your learned behavior patterns. Here the male/female agreement begins to unravel.

"In the Tibetan tradition they say that the power of concentration in normal waking consciousness is increased sevenfold just before orgasm and twenty-five-fold just before death. It has long been known that it is at the edge of sex, death and sleep, loss of consciousness and similar states that we have a momentary glimpse of our True Self."

Li Tse collected his thoughts for a moment, stroked his goatee once again, then looked at me and said, "Dissolving your sense of self and your story is like peeling back the layers of an onion, going deeper and deeper until you reach the state of bliss which then opens you to the mind's natural luminosity."

"What about our emotions? Is bliss an emotion?" I asked.

Silvio took over for a moment, "Emotions are things like anger, fear, sadness, anxiety—these are mechanisms that the body uses to re-align itself, to balance Chi-flow within itself. The feelings we are talking about are much more primordial and less self-conscious. They are overpowering like being on the edge, sensations like terror, shock, and ultimately bliss. Bliss is not really an emotion, or you could say it is the highest of all emotions. It is a feeling, a very refined touching, experienced on the edge of self-awareness. And as such can be used to burn out some of your karmic tendencies."

Li Tse began again, "The lower Dan Tien is where the passion and life-force resides. The upper Dan Tien is where the thinking mind resides. The refined essence of the upper Dan Tien is the bliss of the clear light, and the refined essence of the lower Dan Tien is the bliss of the life-force.

"And it is at the middle Dan Tien where you can mix these two energies. Here you can merge the focus and light of the upper Dan Tien with the feeling and power of the lower Dan Tien. Focus sheds light on feeling and feeling enlivens focus. By mixing them in the middle Dan Tien you can engender a portal to your True Self.

"Be careful, we're just trying to point out a direction here. To point out practical ways for fusing different energies in the body.

"Bliss and spaciousness, at the edge of self-awareness, is where the known sparks with the unknown. This is the realm of the truth-body. Being with bliss and spaciousness is being at the edge of your bubble of perception. Hovering back and forth on this edge creates a friction, a bliss that dissolves karmas.

"Bliss is the instant before realization. When we are in it, it is bliss. When we look back, we notice realizations. Realization happens in hindsight. Realization is the first reflection. If you follow a realization back to its source, you will come to acknowledge that it is the surfacing of the True Self."

He paused, "Do you follow me?"

I was feeling overwhelmed, and by seeing the looks on the faces of Li Tse and Silvio, I must have shown it. Silvio slightly raised his right hand and said, "Jai yen yen! Keep a cool heart and take it slowly!"

Li Tse looked over at Silvio and nodded, then said, "We'll go over it all again now so that you can get a better grasp."

They both got up as if on cue, brushed off their pants and then stood in front of me. Silvio began, "By regulating the breath we first neutralize the 'Four Thieves' and open the 'Hallway to the Ancestors.'"

Silvio gestured at Li Tse, who took up the baton, saying, "This takes our awareness back to the center of the upper Dan Tien, beyond where the four senses meet."

Silvio went on, "This then moves you beyond the breathing patterns that were put into your body after birth, your post-natal patterns."

Slowly they started to circle around me while continuing their explanations, which had me spinning, creating a deep hypnotizing effect.

Li Tse, "You then neutralize the patterns of movement in your body by directing your awareness beyond the heartbeat. This releases your pre-natal patterns—the patterns of fluid flow and muscle movement in your body, that are connected to the heartbeat."

My eyes were almost closed now. I vaguely saw Silvio rub his belly, as they continued circling, "You then direct your awareness down to allow the lower Dan Tien to relax."

As they circled their words came at me from different directions.

I heard Li Tse again, "As you relax the lower Dan Tien, this then opens up the Tai Chi Pole. This moves your awareness to the more subtle refined level of the psychic centers of Chi-flow."

"Next," it was Silvio talking again, "In your middle Dan Tien, you blend the inner feeling of the lower Dan Tien with the inner focus of the upper Dan Tien. This then mixes the highest visual sensation, clear light, with the highest feeling state, bliss."

By now they really had me spinning.

I heard Li Tse saying, as if from far away, "Using breath to nullify the 'Four Thieves' takes you beyond post-natal breathing patterns. Slowing heartbeat and relaxing belly takes you beyond prenatal movement patterns. Then mixing bliss with spaciousness takes your awareness to the edge of the True Self."

They circled around me as if wrapping me in an ever-tightening coil with this body-to-body transmission. Their words leaving a deep imprint.

Then they both slightly raised their voices in unison and said, "Gravity is a series of pressures that spin us around and around and affects us from all sides within the living matrix of the Earth. When your cocoon matches the cocoon of the Earth, both your body and your story disappear."

Silvio then stopped in front of me while Li Tse caught up and play-fully bumped into him. They both then turned to face me, smiling, and giggling as they wiped their hands on their pant legs in a gesture of completion. Then they ceremoniously sat down, both of them beaming.

After a long silence, I finally spoke as a thought suddenly occurred to me. All this talk about patterns reminded me of what Silvio had told me about the path and the trappings of sexuality. This made me wonder whether there was a way of touching the edge of the truth-body through sexual practices. So, I asked, "How are our learned behavior patterns related to our sexuality?"

Silvio looked at Li Tse, then back at me before beginning, "Basically you can say that in essence all of our learned behavior patterns are being transmitted sexually, body-to-body because of the male/female agreement. And yes, sexual practices can be used to take you to an edge beyond those patterns. Sexuality can be used like breath as a way of going through and beyond learned behavior. And breathing techniques actually can amplify and augment one's sexual practices. They can help you to prolong the time prior to orgasm and help you maintain your concentration in that orgasmic state. And it is by staying in this state that you can become aware of and de-charge many of your established patterns and karmas."

Silvio nodded over at Li Tse who then said, "During sexual interaction we create an intense pressure within our being that is amplified by the merging of our individual cocoon with another. We connect and enliven the flow in each other's Tai Chi Pole.

"Thus, if you want to deal with identifying and transcending learned behavior patterns, this is an excellent setting. When two people get closer and closer to orgasm their awareness can go deeper and deeper, closer and closer to the life-force—and beyond.

"When one can remain in the orgasmic state, and prolong it by combining it with the use of breathing techniques that increase concentration, one can release energy that has been diverted by one's learned behavior patterns. This reclaimed energy can then be redistributed joyfully and naturally throughout the body.

"This is how sexual practices can be used as a discipline as it can expose the deeply embodied roots of learned behavior."

Li Tse went on, "In the orgasmic breakdown of our normal consciousness, we begin to understand the makeup and creation of our learned behavior and get a glimpse of what lies beyond. Sexual practices can lead us to states on the edge. Like drugs, accidents, 'Zen sickness,' extreme emotions, exhaustive physical fatigue, and close encounters with death—we can use sexual practices to touch the edge of the truth-body."

I looked over at Silvio who appeared to be completely enraptured by Li Tse's elucidation.

Silvio then said, "And at the end of every good sexual act we will feel enlivened and look at our surroundings with renewed interest. Our senses cleaned and purified, we look and find a world filled with iridescent colors, crystal-clear sounds. The whole world is delicious, permeating all of our senses. It breaks down the fog created by our story and enables us to greet and engage with the world with renewed vigor."

I looked at them as they then both gazed up into the trees with big smiles on their faces.

After a few moments Silvio went over to his pile of paraphernalia, rummaged through it and pulled out a small replica of the picture he had shown me earlier, depicting the different energetic centers in the body, then placed it on the table. He then looked over at Li Tse and nodded, signaling him to begin.

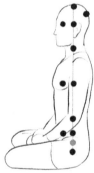

Li Tse started out slowly. Pointing at the five centers above the head, moving his finger downwards along them and down the whole Tai Chi Pole, he exclaimed, "*Focus!* Focus has no breath. Focus exists beyond the breath. You need to move your awareness beyond the breath to really contact it in its pure undiluted form.

"This occurs as your heartbeat gets more and more shallow and your awareness begins to abide at the Chi or psychic level. When your awareness resides at this Chi level, your focus clarifies.

"At the same time as you are moving through and beyond your breathing and heartbeat you are de-charging your patterns—and thus: your story. But as this happens so quickly, you will have to go through it many times before you really notice the results in your everyday life.

"Also, during this process, because you have de-charged your patterns, your awareness will have moved to a place where language no longer is laced with the trappings of learned behavior. It is here that sometimes focus begins to communicate to you via language. It is the evolving voice of your path. It begins to talk to you through an internal voice that will illuminate and advise you. And it gets clearer and clearer as you get clearer and clearer, and your story unravels."

I looked over and saw a smile of appreciation creeping across Silvio's face.

Li Tse continued, "So, language once de-charged can become a conduit of true and essential information instead of being an impediment laced with learned behavior."

He went on, "Strengthening your connection with focus is like building a muscle. It is important to understand that it requires constant and continuous clarifying of focus to give your strivings continuity.

The process of following psychic awareness to its source reveals the nature of focus to us. We begin to understand that listening to it can direct us to the next step on our evolutionary path."

Li Tse stroked his goatee once again, then said, "But be very careful, as focus or the clarifying of the upper Dan Tien is not an end in itself."

"Focus is an illuminating power. But what is most important is— what guides focus and gives it direction? What is directing focus? There is a meditation for you!

"It may be a given that focus runs through us—but it is up to us to decide how to focus and what to focus on, and to look for what or who is focusing. You might even begin to focus on focus." He laughed.

I was so absorbed in Li Tse's words that I hadn't noticed that while Li Tse was talking, Silvio had disappeared into his house. When I looked up, I saw him walking towards us with one of his old books in hand. He sat down again and started flipping through the pages.

After finding what he was looking for, he looked at me and began, "There once was a very famous saint in Tibet called Milarepa. One day his main disciple came by to report with some sense of accomplishment that when he practiced single-pointed concentration, he could remain for seven days in one uninterrupted session.

"Milarepa reproached him, saying, 'You sat for seven days but have not experienced your True Being. If instead you would have directed your focus on the feeling of life-force down in your lower abdomen, not only would you have been able to realize yourself quickly, but also you would have been able to get up after a brief period of time and bring your illumination out into the world.'"

Li Tse then added with a soothing voice, "I'm sure that Silvio shared with you that ancient Chinese sage's proverb: that the bodies of all the eminent monks of great virtue were as soft and supple as a baby's."

He then stopped for dramatic effect before he exclaimed, "But in our training, not only do you want to feel like a newborn when you're sitting but also when you're walking around in the world, and finally when you're relating to other people through learned behavior."

We had been talking for a long time. And the heat of the day was receding. I noticed the shadows were slowly lengthening. And the world felt different, there, under the trees. The trees knowledge of the passing day was being transmitted to us and we were there under their care.

All of a sudden Li Tse nodded to Silvio who got up, put himself into a stance, tightening the internal pulley, that Veronica had shown me, thus activating right structure, and stood there in front of us.

"Let me reiterate," Li Tse said. "After we have moved deeply within it is most important to bring that knowledge out into the world. We want to live in a world of realization. The body was made for moving around in this air/earth environment structured by gravity. Taking a break to understand ourselves and to explore our essence and our potentials beyond learned behavior internally is a necessity. But once you have tapped into your essence this living knowledge needs to be brought back into and permeate the world, and how we relate to it through our standing and moving."

He paused, "It's really quite simple—if you walk in the world in the right way, you will naturally de-charge your story. Every time you pace the Earth correctly you are giving your body a maximum energy charge."

I interrupted, "What do you mean by 'walking in the world in the right way'? I've been walking the Earth my whole life—isn't that natural?"

Li Tse smiled at me approvingly and said, "Excellent question, right to the core of the matter: how to develop correct gravitational alignment, or as we call it 'right structure.' With right structure, when you place your feet on the Earth you will give your whole body a charge—which negates the power of your learned story.

"It is from this correct contact with the Earth that your whole energetic network can be dramatically charged. Working on structure is working on the core problem of how to relate to gravity. It is a long-term project but a worthy one, one that can result in many kinds of unfathomable breakthroughs."

Li Tse then looked over at Silvio who chimed in, "Right structure basically is correct alignment with gravity so that our transformation can take place. Right structure acts as the edifice that stores and directs the flow of energy, or Chi, that allows for the pull of the path to take hold."

He then stopped to look at me and said, "You know that feeling that you have in the morning that gets you up and that pushes you throughout the day? We're trying to get to the essence of that feeling, and where that feeling comes from. Our practices are simply meant to refine and embellish our connection to that force."

"Well, I know that particular feeling in the morning. But when I think about it, I don't know if it's pushing me or pulling me? What's going on here?" I asked smiling.

Silvio responded by twisting his hands in circular movements, forwards and backwards in front of him and said, "Is it inside or outside? We don't really know. Does it matter? It is a force we can feel all around and within that permeates our whole being." He then rolled his eyes a couple of times, smiled, and said, "But what is most important is we feel that it's there! And that we are it. But we need to trace where it comes from."

Li Tse then took over again, laughing, and added, "Right structure provides you with a platform for further exploration as you mine for realizations, for both going deeper, and also bringing energy back out."

He continued as he looked over at Silvio, who I could see was now bristling with energy, "Right structure, functionally, establishes a container for Chi-flow. It strengthens the reciprocal connection between the physical body and the movement-body and their connection to the energy-body and the Earth. And because of this, right structure allows the evolutionary force within us to move through the physical body most efficiently."

Silvio made a slight movement and I looked over. He smiled and said, "Right structure should be the very core of the way you walk on the Earth. In this way you can get more energy from direct contact with the cocoon of the Earth itself. You will begin to see that the more you start walking on the Earth the right way, the more it will tighten up your life, freeing you from the pressures of the learned behavior around you. Build up enough energy and sustain this new level and you will naturally change your relating to people as you align yourself more and more with the nourishing matrix of the Earth."

Off to the side I heard Li Tse clearing his throat. I looked over and saw him pulling on his goatee, then chuckling, "You know Silvio's favorite picture, yes? The one with the frozen cubes? Right structure supplies us with life energy to melt those cubes and release that stuck energy, which then opens our connection to the path coiling around us. And it is there to hold and circulate the energy that is being released from learned behavior. Right structure supplies a bridge that supersedes learned behavior. You can learn to be around others, and not be affected by the pressures exerted by their learned behavior, or in other words not let them throw you back into yours."

"Once you've gathered enough energy from beyond the clutches of learned behavior you naturally begin to stabilize the energy-body," Li Tse said, grinning, as he clutched his hand in front of himself a couple of times. "And by continuously purifying Chi residues you break up the crusts in your body to weave your cocoon."

"Weaving the cocoon, again? What are you talking about? How do I do that?" I asked, a bit overwhelmed, still not clear about this cocoon idea.

Silvio, walking back and forth, explained, "Right structure is the foundation for the weaving of our cocoon. To help establish and strengthen it we practice our Eight Point Chi Gung so that right structure can become a bridge for the flow of awareness. We use our Eight Point Chi Gung to help stabilize that bridge."

Silvio and Li Tse seemed to be always full of energy. And now, as I watched Silvio's moving around, I started to understand why they seemed to be able to maintain right structure whatever posture they were in.

As if reading my mind, Silvio responded, "Right posture is one of the outward manifestations of good internal structure and good Chi-flow. If you build right structure while compacting and reconnecting the body you will create more pressure and naturally move with correct posture. As you increase pressure in the body, Chi will have more places to flow with better quality and more strength. This process develops its own inertia; it works as self-replicating battery through time. Along the bridge of right structure the energy is free to flow through you naturally, out into your life."

Li Tse then said, "To clarify, if you have right structure, you will be most optimally gravitationally aligned, especially while standing and moving. In this way your whole system works more efficiently, which will allow the force of evolution to integrate itself throughout the physical body and out into the world. Right structure creates a kind of exoskeleton for this process to happen."

"An 'exoskeleton'? But I thought that's an outer casing of insects?" I wondered aloud.

"Talking about insects," Silvio said, while rummaging through the thing he had assembled next to us. He pulled out a metal beetle with four legs and a windup key to the side. He wound it up then turned it loose to edge across the table.

Then I looked over and saw Silvio beginning to move. I saw waves of liquefied energy cross his body, pushing the "dough" around. His movements resembled the windup toy that was crawling on the table. I suddenly had a feeling of déjà vu again, a sense of dislocation coming in from another dimension, and a momentary flashing of colors, a remembering of my dream.

As I became entranced by Silvio's movements, I heard Li Tse say, "It's not only good to have toys to help us see how our bodies work mechanically, but also to help us sense how our bodies are related to all creation. You can see now, as Silvio moves, how he is accentuating the lines of structure in his body. You might be able to feel how right structure creates a dynamic container for movement and perception."

I watched Silvio, fascinated until he finally finished his "beetle" movements. He then stopped right in front of me, and bowed ceremonially, before sitting down.

Li Tse continued, "Right structure is the gravitational bridge for integrating the blasts of energy that occur when learned behavior is forced to crack open: during the explosions of puberty and the transitions of 'Zen sickness.' Remember those energetic gateways that Felina described to you?

"As you align yourself more efficiently with gravity the power of your evolutionary path flows through you more strongly. Aligning your body with right structure gravitationally rocks the edifice of your story. It stops the flow, the rhythm, and the patterns of your story, and de-charges the dramas that keep it afloat. And when you override your story that changes everything."

Silvio intervened, "Right structure grows on you in an almost imperceptible way as your path keeps pulling you. One way that you start to observe its effects is as if you're looking through a rearview mirror," he turned his head, looking back over his shoulder.

"I remember when I became aware of it and started working with acupuncture and our Eight Point Chi Gung practices. Imperceptibly my path filled my life. It seeped in and permeated my life without my conscious knowing.

"I can recall one day I found myself running up four flights of stairs in the apartment building I was living in. I stopped and looked at myself in disbelief, asking, 'where did this come from?' I felt like I was seventeen again."

He paused for a moment, then said, "What we notice with people when they get into our practices is like a fog lifting around their bodies. Lifting and being replaced by an ongoing youthful brightness."

I looked over at Silvio and Li Tse and noticed that they were men of age. But they didn't feel old to me at all. They were supple, their minds were pliant and lucid and I was always struck by their vitality. Then I remembered how Silvio had put it in one of our first conversations when he asked rhetorically, "Where are we going to get energy from?" And he had answered himself, saying, "By dismantling learned behavior which has stolen our birth right."

He then went on to say, "When we are free from that we can flow with the energy from beyond."

I could see in both of them the living proof. And I could easily perceive how different their energetic presence was from the other elderly people I knew.

So, I said, jokingly, to them, "Hey, old guys—how come you appear so ageless?"

Li Tse looked over at Silvio, snorted and they both chuckled. Then Silvio said, "Li Tse, you old Chinese fart, this young fellow hasn't even listed to a single word we taught him."

They then both started to cackle. Finally, Silvio waved his hand, as if opening a curtain, setting the stage for Li Tse, once again.

"Let's talk about old age then," Li Tse said smiling.

"We naturally start to become acutely aware of learned behavior at puberty as the sexual energy explodes within us and learned behavior attempts to control it. As we get older the energetic patterns that learned behavior has imprinted on us are still the same, but because they have repeated themselves so many times and there is less energetic pressure within us to feed them. It becomes easier for us to detect and observe them. And since we don't have as much energy as before, we simply cannot so easily ignore the imbalances within us that these patterns create.

But on the other hand, as we get older, we have more opportunity to release these energetic patterns by identifying and detaching ourselves from them. In this way aging can provide us with a medium through which we can deal with our learned behavior and with our story more efficiently."

He paused, before continuing, "You just need to arrange your life so you can keep your exploration going. The physical energy available is less, which makes the balance more precarious, but that can be made up for by greater awareness."

Silvio shared his Cheshire grin with me, then nodded over to Li Tse to continue, "Being on your path is also a protection for your health and vitality. The power of the path can even help you to overhaul death—or at least your learned behavior's idea of death, which takes a lot of your energy. And as you gravitationally align to the cocoon of the Earth with right structure, the associated diseases that were placed upon your body through the misalignments created by your story will start to fall away.

"Basically, by opening to your path and allowing it to pull you along two things will start to happen.

You'll get to the point that on the one hand you'll develop an easier and simpler usage of your learned behavior, while at the same time you'll become much more energized by integrating a much more balanced Chi-flow and thus you'll experience an infinitely stronger life.

"Stay open to the force of evolution by using your path to stay connected to it. The force of evolution is moving through you and it is looking for its natural fruition. And as we have told you, reinforcing right structure allows the path to move through you more fully. It will help you to weave your cocoon and go beyond."

"And get rid of karmas," Silvio chimed in.

I then watched Silvio rushing into his house and returning with a jug of "herbal brew" and three glasses. He had told me about this brew once before. It was a special Chinese herbal formula, soaked for months in high-quality rice wine.

He filled the glasses, looked mischievously into our eyes, then raised his glass and with a grin made a toast, exclaiming, *Fuck the karmas!*"

His actions caught me by surprise, but his exuberance was infectious.

And before we knew it, all three of us had clinked our glasses and were singing out joyfully, "*Yes, fuck the karmas, fuck them all!*"

I was always amazed at how these two could change a serious discussion into a joyous event.

After we recovered and collected ourselves, Silvio looked at me with a smile on his face and started, "In the same way that you can learn to move your awareness beyond breathing and movement to the Chi level you can also move your awareness beyond the learned behavior idea of death to the realm of the evolving energy-body and beyond. The energy-body is made of Chi-flow. Becoming aware of and keeping the awareness on the energy-body enables realization. And realizations are what gives us the power to weave the cocoon of transformation. If we gather enough Chi-flow in our energy-body to weave our cocoon, we can take off on our journey of personal transformation."

I looked at the shadows around us again. They had grown. I could feel the vibrations of the Earth's cocoon around us more keenly. The trees were making their presence felt. Their day's work was almost done. I could already sense their anticipation that in a couple of hours they would be releasing a wave of joyous exhalation. And as I listened carefully, I could detect the minute rustling of insects in the grasses.

I heard Li Tse's voice in a corner of my awareness. It was as if he once again had read my thoughts,

"Remember, it is the pressure inside of the Earth's cocoon that nourishes our physical and energy-bodies.

It is correct gravitational alignment, right structure, that connects us to it. The more we connect with the rhythms of this pressure, the more energy we gather to cultivate our energy-body.

"It takes time to realign our energies with the Earth's cocoon, but once you have reached a critical mass you can then transform those into the healing-body template. Right structure functions as a bridge for that."

Li Tse took in the scene as he immersed himself in reverie for about ten minutes. Finally, I saw him inhale, then exhale deeply before he got around to speaking once again, "As I mentioned to you before when we discussed meditation, going back to and tapping into our source is important, but bringing that awareness back untainted out into the world and beyond is what connects us to the path of evolution.

"Instinctively our body already knows our evolutionary path. As evolution moves through us it is felt at a very deep level. It is a deep almost invisible current all around us. At this level we know what we are to become. Like the monarch butterflies we already know where we are going.

"I will try to describe these feelings," he said, exhaling slowly once again. "They really don't fit into words. But try to get a sense of it through the spaces between them."

Li Tse started, "Evolution is an infinite unfathomable force well beyond our perception and abilities to conceive, not to mention talk about. But the curiosity of our puny little selves sometimes tries to make sense out of it. Or attempts to describe it," he chuckled.

He then began speaking deliberately and slowly, "It is a ceaseless burst, a blind and impersonal force. The force of evolution is like a big spiral falling back in on itself. It orchestrates the dance all around us, and gives us hints. We are but little spirals, amidst all of our sensations, patterns and feelings, connected to its pulsations. Somehow, we know we are its reflection, although infinitely small, yet still knowing that we are a part of it. And at the same time realizing that we will never understand it.

"This force is a force that wants to evolve and move through us. The more aligned we are with it the more it shapes our lives. It can be felt like a pull from beyond, from the outside, and at the same time a push from the inside until it flows through us and becomes us."

He looked at me with piercing eyes, saying, "Just let it pull you—and change your life! And you will attain a level of freedom people will not be able to understand."

Silvio looked at Li Tse and slowly moved his hand over the table as if dusting it. I thought he was using these motions to feel Li Tse's elucidation with his body.

He nodded approvingly and then waved at Li Tse to continue, who did so by saying, "As I said, evolution, as close as we can feel it and try to describe it from this side, is a huge force spiraling in the midst of itself. And the truth-body is our infinitesimal individualized replica or reflection that connects us to it. We can get a true and deep sense of our connection with this force—but not of its immensity. It is refracted down to us and we are opened to it through our realizations.

"You can feel a force pushing us towards our True Self. Our path is the manifestation of this pressure through time. And at the same time, the True Self is pulling us towards itself. We sense this and it manifests as our path.

"The True self is a feeling that permeates everything. It is made of essence beyond perception. But there are many ways that we touch it. Each time this occurs our learned behavior cracks open a little more, sparking realizations. Each time the True Self makes contact we perceive it as an energetic laser of realization, weaving our cocoon.

But really the True Self is everything. It is beyond, yet it is the very fabric of our perception."

Li Tse paused some time to collect his thoughts then took a deep breath, then smiled and said, "To paraphrase an old Buddhist saying,

*There are 10,000 paths to enlightenment, and I will walk them all.*"

"Truth is knocking at you from all sides," Li Tse explained, putting it into perspective. "You're just rolling around inside of yourself, trying to put it together."

I looked over at Silvio who was clearing his throat. Then with a semi-comical intonation, stringing out the words, he began singing a refrain of an old American gospel song as he pantomimed knocking on a door.

*Somebody's knockin',*
*Somebody's knockin',*
*Somebody's knockin',*
*Must be the hand of the Lord.*

Li Tse and I smiled and then clapped with appreciation.

After a pause, Li Tse continued, "Our evolutionary path is knocking. Our evolutionary path, through our truth-body, is knocking on and sometimes cracking the crusts of learned behavior, disrupting the narrative of our story. We find reflections of the True Self in many different things. And this contact is happening to us continuously in our daily lives.

"Reaching the 'Clear Light of Bliss' is a way to contact the truth-body through meditation. But you can't stay in sitting meditation all the time. Even Tilopa, that renowned practitioner of the 'Clear Light of Bliss,' who historically began the linage that brought this teaching to Tibet, knew about this. He was the saint who, after transmitting the essence of his teaching to his main disciple Naropa, left for the charnel grounds with his consort. He was well aware that sitting in meditation was important—but only a taste. A taste of a meal to be devoured out in the world."

"Hitting the edge of the truth-body and sparking realizations is only the beginning of our task. The big test is the integration of the energy of the spark of our realizations into our everyday life. This is the process of weaving our personal cocoon, contacting the truth-body, the body that knows the truth, and then allowing the force of evolution to move through our physical body and out into the action out there," Li Tse said, opening his arms, pushing his chest out, looking over my head and chuckling.

He paused, then continued, "To go over this again: the True Self is all pervasive. And so, it makes contact with our little self in many ways. And every time we touch it, it sparks realizations. When we can begin to become the stream of realization, we are weaving our cocoon. It has happened to us all. We all have experiences of touching truth."

He paused, then said, "But you must stay aware. The point is to take advantage of it and not allow learned behavior to grab your realizations, to co-opt them and change them into something mundane as you bring that energy back into your life. Keep with the spark of realization, don't get fooled by what your little mind devolves them into. Stay alert!!

I looked over at Silvio. And once again I saw him transported by Li Tse's elucidations.

I also listened intently as Li Tse continued, "The act of weaving our cocoon is our own path in motion. We go back to the source by tightening up the inner spiral, then we bring back realization by establishing it throughout our bodies and into the ever-evolving energies around us.

"Realizations are fibers of light, the strands that we use to weave our cocoon. These are created when learned behavior collides with our path. They are the sparks created from this friction. Touching the truth-body can happen in many ways and the frequency of contact increases as you are pulled more and more rapidly along the path, weaving the strands of realization through your body of perception until they become a continuous stream."

When I tried to get a sense of what Li Tse was describing it was a vast feeling—beyond. It was as if I could sense a knowing, an ocean of knowledge, surrounding me, coiled in a spiral exploding with an infinite intimacy in the midst of its blinding, impersonal nature.

It made me ask them, "Would you say that our path is our True Self trying to catch up to us?"

They both looked at me, entertained. My question led to another outburst of laughter. Once they had both settled down, Li Tse replied, "The more you allow yourself to attach to your True Self, the more the force of evolution will pull you along. As the path coils and tightens around you, you start to experience living in a current of realization. The path is pushing you from within and pulling you from without, wringing the truth out of you.

I was caught in the combination of the receding sunlight on the nearby dusty road and the shadows of the trees and buildings that were juxtaposing it. Early sunset colors were just starting to appear over the clouds on the edges of the mountains. Looking at those colors made me reflect upon Li Tse's latest elaborations and metaphors, how realizations are tracers or trailers of our experiences sparked by contact with the truth-body.

I looked around and became aware of Silvio sitting to my right, waiting for my attention. Once our eyes locked, he looked at me with his mischievous smile and started, "What we are talking about is not purely mental. Before we were talking about the whole enchilada—evolution. Now for the second course we want to talk to you about how to make your very own personal enchilada—specifically, weaving your cocoon."

He grinned then said, "I remember when I was a small boy, I helped my Mama in the kitchen to wrap up tortillas into enchiladas filled with the good stuff. And now we're in the Big Mama's kitchen, Mother Earth, and she is pressuring me on. She is helping me now to show you how to wrap your own personal enchilada—blending and mixing the spicy ingredients of your life."

I looked back at him, smiling at his metaphor and asked, "What does this weaving of the cocoon feel like?"

He brightened, "It's very personal. You're working in your own kitchen. Weaving the cocoon is something very intimate. It's like stewing in your own juices!

"As the pull of the path increases you will experience in your body subtle and deep changes occurring every day. You will go around and around, and over and over your personal inventory and dramas, feeling the tightening up of the spiral of your path around you as it de-charges your story.

"We call this 'stewing in the juices of our personal enchilada' or the 'weaving of our cocoon,'" he beamed, "because it feels like you are rolling around in the midst of yourself—your feelings, emotions and patterns. Suddenly something happens in your world that pulls you to touch the truth-body and through it the True Self. Then you find yourself with a resultant realization and feeling that somehow you are being directed by your path to bring this realization out through you, out into the world. This is the process of weaving your cocoon.

"You begin to feel how the path is stirring the mixture. As the path coils and tightens this process progressively self-replicates itself, increasing the pressure that forms into something like a cocoon at the edge of perception.

"Conceive a fluid reality based on moving pressures between the heavens and the Earth. Or think about cooking your beans in a pressure cooker. It's this pressure that mixes and blends the individual tastes."

He grinned, "This is like making your enchilada. The path is the power that is doing the mixing and connecting us more and more with the True Self, and at the same time the path is the True Self," he said with a smile from ear to ear. "Our path activates the juices. Its pressure spirals and mixes as we roll around in our own enchilada," Silvio laughed.

"Following your path comes with a feeling of being drawn or pushed. As our sense of self dissolves, we experience it is as the friction between our path unfolding and learned behavior. This manifests as a sensation of rolling around within ourselves—swirling in the repetitive feelings, dramas, movement patterns and charged language. Twisting and turning, then being pressurized into hitting the True Self and thus sparking realizations.

"Sometimes we feel like we are stumbling along half blind and maimed," Silvio said with a deep knowing smile. "But we are really just trembling at the cusp of half-remembered prophecies."

He stopped, taking a dramatic pause, and looked at me with a twinkle in his eye. Then he said with a Mexican accent in dead pan seriousness, "This is what I do in my kitchen every day."

At that all of us started rolling with laughter.

A couple of minutes later, after we settled down, Li Tse took a deep breath and went on, "You may go along with your latest realization, believing you have it all figured out. Beware, as this is the moment learned behavior has co-opted this new energy. This is when you should re-adjust your focus and allow the pressure to create a new mixture and be waiting for the next chunk of information to hit.

"Get a realization! But don't get stuck, or attached to it! Let it go, move on. Let yourself get into a flow of realization. As the spiral of your path tightens, coiling around you, you will get more and more contact, or create more friction, which then will allow even more answers to come rolling in to open the way for your next step."

Suddenly Li Tse shifted his voice to a more hypnotic cadence. As his words reached my ears my attention split. I was cracked open. It made me feel like a buoy floating in space:

*"The evolutionary process is realization.*

*"Realizations happen more and more frequently. The first few blasts can be devastating as the pains of separation and the jolts of re-ajustment pull you back onto your evolutionary path once again. Most people are not prepared to have their minds changed. This process stretches the boundaries of the learned behavior trained body concept to its very limits and beyond.*

*"When you get revelations, you feel complete for a bit because you've made contact. You feel you're on the path, something you have found and lost so many times before.*

*"Realizations appearing faster and faster, beating down like rain, brushing off old patterns. Become attuned and accustomed to bathing in realization. Keep with it until you live in a constant stream of inspiration and realization and you dissolve more and more.*

*"Your path guides you through realizations, embodying them, weaving them together.*

*"You need to have a strong physical vehicle to contain the stream of realization. It needs to be both malleable and strong as it contracts and expands under pressure. Here is where right structure, acupuncture, and body practices like Eight Point Chi Gung can be very useful as a way to ground and store realization."*

The slowed down hypnotic cadence of Li Tse's voice had flowed through me like waves, meshing with deep currents in my psyche.

Li Tse paused for a moment, then told me to concentrate on my breath, and used this to bring me back to the table under the trees.

After a bit Li Tse looked over to assess my state. When he was satisfied with what he saw he said,

"Silvio wants to show you something."

He then gestured over to our friend.

Slowly Silvio got up, beckoning my attention and began moving like a beetle, the way he had done previously.

I suddenly felt the touch of déjà vu once again, the feelings of my dream:

*I was in a tunnel of intense colored lights. Portentous clouds of brilliant light amidst masses of blackness. My reason rushed in to concoct an explanation that would make sense to me at the moment— but it failed. Then I perceived a glow coming towards me like an enormous slow-motion wave. Finally, it took the shape of a beetle, superimposed on Silvio's body.*

Silvio continued his beetle movements as he moved from his standing/ moving posture bending, his knees to a squatting position, continuing to move his arms back and forth like a beetle. He then rolled back onto the ground with his arms and legs continuing their beetle movements. His body began moving from side to side. He looked like a beetle stuck on his back, rolling back and forth trying to right itself. His eyes bulged as he continued rocking from side to side. He looked at me with a wide grin on his face as if he were really enjoying himself.

Finally, with great effort he rolled forward back into a squatting position and transitioned through a motion that somehow resembled a frog, as he continued to move his arms in that beetle-like fashion until he finally stood up. He then returned to his original beetle movements in the standing posture.

I was surprised how his body still bristled with energy and how he had been able to maintain right structure in his arms and legs as he flowed through all of these postures.

Li Tse spoke, still looking at Silvio, "These beetle movements came to Silvio in dreaming, as movements sometimes do. Bringing movements from the dreaming state back into our waking state can give them an extra transformative power. A deep energetic charge."

Silvio finally stopped. Then after making an expansive gesture with his arms, he bowed.

Li Tse, smiling appreciatively, said, "Silvio was just trying to show you in his humble way what it is like to move structure through the cocoon of realization and connect with the Earth's cocoon."

Li Tse then shifted back to his hypnotic voice, immediately taking me to a deep relaxed state.

> *"We are trying to find our way out of a perceptual maze; fixed fields of perception. We are moving through the morass created by learned behavior, and getting our energy back as we weave our cocoon.*
>
> *"Honestly accept your learned behavior for what it is, with all its foibles. And then look at who is watching this and become that Focus, concentrate on the awareness of that awareness.*
>
> *"We have an impulse within us that seeks to unite with the stream of realization, to weave the cocoon of transformation. Store realizations in your body as you remember—re-assembling your self—weaving the cocoon so you can move beyond."*

As I surfaced back to my normal state of consciousness, I found Silvio had sat down next to me. I looked at him for a moment and then it occurred to me to ask, "How do realizations cure physical ills?"

The words hung in the air for a moment before Silvio responded, "When you're in realization you bring your energy to a higher frequency, thus connect more with your energy-body. It takes a while for the energy-body to work down through to the healing-body template to make an effect in the physical body. However, through time, as you bathe your body in realization, the more connected you will become to your truth-body and naturally physical healing will occur because we know we are meant to be whole."

He looked at me to see if I was following then continued, "When we release energy from the patterns of learned behavior, we get realizations. The energy of realization wants to be stored in the body. If it is not, imbalances occur as its need to find expression becomes more and more demanding, which causes even more even imbalances. Realization is seeking knowledge in the quality and quantity of Chi-flow. When it flows freely it creates pressure which makes the body more pliable and subtle. It makes the body soft and malleable like the body of a child."

The resplendent colors of the sunset were now in full bloom. I felt the coolness of the early evening as the trees began to ooze out fresh air. It had been another splendid day with my friends Li Tse and Silvio, who imbued with this feeling of early evening acknowledged each other.

Then Silvio began talking, "When I told you my history, I was trying to show you how the path has been pulling me through my life."

He then pointed over at Li Tse, "But when I met this one—that definitely sped things up and took both of us to a new level. We were forced to let go of the world we knew."

"What happened to your story?" I asked, wondering what would happen to mine.

Silvio catching my drift, replied, "You'll lose your story to your path."

I heard Li Tse chuckling softly at my side.

Silvio continued, "Your path becomes your story. Remember, your story is that special idea of 'you' created by learned behavior, embedded in your breathing and movement patterns. This is what makes you feel unique and special in relation to others. You can see your path as the unwinding of that 'specialness,' that special relationship with yourself," he grinned. "Your story will no longer obstruct the way you perceive and flow with the world. And the world the way you know it will disappear."

I wondered for a moment, thinking about all the people in my life, and I asked, "So how does one relate intimately with people if not through one's story?"

Silvio nodded over to Li Tse who answered, "You relate to people through your path. This process is so obvious that it is difficult to grasp. Our path disables our story. It's a process of slowly loosening up learned behavior and dissolving it and allowing it to re-assemble itself. The path with its accompanying realizations takes over—you begin to live in a living stream of realization and you don't have time for the internal dialogue of your story anymore. You may not even have time."

Silvio took the baton again and peered at me, "Do you remember—*you are not the mind, you are not the body, there is no personal self?*"

"Whoa, whoa, whoa," I said, as the import of his statement hit me. "After all of this talking about the body, now you are saying the body is not ultimately important. If that is true, why deal with the body at all?"

Silvio look again over at Li Tse who looked at me bemused for a moment then said, "Yes, you are right, in truth the body does not exist. It is just a concept that comes from our karmas and learned behavior. And this is what we are trying to realize all along. But for some of us slow folks." he said as he looked over at Silvio then back at me, "we need to work with and refine the body concept until we can realize that it is only a concept. We need to keep the concept of the body as functional as possible and use this as a steppingstone as we unravel, so we can dissolve gracefully into the True Self.

The more our body concept gets gravitationally lined up with the Earth's gravity, the more the so-called or body-concept body disappears.

From your point of view, or the view from the little self, this is a great paradox. When you realize that there is no body and no self, the realization engulfs us—that all the world you perceive is involuntary."

Again, I was taken aback. "Involuntary? What exactly do you mean?"

Li Tse smiled, slowly spread his hands out in front of me, then put them down. "Normally we say that breathing and heart beat and digestion, etc., are involuntary. We have no 'voluntary' control over them. Right? What I am saying is that when you realize that there is no self then everything you perceive and create through the senses in involuntary also—your thoughts, your actions, the movements of your body are all involuntary. There is just Being."

Silvio beamed me a smile, then bent down, and rummaging through his pile of paraphernalia he pulled out a sign which he then held up in front of me:

## THAT SPECIAL RELATIONSHIP
## WITH YOURSELF
## HAS BEEN TERMINATED!

They both laughed at my reaction and then Li Tse said, "The whole point of doing our practices is to release yourself from the narrative of your story and to allow the pull of the path to envelop you. When your path becomes your story, you realize in a very deep way that the world goes on without 'you'—what a relief," he said as he wiped his brow and chuckled.

Silvio grabbed my attention with a wave of his hand, beaming, and said once again, "You'll lose your story to your path." He then wrinkled his brow, raised his eyebrows a couple of times, donning his mischievous smile, then, waving his hand back and forth at me, he said, "Bye-Bye!"

I walked away from Silvio's home with a new kind of spring in my step. The fireflies in the twilight around me sparked memories of the dream that once had been my life and reminiscences of how it has been transformed.

> *My own Zen sickness–my own enchilada—people in frozen cubes—balls of pressure moving through a world of pressure, being molded by their paths.*
> *The deep knowing of a caterpillar: weaving its cocoon of transformation.*

As my feet hit the Earth, I could sense my story becoming my path, unfolding, pushing, and pulling me.

Then I recited from memory, *"When you realize that there is no self, then the way that the world and the body you perceive moves—is involuntary."*

The body moving of its own accord down the road...

*"When you have become one with the Self, a great power takes you over and runs your life for you. It looks after your body; it puts you in the right place at the right time; it makes you say the right things to the people you meet. This power takes you over so completely, you no longer have any ability to decide or discriminate. The Self simply animates you and makes you do all the things that need to be done."* [3]

—Annamalai Swami

# ACKNOWLEGEMENTS

[1]Annamalai Swami Final Talks – Edited by David Godman

[2]Chuang Tsu/Inner Chapters – Translation by Gia-Fu Feng

[3]Annamalai Swami Final Talks – Edited by David Godman

**Dr. Daniel Santos** has been immersed in the study and practice of Chi Gung, acupuncture, and Chinese Medicine for over 40 years. In the 1970's in California he became one of the first licensed acupuncturists in the USA as an OMD (Oriental Medical Doctor). Dr. Santos then moved to the State of New Mexico where he was appointed to and served as Chairman of the New Mexico State Acupuncture and Oriental Medicine Board. He practiced there in his own clinic for over 25 years. He was also licensed as a private tutor and has lectured in schools, universities, and hospitals.

He is the author of three previous books that have been translated into seven languages: *Luminous Essence/Body talks to Body, Feng Shui for the Body,* and *Cuerpo Luminoso (Luminous Body).*

Dr. Santos' unique psycho-spiritual training began as an apprentice to a psychic healer in the early 1970's. He then went on to further his knowledge of the body by studying and practicing the Chinese healing arts: acupuncture, herbology, Chi Gung, Tai Chi, and other forms of movement arts in the USA, China and Taiwan. His deep interest in herbs and sacred plant medicines also took him to visit the curanderos of Mexico and South America. Here, with indigenous shamans in their own settings, he explored the effects of psychotropic substances.

While in Peru in the 1990's, his probing into ayahuasca and other "master plants" enabled him to do a detailed study of the intricate "science" of the plant medicines there. This, along with the material and interviews he did with various shamans and curanderos in both Peru and Mexico, will form the basis of a future work that will be entitled *The Shaman's Dream.* He has also devoted much time and practice to Theravadan Vipassana, Tibetan Tantrayana, and Vajrayana meditation, and their underlying Buddhist philosophies. His path also took him to vibrant India, where he visited several ashrams and was trained in Kriya yoga, Bhakti yoga, Sound yoga, and most recently to Tiruvannamalai where he lives under the shadow of Arunachala, the mountain that was the guru of Ramana Maharishi.

Dr. Santos has devoted a lifetime of exploration of disciplines concerning body and mind *Chi—The Sixth Sense* presents us with a unique vision of humans as an ever-changing manifestation of energy that is inseparably interconnected with the living Earth.